Environmental Economics

Environmental Economics

Joseph J. Seneca
Rutgers College

Michael K. Taussig
Rutgers College

PRENTICE-HALL, INC., Englewood Cliffs, New Jersey

Library of Congress Cataloging in Publication Data

SENECA, JOSEPH J
    Environmental economics.

    Includes bibliographies.
       1. Environmental policy—United States. 2. Cost
effectiveness. 3. Anthropo-geography—United States.
I. Taussig, Michael K., joint author. II. Title.
HC110.E5S45   301.31'0973   73-8693
ISBN   0-13-283358-1

Printed in the United States of America

10 9 8 7 6 5 4 3 2 1

PRENTICE-HALL INTERNATIONAL, INC., *London*
PRENTICE-HALL OF AUSTRALIA, PTY. LTD., *Sydney*
PRENTICE-HALL OF CANADA, LTD., *Toronto*
PRENTICE-HALL OF JAPAN, INC., *Tokyo*
PRENTICE-HALL OF INDIA PRIVATE LIMITED, *New Delhi*

To Rozy and Nikki

Contents

Preface

The subject of this book is the economics of environmental quality. Our book-length treatment of this subject reflects our feelings about the extraordinary complexity and importance of the topic. We thereby immediately depart from two polar opposing points of view. The first, often expressed by many highly emotional new conservationists, is that economics is completely irrelevant to (if not responsible for) the problems of environmental deterioration. The second, held by some of our purist professional colleagues in economics, is that environmental problems are essentially trivial or "political," and that they can all be solved by the application of simple prescriptions drawn from extensions of traditional economic theory. The latter point of view can be summarized by the following policy recommendation: "Just impose an effluent charge equal to the difference between marginal social and private costs." Although we are conservationists in spirit and loyal economists by profession, we find both positions to be most unsatisfactory. Our own view, as expressed in the book, is that economists have an invaluable potential role to play in helping to solve or alleviate environmental problems. But at the same time we maintain that economists can not undertake this vital role successfully until they first educate themselves both about the very complex physical and biological circumstances of specific environmental problems and about the broader social and legal aspects of these problems.

We therefore take some pains in the book to blend economic theory with environmental facts and social circumstances. The theme of the book is the application of the standard benefit-cost or efficiency criteria of economics to a wide variety of environmental problems. We attempt to make clear to the reader how difficult it is in the real world to apply these criteria to actual environmental problems. We also stress the interaction of efficiency criteria with income redistribution or equity issues. Most important of all, probably, we try to show that environmental policies must take their place in the context of other demands on scarce resources, even in our affluent society.

The book is the outgrowth of a course in environmental economics taught by one of the authors at Rutgers College for the last several years. Thus, the material has been extensively class-tested and refined. The evident success and widespread appeal of this course at Rutgers encourage us to hope that our approach to the subject may have similar appeal outside our own institution. A prerequisite for the course at Rutgers is the micro half of the principles of economics course. Students without this minimum background may find the book beyond their reach. In addition, many students have either taken an intermediate micro-theory course or take it concurrently. Not all of them, by any means, are economics majors. The course has had appeal to students from engineering, the physical sciences, political science, urban planning and other disciplines. We believe that the book can have the same broad audience at other institutions.

The topical organization of the book is detailed in Chapter 1 and need not be duplicated here. Instead let us make some suggestions how the book may best be utilized. At Rutgers, the material in each of the 14 chapters is assigned reading for one week and serves as the main basis for class lectures and discussion. In this way, the whole book fits neatly into a typical college-length semester and can be covered in its entirety without undue haste. We find it useful to supplement the basic core reading in the text with a variety of additional outside readings, and the Selected References at the end of each chapter are intended to guide users of the book to the best available detailed treatments of individual topics. In addition, the Questions for Discussion at the end of each chapter can play a valuable educational role. These questions are designed to help students probe more deeply on their own into the difficult conceptual issues underlying the text discussion. We recognize that our own approach to the subject will not be applicable at all times and places. Users of the book at other institutions will undoubtedly find other ways of utilizing the material to their best advantage.

Many individuals are due our sincere thanks for helping us complete the book. Marshall I. Goldman read the entire manuscript and provided us with a most valuable critique. Professors Paul Gatons, David Fischer, Matthew Edel, and Alan Campbell also reviewed the manuscript and offered sound advice. Our student Sharon Bernstein made many helpful comments on several of the chapters and Jack Worrall also gave us useful assistance. Geraldine Dructor and Irene Matthews typed the bulk of the manuscript with patience and skill. We are also grateful to the Rutgers University Research Council for much needed financial assistance. Finally, we must go beyond our bibliographical citations to make special mention of our intellectual indebtedness to the outstanding pioneers in the new and vital field of environmental economics. We have drawn particularly on the work of J. H. Dales, Allen V. Kneese, John V. Krutilla, Edwin S. Mills and E. J. Mishan. Without their pathbreaking efforts, this book could not have been written.

Joseph J. Seneca
Michael K. Taussig

Environmental Economics

PART 1

Introduction

Chapter 1

The Basic Concepts of Environmental Economics

This is a book about the *economics* of environmental quality. A full treatment of environmental problems would require mastery of basic principles from several different intellectual disciplines: the physical and biological sciences, political science, sociology, the law, and perhaps others. We do not question the value of the contributions from these other disciplines; in fact, we shall make use of them. We do insist, however, that economics has its own unique, valuable role to play in the solution of environmental problems. In taking a narrow economic approach to our subject, we avoid the pitfalls that await those who venture into disciplines in which, unfortunately, they are ignorant, and, more positively, we confirm our faith as practicing economists in the principle that specialization and division of labor generally lead to maximum total output for society.

The theme of this book is that the different aspects of environmental quality are economic goods or, what is essentially the same notion in different words, that they are items of *scarcity*. By scarcity, we mean simply that the demand for environmental *goods* (often perceived as the demand for avoidance of environmental pollution) exceeds the supply at a zero price. Unfortunately, nature does not provide enough of these goods free to satisfy all of man's desires for them. Contrary to the view often expressed in the popular press, economists tend to agree that most environmental problems cannot be solved by passing a law or by exhorting people to be better behaved. Because such environmental goods as nonpoisonous air and potable water are scarce, society can, in effect, *purchase* more of them only at the price of giving up significant amounts of other desirable consumption goods and services. In the language of economics, scarce environmental goods must be *traded off* against other scarce economic goods and services. The *opportunity cost* of obtaining more environmental quality for any society is the sacrifice of doing without other valuable commodities.

In addition, we shall stress throughout the book that the benefits of the enhancement or preservation of environmental quality will, in general, be distributed unevenly among individuals of the present generation and also between the present and future generations, and that the costs of producing environmental quality almost certainly will be distributed differently from the benefits. In common with all other important economic problems, the issue of environmental quality involves the *distribution* of economic welfare. Therefore, it necessarily will provoke conflicts of interest between potential gainers and potential losers from any specific environmental policy alternative.

We shall return continually to these central points throughout the book—with appropriate elaboration, of course—and, in doing so, we shall attempt to make clear to the reader the unique contribution of economic principles to the understanding and the solution of various environmental problems.

A GUIDE TO THE ORGANIZATION OF THE BOOK

The present chapter is intended as an introduction to the rest of the book. The theme of the book has been stated in our introduction. Next, we define some basic terminology in Section A below. Section B then attempts to present modern environmental problems to the reader in the proper historical and quantitative perspectives. Section C is an introduction to the economics of environmental problems; it includes a discussion of benefit-cost analysis, the basic mode of thinking that distinguishes the economic from alternative approaches to these problems. Even the reader who is thoroughly versed in the material in this chapter is urged at least to browse through it in order to assure that he will share a common vocabulary with the authors throughout the later, more difficult parts of the book. Section D contains a brief summary of the chapter.

Following this introductory chapter, Part 2 of the book presents the body of economic theory pertinent to the analysis of environmental problems. The chapters in this part of the book simply adapt basic micro-economic theory, as taught in college-level economic principles courses, to the specific problems involved in achieving environmental quality.

Next, the three chapters of Part 3 of the book survey the actual circumstances of the water (Chapter 6), air (Chapter 7), and assorted amenity (Chapter 8) dimensions of the total environment. These chapters attempt to link the technical, physical, and biological aspects of each environmental resource to the preceding theoretical analysis.

Part 4 of the book examines alternative courses of government intervention intended to improve environmental quality. Chapter 9 analyzes prohibitions on, and regulations of, polluting activities. Chapter 10 deals with tax and subsidy measures designed to encourage environment-enhancing behavior on the part of individual firms and households through the mechanism of monetary incentives and disincentives. Chapter 11 is concerned with the economics of government investments in environmental resources.

The concluding Part 5 of the book treats the relationship between the growth and distribution of population and general economic growth and environmental quality. Chapter 12 discusses the environmental consequences of growth of population, or changes in *levels* of population in any society. Chapter 13 gives a similar treatment of the environmental implications of urbanization, or the *distribution* of population. The final Chapter 14 consists of a general discussion of the relationship between economic growth and environmental quality. This chapter makes some modest attempts to transcend the intentionally narrow economic focus of the book by considering some broad social implications of continued economic growth.

A. SOME DEFINITIONS OF TERMS

Environmental Science Concepts [1]

Ecology is the science of the interrelationship between man and his living and nonliving surroundings. *Ecosystem* is the term applied to a particular, identifiable set of ecological interrelationships. Typical ex-

---

[1] We take most of these definitions directly from *Environmental Quality, The First Annual Report of the Council on Environmental Quality* (Washington, D.C.: Government Printing Office, 1970).

amples of ecosystems are a lake or a mountain meadow. Larger ecosystems, or closely interrelated sets of ecosystems, such as a desert, ocean, or the Great Plains, are called *biomes*. The *biosphere* consists of the earth, its atmosphere, and all life on the planet. The total *environment* of man includes the biosphere and also the relationship of man to nature and to his own created surroundings. Given this definition, the environment clearly can encompass almost every conceivable aspect of life. We shall confine our use of the term to the relationship of man to the atmosphere and waters of the earth, and to a few other specific aspects of his total environment.

Pollution means simply that certain materials accumulate where they are harmful or simply undesirable. Pollution is thus a concept involving individual and group tastes as well as simple technological data. A given level of a certain chemical in a body of water is pollution only if it interferes with a desired use of that water by man. Pollutants are often distinguished as to whether or not they are biologically degradable (*biodegradable*); that is, whether they are readily broken down and dispersed harmlessly by natural biological and chemical processes and thereby cease to be pollutants over some reasonably short period of time. Organic substances such as foods, wood products, and paper are clearly biodegradable; plastics and aluminum cans are not.

Economic Concepts

An *economic good or service* is defined in our introduction as anything that is scarce. Scarcity exists whenever the demand for anything exceeds its supply at a zero price; conversely, any good or service that is free is, by the same definition, not scarce and not an economic good or service. We live, unfortunately, in a world of general scarcity because, with few exceptions, *resources*—the general term applied to anything that contributes to making desired goods and services available for consumption —are limited relative to the desires of man to consume. *Economic welfare* is a part of total human welfare; it is conventionally measured by the value of the consumption of economic goods and services over some specified time period. *Efficiency* is defined as maximum consumption of goods and services given the available amount of resources or, what is logically equivalent, the use of a minimum amount of resources to produce or make available for consumption a given amount of goods and services.

The *benefit* of any good or service is simply its value to a consumer. The benefits of most goods and services are usually measured directly by the market prices at which consumers show themselves willing to buy them. Benefits of goods not bought and sold in the market must be inferred by some less direct method. *Costs* are essentially foregone benefits and, therefore, are most fundamentally regarded as *opportunity costs*. The cost of any economic good or service consists of the foregone benefits from the consumption of some other good or service. The consumption of one unit or more of good A implies the shift of some resources away from the production of good B to produce the additional unit of A. The true cost of A, therefore, is the foregone B caused by the shift in resources from production of the latter to the production of the former. Costs, as well as benefits, are typically measured, more or less accurately, by money prices paid in markets.

We elaborate on the use of these concepts in Section C of this chapter and throughout the rest of the book. Other, less general economic concepts will be defined in context as they are introduced into our later analysis.

B. ENVIRONMENTAL PROBLEMS IN PERSPECTIVE

The Past

Air and water pollution and other environmental problems are as old as civilized man. Historians of ancient Rome have left us a record of the almost unbearable odors prevailing in the imperial capital. More recently, we have available ample documentation of the obnoxious smoke, noise, and odors that plagued the newly industrialized cities of Victorian England. Much of the recent popular writing on current pollution problems naively looks back at nineteenth century America as a golden environmental age. Such a rosy view of our past ignores pertinent facts to the contrary; as, for example, the fact that the exhaust system of the predecessor to the automobile created its own unique brand of pollution.

Despite the frequent recurrence of environmental problems throughout human history, widespread concern about environmental quality is a surprisingly recent and localized phenomenon, beginning only in the late 1960s and largely confined to the United States and a few other economically advanced countries. What explains this apparent paradox? From the perspective of economics, the answer is that the unprecedented high levels of output achieved in a few countries in the last half century have transformed environmental quality from a generally free good into an economic, or scarce, good. At the beginning of this century, the supply of clean air, potable water, and other amenities of life generally exceeded the effective demand at a zero price, despite the presence of often serious, localized pollution problems. Today, in many high-income and densely populated areas, demand exceeds supply at a zero price, and formerly free goods suddenly have become scarce goods. For many people, the shock of this unexpected development has added psychic insult to economic injury and health hazards, resulting in widespread public concern about the *new* problem of environment quality.

The reversal of environmental quality supply-demand relationships in just a few years is the result of two, or possibly three, separate factors. First, economic growth has had the effect of decreasing the available supply of clean air and of other environmental goods through the sheer quantity of effluents generated by high levels of industrial production. Growth in the level of total output has been matched by growth in the amounts of various effluents. Inevitably, the point has been reached where, in some of the most densely populated and industrialized areas of the earth, the quantity of some effluents has overcome the natural, self-cleansing powers of the atmosphere, waters, and earth. If industrial cities in the nineteenth century were grimy and even dangerous to public health, the pleasant countryside was still easily accessible, especially for the middle and upper classes. Today, pollution problems have increased to the degree that polluted air and water follow the would-be urban escapist to his country hideaway. A possibly distinct point is that modern pollutants present unprecedented threats to the health and safety of man. The nature of DDT, nuclear radiation, and mercury pollutants, among others, is sufficiently different from traditional pollutants in technological complexity and in long-run danger to the existence of man that the quality, as well as the quantity, of modern pollution problems merits separate consideration. On the more optimistic side, the technical means for dealing with some of these problems are also much more advanced than in the past. In any case, the important point is that economic growth has steadily diminished the available supply of environmental quality.

In contrast, the demand for environmental goods has increased sharply as a consequence of rising levels of affluence, which, in turn, is simply another byproduct of sustained economic growth. Men at the verge of subsistence care little about the amenities of life, including the various aspects of environmental quality. Once man has assured himself sufficient food and other necessities, plus a good measure of luxuries, he can then turn his attention to satisfying other, less-immediate wants, including the consumption of various environmental goods. In economic terminology, we hypothesize that environmental quality is a highly *income elastic* or *luxury* good, which means that households with relatively high incomes desire to consume a higher fraction of their income in the form of expenditures on environmental quality than do households with relatively low incomes. Thus, on both the demand and supply sides, the effect of economic growth in the most economically developed countries of the world has contributed to the transformation of environmental quality from a free to a scarce good. The fact that industrially advanced socialist countries are plagued by environmental problems suggests strongly that the basic underlying cause of those problems is the supply and demand relationship outlined above and not the private market economic system.

The Present and Future

The modern conservation movement—a term we apply to the many individuals and organizations in this country that are currently demanding more social action to enhance environmental quality—is the intellectual and spiritual heir of the conservation movement of the late nineteenth and early twentieth centuries. The old conservation movement was led by self-styled Progressives, notably Theodore Roosevelt and Gifford Pinchot. The vision of such men was of a country with precious natural resources of all kinds being destroyed by large corporations interested only in exploiting these resources for the sake of maximizing immediate profits. They saw all around them the destruction of great natural beauty and the apparently accelerating depletion of the nation's limited natural resources. Despite the fact that, from today's perspective, the leaders of the old conservation movement were wealthy and staunchly conservative, in the name of conservation they supported the most far-reaching and basic governmental restrictions on the behavior of individuals and business firms within the private market system. This principle of public intervention in private economic activities for the sake of the public interest in conservation is probably the main legacy of the old conservation movement, which now retains very little else of its original force.

The modern conservation movement differs from its predecessor in two important respects. First, the present breed of conservationists is much more broadly based, both politically and socially. The old conservation movement mainly represented the interests of the agrarian society that was made obsolete by the industrialization of the United States during the late nineteenth and early twentieth centuries. These interests were largely irrelevant to the major concerns of the entrepreneurs and laborers of the emerging industrial society. Moreover, the major spokesmen of the old conservation movement can be faulted with a lack of concern for the urban working masses. At their worst, the old conservationists appeared to be satisfied, affluent country gentlemen attempting to halt economic progress in order to preserve the traditional amenities of their country estates. The modern conservation movement in the United States is not entirely free of such class bias, but it has now succeeded in attracting reasonably broad-based public support, largely due to the fact that sustained economic growth has transformed much of the previously poor working class into a moderately affluent middle class.

Second, the modern conservation movement has largely freed itself of the *exhaustion of resources* fallacy that was the intellectual cornerstone of the old movement's beliefs, and has turned its attention, instead, to the more relevant problems of environmental quality. The exhaustion of resources fallacy is the argument that because there exists only a finite amount of any given natural resource in the biosphere, continued economic growth will inevitably exhaust the supply of this resource. The fallacy commonly takes the form of estimating the present annual rate and expected future rates of utilization of some resource, such as coal, then estimating the total amount of coal deposits left in the earth; and, finally, projecting the year in which all coal deposits will be exhausted. Virtually all such projections have proved thus far to be much too pessimistic, and economic growth has proceeded essentially unhindered by raw material shortages.

The flaw in the exhaustion of resources argument is that it fails to take account of the pervasive influence of technological advance in the process of economic growth. As any raw material becomes scarcer, it rises in price. This acts as a signal for profit-maximizing firms to devise more efficient use of it or search for alternative resources as substitutes for it. In the past, technological advance has consistently transformed previously essential resources such as coal into just one of several possible alternative inputs into the productive process. Scientists and economists now envision a future in which the only essential raw materials will be energy and the most basic chemical molecules.

Given the foregoing argument, energy sources remain, in principle, the one truly exhaustible resource. But many careful studies make clear that even energy sources are available in massive quantities for the indefinite future. The important point is that the opportunity costs of developing these resources can be expected to rise sharply in the future as we exhaust the supply of the most economical sources. The consequent rise in the relative price of energy to consumers should encourage various means of economizing on energy use. Energy sources are of interest for our purposes in this book, therefore, not because they are about to run out but, instead, because their exploitation is the root cause of many of our most serious environmental problems.

Widespread recognition of the problem of deterioration of environmental quality has come, understandably, only belatedly, after many years of steadily accumulating pollution. Some perspective on the magnitude of the problem can be given by citing some estimates of the annual costs of producing present pollution controls in the United States.[2] Public

---

[2] These estimates of total costs include annual operating costs plus estimated depreciation and an imputed rate of return on capital. The source for the figures in the text is *Environmental Quality, The Third Annual Report of the Council on Environmental Quality* (Washington, D.C.: Government Printing Office, 1972), pp. 276–277.

and private outlays on water pollution control were over $3.6 billion in 1970 and are expected to increase to $8.0 billion by 1980. Total outlays on air pollution control were estimated at $8 billion in 1970, but this figure is projected to rise to almost $14.7 billion by 1980. Measures to deal with solid waste disposal, noise, and other environmental problems also run into some billions of dollars each year in the United States alone. Total annual costs in 1970 are estimated at $10.4 billion for all public and private pollution control activities, but this figure is expected to almost triple by the end of the decade.

The estimates above are the best available but are acknowledged by the Council on Environmental Quality to be very rough. Although we know too little about the present costs of antipollution measures, we know considerably less about the opportunity costs of producing different specified levels of environmental quality. The relevant technological and economic data are not available to allow us to estimate precisely the costs of achieving a given improvement in the quality of the environment. However, the Environmental Protection Agency estimates that 85 to 90 percent of water pollutants originating from municipal and industrial sources can be eliminated by 1982 with an expenditure of $60 billion. The price tag for an additional 10 percent reduction is another $60 billion, and a return to pristine, zero pollution conditions would cost $200 billion more. Thus, the total costs of removing *all* water pollutants is estimated at $320 billion or about 30 percent of the total annual output of the United States economy.

These costs refer only to improvements in water quality. Presently, equivalent cost estimates for complete air purity are more elusive and the costs for control of other pollutants such as noise, pesticides, and solid wastes are even more speculative. At best, the potential tradeoff between various degrees of environmental quality and per capita standards of consumption of other economic goods and services can only be roughly estimated at the present time.

Given the present state of ignorance on this subject, it is not surprising that views about the gravity of environmental problems differ sharply. Many spokesmen of the modern conservation movement express the doomsday view that our society and the rest of the world face a major crisis, and that only massive social commitments to the environmental cause can preserve human life. In support of their arguments, they observe the widespread serious environmental damage that has already occurred and project present pollution trends into an even more threatening future.

On the opposite side of the question are proponents of the skeptical, business-as-usual view, who deny the overriding urgency of environmental problems and resist all but very modest remedial social actions. They argue that concern with environmental quality is only a fad—just a transitory social cause for youthful idealists. A sophisticated version of this skeptical view argues, first, that Americans, at least, are too materialistic to be willing to sacrifice any significant portion of their high standards of consumption in the long run for the sake of improving environmental quality. In addition, optimistic scientists feel that environmental problems can be reduced to manageable proportions by the application of the same advanced technology that has been so successful in other areas. Granted the validity of both these premises, environmental problems can be expected to fade from the public consciousness, to be replaced by some new cause, and to become the province of technicians and engineers in sanitation and related fields.

The debate between the modern conservation movement and its critics has just begun. Economic growth continues today at customary compound rates in the United States and in most other countries, with the increased flow of output closely matched by increased flows of effluents of all kinds into the absorptive earth, water, and atmospheric media. The full effects of some modern pollutants—DDT, for example—are experienced only with a long lag through complex ecological processes. It remains to be seen whether current policy measures at all levels of government, together with the activities of private parties, will be sufficient to prevent environmental degradation. The environmental policy choices that society makes in the 1970s—either consciously or by default—will determine the quality of the environment we shall live in during this century and our children will inherit.

C. THE BENEFIT-COST APPROACH TO ENVIRONMENTAL PROBLEMS

Benefit-cost analysis is the systematic appraisal of all benefits and all costs of a contemplated course of action, or of several alternative courses of action. The benefit-cost *criterion* for whether to undertake a given course of action is that the additional benefits to be derived from taking the action exceed the corresponding additional costs. In even simpler terms, this criterion means that the course of action be undertaken only if the sum of all the expected advantages outweigh the sum of all the expected disadvantages. Stated in this way, the benefit-cost criterion is nothing more than a description of rational behavior. Who but an irrational man would act in any other way? Despite the deceptive simplicity of this mode of thinking, the benefit-cost approach has proved to be the unique contribution of economics to the solution of social problems; the systematic comparison of benefits and costs and the consideration of all alternatives clearly distinguish the approach of economists to a given problem from the methods of other disciplines. We write this book because we believe that this same mode of analysis will prove fruitful when applied to the special problems associated with environmental quality.

A *benefit* is, as we have already defined it, the value of a good or service to a consumer, and a *cost* is fundamentally a foregone benefit. The private market system, in effect, performs complex benefit-cost analyses every day. If consumers value a given consumption good sufficiently to willingly pay the price that makes it profitable for business firms to produce more of it, then the firms will typically respond by doing so. If, on the other hand, consumers are not willing to pay a price high enough to cover the additional costs of further production, then firms will not produce more. Similarly, individuals perform implicit or explicit benefit-cost analyses in making everyday decisions. The man who asks himself whether it is *worth* taking the time to visit his mother-in-law is implicitly comparing the benefits he expects from the visit to the costs— the foregone time he could have spent watching the football game on television or in some other alternative activity. Benefit-cost types of analyses are now established in federal government agencies since the advent of PPBS (Planning, Programming, Budgeting System) in the 1960s. For our purposes, however, we shall concentrate only on the application of benefit-cost analysis to government activities intended to alleviate or prevent various environmental problems.

The Costs of Waste Disposal

Before presenting a simplified example of applied benefit-cost analysis, let us consider, in some depth, the nature of costs and benefits in environmental problems. Most of the important environmental problems facing man today arise because modern production and consumption techniques of firms and households impose *waste disposal costs* on society.[3] Following the usage of Professor J. H. Dales, we may define waste disposal costs to be the sum of (1) *pollution prevention costs* and (2) *pollution costs*. Pollution prevention costs are those costs incurred, either by firms or individuals in the private sector or by the government, to prevent either entirely or partially the pollution that would otherwise result from some production or consumption activity. The costs incurred by a local

---

[3] The main exceptions to the generalization in the text are the *environmental* problems traceable to human activities that destroy animal and plant life or impair the aesthetic quality of the natural world. The costs due to man's overharvesting a particular species or to the construction of hot dog stands in sites of natural beauty are not waste disposal costs in the usual meaning of the term. They are costs due essentially to the failure of effective enforcement of private or collective property rights, a subject we discuss in more detail in Chapter 4.

government to treat its sewage before dumping it into a river are pollution prevention costs according to this terminology; so are the costs incurred by a firm or by a household to maintain high efficiency furnaces that minimize the residues emitted to the atmosphere.

Pollution costs, in turn, may be broken down into two categories: (1) the private or public expenditures undertaken to avoid pollution damage once pollution has already occurred; and (2) the welfare damage of pollution. Once pollution has occurred, perhaps because of the failure of individuals or government to accept the costs of pollution prevention, society can choose either to avoid the damage of the pollution by undertaking some defensive or remedial actions or it can simply accept the consequences of pollution. The first alternative line of action may take the form of public expenditures on various kinds of clean-up programs or of private expenditures on air filtration systems or on unpolluted drinking water imported from some area free of water pollution. More fancifully, it may take the form of individual purchases of gas masks or of vacations to unspoiled (unpolluted) areas. Over the long run, one of the most socially significant costs of pollution avoidance has been the additional commuting costs accepted by suburban dwellers who work in cities. These commuting costs are pollution damage avoidance costs to the extent that they are incurred for the purpose of avoiding the pollution problems of central cities.

Finally, pollution that is not prevented or avoided causes welfare damage. Such damage is more or less measurable in money terms, but in any case it is a very real phenomenon. The most tangible pollution damage takes the form of the observable deterioration of both physical assets and of living things, including human beings. For example, air pollution may cause paint to peel and thus impose additional painting costs on the owners of commercial and residential structures.[4] It is also likely to increase everybody's cleaning bills as people attempt to maintain standards of cleanliness established in a less-polluted age. Both air and water pollution probably would increase the medical costs of society just to maintain a given level of health. Thus, the explicit money costs of maintenance of physical assets and of human beings will rise as the result of increasing levels of pollution. The more subtle consequences of pollution are the instances of the welfare costs that result from deterioration of physical assets and of human health and are not offset by increased expenditures on maintenance and repair. That is, some physical

---

[4] If the *prospect or threat* of peeling paint causes the owners of property to apply extra coats of paint, our terminology would call the costs of the additional paint pollution damage avoidance costs. Clearly, the line between pollution damage avoidance costs and the welfare damage of pollution is often hard to distinguish.

assets will rust away and some human beings will sicken and even die because of pollution damage that is not counteracted by increased explicit costs. Such costs of pollution damage are conceptually on a par with the explicit money costs of pollution prevention in their effects on human welfare.

The full welfare costs of pollution damage are impossible to measure exactly. How can we evaluate, for example, the welfare cost that results from the polluted water in a stream that once was used for fishing and bathing? Former users and potential users of the stream are *invisible* —they no longer frequent the stream and we can never know how much welfare damage they have suffered from pollution and how much they would be willing to pay to help restore the stream to its former unpolluted state. Despite the fact that we can not measure the full welfare loss of pollution damage in the same way we can measure the costs of pollution prevention or, in many cases, of pollution damage avoidance, we may infer from the stirrings of the modern conservation movement that these hidden costs have recently reached large proportions.

Some implications of the preceding discussion should be immediately obvious. Waste disposal costs, whatever form they take, are real, or opportunity, costs. They are basically foregone benefits to individual consumers in society. Pollution prevention costs involve direct outlays, by the private sector or by government, to purchase resources to inhibit pollution. The resources used for this purpose are thereby diverted from production of some other good and the result is less net output for society. The money costs of pollution damage avoidance are comparable to the costs of pollution prevention, with the exception that they may often be more difficult to identify and to quantify in dollar terms. In contrast, the costs of the welfare damage of pollution are imposed directly on individuals in the form of foregone benefits without the intervening mechanism of explicit money outlays. In any form, however, the costs of waste disposal reduce the level of the net output of consumption goods for society.

The analysis in this section suggests two general observations. First, if society's economic goal is maximization of *net* output of goods and services, it should obviously attempt to minimize *total* waste disposal costs. Government programs involving increases in pollution prevention costs make sense only if they cause pollution costs to decline by a greater amount. Similarly, actions involving higher pollution damage avoidance costs make sense for society as long as they reduce the welfare damage costs of pollution at least dollar for dollar. These obvious points are the rationale underlying the benefit-cost analysis presented in the next section of this chapter. Second, the maximization of output net of total pollution costs may call for a different composition of output than would maximization of output gross of such costs. This same point implies that the set of relative prices of outputs and inputs consistent with maximization of gross output will *not*, in general, be the same set of relative prices required to maximize net output. This latter point will be developed at length in Part 2 of the book.

A Simplified Benefit-Cost Analysis Example

Benefit-cost analysis, in the broadest sense, means a systematic evaluation of all the advantages and disadvantages of any actual or hypothetical change in society's production and consumption arrangements. Ideally, all forms of waste disposal costs would be taken into full account in any benefit-cost analysis of any hypothetical course of action that affects environmental problems. In a narrower sense, benefit-cost analysis is an evaluation of the benefits and costs of a government pollution prevention program. The benefits of such a program are the sum of the reduction of pollution costs—both pollution damage avoidance costs and the more elusive costs of pollution welfare damage. The costs of such a program are the total money outlays of the government, a measure of the value in alternative uses of the resources required to carry out the program.

For concreteness, let us consider the application of benefit-cost analysis to a highly simplified problem of determining the proper dimensions of a government pollution abatement program. We shall assume, to keep matters simple, that each additional dollar spent on this program results in one more unit of *output* of pollution abatement; that is, the removal of a given amount of pollutant from the environment.[5] Assume, in addition, that the public generally values the first few units of abatement more highly than subsequent units. Such an assumption is most plausible in that the first few units of pollutant removed will likely significantly lessen health hazards in heavily populated areas, but the removal of the last units will only mean a reduction in annoyance and perhaps also small increments in aesthetic values. Given both these assumptions, we can draw the marginal social benefit (*MSB*) and marginal social cost (*MSC*) schedules for this pollution abatement program as shown in Figure 1–1. The horizontal *MSC* schedule corresponds to our assumption that every dollar of expenditure on the program yields the same number of units of pollution abatement. The *MSB* schedule represents the sum of all benefits to all households at each level of output of the program; that is, the sum of the amounts each household is willing to pay to remove one more unit of pollutant at a particular level of concentration of the pollutant. The downward slope of the *MSB* schedule

---

[5] We shall drop this highly unrealistic assumption in later chapters.

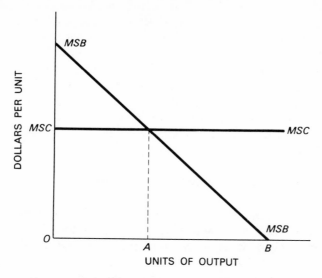

FIGURE 1–1. Marginal Social Benefits and Costs.

reflects our assumption that the first units of abatement output yield more benefits per unit to consumers than do subsequent units. The reader can see immediately that the *MSB* and *MSC* schedules in this simple case are closely analogous to the demand and supply schedules in competitive private markets.

In order to concentrate our discussion on the basic principles of benefit-cost analysis, let us make the heroic assumption that the government has full knowledge of the exact quantitative dimensions of both the benefit/unit and cost/unit schedules.[6] From Figure 1–1, it is then immediately apparent, first, that this program is worth undertaking according to the benefit-cost criterion because *total* benefits (the area under the *MSB* schedule) exceed *total* costs (the area under the *MSC* schedule) at some feasible levels of output. That is, the *MSB* schedule is everywhere above the *MSC* schedule at some levels of output. Second, the optimum level of output is *OA,* because for any lesser level of output, the *additional* benefits of one more unit of output exceed the *additional* costs per unit, and for any greater level of output, the *additional* costs per unit exceed the *additional* benefits per unit. The latter point is especially important, for it contradicts the prevalent notion that society demands complete pollution abatement at all costs (a situation corresponding to

[6] We shall explore the question of how the government may acquire such information in Chapter 5.

output level *OB* in Figure 1–1). The hardheaded, unsentimental view of economists, codified in benefit-cost analysis, is that pollution abatement is justified only up to the point that the additional benefits of more abatement are at least as great as the additional costs per unit. If additional costs exceed additional benefits, as they do at output levels greater than *OA* in Figure 1–1, it implies that households do not value additional pollution abatement more highly than the opportunity costs of the consumption of other goods and services. The implications of this basic point will be developed more fully in Chapters 3 and 4.

Concluding Notes on Benefit-Cost Analysis

As we observed in the introduction to this topic, benefit-cost analysis, in the broad sense, is a term applied to a mode of thinking about social problems. Specifically, it means the systematic appraisal of all the advantages of alternative courses of action. In the narrow sense, however, benefit-cost analysis is a problem-solving tool, and it is used to help in the making of decisions about the best allocation of government resources. For example, a government economist might very well adopt the methodology described in the previous section and, with a great deal of hard and imaginative work, be able to estimate accurately the dimensions of benefits and costs.

The practical application of benefit-cost and analysis is subject to a number of serious limitations that should be made explicit. First, as we have already suggested, the government is, typically, at least partially ignorant of the dimensions of the benefits, and very likely also of the costs. In many cases, decision makers are not even able to specify the nature of the benefits and costs involved in a given program. In addition, many benefits expected from a current budget outlay accrue to society only over various periods of time into the future, and therefore must be discounted to make them commensurable with current costs. Unfortunately, the choice of the correct discounting technique is one of the most difficult and controversial problems in economic theory, one that we shall take up again in Chapter 11. A closely related problem is that the benefits anticipated from a given government program are subject to various degrees of uncertainty, and, again, this factor complicates life for the benefit-cost analyst.

A more basic difficulty is that applied benefit-cost analysis is most useful in situations in which one problem in the allocation of resources can legitimately be treated as independent of the allocation of resources in general. That is, benefits and costs for a hypothetical course of action can most readily be estimated in a *ceteris paribus,* or, other things equal, framework. In our example of the previous section, the estimation of benefits and costs was a tractable problem in part because of our implicit assumption that the allocation of resources in society was given and only the one particular project under study was in question. Such a partial equilibrium framework is appropriate for some environmental problems but not for others. In general, economists in government will have to learn to cope with the biological, physical, and chemical interactions of the total environment before they can usefully apply benefit-cost analysis to serious environmental problems. To illustrate the nature of the problem with a trivial example, suppose that an environmentally naive economist prepares a benefit-cost analysis of a government program intended to alleviate the pollution of a given body of water. If he is careless, he will consider only the outlays of the government as costs and only the value of the pollution abatement in the given body of water as benefits. But if the effect of the government program is simply to cause firms and households to switch from waste disposal into the body of water to waste disposal in some other environmental resource in the ecosystem or biome, this methodology will clearly produce absurd results. The problem of waste disposal costs must ultimately be viewed as a whole, but before this can be done, it will be necessary to understand the basic materials balance theory developed in Chapter 3.

Finally, the most fundamental problem with applied benefit-cost analysis is the analytical treatment of income distribution effects. In brief, a government official cannot limit himself to considering only aggregate benefits and costs. Instead, he must examine the difficult issue of who receives the benefits and who bears the costs of any given program. Because the gainers and the losers from any government action in general will not be identical, the government must determine the magnitude of net gains and losses among various groups and individuals, and then somehow balance the desirability of the distributional effects against the pure economic efficiency effects revealed through straightforward benefit-cost analysis. We shall discuss this point in more depth in Chapter 5.

We have raised several difficulties at this point without any attempt to resolve them. Throughout the rest of the book, however, they will come up repeatedly in several different contexts, and will be given more extended treatment. None of the limitations of applied benefit-cost analysis count as arguments against the more broadly conceived benefit-cost approach to environmental problems. The benefit-cost framework is indispensable to the proper conception of these problems and enables economists to ask the right questions even if they are not yet able to provide the correct answers.

D. SUMMARY AND CONCLUSIONS

This is a book about the economics of environmental problems. The theme of the book is that environmental quality is a scarce, or economic, good. It follows then that the study of environmental problems can proceed along the general lines of analysis economists have successfully applied in the past to similar problems involving the allocation and distribution of scarce goods and services.

Pollution problems have always existed to some degree, but only in the last decade or so has environmental quality become a generally scarce good. The transformation of environmental quality from a free to a scarce good is, paradoxically, the result of man's success in achieving economic plenty. The high levels of pollutants that strain the earth's natural absorptive capacity today are simply the other side of the coin of the high levels of output in economically advanced countries. The combination of the still higher levels of output anticipated in the future and the lack of any effective political response to environmental problems leads us to the gloomy prediction that environmental quality will deteriorate still more in most respects. The major social force for the protection of the environment today is the modern conservation movement, a loosely organized number of individuals and organizations dedicated to the preservation of environmental quality.

Benefit-cost analysis is, in the broad sense of the term, a mode of thinking about problems in the allocation of resources. It is the systematic appraisal and evaluation of all the consequences of a contemplated course of action and of all relevant alternative courses of action.

Most environmental problems today can be linked to the waste disposal costs associated with high levels of production and consumption. Waste disposal costs are the sum of (1) private and public expenditures on the prevention of pollution; (2) private and public expenditures on the avoidance of pollution damage, once pollution has already occurred; and (3) the welfare damage of pollution. For any given level of gross output, society maximizes net output by minimizing total waste disposal costs. This point is the logical basis for a benefit-cost approach to government programs involving pollution prevention or pollution damage avoidance costs. Such costs make sense as long as they result in sufficiently large benefits to society in the form of reduced welfare damage costs of pollution.

Benefit-cost analysis, more narrowly conceived, is a useful problem-solving tool for government decision makers in circumstances where it is feasible and realistic to estimate dollar values for all the benefits and costs of a given government program. In general, the use of applied benefit-cost analysis is limited by a number of complicating factors, the foremost of which are the complex interrelationships between different facets of the environment and the proper analytical treatment of the distribution of benefits and costs.

QUESTIONS FOR DISCUSSION

1. Suppose a body of water A contains m parts per million of a substance X. Is A polluted? Suppose another body of water B contains n parts per million of a substance Y. Is B more or less polluted than A? What criteria are necessary for answering such questions?

2. Spokesmen for less-developed countries have been heard to say that they welcome pollution. What do they mean?

3. Do you think present pollution problems in the U.S. are serious enough to call for drastic measures such as an additional $100 billion a year in government pollution control expenditures? What kind of information would you want to have to answer this question with confidence?

4. Consider the outstanding pollution problems in your immediate area. Can you classify the effects of such problems as either (a) pollution prevention costs, (b) pollution damage avoidance costs, or (c) welfare damage costs?

5. Suppose that air quality at your place of residence greatly deteriorates. What costs would this development impose on you? Outline a benefit-cost analysis of the main alternative courses of action open to you in response to such a situation. Attempt to specify the various benefits and costs for each alternative.

SELECTED REFERENCES

BARNETT, HAROLD J., "Population Change and Resources: Malthusianism and Conservation," in *Demographic and Economic Change in Developed Countries*. National Bureau of Economic Research. Princeton: Princeton University Press, 1960. Contrasts between older and more modern views on the issue of the supply of natural resources.

DALES, J. H., *Pollution, Property and Prices*. Toronto: University of Toronto Press, 1968. An excellent, concise book on the economist's approach to environmental problems. Especially good on the subject of the welfare costs of pollution.

DUBOS, RENÉ, *A God Within*. New York: C. Scribner's Sons, 1972. A philosophical treatment of the relationship of man to his environment.

Environmental Quality, The First Annual Report of the Council on Environmental Quality. Washington, D.C.: Government Printing Office, 1970. A basic source for any student of the environment. Subsequent *Annual Reports* by the Council on Environmental Quality provide up-to-date information on the state of the nation's environment.

KRUTILLA, JOHN V., "Conservation Reconsidered," *American Economic Review,* LVIII, No. 4 (September, 1967). A sophisticated, modern view of conservation.

PREST, A. R., AND R. TURVEY, "Cost-Benefit Analysis: A Survey," in *Surveys of Economic Theory,* Vol. I. New York: St. Martin's Press, 1967. A survey of conceptual problems in benefit-cost analysis.

SAMUELSON, PAUL A., *Economics* (9th ed.). New York: McGraw-Hill, 1973. An excellent elementary textbook. The microeconomic theory chapters should be reviewed before proceeding in this book.

The
Basic Theory
of
Environmental
Economics

Chapter 2

Efficiency
in a
Private
Market
Economy

This is the first of the four chapters of Part 2 of the book, which is devoted to expounding the theory of environmental economics. This material is similar in some respects to the content of a typical undergraduate course in microeconomic theory. We do not attempt to cover the main body of microeconomic theory, but discuss one particular topic—the theory of externalities—in some depth, because of its relevance to environmental problems.

This chapter lays the groundwork for all of Part 2 of the book with a critical discussion of the concept of efficiency in a private market economy; the purpose of the analysis is to review for the reader the desirable *social* properties of a system of private markets under ideal circumstances. Chapter 3 extends the elementary theory presented in this chapter by reconsidering the concept of efficiency in a more realistic, sadly familiar world in which the environmental problems of society, such as air and water pollution, are not satisfactorily resolved by an otherwise ideal private market system. These problems are traced to economic factors operating outside the market system, which we term *externalities.* Chapter 4 then outlines two alternative theoretical solutions to the environmental problems posed by the existence of pervasive externalities. Chapter 5 is devoted to a theoretical analysis of the efficiency and income distribution aspects of government environmental programs.

Our intention, in these four chapters, is to give the reader a coherent theoretical base for the study of environmental economics. The discussion may appear, at first encounter, to be too abstract for the reader who is anxious to go immediately to the substance of environmental problems. In common with research workers in the natural and social sciences, however, we share the prejudice that a carefully worked out theory is a prerequisite for the successful study of a complex subject. The various phenomena that can be classified under the general rubric of environmental economics are too numerous and too varied to be comprehended by any human mind, however powerful, if each fact and empirical relationship is taken up one by one without a prior attempt to relate each to some central organizing concepts. In fact, it is a fallacy to assert that the study of environmental economics, or of any reasonably difficult subject, can be conducted successfully without the aid of theory. The real issue is between an explicitly stated, consistent set of organizing concepts and an implicit, *ad hoc,* probably inconsistent, and misleading set. The phenomenal successes achieved by implementation of the scientific method in other fields make a strong argument for explicit, rigorous formal theory as one ingredient of progress in solving complex environmental problems. The second basic ingredient—the subjecting of theoretical hypotheses to the tests of factual verification and the consequent refinement and elaboration of the existing body of theory—is still in a rudimentary state in the infant science of environmental economics, as will be painfully clear throughout the book.

This chapter proceeds according to the following outline: Section A begins with a discussion of the basic problem in modern welfare economics—the relationship of the interactions between individual markets in a private market system and of the efficiency of resource allocation from the viewpoint of all of society. We shall outline, very briefly, in this section, the traditional analysis leading to the conclusion that, under ideal circumstances, the private market system tends to produce optimal *social* results. In Section B, we turn a critical eye on the results of the analysis as stated in Section A, and attempt to make clear the strong assumptions that underlie these results. A final Section C summarizes the chapter.

A. PRIVATE MARKETS AND SOCIAL WELFARE

1. Definitions of Terms

This section discusses the *social*, or aggregate, implications of a hypothetical private market economy in which *individual* households and firms take into account only their own, individual welfares. Hopefully, much of this discussion will merely review material covered in the reader's first course in economics. A few definitions of terms must precede our analysis:

The *household*, consisting either of individuals or a larger family unit, is the ultimate consumer unit in society. We assume that each household attempts to maximize its welfare (often called utility), and that welfare is a positive function of the consumption of goods and services sold in markets.

The *firm*, although owned by households, is, for analytical purposes, best treated as an independent entity whose major goal is the maximization of profits. Firms hire productive services and combine them to produce the goods and services then sold to the ultimate consumers, households.

Firms and households interact as economic units in *markets*—the institutions through which potential buyers and sellers of goods and services deal with each other in the process of exchange. Markets exist both for *outputs* and *inputs*. Firms are suppliers of consumer goods and services to output markets, and households are demanders. In contrast, households supply the services of their labor and capital to firms in input markets, and firms are the demanders of these services.

Consumer *expenditures* in output markets are the *revenues* of firms. Wages, salaries, dividends, rents, and other payments by firms in return for household labor and capital services in input markets are the *costs* of firms and the *incomes* of households. *Profits* (losses) are simply the algebraic difference between firm revenues and costs.

Markets may be characterized as *perfectly competitive* if no buyer or seller can affect the market price by varying its own individual supply or demand. Roughly speaking, a market will be perfectly competitive if the number of potential buyers and sellers is sufficiently large to ensure that no one household or firm can affect the market price by varying the amount it demands or offers. If a market is perfectly competitive, it follows from the above definition that every household and firm is a *price taker* in the sense that it can buy or sell all it wants at the going market price.

2. General Equilibrium in a System of Private Markets

As the reader will recall from his introductory course in economics, equilibrium prices in individual, perfectly competitive markets are determined by the impersonal forces of market supply and demand. In a state of *general equilibrium* in a hypothetical system of perfectly competitive markets, the prices of all goods and services in output and input markets alike are determined simultaneously, with complex interactions occurring between different individual markets, some of them apparently completely unrelated. Abstracting from the most complex dynamic processes that bring about price adjustments in interrelated markets, let us concentrate on a hypothetical economy in which all adjustments have already occurred and prices in all markets have attained their equilibrium values. Assuming that the level of technology, tastes, and other underlying variables affecting the supply and demand of all goods and services remain unchanged and do not disturb the state of general equilibrium, let us examine some of the implications of the general interrelationships between prices, costs, and individual household and firm decisions.

A. HOUSEHOLD EQUILIBRIUM IN CONSUMPTION. First, consider the adjustment of the individual consumer unit, the household, to the pattern of relative prices that exists in output markets—the markets for consumption goods and services. We assume that households behave rationally; that is, that they purposefully attempt to maximize their economic welfare by searching for the largest and best collection of

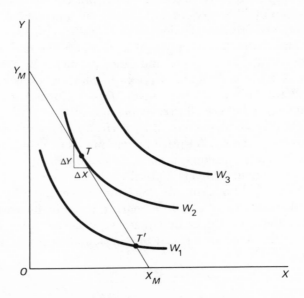

FIGURE 2–1. Household Equilibrium.

consumption goods and services they can afford. Figure 2–1 depicts the process of rational choice for an individual household allocating its expenditure between just two goods or services—X and Y. Our assumption of perfect competition in all markets implies that the prices of X and Y, P_X and P_Y, are constants for the household (it can buy all of X and Y it desires at these prices.) Thus its *budget line*, $Y_M X_M$ in Figure 2–1, is a straight line. Points X_M and Y_M represent the maximum amounts of X and Y, respectively, that it can purchase if it devotes its whole income to just one good or the other. Intermediate points along $Y_M X_M$ represent the various combinations of X and Y it can buy with the same total expenditures.[1] As shown in footnote 1, the slope of the budget line— the rate at which a household can substitute Y for X in its budget by shifting from the purchase of one to the other in the market—is equal to $-\dfrac{P_X}{P_Y}$, with the minus sign having the economic interpretation that, with a given income, the household can spend more on Y only by purchasing less of X.

Superimposed on the budget line in Figure 2–1 are three *indifference curves*, W_1, W_2, and W_3. Each of these curves is the locus of a given level of welfare for the household, with the level of welfare increasing as the household moves to the northeast, away from the origin; that is, as it consumes more of *both* X and Y. W_3 represents a higher level of welfare for the household than W_2, and W_2 a higher level than W_1. The slope of any indifference curve, called the marginal rate of substitution (MRS), can be given the economic interpretation of the subjective rate of tradeoff by the household between X and Y that will leave its economic welfare unchanged. The MRS between Y and X (MRS_{YX}) is equal to the ratio of the marginal welfares of X and Y at any point on the curve, or $\dfrac{MW_X}{MW_Y}$.[2] The implied negative slope of MRS_{YX} means that an increase

---

[1] The equation of the budget line is $I = P_Y Y + P_X X$, where I is total income or expenditure. Solving for Y as a function of X, we obtain:

$$Y = \frac{I}{P_Y} - \frac{P_X}{P_Y} X.$$

This is the equation of a straight line with $\dfrac{I}{P_Y}$ equal to Y_M, the Y intercept, and $-\dfrac{P_X}{P_Y}$ the constant slope. Note that $Y = Y_M = \dfrac{I}{P_Y}$ when $X = 0$, and $X = X_M = \dfrac{I}{P_X}$ when $Y = 0$.

[2] A small movement along any indifference curve leaves welfare unchanged. The change in total welfare for any change in X and Y consumed may be expressed as

$$\Delta W = \Delta Y \cdot MW_Y + \Delta X \cdot MW_X$$

where MW_Y and MW_X are the marginal changes in welfare associated with each unit of additional Y or X, and the Δ symbol signifies small changes in the variables. Thus $\Delta Y \cdot MW_Y$ is the change in welfare associated with a small change in the consumption of Y. Along any indifference curve, it follows that $\Delta W = 0$

in welfare due to an increase in the consumption of either X or Y must be offset by a decrease in welfare due to a decrease in the consumption of the other if the household is to remain at the same level of economic welfare (on the same indifference curve)—an increase (decrease) in both X and Y would make the household unambiguously better (worse) off. Finally, the indifference curves are assumed to be convex in Figure 2–1, which implies a *diminishing* MRS_{YX}. This means simply that we assume that the household's subjective rate of tradeoff between Y and X varies systematically with the relative amounts of Y and X it is already consuming. As we move down and to the right along any indifference curve, the slope, or MRS_{YX}, decreases (in absolute terms), which means that it takes increasingly greater amounts of additional X to compensate the household for the loss of one unit of Y as the household consumes a greater ratio of X to Y.

With the above assumptions and definitions, we can inspect Figure 2–1 to find the mix of X and Y it chooses in order to maximize its welfare. We see that the household can, in effect, move along (or inside) its budget line until it obtains its most advantageous market basket of X and Y. The best combination, given its income, is clearly at point T, where it attains a subjective welfare level of W_2. Welfare levels to the northeast of W_2, such as W_3, are preferable, but it can not attain these higher levels given its current income and the prices at X and Y, as embodied in the budget line $Y_M X_M$.

Note that the crucial result of this analysis is that the best attainable combination point T must occur at a tangency between the budget line and an indifference curve. From our previous results, we know that we can describe this outcome by an equality of the two slope coefficients. At the optimal point, T,

$$\begin{array}{c} \text{Slope of Indifference} \\ \text{Curve} \end{array} = MRS_{YX} = -\frac{MW_X}{MW_Y} = -\frac{P_X}{P_Y}$$
$$= \text{Slope of Budget Line}$$

Rearranging terms, we obtain:

$$\text{either } \frac{MW_X}{P_X} = \frac{MW_Y}{P_Y} \text{ or } \frac{P_X}{P_Y} = \frac{MW_X}{MW_Y}$$

---

or

$$\Delta Y \cdot MW_Y = -\Delta X \cdot MW_X$$
$$-\frac{\Delta Y}{\Delta X} = \frac{MW_X}{MW_Y}$$

Note that $-\dfrac{\Delta Y}{\Delta X}$ is simply the slope of the indifference curve; so we have the result in the text for the MRS_{YX}.

Because our analysis was general for all perfectly competitive markets, we know that this last expression must hold for any household between any pair of goods and services, and, therefore, *all* goods and services in its budget. The allocation of the budget among alternative goods and services will, of course, vary across households, both because of differences in tastes (different indifference curves) and differences in incomes (different budget lines).

In words, *in general equilibrium in an economy of perfectly competitive markets, the maximization of welfare by a household implies that it has a common* $\dfrac{MW}{p}$ *for all commodities.*[3]

The logic of this rule can best be understood by observing that if any household does not consume any pair of goods and services so as to meet this maximization condition, it can always increase its level of economic welfare by shifting some of its expenditures from the commodity with a relatively low MW/P to one with a higher MW/P. In Figure 2–1, such a shift would be depicted by a movement from T' to T along budget line $Y_M X_M$, because at point T', $\dfrac{MW_X}{P_X} < \dfrac{MW_Y}{P_Y}$, and Y can be substituted for X in the household's budget to increase the household's level of welfare from W_1 to W_2. We remind the reader that this important result holds only under the assumption of perfect competition in which the price ratio $\dfrac{P_X}{P_Y}$ is a constant parameter for any household.

The result derived above has a very important implication for the interpretation of the role of relative prices in a perfectly competitive economy in a state of general equilibrium. All relative prices, such as $\dfrac{P_X}{P_Y} = (MW_X/MW_Y)$, measure exactly for every household the relative subjective contributions to its economic welfare of the last units of the goods and services it consumes. The price of every good or service measures the benefit of the last unit consumed—the marginal benefit—for every household in the economy in equilibrium. This result is, in effect, the outcome of individual benefit-cost types of decisions made by millions of households.

The economic theory underlying this discussion is somewhat subtle and bears some elaboration. Each household is assumed to be a price taker in this theory. Because the quantity of any output it is capable of buying is very small relative to the total market demand, it merely

---

[3] The conclusion assumes that all households consume positive quantities of both X or Y. If they do not, corner solutions at Y_M or X_M in Figure 2–1 will be relevant. For the rest of this chapter, we shall not concern ourselves with such theoretical fine points, but the reader may consult the more advanced treatments of this subject cited at the end of the chapter.

adjusts the quantity it consumes of any commodity to whatever price obtains at the moment in the market, without affecting the price. The aggregate of all households behaving in this way, however, determines the total market demand for every commodity. The total market demand interacts with the total supply in each market to determine the price that clears the market in an equilibrium situation. Each individual consumer is a passive price taker, but the aggregate of the *passive* behavior of all consumers *actively* helps, together with supply, to determine the equilibrium market price. The strong conclusion stated in the previous paragraph holds, therefore, only in a state of general equilibrium in a system of perfectly competitive markets.

B. FIRM EQUILIBRIUM IN PRODUCTION. Consider the decisions required of the manager of a profit-maximizing firm in response to a set of input-market-determined prices for all productive input services and another set of output-market-determined prices for all potential outputs. The manager must decide simultaneously what outputs, if any, to produce, the quantities to be produced, and the necessary quantities of various productive input services to hire. A simple, crucially important rule summarizes the outcome of his profit-maximizing decisions in perfectly competitive markets. The firm will produce any good or service only up to a level at which the selling price just covers the incremental or marginal costs of production.[4]

Figure 2–2 depicts the reasoning underlying this basic relationship.

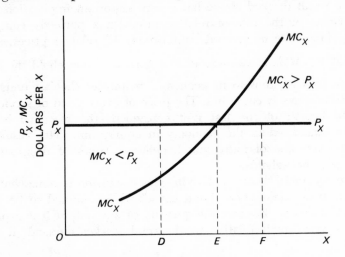

FIGURE 2–2. Equilibrium of the Firm.

[4] Over the long run, the selling price must also exceed the average, or per unit, cost of production if the firm is to have positive profits.

The firm in Figure 2–2 faces a market price of P_X. Note that the horizontal line P_X is the firm's demand curve, which is the geometric representation of our assumption that a firm in a perfectly competitive market can sell as much as it wishes at the going market price without affecting the price. The firm's marginal cost (MC) of production must be increasing at a level of output that is a very small fraction of total industry output in order for perfect competition to be viable in the industry. If such were not the case, it would be impossible for many small firms to survive and compete with larger firms, and the industry would be made up of large firms each of which has some control over market price. Thus, the upward slope of the MC curve in Figure 2–2 is necessary for consistency with our assumption of perfect competition.

Given the assumptions stated above, the profit-maximizing firm in Figure 2–2 will produce at an output of OE units, where $P_X = MC_X$. At any lower level of output, say OD units, $MC_X < P_X$, and each additional unit of X the firm sells yields it a net profit of $(P_X - MC_X)$ per unit. Similarly, a firm will not produce at a higher level of output than OE units, such as OF, because at this level of output, $MC_X > P_X$, and the firm loses $(MC_X - P_X)$ on each additional unit it sells. Only at output level OE, where $P_X = MC_X$, does the firm maximize profits. Stated more carefully with proper attention to the internal logic of the theory, the assumption that a firm maximizes profits in a perfectly competitive market *implies* the important result that production of any good or service will be at a level at which

$$P = MC.$$

The result derived above holds for every firm in a perfectly competitive economy. That is, every firm in the economy produces its outputs to a point where $P = MC$. Because $P_X = MC_X$; $P_Y = MC_Y$; $P_Z = MC_Z$ . . ., it follows that relative prices such as P_X/P_Y will be exactly equal to relative marginal costs for all products. In symbols,

$$\frac{P_X}{P_Y} = \frac{MC_X}{MC_Y}$$

The economic interpretation of this last result is that relative prices in general equilibrium in a perfectly competitive economy exactly measure the relative marginal costs of all goods and services. Combined with our previous result about the interpretation of relative prices from the standpoint of consumers' relative MWs, we are now in a position to put together the pieces of our analysis in order to draw some conclusions about the meaning of efficiency and social welfare in a perfectly competitive economy.

3. Social Welfare in a Perfectly Competitive Economy

What is the meaning of the concept *efficiency* for a whole society? An individual firm or household is said to be efficient if it maximizes output or consumption for a given level of resources or if it minimizes its expenditure of resources to attain a given level of output or consumption. Intuitively, a whole economy may be called efficient if it too can maximize some kind of aggregation of individual welfares for the given amount of resources available to the whole society at any point in time. Individual welfares, in turn, depend on individual household evaluations of the consumption goods and services each is able to consume.[5] Thus, social efficiency is not measured by aggregating physical quantities of goods and services, such as tons or yards, but rather by somehow aggregating the subjective values placed on different goods and services by individual consumer units. Thus, in our usage, (maximum) economic efficiency for a society is identical with a term we prefer to use, *maximum social welfare*, or MXSW.

MXSW can be defined tentatively as a situation in which it is impossible, even conceptually, to make any readjustment of production or consumption arrangements that would make even one household better off without making some other household worse off.[6] As long as such a "costless" readjustment could be effected in a society, it has not attained a state of MXSW. This concept of MXSW is usually termed a *Pareto Optimum*, after the famous Italian sociologist, Vilfredo Pareto (1848–1923).

With the results we have already derived, it is possible to show that a state of general equilibrium in a perfectly competitive market economy satisfies the necessary conditions for MXSW. To demonstrate this proposition, all that is necessary is to prove that the consumption and production relationships established by a perfectly competitive market system are such that it is not possible to make any household better off without making any other household worse off. We shall give the necessary proof very briefly by first establishing the necessary conditions for MXSW, and then showing that these necessary conditions are fulfilled in a state of general equilibrium in a perfectly competitive economy. Our arguments below will be largely on an intuitive level and grounded only on examples, because the full, rigorous proof of these conditions is

---

[5] A more complete treatment of this subject would include the value of leisure time, as well as consumption, in individual and social welfares.

[6] We should note immediately that the definition of MXSW in the text is an overly narrow one, and we present it only on the grounds of expository convenience. In Section B, we shall reconsider the concept of MXSW within a broader perspective.

beyond the scope of the book. The interested reader is urged, however, to consult one of the more advanced references cited at the end of the chapter.

The first necessary condition that must hold for MXSW is that all households consume each good and service to the point at which the individual subjective estimation of the tradeoff between the last units of any pair of commodities—the ratio of MWs—is equal for all families. If this condition is not met, a reallocation of consumption could make at least one household better off without making any other household worse off.

To see this point, suppose that some households (Group I) are just willing to trade (indifferent between) their last 2 units of commodity X for 1 more unit of commodity Y, and all other households (Group II) are just willing to trade just their last 1 unit of X for 1 more unit of Y. Stated from the opposite perspective, the Group I households are just willing to trade their last 1 unit of commodity Y for $\frac{1}{2}$ more unit of commodity X and the Group II households are just willing to trade their last 1 unit of Y for 1 more X. For Group I, then, the $MRS_{YX} = \frac{1}{2}$, and for Group II, the $MRS_{YX} = 1$. (For convenience, henceforth we shall ignore the minus sign in the MRS). In these circumstances, suppose that A and B were traded on a 1 to 1 basis between Groups I and II. Group II would, by assumption, remain as well off as before the trade in giving up 1 unit of X in exchange for 1 unit of Y; the loss in economic welfare from giving up 1 last unit of X would be just offset by the gain in economic welfare derived from gaining one more unit of Y. Group I, on the other hand, would, by assumption, be better off as the result of the exchange. The gain in economic welfare from obtaining one more unit of Y would be twice as great for them as the loss in economic welfare from giving up one last unit of X. By the same reasoning, if X and Y were traded on a 2 to 1 basis, Group I would remain just as well off as before the trade, and Group II would be better off. Following the same logic further, if X and Y were traded on a 1½ to 1 basis (or in any ratio between 1 to 1 and 2 to 1), both Group I and Group II would be better off as a result of voluntary exchange.

The general conclusion from the foregoing example should now be intuitively reasonable; unless the ratio of individual MWs is the same for all households for any pair of commodities, the reallocation of consumption commodities among households potentially can improve the welfare of some, and perhaps all, households without decreasing the welfare of any other household. In general equilibrium in a perfectly competitive economy, all MW ratios will be equal for any pair of goods for all households, as demonstrated in Section 2A. Recall that the rule describing the outcome of rational consumer behavior by households is:

$$\frac{P_X}{P_Y} = \frac{MW_X}{MW_Y},$$

for any two commodities, X and Y. The economic logic behind this rule is, again, that all households can maximize their own welfare only if they adjust their expenditures on all commodities until all their MRSs are equated to the relative prices established in output markets. In short, the perfectly competitive market system assures that, in general equilibrium, the ratio of MWs for all households will be equal for any pair of commodities—equal exactly to the general equilibrium relative prices.

A second necessary condition for MXSW to exist is somewhat more complex, because it involves production and consumption relationships simultaneously. Recall the result established previously that all profit-maximizing firms will produce a level of output at which the MC of the last unit produced will be just equal to the market price of its output. To see intuitively the relationship between this profit-maximizing rule for an individual private firm and MXSW, suppose that for any reason, $MC \neq P$ for some commodity. If, for example, $MC > P$, we could say that the last unit produced of the commodity requires the use of productive input services of greater value than the market price, which is a measure of the subjective value placed on the last unit consumed of that commodity by all households. Therefore, we could say that from the point of view of the whole economy, too much of the commodity is being produced, suggesting that production be cut back to release some of the productive input services employed by the firm and free them for use by some other firm in the production of some more socially valuable commodity. The perfectly competitive market system performs millions of such *benefit-cost* tests simultaneously to determine the optimal levels of production for all goods and services in the economy. These arguments suggest that $MC = P$ is a necesary condition for MXSW as well as the outcome of the process of profit maximizing behavior by individual firms under perfect competition.

We can develop these points more rigorously by inquiring into the economic significance of the ratio of the marginal costs of any two goods and services in equilibrium. Let us suppose that X and Y are the only two outputs in a perfectly competitive economy, and examine the ratio $(-)\,MC_X/MC_Y$. We call it the *marginal rate of transformation of X into Y*, or MRT_{YX}. It can be interpreted as the (negative) change in the production of X—the foregone production of X—required to produce one more unit of Y. (For simplicity, we shall henceforth ignore the minus sign in the MRT.) Suppose that the market price of commodity X is \$3, and the market price of commodity Y is \$1. The fact that X is three times more costly than Y reflects the fact that in equilibrium, MRT_{YX}, the ratio of MC_X to MC_Y, is 3 to 1. The economic sense of this ratio is that if the productive input services devoted to producing the last unit of X were reallocated to producing more of Y, 3 more units of Y could be produced. In other words, the MC_X/MC_Y ratio measures the rate at which X can be transformed into Y by means of shifting productive resources from the production of X to the production of Y. If MC_X is 3 times as great as MC_Y, this means that the same productive input services that produce the last 1 unit of X are capable of producing 3 more units of Y.

Figure 2–3 gives the MRT_{YX} a geometric interpretation as the slope

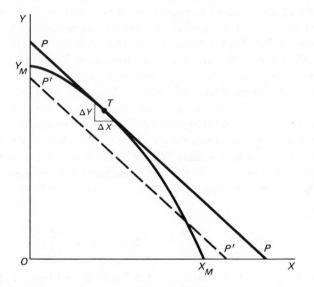

FIGURE 2–3. Maximization of Social Welfare.

of a *transformation* (or production possibilities) curve between X and Y. This curve is a locus of the maximum combinations of X and Y that can be produced with given resources and technology. The slope of the transformation curve $Y_M X_M$ at any point, $-\Delta Y/\Delta X$, can be interpreted as the social marginal opportunity cost of Y in terms of foregone X. From the analysis of the previous paragraph, we know that this slope value must be equal to the MC_X/MC_Y ratio. Superimposed on the transformation curve in Figure 2–3 is a relative price line, PP, with slope $= -P_X/P_Y$, established by the interaction of supply and demand in perfectly competitive markets for X and Y. The optimal production mix of X and Y

occurs at point T in Figure 2–3, the point of tangency between the relative price line and the transformation curve; that is, where $P_X/P_Y = MRT_{YX}$.[7] This result is general for *any* two goods or services in a perfectly competitive economy. Relative prices for any pair of goods or services measure the marginal opportunity cost of producing more of one in terms of less production of the other.

The relevance of the result derived above to MXSW can best be brought out by asking the question: What must be the relationship of MRS_{YX} to MRT_{YX}, where X and Y are again any two goods or services, in a state of MXSW. Suppose, for example, that the $MRS_{YX} = 2/(1)$, and $MRT_{YX} = 1/(1)$. Interpreted verbally, this means that all households can trade the last unit of X consumed for 2 additional units of Y (or 1 unit of Y for ½ unit of X) and remain equally well off in their own estimation, and firms can produce one more unit of Y at the cost of producing 1 less unit of X (and of course, one more unit of X at the cost of 1 less unit of Y). Under these assumed circumstances, the economic welfare of all households can clearly be improved by shifting some productive input services away from the production of Y to additional production of X. Households will have 1 less unit of Y available after such a shift in production in exchange for 1 more unit of X, but, by assumption, they value another unit of X twice as much as the last unit of Y consumed, and, therefore, they clearly will be better off. By reasoning closely analogous to the first MXSW condition for the allocation of consumption commodities, it can be demonstrated mathematically in advanced treatments of this subject that a second MXSW condition is that:

$$MRS_{YX} = -\frac{MW_X}{MW_Y} = MRT_{YX} = -\frac{MC_X}{MC_Y}$$

In words, the rate at which all households are willing, at the margin, to trade all consumption goods and services must be equal to the ratio of the MCs of all goods and services—the marginal rate at which goods and services can be productively transformed from one to another by the shift of productive input services between alternative uses.

The perfectly competitive market system assures that this second condition of MXSW also will be satisfied. As we have already shown:

$$\frac{MW_X}{MW_Y} = \frac{P_X}{P_Y} \text{ and } \frac{P_X}{P_Y} = \frac{MC_X}{MC_Y}$$

---

[7] Point T is optimal because total product is at a maximum along the transformation curve as measured either in terms of X or in terms of Y. That is, any other price line parallel to PP, such as $P'P'$, that intersects $Y_M X_M$ must lie to the left of PP.

in general equilibrium. By definition, the above equality implies, of course, that

$$MRS_{YX} = MRT_{YX}$$

where X and Y are *any* two commodities. Thus, we have accomplished our purpose of establishing that the necessary conditions for a state of MXSW are identical with the general equilibrium outcome of individual household and firm behavior in a perfectly competitive market system.

The idealized perfectly competitive market economy may be viewed as a completely decentralized mechanism that attains the social end of maximum economic efficiency. Each household and firm strives only to maximize its own economic well-being, with the aggregate of all such individual behavior reflected on opposite sides of all output and input markets in supply and demand forces. The impersonal factors of supply and demand interact in the markets of the economy to determine a set of relative output and input prices that satisfy the necessary conditions for MXSW. Adam Smith, the first economist to understand this remarkable social result of apparently uncoordinated private individual behavior, stated his version of the process most eloquently:

> . . . every individual necessarily labours to render the annual revenue of the society as great as he can. He generally, indeed, neither intends to promote the public interest, nor knows how much he is promoting it . . . he intends only his own security; . . . he intends only his own gain, and he is in this, as in many other cases, led by an invisible hand to promote an end which was not part of his intention. Nor is it always worse for the society that it was no part of it. By pursuing his own interest he frequently promotes that of the society more effectually than when he really intends to promote it.[8]

B. PRIVATE MARKETS AND SOCIAL WELFARE: DIFFICULTIES OF INTERPRETATION

The previous section reached strong and unambiguous conclusions about the relationship between MXSW and a private market economy at the cost of neglecting important problems. The purpose of this section is to indicate to the reader the limitations of the analysis in Section A. We shall take up in turn four important problems left out of the previous discussion in order to reduce to manageable proportions the complexity of the analysis.

[8] Adam Smith, *The Wealth of Nations* (New York: Random House, Modern Library Edition, 1937), p. 423.

1. *Imperfection of Competition*

In Section A, we defined perfect competition as a situation in which no buyer or seller in a market was sufficiently large to have any influence on the market price. Each buyer or seller simply accepted the going market price as a parameter and could buy or sell all he wanted at that price. In contrast, *imperfect competition* is said to exist if any buyer or seller in a particular market does have some power to affect the market price—*monopoly power*. Imperfection of competition and monopoly power are matters of degree, varying greatly among different markets. General Motors, with about half of total sales in the United States automobile market, can, obviously, influence the price of automobiles. It cannot, despite its best efforts, sell all the automobiles it would like at its established market price. To sell more automobiles, it would have to cut its price, an action it does not ordinarily deem to be most profitable. On the other hand, the local neighborhood supermarket usually has a lesser degree of monopoly power over the prices of various food items, because of the existence of many alternative food retailers in the neighborhood. If the degree of monopoly power in a market is only slight, the assumption of perfect competition is often a useful abstraction from the unimportant details of actual market circumstances because of its great relative simplicity. In many important problems, the monopoly power of just one or a few buyers and sellers is too significant to ignore, making it necessary for economists to revise theoretical analysis based on the assumption of perfect competition.

The existence of imperfect competition severely modifies our conclusion in Section A about the identity of general equilibrium conditions in a private market economy and the necessary conditions for MXSW. The most straightforward approach to revising our previous result is simply to show that, in imperfectly competitive markets, prices will not be equal to marginal costs in general equilibrium. Consider the typical case of a supplier of a commodity in an imperfectly competitive market. The assumption that a supplier has some degree of monopoly power can be given precise meaning in the assumption that the firm faces a downward sloping demand curve for its output. That is, the demand curve facing the firm with some monopoly power looks like the one in Figure 2–4, showing that the firm can sell more to its customers only at lower prices. In contrast, under perfect competition, the individual supplier faces a horizontal, or perfectly elastic, demand curve (Figure 2–2); that is, the firm can sell all it wants at the going market price.

We assume that the basic motivation of a firm under imperfect competition is the same as under perfect competition, the maximization of profits. Therefore, the general rule for determining the output of the

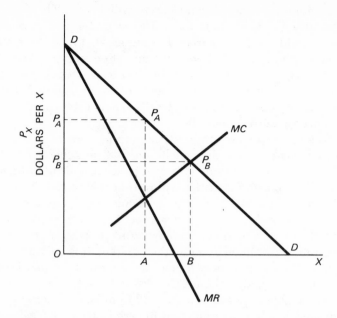

FIGURE 2–4. Equilibrium of the Imperfectly Competitive Firm.

firm does not change; the firm should produce and sell a quantity such that the incremental or marginal revenue derived from the last unit of output sold is at least as much as the incremental or marginal cost of producing that last unit.

Given the circumstance that the supplier must, in general, sell all his output at one price to all customers, the profit-maximizing firm with some degree of monopoly power must take into account the fact that an increase of one unit in the amount it sells will always yield it an additional revenue less than the new (lower) market price. This will be the case because in order to sell one more unit of output, the market price the firm charges its customers for *all* items must fall to the new, lower price. The additional revenue need not even be greater than zero. If demand conditions are such that a seller can sell nine units at ten dollars a unit, but can sell ten units at only nine dollars a unit, then the incremental revenue from the tenth unit is zero, because total revenue remains constant at ninety dollars. Thus, in Figure 2–4, we draw an incremental or marginal revenue curve (*MR*) that lies always below the demand curve, reflecting the fact that a movement down and to the right on the demand curve always adds less to total revenue than the going market price. We can see from Figure 2–4 that the profit maximizing output level for the firm will be *OA*, where *MR* = *MC*, and the selling price in equilibrium, found on the demand curve, will be P_A. The firm will not produce an output of OB, where $P_B = MC$, as under perfect competition, for to do so would *spoil the market* and reduce its profits from the maximum possible at output OA. For every unit produced beyond a level of OA, $MC > MR$, which means that the firm loses money on each additional unit sold and that total profits fall. In fact, as Figure 2–4 is drawn, before the firm reaches an output of OB, MR becomes negative, which means that even total revenue falls.

This very brief investigation of the implications of imperfect competition is sufficient to give the conclusion that, in general $P \neq MC$, in contrast to perfect competition. This results because firms with some degree of monopoly power over price will restrict their output below perfect competition levels in order to maximize profits. Thus, our previous assertion that the existence of imperfect competition negates the conclusion that the workings of a market economy result in MXSW. If price is not equal to marginal cost in every individual market, it is no longer true that relative prices for any pair of commodities are exactly equal both to the MRSs of households and to the relative MCs of firms.

Private monopoly power is a fact of life in any economy with a private sector, and much of it is inherent in certain technological and social conditions. The economic rationale for government intervention in a private market economy rests partly on the grounds that, under such circumstances, the private economy, itself, cannot achieve an acceptably efficient solution to some economic problems.

2. Dynamic Problems and Uncertainty

The microeconomic theory expounded in Section A of this chapter is purely static. The analysis is timeless in that it says nothing about dynamic movements of supply and demand conditions over time, such as the introduction of new products, the systematic development of more advanced technology, and sweeping changes in tastes for consumer goods and services. Although we shall not attempt to do so here, it is possible to develop more fully traditional microeconomic theory beyond a purely static framework. Intricate formal theories of markets extending over time have been formulated in a branch of economics called capital theory. The determination of the price called an interest rate in a dynamic market economy turns out to be a problem formally analogous to the determination of the price of apples in a static market economy. In perfectly competitive markets, for commodities to be exchanged either in the present or at some specified time in the future, demand and supply forces serve equally well as the proximate explanatory variables. Useful work in capital theory has done much to clarify aspects of saving and investment behavior, as well as other important topics that require explicit theoretical recognition of the fact of the passage of time.

For our purposes, however, it is sufficient to note only that the link between even a perfectly competitive market economy and the attainment of MXSW holds in a dynamic setting only under strong assumptions, the foremost of which is perfect *certainty* about the course of the future. Once we admit that the future is uncertain, the identity between general equilibrium in a perfectly competitive economy and MXSW cannot be logically demonstrated. In fact, it becomes difficult even to specify the meaning of social welfare in an uncertain, dynamic world. To mention just one problem, a useful definition of social welfare in a dynamic world must include not just the present consumption of existing households, but also the consumption of future households, which may include individuals not yet born. Another problem in dealing with the future theoretically in an uncertain world is that markets for certain essential insurance services in such a world are not viable, so that even individuals who wish to do so cannot deal effectively with all uncertain contingencies. Other, similar complexities are still the subject of much dispute in capital theory. In such a world, government intervention in the private market economy may be necessary to achieve a socially desirable time configuration of production and consumption.

3. The Problem of the Equity of Income Distribution

In Section A of this chapter, we defined the concept of maximum social welfare (MXSW) conventionally as a situation in which it is impossible to change the allocation of production or consumption in any way that would increase the economic welfare of any household without decreasing the economic welfare of any other household. As we have already noted, however, the implicit conception of social economic welfare embodied in the conventional definition of MXSW is exceedingly narrow; it is tenable only if the problem of the *equity* of the distribution of income among the households in a society is swept under the rug. Once explicit social concern with the distribution of economic welfare between households is admitted, it becomes immediately evident that government intervention will be necessary in some degree to improve on the outcome of a free, private market economy.

The reader will recall from his first course in economics the simple circular flow model of market relationships in a market economy. The incomes of households are the costs of firms—the payments by firms to purchase the productive labor and capital services owned by households. Each household's money income level is determined in a pure market economy solely by the quantities of productive services it is willing and able to sell to firms and the input market prices of these services. The money income of a household will be higher the more capital services it owns and has available to supply to firms, the more its members of working age are able and willing to work, and the higher the prices of the particular services it offers in the market. The higher its money income, the higher, normally, will be its level of economic welfare.[9]

Now, consider how this briefly sketched analysis of the determinants of the distribution of incomes in a market economy fits into our conventional definition of MXSW. We have shown that, in general equilibrium, in all markets under perfect competition, no household's economic welfare can be improved without diminishing the economic welfare of some other households. To grasp the narrowness of this conception of social welfare, it is sufficient to observe that if all existing property (the legal rights to the proceeds of the sale of productive capital services) were *randomly* redistributed among all households in society, a new state of general equilibrium incorporating the new distribution of income in the economy would also satisfy the necessary conditions for MXSW. Because there are an infinite number of random redistributions of property in any society, it follows that there are also, literally, an infinite number of states of MXSW, each corresponding to a different initial distribution of property rights. Economists have resolved this apparent paradox by recognizing that the conventional conditions for a state of MXSW are only *necessary*, as opposed to *sufficient*, conditions. In a broader view of this very difficult concept, most economists now agree that sufficient conditions for a state of *true*, or *general*, maximum social welfare include some prior specification of the appropriate distribution of incomes among households as well as the more technical necessary conditions for the *Pareto Optimum* version of MXSW.

In the study of political economy, as opposed to narrowly conceived *value-free* economic theory, the issue of income distribution must be primary. A pure private market economy, without government intervention, will generate a distribution of incomes and economic welfare related only tenuously to the ethical norms of the great majority of the populace. Such a pure market economy has never existed and is inconceivable because of its harsh and inhuman treatment of individuals unable to earn sufficient incomes by selling their productive services in the marketplace. The aged, the disabled and chronically ill, children without parents, and the just plain unlucky would literally starve in a pure market economy without the intervention of government and private, nonprofit organiza-

---

[9] The major qualification of this statement is that differences in the amount of voluntary leisure are also important in determining differences in the economic welfare of households.

tions. Thus, it is neither a controversial nor a difficult point that the private market economy, by itself, cannot attain a state of maximum social welfare that is broadly conceived to take account of the distribution of economic welfare. As we shall see in Chapter 5, government environmental policies inherently raise most complex income distribution issues.

4. Full Employment of Productive Resources

If government fiscal and monetary policies do not succeed in maintaining aggregate demand sufficiently high to assure full employment of all the productive input services that households are willing and able to supply, then the private market economy will fail to attain a state of MXSW. That is, with unemployed resources, the economy will operate inside the *PP* transformation curve in Figure 2–3. Productive resources that remain idle involuntarily, although households desire the commodities these resources could be used to produce, represent pure social waste. From the whole society's point of view, the opportunity cost of idle resources is literally zero, whatever the market prices of these resources happens to be. We shall not pursue this point further here, other than to observe that full employment of an economy's productive resources is an obvious prerequisite for MXSW.

C. SUMMARY AND CONCLUSIONS

This chapter reviews some basic principles of standard welfare economics in order to establish the connection between the workings of a private market economy and the concept of efficiency. Under the assumption of perfect competition in all markets, we show that in a state of general equilibrium two important conditions must hold: (1) Each household will maximize its economic well-being only if it equates its subjective marginal rate of substitution between any pair of goods to the relative prices of these goods, as established in perfectly competitive output markets; (2) Each firm will maximize profits only if it produces its output to a point at which price equals marginal cost. Every firm, in common with every household, takes all output market and input market prices as constant parameters in making its economic decisions.

With the above implications of a perfectly competitive economy established, we proceed to define the concept of social efficiency tentatively as a situation in which it is impossible to make any change in the economy's consumption, distribution, or production arrangements that could improve the welfare of any one household without diminishing the welfare of any other household. The necessary conditions for such a situation—termed either a state of maximum social welfare (MXSW) or a *Pareto Optimum*—turn out to be identical with the outcome of a perfectly competitive private market economy in general equilibrium. Viewed from the perspective of social welfare, the perfectly competitive market economy is an impersonal, completely decentralized mechanism that establishes a set of relative prices consistent with the most efficient use of society's resources.

The above conclusion about the social implications of a private market economy holds only under strong and unrealistic assumptions. First, perfect competition in all markets is a condition that can never be fully satisfied in any real economy. Second, a private market system does not guarantee socially optimal results in the allocation of resources over time in a dynamic world rife with uncertainty. Third, a state of MXSW is not unique, and, in fact, an infinite number of MXSWs are possible conceptually, each corresponding to a different initial distribution of the legal rights to productive resources. A *general* state of maximum social welfare must, therefore, involve some specification about the equity of the *distribution* of welfare among individual households. Fourth, a private market economy does not necessarily generate full employment of an economy's resources, which is a necessary condition for MXSW.

In conclusion, it is clear that the concepts of efficiency and social welfare involve great practical difficulties and that the connections between them and the private market economy are most ambiguous. We can work with market prices as indicators of social value in benefit-cost analysis and in other applications only if we are very careful to take full account of the various problems outlined above. We reserve discussion of one further difficulty—the problem of externalities that is central to environmental problems—to the next three chapters of Part 2.

QUESTIONS FOR DISCUSSION

1. Suppose that household A pays a higher price for good X than does household B. Why is this situation inconsistent with MXSW?

2. "The market price of a good is a measure both of its costs of production and its value to consumers." Why is this statement correct only under perfect competition?

3. "Individual selfishness results in a socially desirable outcome." Under what circumstances is this statement valid?

4. Figure 2–3 depicts maximization of social welfare in perfectly competitive markets for two goods, X and Y. Suppose, instead, that good X is produced by a monopoly firm and good Y is produced by many perfectly competitive firms. How would this change in assumptions affect the diagram?

5. Suppose that X and Y are the only two goods produced in a perfectly competitive economy. Would you favor a government subsidy for the production of X if you knew that X was consumed mainly by the poor and Y mainly by the rich? What are the implications of such a subsidy for MXSW?

SELECTED REFERENCES

BATOR, FRANCIS M., "The Simple Analytics of Welfare Maximization," *The American Economic Review*, XLVII, No. 1 (March, 1957). An advanced treatment of the material in this chapter.

BAUMOL, WILLIAM J., *Economic Theory and Operations Analysis* (2nd ed.). Englewood Cliffs, N.J.: Prentice-Hall, Inc., 1962. An excellent intermediate-level textbook in microeconomic theory.

FERGUSON, CHARLES E., *Microeconomic Theory* (Rev. ed.). Homewood, Illinois: Richard D. Irwin, Inc., 1969. An alternative to the Baumol text.

HIRSCHLEIFER, J., *Investment, Interest and Capital*. Englewood Cliffs, N.J.: Prentice-Hall, Inc., 1970. A very advanced, comprehensive treatment of neoclassical capital theory.

LANCASTER, KELVIN, *Introduction to Modern Microeconomics*. Chicago: Rand McNally & Co., 1969. Another alternative to the Baumol text.

SCITOVSKY, TIBOR, *Welfare and Competition* (Rev. ed.). Homewood, Illinois: Richard D. Irwin, Inc., 1971. Probably the best overall treatment of the topics covered in this chapter.

Chapter 3

Externalities,
Efficiency,
and
Social Welfare

The traditional microeconomic theory developed in Chapter 2 relates the functioning of a competitive market economy to the concept of social economic welfare without any references to the social welfare effects of environmental deterioration. The simple theoretical model of Chapter 2 is not, therefore, logically wrong—it is simply incomplete. This chapter develops some extensions of the simple model that will enable us to analyze a wide variety of environmental problems. For the sake of simplicity, we do not include in this chapter some of the difficulties raised in Chapter 2—specifically, the problem of uncertainty in a dynamic world, the equity of income distribution changes, and the possibility of less than full employment of society's resources. We shall demonstrate that, even in the absence of these problems, a perfectly competitive market system maximizes social economic welfare only under unrealistic assumptions about the technological conditions of production and consumption. In brief, a private market economy will systematically produce too much of some commodities and too little of others because relative market prices of goods and services are incomplete indicators of total social benefits and costs.

The substance of this chapter is developed according to the following plan: Section A discusses the central distinction between the concepts of total social costs (benefits) and private costs (benefits), the differences being defined as *external* costs (benefits), or more generally, externalities. Section B discusses the concept of *materials balance* in the processes of consumption and production. This concept emphasizes the intimate interdependence between economic activities and most environmental problems. Section C then examines the relative price and resource allocation effects of externalities, with emphasis given to the divergence of the social welfare implications of a system of private markets in the presence or absence of externalities. Section D gives a brief summary of the chapter.

A. THE CONCEPT OF EXTERNALITIES

Economists have long recognized that the private market system often produces undesirable *spillover* effects on man's environment.[1] Typical and too familiar examples of such spillover effects are the noxious smoke and polluted water emissions of modern industrial plants. In such circumstances, the technical nature of the production process generates an *output* effect distinct from the final marketed product of the firm. The spillover effects of modern industrial production result in deteriorating environmental quality, an output that the firm does not, and, of course, could not, sell. On the contrary, households and other firms affected by the pollutant spillovers experience real opportunity costs in many different forms and would be willing to pay varying amounts if they could effectively end or lessen the firm's polluting activities.

We define any costs that are additional to the costs resulting from the production outlays of the firm as *external*, or spillover, costs. *Total social costs* (social costs, for brevity) are defined as the sum of the private costs of the firm and any external costs. The use of the word *external* implies that some costs do not accrue to the firm that produces the good, but are imposed on all of society or, at least, on a subset of the households or firms in a society. Such costs are outside the market system and are not reflected in relative market prices.

[1] The classic treatment of this problem is given in A. C. Pigou, *Econmics of Welfare* (4th ed.) (London: Macmillan & Co., Ltd., 1960). The term *spillover* indicates that the full effects of production or consumption are not confined to the firms or households directly involved, but spill over onto third parties.

Examples of external costs are easy to find in any modern industrial economy. The paper firm that pollutes a river and destroys the game fish population imposes external costs on fishermen, boaters, and swimmers; so does the chemical plant that plagues the local community with constant stenches. The residential developer who denudes the landscape and constructs row on row of similarly built homes may impose psychic costs on many individuals by affronting their esthetic sensitivities. The individual who misses a number of work days each year due to illnesses caused by impure air bears a personal external cost, equal to his lost wages. Society, which loses the worker's production for the work days lost bears an additional external cost, equal to the net difference between the worker's average product and his wages over the relevant time period. Even the charcoal cookout of the suburbanite that soils his neighbor's drying laundry involves a (perhaps) small external cost. The common theme in all of these hypothetical situations is that firms or households other than those responsible for the initial act of production or consumption suffer uncompensated monetary or psychic costs.

At the same time, the general term *externalities* suggests that it is possible for the production or consumption of some commodities to bestow spillover benefits on fortunate firms and households not immediately involved in the actual production or consumption process. The recipients of such external benefits are not charged the monetary value of these benefits. No markets exist that enable the producers of the spillover benefits to exclude potential beneficiaries from consuming the spillovers if they fail to pay the market price. For example, health immunization services provide benefits to all of society in addition to the individual consumer in the form of better protection from contagious diseases. Similarly, everybody in the neighborhood benefits from the beauty of a well-designed building, and these benefits are all supplementary to the benefits derived from the owner of the building himself. Because this book is concerned mainly with problems of environmental pollution, our main focus will be on those externalities that have negative spillover effects; that is, external diseconomies. We shall note later, however, that the economic welfare implications of external economies are logically symmetric to those of external diseconomies.

B. THE MATERIALS BALANCE APPROACH TO ENVIRONMENTAL PROBLEMS

Until recently, economists have tended to consider externalities an interesting intellectual footnote to the main body of economic theory with little practical relevance to most economic policy issues. The emergence of serious environmental problems in the 1960s in the United States has induced many economists to reexamine their old views and prejudices on this issue. The work of Allen V. Kneese and several coworkers at Resources for the Future, Inc. has been especially influential in reshaping traditional views. Kneese and others have advanced a new theoretical model of the economy—the *materials balance* approach—that emphasizes that the external effects associated with waste disposal are general and pervasive in a modern economy rather than being trivial or exceptional phenomena.[2]

The point of departure for the materials balance approach is the self-evident relationship between the principle of the conservation of matter and the production process. Because physical matter cannot be destroyed, it follows that any economy will eventually have the same amount of material to dispose of as it initially uses as raw material inputs in production. Indeed, the economist's use of the term *consume* is, strictly speaking, a misnomer, because it suggests that economic goods somehow disappear as they are used. Obviously, as a society, we do not physically consume our output of economic goods. The owner of a car, for example, does not in any physical sense consume the car; he does utilize its services as a means of transportation, but the physical entity of the car remains intact after its useful life as a transport device is over. This is true of all goods, even though some goods (or parts of them) may be transformed from solid matter into gases via combustion processes or become diluted or dispersed in bodies of water instead of remaining simply as solid refuse matter. The disposal of physical goods poses an immense waste disposal problem for an industrialized economy. Obviously, different mixes of total output between physical goods and what we presently call services (that is, legal and financial services, repair services, medical services, and so on) in our national accounts will result in different magnitudes of waste disposal.

The materials balance approach conceives of the total economic process as a physically balanced flow between inputs and outputs (and the byproducts associated with generating outputs). In Figure 3–1, the materials balance view of the production process is depicted to begin with some level of organic and inorganic inputs from the resource base of the economy; then, through the various energy conversion and productive processes (determined by the available technology), the economy generates some output level of final goods. During both the energy conversion and productive processes, various waste residuals are generated that are discharged into the environment. Eventually, the final

[2] The material in this section draws heavily on R. U. Ayers and A. V. Kneese in "Production, Consumption and Externalities," *American Economic Review*, LIX, No. 3 (June 1969).

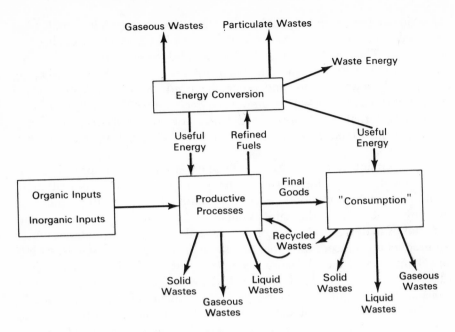

FIGURE 3-1. The Flow of Materials.

Reprinted with the permission of the authors and the American Economic Review.

outputs, after they have been *consumed* (that is, after their services are utilized), also reappear in various waste forms (trash, garbage, sewage, gases, junk, and so on) in the environment.[3]

The laws of conservation of matter and energy tell us that these residual wastes will be virtually identical in amount to the physical masses of all the inputs. Some of these wastes may be recycled into the productive process to reappear as inputs. Natural biological processes also may convert some wastes into inputs after varying periods of time. The amount of recycling of wastes is influenced by the available technology and existing economic incentives. This amount can be altered by appropriately designed policies, a subject we shall discuss in Chapters 8 and 10. However, all of the wastes that are not recycled into inputs must be discharged into the environment in various physical forms (liquids, solids, gases). The distribution of the residual wastes among these various forms is, of course, not fixed by natural processes or by the law of the conservation of matter and we shall discuss the important

---

[3] We abstract, for simplicity, from the existence of net imports or exports or net changes in inventories of either inputs or outputs.

implications of this point. The essential point at present, however, is that the amount of waste residuals generated as byproducts of the production process or at the end of consumption activities, is essentially *equal*, in physical weight, to the amount of basic materials entering into the production process over some period of time.

The environment has a large but *finite* capacity to absorb these waste residuals. With increases in the production levels of physical goods in an economy, we can deduce from the law of the conservation of matter that there will be corresponding increases in the waste loads placed on the assimilative media of the environment. As these increases in production (and, hence, potential waste) impinge on the assimilative capacity of the environment, society will begin to incur significant costs associated with environmental pollution. These costs are *external* costs in the sense of the definitions given in Section A above. That is, the external nature of these costs arises from the fact that individuals and firms that use the waste assimilative capabilities of the environment in the course of production or consumption are not charged for this use. They are, in essence, using a scarce good at a zero price at the expense of the rest of society. The reason why these costs are external to those responsible for their creation is that the rights to use the environmental media are, in general, not owned. We shall discuss further the role of ownership and property rights in externality problems in Chapter 4. At present, we can simply assert that because, for various reasons, ownership rights to the assimilative capabilities of the environment are incomplete, the disposal of the residuals from production and consumption processes will impose external costs on society. Further, the principle of the conservation of matter indicates that the amount of residuals to be disposed will be roughly of the same order as the amount of basic inputs. This is an enormous figure, running to the order of 2.5 billion *tons* for the U.S. economy in 1965.[4] Thus, it is certain that the disposal of this material in solid, liquid, and gas form represents a formidable undertaking and one whose effects will be widespread throughout the economy, particularly as the capacity of the environment in any given geographical region to absorb these materials in a costless way is surpassed.[5]

As a final point, we can note that the form in which the residuals

---

[4] This amount is estimated with some given basic definition of inputs (it also includes net imports). See R. U. Ayers and A. V. Kneese, "Environmental Pollution," U.S. Congress Joint Economic Committee, *Federal Programs for the Development of Human Resources*, Vol. II (Washington, D.C.: Government Printing Office, 1968).

[5] We also take as given, in this elementary analysis, the durability or length of useful life of final consumer goods. Obviously, if goods have longer rather than shorter useful lives, the amount of wastes to dispose of in any given time period will be lower than if goods are used up more rapidly.

are discharged into the environment can be determined, to a considerable degree, by society. Even with a given state of technology for waste disposal, society can choose how it desires to allocate the total amount of wastes between alternative media. Should the wastes be primarily gaseous (that is, use combustion processes); in liquid form, using water resources to dilute and disperse the wastes; or in solid, compressed forms, and disposed of on land? With proper information on the relative costs and benefits, a choice can be made of the most efficient disposal solution. Accordingly, it is inappropriate to analyze air, water, or land pollution as separate and distinct problems. For example, if an economy burns most of its wastes, the problems associated with poor air quality will be relatively greater than those of water and land pollution. Thus, the choice of using primarily one environmental medium for waste disposal does affect the qualities of the other media in any ecosystem. The implication of these physical interrelationships of waste disposal is that environmental problems must be considered simultaneously and not as independent problems.

Economists are just beginning to analyze environmental problems in terms of a systems approach that treats the external costs associated with pollution within elaborate simultaneous-equation models of the economy. Such models are too complex for our introductory treatment of environmental problems, however, and we shall, therefore, now return to a fuller development of the concept of externalities within a relatively simple partial equilibrium context.

C. THE ECONOMICS OF EXTERNALITIES

A simple, hypothetical example best illustrates the economic effects of an external diseconomy. To begin, let us assume the existence of a small river valley ecosystem in which the land along the upstream portion of the river is unsuitable for cultivation and, initially, lies idle. The downstream land is owned by a single farmer who uses the river water to irrigate his corn fields. The corn yields an average return that is sufficient to keep the land from being used in any alternative use and to keep the farmer from changing his occupation. Now, let us suppose that the upstream land is acquired by a textile producer who proceeds to utilize the river water as a waste disposal resource and, in doing so, degrades the water quality to a point that lessens its productivity for the farmer downstream. We may also assume that the loss of the river water resource decreases corn yields and may even force the farmer out of the corn production business. The assumed circumstances in this highly simplified example present a relatively unambiguous case of a readily identifiable external diseconomy of production in a private market economy.

Some preliminary general observations may be useful before proceeding to a more detailed formal analysis. Society gains from the production of textiles, on the one hand, by the additional textile production and loses, on the other, by the decrease in the farmer's corn crop. The net social gain from the textile production in a fully employed economy is equal to the excess of the value of the textile products over the value of the factors of production used by the textile firm in their best alternative uses. The net social loss associated with the textile production is equal to the excess of the decrease in the value of the corn crop over the value of the land and the farmer's labor in their best alternative uses. (If we make the extreme assumptions that the farmer is driven out of the corn business and that the land is valueless in all other uses and that the farmer becomes unemployed, then the value of the loss is simply identical to the full value of the corn crop.) The external diseconomy of textile production (literally a spillover effect, in this example) is easily measured in any event as the farmer's net income loss. Note that, in this example, the net social gain from the partial or full substitution from corn to textile production is not necessarily greater than zero. The random factor of the upstream geographic location of the textile plant precludes a market test of whether such a substitution makes the most efficient use of the water resource and yields a net social benefit.

The possibility that the switch from corn to textile production results in a net social loss is a form of (potential) market failure. Such a possibility would not arise, of course, if the corn farm and the textile plant were owned by the same profit-maximizing firm. A rational economic calculation by a conglomerate corn farm-textile firm would determine whether the substitution of textile for corn production was, or was not, profitable. Such a calculation would yield the desirable private market solution insuring that river water, like all other productive resources, is allocated to its most socially efficient use. Our assumption of two independent firms is clearly the villain in preventing the invisible hand of profit-maximizing behavior in a competitive market system from allocating resources most efficiently. Also implicit in this example is the crucial assumption that no market exists for the sale and purchase of water rights (that is, that the farmer cannot contract with the textile producer *not* to pollute). This last assumption insures that the textile producer has no rational (gain versus loss) incentive to include in his cost and profit calculations the amount of external costs he imposes on the farmer as a consequence of his mode of production.

The assumptions in this example are obviously too restrictive to yield insights into more complex real world environmental problems. The possibilities of a viable private market for water rights or various kinds of government intervention in water resource use by private parties would make our simple example much richer and more generally applicable. For the time being, however, we shall postpone consideration of these possibilities and other complexities until Chapters 4 and 5 and shall pursue, instead, the resource allocation implications of externalities in an otherwise ideal private market system.

Price and Quantity Effects of External Diseconomies

As argued in Chapter 2, the goal of profit maximization leads perfectly competitive firms in equilibrium to produce at a level of output at which price equals marginal cost (Figure 2–2). This equality between price and marginal cost is a crucial link in the chain of logic that concludes with the identification of maximum social economic welfare with the outcome of a system of competitive private markets. We are now interested in reexamining the validity of this result once externalities are introduced into the simple model presented in Chapter 2.

In most contexts, the marginal cost schedule of a firm represents all the additional costs incurred to produce a given unit of output. The implicit assumption is that all costs are borne by the firm and thus may be termed private costs. Given this assumption, then in Figure 3–2 the full incremental costs of production could be shown as the *marginal private cost schedule* (*MPC*). Profit-maximizing behavior by the firm then yields the socially optimal output of *OE* units. The *MPC* schedule in-

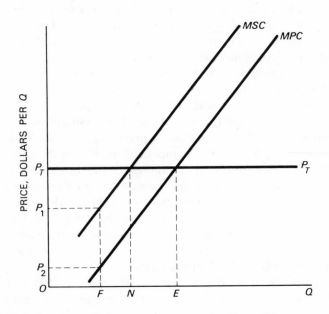

FIGURE 3–2. Equilibrium of the Firm Reconsidered.

cludes the incremental costs to the firm of labor, materials, and capital. If these are the only variable costs of production, then MPC is identical to the full marginal costs of production for the whole economy. By emphasizing the word *private* in the firm's marginal cost schedule, we intend to indicate the possibility that other costs of production may exist. If we use Figure 3–2 to represent the textile producer in our example, we know that the MPC understates the full variable costs of its textile production. The net income loss of the farmer is an additional cost from the standpoint of the whole society, but this cost is not included in the MPC schedule of the textile firm.

Thus, we can conceive of another marginal cost schedule that includes all the costs of textile production, both private and external. We shall call this alternative, the *marginal social cost schedule* (MSC). As drawn in Figure 3–2 in accordance with the assumption of our simple example, it lies above the MPC schedule at every quantity. The vertical difference between the MPC and the MSC schedules at any given quantity measures the external costs (that is, the farmer's net income loss) per extra unit of output of textile production. For example, the MPC of producing the OF^{th} unit of textile is P_2 dollars but the MSC of this unit is P_1 dollars. The difference, $P_1 - P_2$ dollars, is the marginal external cost of producing the OF^{th} unit of textiles. As the two schedules are drawn in Figure 3–2, the marginal external cost of textile production is a constant per unit of output and does not depend on the level of output. (Geometrically, the vertical distance between the MSC and MPC schedules is equal at all levels of output.) Probably a more realistic assumption is that higher levels of textile production cause at least proportional increases in water pollution with more than proportional damage to the fertility of the downstream land. Under such circumstances, the MPC and MSC schedules would begin from the same point on the vertical axis (at a zero level of output of textiles) and would diverge at higher levels of output. The limit of such a case would be the level of textile production at which water pollution destroyed the whole corn crop. However, the precise relationship between the MPC and MSC schedules does not affect the basic results we are attempting to establish here.

As we are assuming that all markets are perfectly competitive, we know that the textile producer cannot affect the going market price, shown in Figure 3–2 as the horizontal line P_T. Because the manager of the textile firm takes account only of the firm's private costs, he maximizes profits by producing an output of OE units, where $P_T = MPC$. From society's standpoint, however, all costs—private and external—should be accounted for in determining optimal levels of output. Ideally, the price-marginal cost equality should occur at the output level where $P_T = MSC$, or ON in Figure 3–2. This reasoning allows us to conclude that the excess of NE units between the private optimal level of production OE and social optimal level ON represents overproduction of textiles. Society would be better off with ON units of textile production than with OE units because the resources used to produce the last NE units have greater net productive value in other employments. The same reasoning implies, of course, that some other good or goods in the economy are being underproduced, or not produced at all. Thus, the first result of our analysis is simply that an external diseconomy in an otherwise ideal competitive market system distorts the optimal allocation of resources; the quantities produced of some goods are too great and the quantities produced of other goods are too small.

The distortion in resource allocation seems trivial in our example as developed thus far because we have assumed that only one small firm's production causes external diseconomies and that the marginal changes in output associated with this one firm's activities have no effects on relative market prices. We shall now extend the analysis one step further by assuming that all textile firms cause exactly the same degree of external diseconomies in their production activities. This assumption permits us to shift our analysis from the firm to the industry level. We may suppose, for example, that the state of textile technology requires water as an input and the use of the water in textile production degrades its quality. In every case, the pollution discharges of textile producers impose monetary or psychic costs on other firms or households. For example, the discharges of some textile producers may fully or partially destroy commercial fishing grounds. In other cases, the discharges may degrade water quality to the point that downstream communities are forced to spend greater amounts on water treatment plants just to continue to provide their residents with potable water. Or the water pollution caused by textile firms may degrade downstream water used for recreational purposes. With our assumption about the similarity of the polluting activities of all textile firms, we may represent the cost conditions of all textile firms in the economy by the MPC and MSC schedules in Figure 3–2.[6]

The aggregate of all textile firms with similar marginal cost conditions can be summarized in the industry supply schedule. The MPC schedule of each textile firm is its supply schedule at all price levels that exceed average variable costs.[7] The textile industry supply schedule is

---

[6] A more realistic assumption is that textile production results in varying degrees of discrepancy between marginal private and social costs. Our assumption of homogeneous firms with respect to external diseconomies of production is based on simplicity of exposition and does not affect the main line of our analysis. All that is really necessary for our purposes is that a large number of textile firms impose varying amounts of external costs on others.

[7] If the reader is not familiar with this point, he should consult one of the economics texts cited in the *Selected References* at the end of Chapter 2.

simply the horizontal summation of the *MPC* schedules of all the individual textile firms. For example, if each firm produces *OE* units at a price of P_T, as in Figure 3–2, then *n* identical firms will produce $n \times OE$ units at this price. The reader should see intuitively that any point on the industry supply schedule can be obtained conceptually by adding the quantities that each firm would offer for sale at the relevant price. Such a supply schedule is drawn for the textile industry as its (*private*) *supply schedule* (*PSS*) in Figure 3–3.

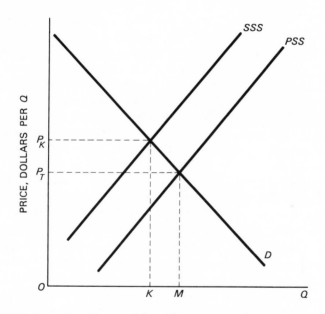

FIGURE 3–3.   Equilibrium of the Industry Reconsidered.

A similar summation of the *MSC* schedule of all textile firms is also shown in Figure 3–3 and is labeled *SSS*, short for *social supply schedule*. The *SSS* curve lies above the *PSS*, reflecting the difference between marginal private and social costs for all firms in the industry. The vertical distance between these two industry schedules is the aggregate of the external costs imposed on society for any given level of output by the industry. The reader should note that although the *PSS* curve could be obtained by observing the supply response of the textile industry to different prices, the *SSS* curve locus is dependent on extraneous, nonmarket information. According to our assumptions, firms base all their behavior on private costs alone, and are ignorant or indifferent about the external costs of their activities, as reflected in the *SSS* curve.

The *PSS* and the *SSS* schedules, together with the industry demand schedule (D) in Figure 3–3, can be used to analyze the full effects of the external diseconomies of textile production on relative prices and resource allocation. The demand schedule intersects the private supply schedule in Figure 3–3 at a price of P_T and a total quantity of OM. The equilibrium industry price P_T is the going market price that faces each textile firm in the industry, as shown in Figure 3–2. Total industry output of OM is just equal to the sum of all firm outputs of OE in Figure 3–2.

According to our previous assumptions, the SSS schedule, not the PSS schedule, reflects the social marginal costs of textile output. Embodied in the SSS schedule is the value of the foregone corn production and all the other external costs imposed on firms and households in society by textile producers. If SSS were the industry supply schedule in Figure 3–3, the level of industry output would be OK units and the market price would be P_K. Comparing this result with the actual industry price and output in equilibrium, we can conclude that the private market for textiles leads to too high a production of textiles (by $KM = OM - OK$) units and too low a price (P_T instead of P_K). Also implicit in this conclusion is that some other industries are precluded from producing enough. Society, as a whole, would be better off if textile firms behaved as if SSS, and not PSS, were the industry supply schedule.

As a final observation, we may note that in the absence of any government intervention, the external diseconomies of textile production lead, via the invisible hand of the profit incentive, to very visible pollution and the burdensome social costs due to pollution. This conclusion holds, remember, even under the assumption of an otherwise ideal private market system. No evil or sinister motives need be ascribed to the producers in our example in order to explain the malfunctioning of private markets. Given the monetary reward structure of a private market system, the manager of a textile firm in our example simply makes the rational economic calculations required to minimize costs of production that firm managers in all other industries also make. But least cost in the private market framework means least cost to the firm, not necessarily to society. If external costs of production exist, but firms are not required to pay the costs of compensating those who suffer from the externalities, then such costs do not enter the rational profit-maximizing calculations of managers. Any individual manager who exhibited *social concern* and did attempt to pay the external costs imposed on others by his firm would be placing himself at a severe competitive disadvantage relative to other firms and would be risking his own job at the hands of angry stockholders. Indeed, in many cases, it is possible that the manager does not even know that his firm is responsible for generating external costs and it is generally true that he does not know the exact dimensions of such costs. In later chapters, we shall emphasize methods that provide profit and loss incentives for managers of firms to take full account of their external costs of production, in much the same way that the private market system forces them to account for the private costs of production.

A Note on External Economies

As noted previously, external economies are formally symmetric in their economic significance to external diseconomies. External economies arise whenever firms or households other than those directly involved in market activities experience benefits from those activities. Just as the unfortunate individuals who bear the costs of external diseconomies are not compensated for these costs, the recipients of external economies do not pay for their benefits.

We have previously cited health immunization programs and superior architectural design as examples of goods and services that generate external economies. Other examples of external economies more directly relevant to pollution problems should be mentioned briefly. Suppose that a private firm purchasing land for a new plant site determines that the ground is too swampy for immediate use and first must be drained. During the draining process, the firm effectively destroys a large mosquito nesting area on this land that has *no other* ecological values. Previously, this area required regular treatment by the local community in order to control the mosquito population. With the draining of the land, the local community no longer has to incur the expense of mosquito control. The value of the savings in mosquito treatment is an external economy to the community. These savings can be used for other public expenditures such as improved roads, more parks, or better schools, or can be passed on to the individuals of the community in the form of lower taxes. Another example might be the damming of a small stream for irrigation purposes. The resultant lake provides new recreational opportunities for boaters, fishermen, and swimmers. Accordingly, the value of the recreation created is a spillover benefit of the dam. As a final example, consider the firm that provides its workers with a driver safety training course. The firm is attempting to prevent injuries to its workers and avoid the subsequent expenses associated with employee accidents (that is, work days lost, injury benefit payments, hiring and training costs of new workers). Society in general, however, also receives an external economy in the form of the general reduction in the number of accidents and their associated costs.

The economic effects of external economies are exactly the obverse of those of external diseconomies. For example, consider the firm that is providing the driver safety course for its workers. In general, each additional unit of output produced requires some labor input. Units of effective labor input can be expected to vary positively with additional hours of driver training instruction. Given the per unit costs of driver training, the firm manager can determine the optimal level of such training by the usual profit and loss criterion. But under these assumed circumstances, the marginal private cost function of the firm does not take into account the value of the accident savings to society. Thus, the true marginal social costs of production are less than the marginal private costs. The external benefits of the driver training should be *subtracted* from the *MPC* schedule of the firm to obtain its *MSC* schedule.

Accordingly, the *MSC* schedule lies below the *MPC* schedule at every output level (that is, the two curves reverse positions in Figure 3–2). Following our previous reasoning, we conclude that the firm is producing too few units of output. If all firms in the industry are similar to the firm under discussion, then the aggregate industry private supply schedule lies above the industry social supply schedule at every level of industry output (that is, the positions of the *PSS* and *SSS* schedules in Figure 3–3 should be reversed). By our previous argument, the industry is producing below the optimum quantity and the equilibrium price for the industry's output is too high. Again, the private market system malfunctions because of the existence of externalities. Only the direction of distortion differs.

A Note on Externalities and Imperfect Competition

Our discussion of the economic effects of externalities, thus far, has assumed perfect competition in all markets. What difference does it make to the analysis if we take account of the fact that a great deal of monopoly power exists in any market economy, especially in heavily concentrated industries? Our discussion of this problem can be very succinct. We know that departures from a state of perfect competition vary greatly among industries, even if we cannot measure perfection or imperfection of competition precisely. We also know that a firm with some degree of monopoly power—that is, a firm facing a less than infinitely elastic demand curve for its output—will take account of its influence on the market price of its output by setting a price higher than that of an identical firm without monopoly power. That is, its profit-maximizing price will exceed its marginal cost. Because of the downward slope of the demand curve facing an industry, a higher price implies a lower level of industry output, relative to the situation for a perfectly competitive industry. We can conclude that imperfection of competition distorts the allocation of resources in an economy because too little output will be produced in heavily concentrated industries with important elements of monopoly power relative to the level of output produced in less concentrated and more competitive industries.

If external costs prevail predominantly in heavily concentrated industries, then the resource allocation distortions caused by monopoly power and externalities will tend to offset each other. Relatively high external costs are associated with inefficiently *high* levels of output, and the existence of relatively great monopoly power causes inefficiently *low* levels of output for an industry. Thus, it is possible, on the basis of this abstract reasoning, that externalities may actually improve the overall allocation of resources in an economy. On the other hand, if external costs are found mainly in competitive industries, then both the monopoly and externality effects reinforce each other in distorting the allocation of resources. Unfortunately, we cannot go beyond stating the above theoretical possibilities on this issue because we are ignorant about even the qualitative correlation between the extent of monopoly power and externalities across industries. Furthermore, we know nothing about the quantitative importance of the effects of either of these two influences in distorting the allocation of resources. Until we know more, this issue must remain a theoretical fine point, with relevant empirical work clearly having high priority on the research agenda of economists concerned with environmental problems.

Externalities and the Necessary Conditions for Maximum Social Welfare

In Chapter 2, we demonstrated that the allocation of resources in an ideal market system without externalities satisfies the necessary conditions for MXSW, or a *Pareto Optimum*. The main link in the reasoning behind this conclusion is that in a competitive market economy in general equilibrium, an equality will exist between the marginal rate of substitution in consumption between any two goods and the marginal rates of transformation in production between the same two goods. For any pair of goods X and Y, this key result can be expressed in symbols as:

$$MRS_{YX} = MRT_{YX}$$

Now, as shown in Chapter 2, the MRT_{YX} is simply equal to the (minus) ratio of the marginal costs of X and Y:

$$MRT_{YX} = -\left(\frac{MC_X}{MC_Y}\right)$$

Implicit in our previous analysis, however, was the key assumption that the MC_X and MC_Y included all social costs, both private and external. Let us briefly indicate the implications of modifying this implicit assumption.

Profit-maximizing behavior by private business firms will lead to the equalization of price and marginal private cost (MPC), as argued in this chapter. Thus, in general equilibrium, the marginal rate of transformation between any two goods X and Y will be equal to the (minus) ratio of MPC_X and MPC_Y, or

$$MRT_{YX} = -\left(\frac{MPC_X}{MPC_Y}\right)$$

Now, let us suppose that the production of X imposes external costs on society but the production of Y does not. In symbols, these assumptions can be stated as:

$$MPC_X < MSC_X$$
$$MPC_Y = MSC_Y$$

It immediately follows, too, that the ratio of marginal private and social costs of X and Y are not equal:

$$\frac{MPC_X}{MPC_Y} < \frac{MSC_X}{MSC_Y}$$

Thus, the marginal private rate of transformation between X and Y will not be equal to the true social rate at which these goods can be substituted for each other in production, taking full account of externalities. Furthermore, the equality between the MRS_{YX} and the true social MRT_{YX}, including all external costs, will not hold. If the production of X involves external costs, society will not be in an MXSW situation in which a costless improvement in the allocation of resources could not be effected. Under the circumstances assumed in the present example, total economic welfare could be improved by somehow adjusting the MPC of X upwards to reflect the external costs included in MSC. Raising the perceived marginal cost of X would increase its market price and reduce the level of its consumption and production, thus freeing some resources used in its production for more socially valuable employments.

The necessary conditions for MXSW can now be restated very simply. The essential equality between the MRS and MRT for any two goods must still hold, but all external benefits and costs must be included as well as purely private benefits and costs. As external costs and benefits will not, in general, be included in private marginal costs, we can restate our previous conclusion that a private market system, by itself, will not allocate resources with full social efficiency.

D. SUMMARY AND CONCLUSIONS

This chapter introduces the concept of externalities and demonstrates its significance for the efficiency of resource allocation. External costs are defined as costs not borne by a firm in the course of production but imposed on other firms and households in society. Total social costs are the sum of private costs and external costs. Analogously, externalities may be external benefits bestowed on other firms and households in society, in which case total social benefits are the sum of private and external benefits.

The materials balance approach to the modern economy stresses the point that all material inputs into production and consumption are not literally consumed but, instead, eventually become potential wastes needing disposal. This approach emphasizes the pervasiveness of externalities in our economic system. Economic policies help determine the lag between production and waste disposal and the methods and media for disposal, and thus affect the total social costs of pollution.

When production or consumption generates externalities, the private market system fails as a mechanism for socially efficient resource allocation. Too much of some goods and too little of others are produced. Because the market system responds mainly to the rewards of private profits, the external costs of producing a good will not be taken into account by firms. Therefore, the market price of the good will be too low from society's standpoint because it does not include the full social costs of production, and too much of the good will be produced. Similarly, the private market system produces too little of goods generating external benefits because such benefits cannot contribute to firm profits. The market price of goods that involve external benefits will be too high for a socially efficient allocation of resources. These points about externalities argue the need to reinterpret the necessary conditions for maximum social welfare. Equality of the marginal rates of substitution and transformation between any pair of goods is a necessary condition for maximum social welfare only if externalities are included in the relative marginal costs that determine the marginal rate of transformation. The private market system that does not take full account of externalities cannot satisfy the necessary conditions for maximum social welfare thus reinterpreted, even assuming otherwise ideal circumstances.

QUESTIONS FOR DISCUSSION

1. Governments often build roads through populated areas. Identify the *external* costs and benefits associated with such road building. Which externalities do you think usually predominate, benefits or costs?

2. The Office of Business Statistics of the Department of Commerce reports that households *consumed* over $40 billion of furniture and household equipment in 1972. Evaluate this statistic critically.

3. What externalities can you think of that are associated with (a) durable consumption goods and (b) consumer services? Does your answer lead you to any generalization about systematic departures from MXSW in the United States economy?

4. "Our economy produces too much pollution because big corporations have no concern for the public interest." Evaluate this statement critically.

5. According to Chapter 2, sufficient conditions for MXSW are that every firm produce its output to the point where $P = MC$ and that markets for consumption goods are perfectly competitive. Reevaluate this statement.

SELECTED REFERENCES

AYRES, R. U., "A Materials-Process-Product Model," in *Environmental Quality Analysis*, eds. A. V. Kneese and B. T. Bower. Baltimore: The Johns Hopkins Press, 1972. A systems application of the materials balance concept.

BAUMOL, WILLIAM J., *Welfare Economics and the Theory of the State* (2nd ed.). Cambridge, Mass.: Harvard University Press, 1967. A classic work, which includes good discussions of the output and price effects of externalities.

DAVIS, OTTO A. AND A. WHINSTON, "Externalities, Welfare and the Theory of Games," *Journal of Political Economy*, LXX, No. 3 (June, 1962). An examination of the complex issues raised by externalities.

LIPSEY, R. AND K. LANCASTER, "The General Theory of Second Best," *Review of Economic Studies*, XXIV, No. 63 (December, 1956). An advanced treatment of the welfare implications of general market distortions, with externalities only a special case.

MEADE, J. E., "External Economies and Diseconomies in a Competitive Situation," *Economic Journal*, LXII, No. 245 (March, 1952). A discussion of the economic effects of externalities.

MISHAN, E. J., "The Postwar Literature on Externalities: An Interpretive Essay," *The Journal of Economic Literature*, IX, No. 1 (March, 1971). A survey article containing some of the author's contributions.

PIGOU, A. C., *Economics of Welfare* (4th ed.). London: MacMillan & Co., Ltd., 1960. The classic work on externalities.

WHITCOMB, D. K., *Externalities and Welfare*, New York: Columbia University Press, 1972. Analyzes externalities in the context of welfare theory.

Other relevant references are given at the end of Chapter 4.

Chapter 4

Alternative Solutions to the Externalities Problem

Externalities result when firms and households do not appropriate the full costs or benefits of their productive or consumptive activities. The benefits or costs that accrue external to the system of private exchange markets do not enter into the rational gain and loss calculus of individual suppliers and demanders. The central point of Chapter 3, and the point of departure for this chapter, is that, in the presence of externalities, the private market system fails to allocate resources with maximum efficiency, even under otherwise ideal circumstances.

The purpose of this chapter is to explain the alternative mechanisms that allow society to correct, partially or fully, for the allocative distortions caused by externalities. The first possibility we explore is simply an extension of the private market system through the creation of new markets. The basic notion involved in this discussion is simple. If externalities are the consequence of incomplete ownership of specific kinds of property, the profit incentives of a market system will automatically tend to encourage the establishment of newly defined property rights and the trading of such rights in new private markets. If private markets can be extended in this way, then all benefits and costs initially external to the market system will become internal, just like the benefits and costs of other goods and services already traded in private markets. A discussion of this possibility calls for an analysis of the concept of property rights, a task given first priority in this chapter.

An alternative mechanism of responding to the externalities problem is to use the coercive powers of the government to force private firms and households to take full account of the external costs and benefits that result from their economic activities. Governments can, in effect, establish and enforce property rights to various environmental resources that have previously been treated as commonly owned property or, more accurately, unowned property. This solution may involve relatively crude prohibitions or regulations on the use of such resources or a more subtle system of monetary incentives designed to alter their allocation among different users. In either case, the intent of such government intervention into the private market system is to internalize, for society, benefits and costs otherwise external to private firms or households.

This chapter discusses the above possibilities according to the following outline. Section A begins with an analysis of the concept of property rights and the problems associated with common property resources. Section B then demonstrates the tendency of the private market system to internalize externalities by the generation of new markets. Section C next examines the limitations of a private market system with respect to the internalization of externalities that cause typical environmental problems. Section D discusses the rationale of government intervention to inhibit activities that destroy or impair environmental quality. The ideal form of government intervention is a system of charges designed to provide the economic incentives lacking in the private market system for inducing socially desirable results from the aggregate of the many individual activities of firms and households. We demonstrate that, under certain assumptions, the allocative results from such a system of charges are equivalent to the private market solution outlined in Section B. Finally, Section E is a brief summary of the chapter.

A. THE CONCEPT OF PROPERTY RIGHTS

Economists often speak loosely about the private or public ownership of various kinds of property, but the more appropriate legal terminology is ownership of property *rights*. The legal system of the United States, and of other countries sharing the English common law heritage, recognizes only limited and qualified ownership of property. Individuals who own a piece of property are legally entitled to use it only within certain defined limits.[1] For example, any individual who owns a rifle has the right to use it as the law permits, to restrict others from using it without his expressed permission, and to transfer his rights to it to other individuals on mutually agreeable terms. His purchase of the rifle does not entitle him, however, to fire his rifle at three o'clock in the morning in an urban area or to use it to hunt squirrels in a city park. Similar sets of limited rights adhere to all other kinds of property. A large body of law has developed in response to potential conflicts of individual interests related to the exercise of property rights. Such conflicts arise because of what economists term externalities.

From a legal perspective, the private market system may be viewed as a social mechanism for the voluntary transfer of property rights through contracts that are legally enforceable by appeal to the coercive power of the state. Furthermore, externalities may be explained as the consequence either of an incomplete set of property rights or by the failure of the state to enforce public or private property rights.

Consider again the example of Chapter 3. What is the fundamental cause of the external cost imposed by the textile plant on the downstream farmer? In effect, the textile firm in this example simply appropriates a valuable water resource by disposing of its wastes in the river, and thereby inflicts heavy losses on the farmer downstream. If the textile firm instead had taken its wastes directly to the farmer's land by truck and dumped these wastes on the farmer's land, our example of the previous chapter would have been patently absurd. The farmer would surely have an overwhelming legal case against the firm in the latter instance because of the prevailing system of enforceable property rights. The textile firm can dump its wastes on the farmer's land legally only if it can first contract with the farmer to transfer the waste disposal rights to the land. Presumably, the firm would be granted such rights only in return for mutually agreeable compensation. We shall explore further this possibility of accommodation between private parties as a possible solution to the externalities problem in Section B, but, for the time being, let us return to the question of why the two hypothetical alternatives, outlined above, differ. That is, how is it possible that the textile firm can impose costs on the farmer through the medium of the water in the river when he cannot impose such costs directly by dumping his wastes on the farmer's land?

There are two possible answers to this question. First, if either

---

[1] For a fuller discussion of this topic, see J. H. Dales, *Pollution Property and Prices* (Toronto: University of Toronto Press, 1970), Chap. 5.

public or private property rights are defined for the river in such a way as to prohibit waste disposal into the water, then the example of Chapter 3 is simply a matter of nonenforcement of the law.[2] Second, if the river is considered by the legislature and the courts to be a *common property resource*, then the farmer is just an unfortunate victim of the consequence of the absence of property rights to the river. The apparently irrelevant circumstance of the direction of water flow in the river allows the textile firm to appropriate the valuable water resource at the farmer's expense. Even if this second possibility is the relevant case, the farmer can still attempt to bribe the textile firm to find another means of disposing of its wastes. That is, he can contract with the firm not to appropriate the river water if both sides find such a transaction mutually profitable. Unfortunately for the farmer, this kind of private market arrangement is unlikely to be of much help. First, it is not clear that the contract between him and the firm can be effectively enforced, a problem we discuss in more detail in Section B. Second, and much more fundamental, the supply of *potential* polluters is virtually inexhaustible. Any unscrupulous individual can threaten to pollute the water upstream from the farmer and attempt to use such a threat to extort money from him without any violation of law. Such threats are almost costless, and if they are credible, a small number could quickly bankrupt the farmer just as surely as the water pollution from the textile firm's waste disposal. In summary, the externality imposed by the textile firm on the farmer is the result either of the lack of enforcement of property rights to the river (if they exist) or of the failure of society to define adequately property rights to resources like river water. The latter case is the fundamental basis of externalities that lead to perceived environmental problems.

The Common Property Resource Problem

Environmental problems arise because of incomplete ownership of rights to use valuable property in specific ways, as illustrated above. More specifically, some property rights are held in common by everybody. The atmosphere, most large bodies of water, and some land sites have long been commonly owned property. Only recently has the law begun to place limits on the use of such resources. For some time, economists have observed that when everybody shares ownership of a resource, there is a strong tendency to overexploitation and general misuse of that resource. Thus, common ownership may be better described as effectively *no* ownership. This legal fact is the key to understanding the common characteristics of apparently unrelated environmental problems.

---

[2] See the Appendix to Chapter 6 for a discussion of water law in the United States.

Some familiar examples of the use of common property resources may help to illustrate our point. Common ownership of the air makes it virtually costless for any firm or individual to dispose of wastes by burning them. The gaseous residuals from the inefficient combustion of wastes is experienced as an external cost by everybody in society. The individual responsible for the waste residuals bears only as infinitesimal share of the total cost. Common ownership of the ocean makes it costless for tankers to flush their fuel tanks at sea. The oil slicks impose external costs on firms and households that also attempt to use the ocean either as a commercial or recreational resource.

Nobody owns the rights to whales. If any one country delays in getting its fair share of the available supply of whales, other countries may not be so slow. Thus, there is a strong incentive for overharvesting of the whale population and a consequent threat to the survival of the species. What is true on an international scale for whales is true also for other species within individual countries. Note that the endangered species are all wild and undomesticated; there is no concern about the survival of privately owned livestock. Finally, common ownership of land resources, such as parks and streets, is the source of other environmental problems. People who litter in public parks and public thoroughfares do not, in general, dump trash on their own real estate holdings. The lack of enforceable property rights to commonly owned resources explains much of what John Kenneth Galbraith has termed "public squalor amid private affluence."

B. A MARKET SOLUTION FOR THE EXTERNALITIES PROBLEM

The existence of external effects does not necessarily imply that a private market system will fail to allocate resources efficiently. The central feature of a market system is the existence of property rights and enforceable private contracts for the voluntary exchange of these rights. Contracts are explicit or implicit in any market transaction. For example, a businessman may formally contract to deliver a certain number of goods of specified quality at a given time and place. A casual worker may have an implicit contract to provide labor services for a certain number of hours under specified working conditions in exchange for some mutually acceptable wage. Other, similar contracts are applicable to all other market transactions and are a vital element of a viable market system.

External effects of production and consumption, in contrast, can be viewed conceptually as benefits and costs that do *not* have a market and hence are not transferred between parties through the mechanism of private contracts. Consumer goods and services of all kinds, labor services, and capital goods all are marketed and exchanged between buyers and sellers. Well-defined markets for most of these goods and services aid greatly in providing information about the possibilities of mutually beneficial exchange to all potential buyers and sellers. Households and firms can readily buy or sell goods or services in markets according to clearly established procedures.

In contrast, externalities are not subject to private contractual arrangements within the market mechanism. Consider, for example, an individual who attempts to spend a day of leisure fishing in a nearby lake. A well-defined market exists for him to purchase fishing equipment, as elaborate and varied as his tastes dictate. He can purchase his transportation, picnic lunch, and even the fishing bait he needs for the day's activities in readily accessible markets for these items. In the terminology of economics, he can contract with sellers for the purchase or lease of virtually all the complements for a day's fishing. But, suppose that when he arrives at the lake ready to begin fishing, he discovers a lifeless, polluted body of water. Let us further suppose that a chemical plant situated on the lake shore is responsible for degrading the water quality in the lake to the point that all or most fish in the lake are destroyed. Initially, we shall make the important assumption that the firm owns exclusive rights to all uses of the lake.

The fisherman obviously values unpolluted water for his day of fishing. The potential benefit to him of unpolluted water may be measured by the amount he would willingly pay to be able to fish in a body of water clean enough to permit the survival of some fish. But, in contrast to the items he can purchase in existing markets, no market exists for him and others to purchase *no pollution* or *less pollution.* Thus, fishermen collectively bear the external costs of chemical production in the form of foregone recreational opportunities. Total external costs will be the sum of the subjective values placed on lost fishing opportunities by all fishermen affected, and will, obviously, depend heavily on the accessibility of alternative, unpolluted fishing sites. The losses suffered by the fishermen do not influence decisions of the chemical plant, because its profit and loss incentives are affected only by potential sales and purchases contracted through markets. Thus, the fishermen are economically powerless to better their situation and the market system apparently fails to allocate resources efficiently.

Our example is critically incomplete, however, as developed thus far. The most important omission in the story is that we have neglected the *possibility of the formation of a new market.* Let us suppose that the chemical firm realizes the potential for a market transaction with fishermen who are willing to pay for the opportunity of fishing in an unpolluted lake. It can then attempt to increase its profits by charging an entry fee to fishermen and, at the same time, reducing the pollution of the lake to increase the fishermen's demand for its use. If the management of the chemical firm is economically rational, it will estimate the least-cost combination of the methods of producing no pollution with the available technology. This combination would be derived from the relative costs of different techniques of water treatment, the net reduction in revenue from a cutback in the level of output of chemicals, and, at the extreme, even the cost of relocating the whole plant. The least-cost combination of producing no pollution in the lake is both the private cost of the firm and, under the assumptions discussed in Chapter 2, also the cost to society measured in terms of the value of treatment equipment and operations, foregone chemical production, or the resources expended in relocating the plant site. If this least-cost method of providing no pollution is less than the maximum revenues that could be obtained from charging admission to fishermen, the firm rationally will elect to produce and sell no pollution and thereby provide fishermen with the opportunity to use the lake.

The profit motive thus may lead to a solution of no pollution. The firm responsible for pollution has an incentive to internalize the external cost it was previously imposing on other firms and households. Once the firm recognizes the possibility of selling clean water, it will see that it is not costless to dispose of its wastes. The cost of waste disposal is the opportunity cost of the foregone revenues it cannot collect if it continues to pollute. The creation of new markets to produce no pollution eliminates the *external* aspect of waste disposal costs and makes them *internal* to the firm, just like the costs of labor and capital services.

Note that it is certainly possible that after the firm in our example estimates the costs of waste reduction and the likely demand for no pollution, it may continue to pollute. The continuation of polluting activities under these circumstances indicates simply that the total social cost exceeds the total social benefits of no pollution. In other words, the value of the resources required to end pollution may be greater than the value fishermen place on a nonpolluted lake, perhaps because water treatment costs are prohibitive or because good alternative fishing sites are readily available in the area. Provided that a market can exist for the sale of rights to no pollution, the failure of the two sides to transact a mutually agreeable bargain is, indirectly, an indication that no improvement in the allocation of resources is possible. In our previous language, transactions in pollution rights will tend to take place until it is impossible for any party to gain without loss to the other party; that is, until a *Pareto Optimum*, or a state of MXSW is established.

The above analysis has been presented in terms of fixed sum comparisons. That is, we have assumed that the firm makes a simple two-way comparison between the costs of ending pollution and the potential revenue from the fishermen. This comparison results in a decision either to continue pollution with no fishing or to halt waste discharges and provide fishing opportunities. More generally, we can conceive of measuring the degree of water pollution on a continuum. The quality of water is neither *good* nor *bad* in any single dimension, and the number of dimensions of water quality matches the number of potential water uses. The chemical firm may treat its water discharge in degrees and thereby create various levels of water quality. Obviously, the higher the water quality in any dimension, the higher will be the costs of treatment. On the other side of the market, we can think of fishermen collectively offering various dollar amounts for different levels of water quality, with more offered for higher qualities than for lower qualities.

These more realistic assumptions are depicted in Figure 4–1. An

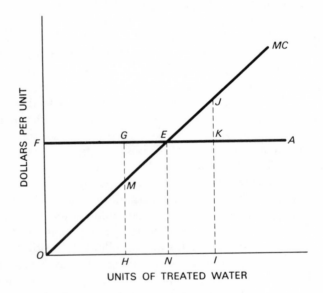

FIGURE 4–1.   A Clean Water Market.

index of water quality on the horizontal axis represents levels of water quality ranging from zero at point O (polluted, lifeless water) to higher levels of water quality to the right. The horizontal axis is measured in terms of physical units of water that are treated to some given standard of water quality. Thus, increasing levels of water quality are directly related in Figure 4–1 to the number of units of water treated. The marginal cost to the chemical firm of producing different levels of water quality is represented by the marginal cost (*MC*) schedule. As drawn in Figure 4–1, the marginal cost of producing higher water quality increases with the number of units of water treated.

On the demand side, Figure 4–1 assumes that fishermen are willing to pay a constant amount per unit of water quality. The horizontal curve *FA* indicates a constant average and marginal benefit of water quality to fishermen, as measured by their willingness to pay, for each additional unit of water quality.[3] For example, to obtain a water treatment level of *OH* units, fishermen are willing to pay *GH* dollars per unit, or a total amount equal to the area *OFGH*. The chemical firm incurs a total dollar cost of *OMH* (the area under the *MC* curve) to treat *OH* units of water. As *OFGH* > *OMH*, the firm profits by providing at least *OH* units of treated water.

The relationships shown in Figure 4–1 thus give a simplified description of a market for clean water or, equivalently, a market for reduced pollution. Such a market is identical, as far as a firm's profit and loss incentives are concerned, to more conventional markets for goods and services. The chemical firm will be induced, by profit incentives, to provide water treatment up to the point where the marginal cost of producing water quality is just equal to its marginal revenue—the amount fishermen are willing to pay for the last unit of water quality sold. In Figure 4–1, the optimal level of output occurs at point *E* and a water treatment level of *ON*. At all levels of water quality less than *ON*, *MC* is less than the marginal revenue of the last unit produced, and the firm can increase profits by treating more units of water. At all levels of water quality greater than *ON*, *MC* is greater than the marginal revenue of the last unit produced, and the firm can increase profits by treating fewer units of water. At point *E*, the firm receives a revenue of *OFEN* and inurs a cost of *OEN* from its water treatment for a net revenue gain of *OFE*.

Again, in this more general case, profit incentives lead to the creation of a new market and to the elimination of a previous externality. The firm that can sell reduced pollution will take into account the true social costs of its polluting activities. Once external costs are perceived as potential foregone revenues, the firm fully internalizes them as private opportunity costs. Then, through the market mechanism, the water re-

---

[3] A more complex analysis, involving monopoly considerations, would be required if we assumed that *FA* sloped downwards. If such were the case, the chemical firm would have to take into account the fact that the amount of water quality it produces affects the final price it can charge fishermen for admission to the lake. Our assumption of a horizontal *FA* schedule is probably a good approximation of reality if the lake is just one of a large number of closely substitutable fishing sites within a small area.

source or, more generally, any environmental resource, will be allocated efficiently among alternative uses.

Note once again the crucial assumption in this example of well-defined and enforceable property rights. If the chemical firm did not have the right to exclude fishermen from the use of the lake, it would have no profit incentive to reduce its pollution. Equally important is the firm's right to exclude others from disposing of wastes in the lake. Without the latter exclusionary right, it could not effectively offer to sell cleaner water to the fishermen. With other potential pollutors of the lake a credible threat, the firm could not guarantee delivery of cleaner water. As explained in the previous section, a market for no pollution rights would not be viable if the lake were a common property resource.

Nothing in the foregoing analysis refers to the initial assignment of property rights to one party or another. The ownership of property rights to the lake is crucial for the viability of a pollution rights market and to the efficient allocation of resources. But it is not necessary that the chemical firm initially owns the rights to use the lake. Suppose that a fishermen's club had previously bought the lake to preserve it for sports fishing. If such were the case, then the chemical firm would appear in the scene as a potential demander of pollution rights and the fishermen would now be the prospective seller of these rights. The same prospects for mutual gain would encourage creation of a market for use of the lake, and the optimal result of trading could be (a) sale of the lake to the firm, with the club disbanding or moving on to another site; (b) no sale and continuation of the status quo: or (c) a limited sale of rights to the firm for disposal of wastes, with only minor effects on sports fishing opportunities. Except for considerations of bargaining power, the results of the transactions in this later case are equivalent to the previous results in which we assumed that initial ownership of the lake belonged to the chemical firm. Indeed, the original owner of the lake could be a third party, who auctions off use of the lake to the highest bidder or bidders. The lake resource would, in any case, be allocated with maximum efficiency, whatever the initial distribution of property rights, provided that market transactions are feasible. The reader should note carefully that this conclusion does not imply, by any means, that the chemical firm and the fishermen are equally well off independent of the initial ownership of the lake. Clearly, the initial ownership of the lake puts the original owner in the enviable position of allowing others to attempt to pay him sufficient compensation to relinquish, wholly or partially, his property rights. More needs to be said on the distributional aspects of environmental problems, but we shall defer a full analysis to Chapter 5.

Two final points can conclude this section. First, we have not yet explored the issue of the *viability* of markets for pollution rights or their opposite, which we may call *amenity* rights (a more general term than *no pollution* rights). This subject is our next concern in Section C. Second, the reader should not conclude that the establishment of *private* property rights is necessary for a solution to pollution problems. All that is necessary is *effective* property rights, private or public. Section D discusses a situation in which the government, in effect, leases public property rights to the highest bidder, which turns out to be another means of maximizing efficiency of environmental resource allocation.

C. THE FEASIBILITY OF A MARKET SOLUTION

The analysis of the previous section suggests that the environmental problems traceable to externalities can be corrected within the framework of a private market system. The profit and loss incentives of private firms and households tend to restore efficiency of resource allocation through the establishment of new markets wherever the opportunities of mutual gains are present. This process of market extension tends to provide a comprehensive accounting for all of the economic consequences of production and consumption activities. The market solution essentially requires the existence of enforceable property rights to all environmental resources and the possibility of contractual agreements between the parties affected by an externality and those responsible for its creation. Given these prerequisites, new markets can internalize the costs and benefits of an externality and induce firms and households to include the consequences of their polluting activities in their rational economic calculations. Our discussion, thus far, has been limited to the case of water pollution, but, in principle, similar markets could form for air pollution rights and for other aspects of the environment. The theoretical arguments are perfectly general and apply, therefore, to all environmental problems involving externalities.

The market solution for environmental problems has great appeal, because it appears to involve no basic changes in the organization of economic activities in the private market sector of the economy. The only task for the government would be to extend its traditional role in a market economy by assigning and enforcing property rights to environmental resources. Unfortunately, conditions in the real world are not as simple as our textbook discussion has thus far indicated. Some important considerations argue strongly that private markets for most externalities are not viable.

Perhaps the single most important characteristic of environmental pollution as we understand it today is that it involves externalities that are *not* limited to well-defined, and identifiable, individuals or groups.

In our previous examples of the effects of externalities, we have assumed explicitly just the opposite; that is, that textile firms impose external costs on downstream farmers or that a chemical firm destroys the fishing potential of a lake. The two-party assumption permits a tractable analysis of the economic implications of externalities in general, but it does not capture the essence of the externalities relevant to *environmental* problems.

In general, pollution in a modern, industralized economy is the consequence of the byproducts of consumption and production by innumerable households and firms. The disposal of wastes into the various environmental media becomes diffuse and affects many unrelated individuals by ecological processes that, as yet, are not all well understood. This is particularly true in metropolitan areas where there are large concentrations of people and industrial plants. In modern urban life, the effects of externalities are not generally confined to identifiable and distinct parties. Instead, they are pervasive and collectively form the urban environment affecting millions of individuals.

Are markets for pollution rights or amenity rights feasible under these realistic conditions of the present-day world? The fact that such markets do not exist anywhere suggests a negative answer. Even within a single urban area, for example, thousands of air pollutors may impose external costs on millions of individuals. Demanders of reduced air pollution could not call forth a corresponding supply unless they could contract with virtually all polluters and potential polluters simultaneously. Furthermore, as we shall show in Chapter 7, *clean air* is a most ambiguous and complex concept. A market for reduced air pollution would have to cope with many different air pollutants. The demand and supply relationships for each dimension of air quality would surely differ significantly, and this fact, too, would be part of the information requirements for a market for reduced air pollution.

A broker for air pollution rights could gather the requisite information and bring buyers and sellers together to sign meaningful contracts only at enormous costs. The costs of organizing and operating private markets for pollution or amenity rights are not unique. Similar costs exist to some degree for every marketed good or service. For an ordinary good, however, say toothbrushes, such costs are comparatively trivial and private markets are viable. The opposite is true of environmental goods like air quality because of the diffusion of the various polluting effects of production and consumption. Under such circumstances, too many complex bargains and private contracts are required for a feasible market to operate.

Matters are even more difficult, however, than we have yet indicated. First, consider the problem of sanctions against lawbreakers in any hypothetical market for air pollution rights. That is, suppose that contracts to provide cleaner air were somehow negotiated in spite of the large information and transactions costs discussed above. Successful delivery of clean air to buyers would depend critically on the ability of the police and the courts to enforce the terms of such contracts. Effective enforcement would depend, among other things, on detection of innumerable potential violators on the sellers' side of the contracts. Enforcement probably would be prohibitively expensive, especially if the general public feels that everyone has an inalienable right to burn his garbage or drive his car and refuses to cooperate with law enforcement officials. Indeed, it is the lack of a feasible technology to enforce prohibitions against use of a common property resource like the air that explains the very existence of socially abused common property resources. A second fundamental problem is how the entrepreneur or any government could possibly obtain *true* evaluations of the value of cleaner air from potential individual consumers. We defer this latter issue, sometimes called the public goods problem, to Chapter 5.

We conclude that a private market system can correct efficiently for externalities only under very simple technological conditions. Unfortunately, environment pollution problems involve complex ecological relationships that make the market solution generally inapplicable. The pervasive nature of the externalities of real world environmental pollution problems makes the costs of organizing private markets to provide pollution or amenity rights prohibitive relative to potential benefits. Enforcement of property rights may also not be possible for some environmental media, which effectively quashes prospects for a viable market under any circumstances. With this pessimistic diagnosis, let us now proceed to examine an alternative nonmarket solution to environmental problems.

D. THE MARKET SOLUTION IMPOSED

This section outlines a public sector analogue to the market solution for externalities present in Section B. We have shown, thus far, that profit incentives tend to internalize externalities within an extended market system, provided that private property rights to the relevant resources can be established and enforced. Given the practical difficulties of organizing markets for the externalities that cause environmental problems, a natural next step in our discussion is to examine alternative nonmarket solutions. The objective of our discussion remains the same; namely, to find some means of achieving efficient resource allocation in the presence of the externalities that cause environmental problems. The market solution ideally accomplishes this objective by inducing firms to internalize the external effects of their production activities. In our example, the firm becomes aware of the additional profit opportunities available to it from selling reduced pollution to the parties who bear the external costs of its activities. The prospective payments to the firm from potential consumers of reduced pollution thus become an explicit, internal cost to the firm in the form of the foregone revenue that results from its waste disposal practices. Our problem in this section is to devise a similar, non-market device that will accomplish the same goal of internalizing, to the relevant decision maker, the external effects of his activities.

Let us consider once more the example of the chemical firm whose wastes impose external costs on individuals who desire to use a lake for fishing. Suppose that the state government owns the lake and all its tributaries and is not willing or able to dispose of its property by sale to the private sector. What actions can it take to assure efficient use of the lake? The perhaps obvious answer is a simple one; it should *charge* the chemical firm for every unit of polluted water that it discharges into the lake. (It should also charge for all uses of the lake perhaps, but this is a separate issue that is not our present concern.) The firm will then take account of (internalize) the previous external costs of the pollution associated with its waste disposal, as it will have to pay a certain dollar amount for each unit of polluted water it produces. The theoretically correct level of this *effluent charge* is the per unit external cost of the untreated water discharge of the firm. We shall pass over, for the time being, the practical difficulties of determining the correct effluent charge amount. The important point for the moment is simply that an effluent charge is an appropriate device for internalizing previously external effects that lead to an inefficient allocation of environmental resources.

We can analyze the effects of an effluent charge by reinterpreting Figure 4–1. Let us assume that the government has a good estimate of the external costs of each unit of pollution discharged by the firm. By our previous assumption, the true value is a constant amount, equal to *OF* dollars. If the government is assumed to know this exact amount, it can charge the firm *OF* dollars for each unit of water discharge that it *fails* to treat. The horizontal line *FA* then will represent the (constant) cost of a unit of untreated water to the firm. Note that the firm must *pay* *OF* dollars per unit of untreated water discharge instead of, as in the market solution, being paid *OF* dollars per unit of treated discharge. The effluent charge thus becomes an internal cost to the firm exactly like the costs of labor, capital, and all other factor inputs into the production process. The firm is induced to make a profit and loss calculation to determine its best response to the imposition of the effluent charge. One alternative open to it is to treat its wastes, incurring the marginal treatment cost given by the *MC* schedule in Figure 4–1. Another alternative is to continue to discharge untreated water and to pay *OF* dollars per unit of discharge. The profit-maximizing (or loss-minimizing) solution for the firm is to treat the water until the cost of treating one more unit would exceed the effluent charge it pays per unit for the discharge of untreated water. In Figure 4–1, this solution occurs at the treatment level of *ON* units, at which point the *MC* schedule intersects the constant effluent charge, *FA*. At all water treatment levels less than *ON*, the effluent charge exceeds the marginal cost of treating more units of water, and the firm can reduce its total costs by further treatment. At all levels of treatment beyond *ON*, it costs the firm more to treat the water than it does to discharge untreated water and pay the effluent charge. Therefore, *ON* is the profit-maximizing water treatment level for the firm, given the *OF* level of the effluent charge.

The imposition of the effluent charge does not mean that pollution will necessarily, or probably, be reduced to zero. Zero levels of pollution will result only when the marginal cost of treatment is less than the effluent charge at all levels of treatment or if the firm's loss-minimizing solution is to close or relocate its plant. The latter extreme response will be appropriate from an economic efficiency standpoint only in cases in which fishing is incompatible with any pollution and the lake is clearly more valuable when used for fishing than when used as a waste disposal resource. The opposite extreme response by the firm would be to continue its previous level of pollution and to pay the effluent charge in full. This latter extreme response would be evidence both that water treatment costs are prohibitively high and that the lake is clearly more valuable as a waste disposal resource than as a fishing site.

The more general response is some degree of treatment of waste water together with some payment of the effluent charge, as shown in Figure 4–1. In this general case, pollution abatement will occur to some degree, probably to a point at which both the chemical firm and fishermen share use of the lake for different purposes. Whatever the firm's response, however, the imposition of the effluent charge of *OF* dollars assures the most efficient use of the lake, assuming again that *OF* is a true measure of the external costs of the firm's waste disposal activities.

The reader can easily see that the result of a per unit effluent charge of *OF* dollars is exactly identical theoretically in its allocation effects to the market solution analyzed in Section B. Indeed, because the two solutions are conceptually identical, they can both be depicted by the same Figure 4–1. Both solutions yield a level of treated water discharge of *ON* units, which is the optimal amount of pollution abatement for the firm and for society alike. In the market solution, the firm must be paid *OF* dollars for each unit of treated water. In the effluent charge solution, the firm must pay OF dollars for each unit of untreated water. Thus, the two solutions are equivalent in their allocational effects; both lead to the most efficient use of resources.

On the other hand, the distributional effects of the two alternative solutions are radically different. If the firm owns property rights to an environmental resource, it can in effect sell a new product—less or no pollution—to potential users of that resource, and thereby *add* to its previous profits. The users of the environmental resource bear the cost of pollution abatement. If the government owns the property rights, then the firm must compensate the government for the lease of public property rights. The cost of pollution abatement will be borne largely as a capital loss by the owners of the firm. If an entire industry is subjected to an effluent charge, then in the long run, the costs will be shared more widely among factors of production specialized to the industry and the consumers of the output of the industry. The analysis of the long-run incidence of the effluent charge is the same analysis given in most elementary economic textbooks for the incidence of any tax that increases the per unit costs of an industry. The supply curve of the industry shifts upward and to the left but the demand curve is unaffected. In long-run equilibrium, the effect of such a tax is to raise the gross price of output paid by the consumer and to lower the net price received by the industry, with the tax paid per unit of output a wedge between the gross and net prices. Because the gross price to consumers must rise, industry output and sales will fall, as will industry employment of labor and capital. Some firms may be forced out of business as the industry contracts in response to the tax. The reader should note that, in general, the beneficiaries of the effluent charge (the fishermen, in our example) are not the same people who bear its cost. The income distribution consequences of the two solutions are clearly *not* equivalent. We shall further elaborate on this issue in Chapter 5.

An Output Tax as an Effluent Charge

The preceeding analysis has assumed that the government charges a firm for each unit of waste disposal emitted into an environmental medium. An alternative policy is a tax levied on each unit of the *output* of an industry that is emitting pollutants. If output reduction is the *only* method available to an industry to reduce pollution, then an output tax is conceptually equivalent to a direct effluent charge. If one unit of output is associated with k units of waste, an output tax of $1 per unit of output is equivalent to an effluent charge of $1/k$ per unit of waste. Other methods of pollution reduction are generally available to firms, and we shall discuss some of these alternatives in later chapters. Our purpose in making this restrictive assumption here is to simplify our discussion below of the relationship of effluent charges to the more general analysis of externalities in Chapter 3.

Let us return to the chemical firm-fishermen example developed in this chapter, and assume that output and waste disposal can be defined in such a way as to be linked in a one-to-one relationship. That is, suppose one unit of output is associated with one unit of polluted, untreated water. Then an optimal per unit output tax imposed on the chemical industry will be equal to the external cost associated with each unit of the output of the industry, if we assume that all firms in the industry are exactly alike. In our example, this output tax would be OF dollars per unit of output, precisely equal to the value of a unit of clean water to fishermen. We can relate this output tax on the chemical industry to our previous discussion of externalities by referring to Figure 3–3. The per unit tax on output shifts the industry supply curve from the private supply schedule (PSS) to the social supply schedule (SSS). The vertical distance between the two schedules is simply the value of the external costs to fishermen associated with each unit of industry output, which, by construction of Figure 4–1 is just equal to OF dollars. Thus, the per unit output tax (equivalent to an effluent charge under our restrictive assumptions) fully internalizes the previously external costs associated with the industry's production. The tax adds to the industry's costs of production and leads to a higher industry price and a lower industry output. The lower level of industry output reduces the level of pollution caused by the industry. If the tax is set exactly equal to the external costs of industry output, the resulting lower level of pollution will be at an optimal level for society. Finally, note that the presence of external economies for some industry would call for a per unit subsidy for the output of the industry. By the same reasoning applied above to the case of external costs, it follows that the subsidy should be set equal to the value of external benefits associated with each unit of industry output, with the result being a lower price and a higher output for the industry.

Dynamic Adjustments of Effluent Charges

Let us now return to the more general case in which effluent charges are imposed directly on waste disposal effluents rather than on output and firms can reduce wastes by various treatment methods or by relocation of a plant as well as by output reduction. Suppose an effluent charge is imposed that initially is just equal to the value of the external costs associated with an industry's output. How should the effluent charge be adjusted in response to changes in economic conditions?

First, suppose that the demand for fishing sites increases over time because of general increases in per capita income and, perhaps, also because of a change in tastes towards more participation in outdoor recreational activities. Fishing sites will become scarcer as increased demand impinges on a virtually fixed supply. The increased demand for fishing sites raises the level of external costs, because the value of fore-gone fishing opportunities rises, even under the assumption of an un-changed level of pollution. In such circumstances, the level of the effluent charge should be raised to conform to the new higher value fishermen collectively place on clean water. Consider this situation as depicted in Figure 4–2, which is only a slight variation of the Figure 4–1 description of the chemical firm-fishermen example discussed previously. The origi-nal effluent charge—equal to the per unit marginal social benefit of water treatment—is again drawn as the horizontal line FA and the marginal cost schedule of treatment remains at MC. However, with the increase in demand for fishing sites, the increase in the external costs of pollution raise the FA schedule to $F'A'$, where $F'A'$ is now the new per unit value fishermen place on clean water. As drawn, $F'A'$, is higher than FA at any given level of water treatment, reflecting our assumption of the increased ability and willingness of fishermen to pay for fishing sites. The efficient water treatment level increases from ON units to OI units, where the new marginal benefit schedule intersects the MC schedule. If the effluent charge remains at OF, the firm has no incentive to increase its level of water treatment. From Figure 4–2, it is clear that the effluent charge must

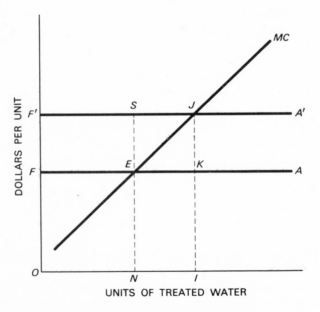

FIGURE 4–2. Increase in Value of Clean Water.

be raised by FF' dollars, to a new level of OF' dollars. The higher effluent charge will induce the firm to treat OI units of water rather than ON
units in order to minimize its total waste disposal costs.

As demands for environmental amenities of all kinds can be expected to increase over time in response to sustained increases in per
capita income, firms could expect with reasonable certainty that the
optimal level of effluent charges would also increase over time in conformity with these increased demands. The existence of effluent charges
and the expectation of increases in their level over time would provide
incentives for firms to develop more efficient methods of pollution reduction. In Figure 4–2, the marginal cost of water treatment schedule would
be expected to shift to the right over time as firms developed more efficient techniques of waste reduction. Thus, the imposition of effluent
charges, expected to rise over time, would promote efficiency in the use
of environmental resources just as secular increases in wage rates now
induce firms to invest in the development of technically more advanced
capital equipment in order to economize on the use of labor. As a footnote to this discussion, the reader should recognize that there is a close
analogy between the appropriate effluent charge response by governments to changes in demand for environmental resources and the automatic response of prices to changes in demand in competitive markets.
The important difference between the two situations is that governments
must invest resources to discover the true external costs of pollution at
any point in time, whereas changes in demand are reflected more directly
in markets through the automatic signals of shortages or surpluses per-
sisting at existing price levels.

The Feasibility of Effluent Charges

The first problem governments face in implementing effluent charges is
the determination of the level of the charge appropriate for the use of
each environmental medium. The correct level of an effluent charge is a
most complex issue once we move away from abstract and highly simplified textbook examples. First, as we have already observed, the pervasiveness and diffuseness of the external costs of pollution make it difficult
to estimate the total value of these costs. The distribution of external
costs is probably highly uneven among the total population and, to a
lesser degree, also among the population in a small area. No perfect substitute for the private market has yet been devised to measure accurately
the demand for goods and services like environmental quality that cannot
be marketed. *Some* measure of the external costs of pollution must be
made, for better or for worse, before setting the level of effluent charges.

A second problem is that environmental problems cannot effectively
be dealt with on a piecemeal basis. As we have already indicated, an

effluent charge for use of one environmental medium such as a lake may merely shift waste disposal to an even more vulnerable alternative medium in an ecosystem with no guarantee of any net social improvement in the allocation of resources. A systems approach, taking full account of the materials balance conception of economic activities, is required to insure adequate recognition of the interrelatedness of environmental problems. A large body of emerging literature currently is attempting to analyze the full ecological relationships that have to be understood before economic policies can be made fully effective. As the reader can see, the implementation of a *system* of effluent charges will be a difficult undertaking in the immediate future.

A related problem in implementing effluent charges concerns the measurement of effluent standards and environmental quality. In Figures 4–1 and 4–2, for example, the horizontal axis is labeled *units of treated water*. The concepts of *unit* and *treated* must be given operational content before implementation of any system of effluent charges. Units of water can be thought of as some quantitative measure, such as 1000 gallons or 55 cubic feet per second. But the determination of an appropriate treatment measure represents considerable difficulty for researchers in both the physical and biological sciences and in economics. Water quality involves such issues as life tolerances, disease levels, toxicity, and aesthetic norms. A standardized treatment of the effluent must be determined in conformity with agreed on quality standards. Quality standards, in turn, may depend largely on subjective attitudes of individuals towards the value of water. This point brings us back full circle to the issue of how we can determine individual valuations of environmental quality in the absence of a market. We shall examine some of the physical properties of various pollutants in Chapters 6, 7, and 8, where we shall also discuss in more detail the problems of determining quality and treatment standards for effluents.

Finally, beyond these technical problems, there remain the considerable problems of administering and enforcing a system of effluent charges. The basic problem is, once again, the enforcement of property rights, which, in this context, are the property rights of the public to various environmental media. The long tradition of free air, water, and public land resources, especially strong in the United States, is a difficult obstacle for effective implementation of effluent charges. Laws cannot be enforced unless the great majority of the people believe in them and see the necessity of enforcing them. A long period of environmental education has just begun in the United States and in other countries. In addition to the problem of enforcement of public property rights, there is a separate issue of whether governments realistically can be expected to administer a sophisticated system of effluent charges through bureaucratic agencies. We shall discuss aspects of this latter issue in Chapter 5.

Obviously, the above list of problems is a formidable one. Whether or not they can be resolved satisfactorily remains an open issue. The impetus to solve the problems and to implement a workable, reasonably acceptable system of effluent charges depends on the effective demands of the population for an amelioration of environmental conditions through the political process. Such demands presumably are related directly to the severity of the external costs borne by the population as a result of environmental degradation. As these costs rise in the future, we can predict that the political pressures for effective measures to deal with pollution will be difficult to resist.

E. SUMMARY AND CONCLUSIONS

Externalities arise when property rights are not defined for certain scarce resources or when nominal rights are not enforced in practice. Certain resources, such as the air and many bodies of water, are, in effect, common property. Even though these resources are scarce—the demand for them exceeds the supply at a zero price—no individual has a profit incentive to ration them efficiently among alternative users. The common property characteristics of these resources are due, in part, to tradition, beginning in times when high quality air, water, and other natural resources were not yet scarce, and, in part, to a lack of technology to enforce exclusive private or public property rights to these resources.

When private property rights can be enforced, externalities tend to disappear because profit opportunities for firms encourage them to internalize the externalities. Once a firm recognizes that its use of a resource such as water prohibits others from using it, the possibility of selling reduced pollution will be taken into account in the firm's profit and loss calculations. The foregone revenue from not being able to sell the rights to an unpolluted or less polluted resource to others becomes an internal opportunity cost for the firm and induces it to ration the resource efficiently among alternative uses.

Unfortunately, the market solution is not of much help for the kinds of externalities relevant to real world environmental problems. The market solution is feasible in simple cases of externalities, in which markets can be readily created among just a few easily identifiable buyers and sellers. The market solution is not feasible when externalities are pervasive and diffuse throughout society and the costs of organizing a market become prohibitive. But this means that the extension of the market is not a realistic solution to actual environmental problems, which, almost by definition, involve the most complex kinds of externalities.

An alternative nonmarket solution is for governments to assert their sovereign rights to environmental resources by charging private parties for their use. Effluent charges are essentially rents charged for the lease of rights to dispose of wastes in publicly owned environmental resources. The theoretically correct level of effluent charges is the external cost of the marginal unit of unpolluted air or water or some other environmental resource, which is equal to the sum of the marginal valuations of the unpolluted resource to potential consumers. If this level of effluent charge is set individually for the use of all environmental resources, then these resources will be allocated efficiently among alternative uses. Adjustments in effluent charges must be made over time to respond to changes in economic conditions. The ideal effluent charge solution theoretically is equivalent in its allocational or efficiency effects to the ideal market solution, but differs greatly, of course, in its distributional effects.

The effluent charge solution is no panacea for environmental problems. Like the market solution, it is most feasible in the simplest cases of externalities, not in the more complex cases relevant to modern environmental problems. The most fundamental problem is the determination of the correct effluent charge in the absence of the information provided automatically in a viable market. Another serious problem is effective coordination of a number of effluent charges into an overall system in a world of interrelated environmental problems. In addition, the technical complexities of defining quality standards for various environmental resources have yet to be fully solved. Despite all these problems, a workable, if less than perfect, system of effluent charges appears to be a vital component of a more comprehensive policy to allocate environmental resources with greater efficiency.

QUESTIONS FOR DISCUSSION

1. Ordinances in most communities prohibit individuals from using their own back yards as dumping grounds for refuse. Some libertarians argue that such ordinances are examples of *big brother* government infringements on the individual's rights to use his own property as he sees fit. What is your own view, and why?

2. "The way to save the mountain lion from extinction is to grant a single firm exclusive rights to issue hunting licenses." Does this assertion make any economic sense?

3. Local seaside communities in the New York metropolitan area have sometimes attempted to exclude nonresidents from their beaches by charging the outsiders prices above those paid by the natives. These communities now face lawsuits challenging the legality of such discriminatory pricing schemes. What is your own view of the efficiency and equity issues involved in these lawsuits?

4. Professor J. H. Dales has proposed that a government agency in Ontario set up a market for water pollution rights. (See the Selected References.) What would be the purpose of such a government-created market? How do you think such a market would work in practice in the United States?

5. Spokesmen of the modern conservationist movement have sometimes argued against an environmental policy based on effluent charges on the grounds that "such charges are licenses to pollute and the environment is not for sale." Evaluate this argument critically.

SELECTED REFERENCES

COASE, R. H., "The Problem of Social Cost," *The Journal of Law and Economics,* Vol. III (1960). A classic article on the nature of externalities.

DALES, J. H., *Pollution, Property, and Prices.* Toronto: University of Toronto Press, 1968. An excellent treatment of the importance of property rights in pollution problems. Presents a detailed proposal for the sale of pollution rights.

DAVIS, O. A. AND M. I. KAMIEN, "Externalities, Information and Alternative Collective Action," *The Analysis and Evaluation of Public Expenditures: The PPB System,* Vol. I. U.S. Joint Economic Committee. Washington, D.C.: Government Printing Office, 1969. A discussion of many of the issues raised in this chapter.

DEMSETZ, H., "The Exchange and Enforcement of Property Rights," *The Journal of Law and Economics,* Vol. VII (October, 1964). A basic article on the subject.

KNEESE, A. V. AND B. T. BOWER, *The Economics of Regional Water Quality Management.* Baltimore: Johns Hopkins Press, 1968. Discusses the issues of this chapter thoroughly.

KNEESE, A. V. AND R. U. AYRES, "Production, Consumption and Externalities," *American Economic Review,* LIX, No. 3 (June, 1969). A generalized analysis of the full implications of production activities, with the presentation of the materials balance approach to the economy.

RUFF, L., "The Economic Common Sense of Pollution," *The Public Interest,* No. 19 (Spring, 1970). A brief overview of the issues of this chapter written for the noneconomist.

SAX, J. L. "Legal Strategies Applicable to Environmental Quality Management Decisions," in *Environmental Quality Analysis,* A. V. Kneese and B. T. Bower, eds. Baltimore: The Johns Hopkins Press, 1972. A treatment of property right issues in the environmental area.

SCHULTZE, C. L., "The Role of Incentives, Penalties and Rewards in Attaining Effective Policy," *The Analysis and Evaluation of Public Expenditures: The PPB System,* Vol. I. U.S. Joint Economic Committee, Washington, D.C.: Government Printing Office, 1969. A discussion of the basic issues of the use of effluent charges.

Chapter 5

Environmental
Quality
as a
Public Good

Government intervention into a private market system for any purpose raises many difficult theoretical and practical issues. This chapter explores a few of these issues relevant to the public provision of environmental quality. The purpose of our discussion is to make clear to the reader the complexities involved in collective, nonmarket, economic activities. The market system by itself fails to allocate environmental resources efficiently, but corrective action by government agencies does not *necessarily* make things any better.

The central new concept in this chapter is *public goods*. We define a (pure) public good to be the limiting, or extreme, case of externalities. Suppose that it were possible to array all possible goods and services along a continuum running from pure *private goods* to pure public goods. What characteristics distinguish a pure private good, say, television repair services, from a pure public good, such as national defense? The answer lies in the degree of externalities involved in the production and consumption of the two goods. Television repair services involve a minimum of externalities, as do virtually all other services. Most goods involve only some degree of externalities, because of disposal problems. In contrast, national defense involves maximum externalities of consumption in the sense that all the benefits from the production of national defense accrue automatically to everybody in society. Once a given level of protection is provided for any one individual in society, the same level of protection is available for more than 200 million other individuals without additional cost. The marginal cost of providing national defense services for one more individual is literally zero. Indeed, society can exclude any individual from sharing the consumption of these services only by incurring costs to remove him beyond its protected boundaries.

Thus, the degree of externalities inherent in goods and services, and, therefore, the degree of *publicness*, varies over an extremely wide range. It is difficult to conceive of more than a very few goods or services that are either purely private or purely public on the basis of our definition. For our purposes in this book, however, it is sufficient to note that environmental quality lies near the extreme public end of the private good-public good continuum. This is the case because, like national defense services, once most aspects of environmental quality are made available to any one individual, they can be extended to others in society at virtually zero additional cost. The best example of this point is the provision of clean air; once provided for any one individual, it is also available automatically to everyone else within a broad area. Again in common with national defense services, any individual can be excluded from the benefits of purer air only by expelling him from a given area.[1] In summary, then, environmental quality justifiably may be termed a public good.

A well-developed literature on the economics of public goods may be applied directly to the problem of environmental quality. As we shall argue in this chapter, although it is futile to expect any form of adequate private market solution to the provision of environmental quality or of any other pure public good, the alternative of government provision is not free of grave problems of a different sort.

Section A of this chapter gives an analysis of the efficiency aspects of the provision of the public good, environmental quality. Section B

---

[1] Some confusion persists in elementary texts about identifying a public good with the *impossibility* of exclusion. It is almost never impossible to exclude individuals from sharing in the consumption of any good or service. The more fundamental point is that, in the case of public goods, exclusion is too costly to be *worth* enforcing on the basis of the efficiency criterion. As we emphasize in the text, for example, an individual *can* be excluded from the benefits of air pollution control, but it is not worth enforcing exclusion when the marginal costs of providing such benefits to any individual are zero or very close to zero.

takes up the problem of the income redistributional effects of government intervention in the production of environmental quality. We emphasize the possibility that the efficiency and equity goals of society may conflict as the government attempts to achieve environmental policy objectives. Section C discusses a quite different subject, the effectiveness of the government sector as an alternative to the private market system in the provision of environmental quality. We argue that any government will encounter great difficulties in defining the public interest in environmental problems and perhaps even greater difficulties in achieving specified environmental objectives with reasonable efficiency. Section D gives a brief summary of the main points of the chapter.

A. ENVIRONMENTAL QUALITY AS A PUBLIC GOOD

Let us assume, for our discussion in this section, that the government recognizes the inability of private markets to function efficiently with relation to environmental problems, and that it decides to intervene to provide higher levels of environmental quality directly. The particular methods the government uses to achieve its environmental objectives—prohibitions, regulations, effluent charges, or others—need not concern us here, for this policy choice problem is the subject of all of Part 4 of the book. Instead, we shall concentrate for the present on some general theoretical aspects of government provision of environmental quality.

In Chapter 4, market failure in the provision of environmental quality was shown to be due in part to the problem that information costs and transaction costs are too high for mutually advantageous private contracts to be negotiated for the rights to environmental resources. Ideally, the government can use its fiat powers to cut through the maze of information and transaction costs and enforce any given environmental quality standards it establishes as its proximate goals. At issue here is the economic *efficiency* of any hypothetical government-imposed solution.

The basic allocation problem is the determination of the socially optimal level of environmental quality in all relevant dimensions. The general efficiency rule is that more environmental quality should be provided only up to the point at which additional social benefits are equal to the additional social costs. Problems arise, however, in determining the magnitude of the relevant benefits and costs in the absence of information provided automatically in market transactions. Once the government abandons the market as an allocation mechanism for environmental resources, it must find some other means of obtaining information on the benefits and costs that result from its actions.

We began the chapter by defining a pure public good to be the limiting case of externalities and observing that environmental quality fitted well into this conceptual category. The case of clean air was cited as perhaps the best example of an environmental good meeting the pure public good criterion. Once a given quality of air is provided for any one individual in an area, it is automatically available without additional cost to all other individuals in the same area. Recognizing this technological fact, how can a government estimate a demand or benefits schedule for clean air in determining the efficient dimensions of an air quality program? Two possible conceptual demand schedules for a public good are outlined below; the estimation of either one raises profound problems for public policy.

Demand as the Sum of Willingness to Pay

Let us begin by attempting to give precise meaning to the concept of the demand for a given level of air quality. We might define the *demand price* for any air quality level by appeal to the private market analogy; that is, as the sum of the amounts all individuals are willing to pay per unit of output. In markets for private goods, the demand price (P_i) for the ith unit of output (Q_i) is simply the price at which the sum of all individual demands exactly equal Q_i. That is, for a given level of output Q_i, the average value of output to consumers is the price P_i at which consumers are collectively willing and able to buy the total amount Q_i. Figure 5–1A illustrates the conceptual derivation of a private market demand curve for the three-person case. Total quantity Q_i corresponds

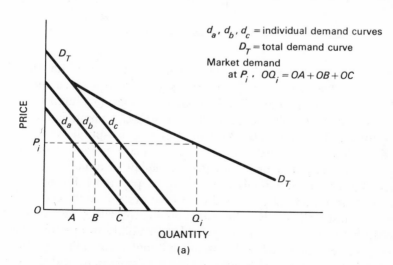

FIGURE 5–1A. Private Good Demand Curve: Horizontal Summation.

to the *horizontal* summation of individual demands OA, OB, and OC at price P_i. The locus of all such (P_i, Q_i) points is the market demand curve D_T.

For a pure public good, however, individuals cannot choose to vary the amount they consume independently of each other. If any individual consumes a given amount Q_j of a pure public good, then *everybody* necessarily also consumes exactly Q_j. Figure 5–1B shows the conceptual

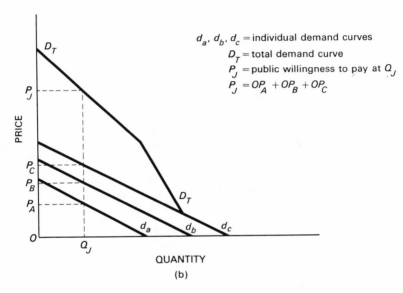

FIGURE 5–1B. Public Good Demand Curve: Vertical Summation.

derivation of a pure public good demand curve, again for the three-person case. The demand price P_j corresponding to a given quantity Q_j is the *vertical* summation of individual valuations (willingness to pay) OP_A, OP_B, and OP_C. The locus of all such (P_j, Q_j) points is the demand curve for a public good, D_T. We would expect this public good demand curve to slope downwards just like an ordinary private good demand curve. For either public or private goods, the law of diminishing marginal utility states that individuals are willing to pay more for the first few units of consumption of any good than they are for additional units. For example, most individuals value clean air highly if they see a clear relationship between very polluted air and their ability to breathe. Once the air is clean enough to allow breathing without great difficulty, the relationship between air quality and health is less obvious, and the willingness to pay for clean air therefore diminishes.

How *good* an estimate of the demand for a pure public good like clean air can the government hope to obtain? If a government agency attempts to ask directly for individual valuations of different air quality levels through some sort of survey, it will undoubtedly obtain a very poor estimate. First, it may find that the costs of gathering such information are unacceptably high. The private market is an efficient instrument for generating high quality information, and nonmarket substitutes like questionnaires are distinctly inferior. A more fundamental problem, however, is that individual valuations of a public good cannot be trusted as true valuations if individuals see any systematic relationship between their answers to hypothetical questions and the amounts they may be charged (through taxes or prices) to pay for the provision of the good. Any intelligent individual realizes that the total estimated demand price for a given air quality level will be virtually unaffected by his own individual valuation, and therefore that his failure to reveal his own true valuations will not affect the demand price for the whole population. He also knows that if the government does proceed to provide better air quality in the area, he will share it equally with everyone else as a *free rider* regardless of the amount he pays to help finance antipollution measures. If he suspects that his share of the cost of any government programs will be related to the amount he says he is willing to pay, he will have a strong monetary incentive to understate his true valuation. (Note that he cannot conceal his true valuation of a private good. If he does not pay the going market price for a private good, he is excluded from consuming it.) Even if he is otherwise a public-spirited citizen, he knows that all other individuals are aware of the situation and are subject to the same incentives to understate their true valuations. He may therefore consider himself foolish to reveal his true preferences if he has reason to believe that others will not be so forthright. The competition of all individuals to minimize their share of total payments in these circumstances is not coordinated by a benevolent invisible hand to lead to an optimum result. Thus, it seems almost inevitable that total demand for public goods would be greatly understated if the government attempted to obtain demand information by means of sample surveys or by other nonmarket devices. Alternatively, if people believe that their responses to hypothetical questions cannot affect their tax burdens, they may *overstate* their true valuations of public goods. Thus, public opinion polls often find large majorities in favor of all kinds of social welfare programs when they are presented in a costless guise.

This analysis helps explain why the dominant mode of government provision of public goods takes the form of largely *noneconomic* legislative and administrative determinations of quality and quantity levels together with financing through general taxation. The political process thus substitutes for the private market system as a resource allocation device for public goods. Everyone in society shares in the financing of the costs of any public good according to his position in the total tax structure, but his tax share of the total cost may be far from his own individual valuation of any particular public good. At best, an individual's total tax burden may correspond roughly to his valuation of the total package of public goods provided by the government, but even this weak correspondence does not necessarily hold. In general, nothing in the political process guarantees that the total package of public goods provided meets the test of efficiency of resource allocation.

Demand as the Sum of Willingness to Sell

The *willingness to pay* approach to the determination of the demand for public goods, outlined above, is explicitly based on the analogy of the determination of private market demand. Private market demand curves, in effect, measure the value of a good by the amount of income individuals are willing and able to give up to obtain it. Thus, in our previous discussion we implicitly treated the demand curve for clean air as a measure of the willingness and ability of the population to give up income for cleaner air. This approach to the determination of demand for a public good follows the private market analogy so closely and naturally that it may tempt the reader to believe that it is the one correct approach. But if we probe deeper into the question, we can see that the willingness to pay approach to demand determination yields only a *minimum* estimate of the value of a given level of environmental quality to the public. More fundamentally, it depends on the assumption that the public must pay for the property rights to environmental resources.

Suppose that we begin, instead, from the plausible assumption that property rights to the air and to other environmental resources reside in the general public and cannot be appropriated by any private parties without adequate compensation. With this assumption, it no longer makes sense to value a given level of air quality by asking how much individuals in society are collectively willing to pay for it, as they already own it. Instead, it is natural to ask for the minimum amount all individuals collectively would be willing to accept as compensation to give up their rights to all higher quality levels. The latter approach yields a *maximum* estimate of the value of a given level of air quality, and of the quality of environmental resources in general.[2] Why does the latter approach give a higher valuation than the willingness to pay approach?

---

[2] This point is developed more fully in E. J. Mishan, "The Postwar Literature on Externalities: An Interpretative Essay," *The Journal of Economic Literature*, IX, No. 1 (March, 1971).

The answer is that the original assignment of property rights to the public gives it greater financial ability to achieve a higher standard of consumption, including consumption of environmental quality.

A specific example can illustrate this point. A man's willingness to pay for a minimum level of air quality just sufficient to sustain life is bounded by his current income, his net assets, and his ability to borrow. But *no* conceivable price could compensate him for the loss of his life if air quality is his to sell. A great gap may exist between the two alternatives of the willingness to pay and the willingness to sell, as measures of the value of environmental quality.

The reader should note that the *willingness to sell* approach to the valuation of environmental resources poses the same basic information problems as the willingness to pay approach. In either case, the government cannot count on the self-interest of individuals to obtain an unbiased measure of total demand for environmental quality. If the government attempted to use direct survey methods to obtain individuals' valuations of environmental quality according to the willingness to sell concept, individuals would be tempted to overstate their true valuations if they believed that their tax liability might be reduced according to their response. The analogy to our previous discussion of the willingness to pay approach should be obvious without further elaboration. The important difference between the two approaches lies in the conception of property rights to environmental resources and not in the fundamental difficulty of obtaining true evaluations in the absence of private market transactions.

Thus, it should now be evident to the reader why resource allocation in the public sector is determined largely through the political process. Political judgments have been supplemented in recent years by formal benefit-cost analyses that make use of information derived indirectly from market transactions. However, the role of market-type information is still relatively insignificant. We take up the subject of the political and administrative processes as mechanisms of resource allocation briefly on a general level in Section C of this chapter. Next, however, in Section B, we shall discuss the income distribution aspects of government provision of the public good, environmental quality.

B. EQUITY PROBLEMS IN GOVERNMENT ENVIRONMENTAL PROGRAMS

Government environmental programs raise complex issues of distributional justice, or *equity*. As observed in Chapter 2, a state of maximum social welfare—a *Pareto Optimum*—can be defined as a necessary condition for maximum efficiency in resource allocation, for a given distribution of income among all households. But there are an infinite number of *Pareto Optimal* states—at least one for each of an infinite number of different income distributions. Any significant intervention by the government in economic affairs will not be distributionally neutral. Some individuals will always enjoy windfall gains as other individuals suffer windfall losses. Government environmental programs, in common with all other government economic activities, cannot, therefore, be judged solely on the basis of pure benefit-cost or efficiency criteria. Considerations of distributional justice should also count to some degree in the decision-making process of a government environmental protection agency.

Efficiency is a deceptively simple and attractive objective for a government official. Who can oppose the principle that more of every good for everybody is desirable? Careful economic theorists point out, of course, that greater efficiency in the *Pareto Optimum* sense means only that more of everything is potentially available for everybody. The distribution of the actual gains from efficient changes in society's mode of production often is quite unequal. As a rough generalization, it seems that many government programs result in large gains for a few beneficiaries and small losses for the general public, with the total value of gains perhaps somewhat larger than the total value of losses. In an attempt to separate efficiency from equity considerations, economists have devised various compensation tests that say, in effect, that any given change is socially desirable (more efficient) if the gainers *could* fully compensate the losers for their losses and still come out ahead. Unfortunately, these compensation tests suffer from a large degree of theoretical ambiguity. More fundamentally, the hypothetical compensation of losses is, in general, impossible in the world outside the covers of economic textbooks. We may conclude, then, that equity and efficiency effects of government programs are inextricably interrelated in practice and must be considered jointly in the formulation of economic policy.

The meaning of efficiency can be defined with precision, but what are the criteria for distributional equity? Moral philosophers have long debated this issue without, unfortunately, reaching any consensus. Let us venture two relatively simple criteria acceptable to many, but not to all:

(1) A redistribution of income is socially desirable, other things equal, if it raises the incomes of the very poor closer to the average level of income in society. A more controversial extension of this criterion would deem any change desirable, other things equal, if it reduces the inequality of the whole income distribution; that is, if it narrows the gap between very high and average incomes as well as the gap between very low and average incomes.

(2) As opposed to the above *vertical* redistribution criterion, no comparable general rule applies to what are largely *horizontal* redistributions of income; that is, transfers of income between individuals at the same level of income. Horizontal redistribution may be said to occur when income is transferred between two groups differentiated *principally* by characteristics other than size of income, even if the average income of the two groups is not precisely equal. We can only suggest the criterion that gains and losses from such horizontal redistributions of income should not be arbitrarily bestowed or imposed on minorities in the population unless other considerations of government policy are of overriding importance. As far as possible, the losers should have recourse to the full procedural protections traditionally afforded them by our common law traditions.

As the reader can recognize, distributional equity is a thorny issue that is not easily susceptible to analytical treatment. Indeed, no completely satisfactory method of making the efficiency and equity effects of government programs commensurable in the social decision-making process has ever been devised. A dollar's worth of greater efficiency cannot readily be compared with a dollar's worth of redistribution between the rich and the poor or between, say, the East and the West. Such an agnostic view is cold comfort, however, to public officials, who *must* make decisions between various options involving complex mixtures of efficiency and redistributional effects, including the option of making no changes at all from the status quo. With these general considerations as background, we turn to equity problems related to government environmental programs.

Gains and Losses from Environmental Programs

The identification of gains and losses can be extremely complex in the general case in which the parties affected by an environmental program are large in number and geographically diffuse. We shall attempt to bring out the essential points by use of a relatively simple example, however, in which the benefits and costs of an environmental program can be readily identified.

Let us assume that a metropolitan airport authority acquires some land in a convenient site located in a previously peaceful suburban community, Jetportville, and proceeds to construct an airport. The noise from jet aircraft landing and taking off from the airport turns out to make life very unpleasant for the inhabitants of Jetportville. In response to the anguished complaints of its constituents, the local government successfully asserts its sovereign local air rights and institutes a schedule of landing and takeoff fees—called *noise control* fees—designed to reduce the noise pollution problem of the community. The mayor of Jetport-ville fortunately happens to be an economist, and recognizing that the noise control fees are a variety of effluent charge, he sets up a complex schedule of fees that vary with type of aircraft and time of day. Because of his cleverness, the program turns out to be a great success. Who gains and who loses from Jetportville's noise reduction program?

The most obvious gainers are the residents of Jetportville. The noise control fees not only reduce the psychic costs from noise pollution but also raise additional revenue for the local government. The additional revenue can be used either to finance additional local services to lower local property taxes that finance the existing level of services or to sub-sidize soundproofing of homes. Both the reduction in noise pollution levels and the additional revenue will result in higher real incomes (including psychic benefits from noise reduction) for the residents of Jetportville. Probably the best direct measure of the increase welfare of the citizens of Jetportville is the observed increase in property values in the community. The impact of noise control fees should, at least, offset the initial loss in property values caused by the construction of the air-port and the excess noise problems associated with it. The *worst* Jetport-ville could do would be to set the noise control fees so high as to close down the airport, but it is likely that the residents could do better by trading off some peace and quiet for the additional revenue that could be derived from the noise reduction fees.[3]

Who are the other gainers and who are the losers from Jetport-ville's noise reduction program? Let us assume for this discussion that the situation in Jetportville holds more generally for all airports in the country. In the short run, the airlines and, perhaps, the airport authority are likely to suffer a reduction of profits, because they cannot avoid the extra costs of the noise reduction fees and of the shifting of flight schedules in response to the fee schedule. In the longer run, however, the price of airline tickets must rise to include the costs resulting from the noise reduction fees so that the return to capital invested in the air-line industry will not fall below the normal level for the industry. The eventual higher price of airplane tickets will impose additional costs on all airline travelers, however, including those business firms for whom air travel is a business expense. If we can presume that the demand curve for airplane travel is downward sloping, the higher price for airplane

[3] Our previous discussion of distributional effects in Chapter 4 should make it clear to the reader that the gains and losses from the government's noise control fees are just the opposite of the gains and losses that would result if the city had to compensate the airport authority for any noise reduction. To restate our previous fundamental point, the distribution of gains and losses from environmental programs turns on the assignment of property rights to one side or the other.

tickets will reduce the amount of air travel and, therefore, will also indirectly reduce the demand for all the resources hired by the airline
industry. Resources that are highly specialized to the industry—airline
pilots and skilled jet engine mechanics, for example—may experience a
reduced demand for their services and many individuals in those groups
will suffer a loss in income. Other resources, such as unskilled labor and
basic raw materials, that are not highly specialized to the airline industry,
will, in general, be reabsorbed into other industries at much the same
prices and will suffer relatively small losses, if any.[4]

Even in this simple example, the analysis of the full redistributional
effects are not yet complete. The rise in the price of airplane tickets
implies an increase in demand for alternative forms of travel and communication as substitution away from airline travel occurs, and the
increased demand will result in some indirect gains for the resources
employed in alternative transportation industries. For exactly the same
reasons discussed above, resources specialized to, say, the railroad industry will experience gains comparable to the losses suffered by the resources specialized to the airline industry. Of course, all of these indirect
gains and losses may be quite small, depending on the size of the noise
reduction fees and the elasticity of supply and demand schedules for the
airline industry.

Finally, we should observe that the direct gainers from the noise
reduction program, the residents of Jetportville and other airport communities, will, in general, share the gains unequally. The big gainers
will be the individuals who initially suffered the most from noise damages, those who enjoy the largest actual reduction in experienced noise
levels, and those who derive the most benefits from the additional fee
revenue, either through expansion of local government services or from
tax reduction. Note also that the set of gainers may overlap with the
set of losers. The resident of Jetportville or some other community who
gains from the noise reduction program in the form of reduced noise
damages and higher property values may also lose in his role as an employee of the airline industry or as an airline passenger.

In general, the best economists can do is to trace out the likely
major gainers and losers from environmental programs; benefit-cost
analysis will rule out the high costs of attempting to specify in any detail
all the indirect distributional consequences of environmental programs.
More complicated cases than the example considered in this section will
involve correspondingly more complex redistributional effects. The most
useful contribution an economist can make in this area is to present to

---

[4] This discussion assumes full employment of all resources.

the policy decision makers comparisons of the major distributional differences expected to result from major environmental policy alternatives.

Efficiency and Equity Tradeoffs

Much of the popular literature on environmental problems suggests that only the *bad guys* or the *interests* lose when the government intervenes in the private market system to improve environmental quality and the public gains. Unfortunately, the truth is much more complex. Let us now attempt to apply the two distributional criteria suggested in the introduction to this section to problems that face society in choosing between environmental policy alternatives.

To begin, let us first examine more deeply the noise reduction example presented above. As the example stands, most readers probably would not question the noise reduction fee program on distributional equity grounds, because the gains to the residents of Jetportville largely go to reimburse them roughly for the psychic and dollar losses of noise pollution arbitrarily imposed on them by the construction of the airport. In addition, it is well established that the typical airline passenger enjoys a much higher than average income. In comparison to the residents of Jetportville, then, the direct losers from the noise reduction fees are likely to be able to afford their losses, that, in any event, probably are very small for any individual because of their wide dispersion among the many thousands of passengers using the airport facilities. Thus, the most direct redistributional effects of the noise reduction program appear to violate neither of our two sugggested criteria; both vertical and horizontal redistributional effects appear to be acceptable and, perhaps, even desirable.

The reasoning above is faulty, or at least incomplete, on two grounds. First, the example implicitly assumes that the residents of Jetportville at the time the noise reduction program takes effect are identical to the people who initially suffered losses. Such a situation is possible, but it should be recognized realistically as an extreme case. To take an equally extreme counter-example, suppose that all the original residents of Jetportville responded to the announcement of the site of the airport by selling their properties to large industrial corporations at prices that fully reflected the capitalized losses in property values due to the anticipated noise pollution. If each original resident of Jetportville valued the expected psychic loss of noise pollution from the airport at, say, $500 per year, he would have been willing to sell his property at the previous market value minus the present value of a perpetual annual flow of $500 per year (about $10,000 at a 5 percent rate of discount).[5] Given this admittedly extreme assumption, the full loss from the location of the airport is borne by the original residents who sell their properties and move away. Other people, the owners of corporations in this example, acquire the affected property at reduced prices that fully capitalize the cost of noise pollution and can suffer losses only if the level of noise pollution turns out to be greater than expected at the time the properties are purchased. Thus, the gains from the noise reduction program accrue to the *new* owners of property in Jetportville and are obviously pure windfall gains. These gains are just as arbitrary a redistribution of income as the losses originally imposed on the previous residents. In reality, the gains from the noise reduction program will undoubtedly be some mix of more or less justifiable compensation for previous losses and of windfall gains, with the degree of the mix depending on specific factors such as the extent of capitalization of the losses in value due to noise pollution and the volume of turnover of properties after the airport site is first announced.

The second complicating factor in our simple noise reduction example has already been raised in our previous discussion. The losses due to the noise reduction fees are borne in part by the consumers of airline services, but additional indirect losses fall on resources specialized to

[5] The value or market price of any asset traded in a competitive market tends to equal the present discounted value of the expected income flows from that asset. In symbols:

$$P_A = \sum_{t=0}^{n} \frac{Y_t}{(1 + r)^t}$$

where P_A is the market price of the asset, Y_t is the expected net income yield of the asset in time period t, r is the rate of discount, and n is the number of time periods in the expected life of the asset. If n is very great—a realistic assumption for a long-lived asset such as real estate—and if Y_t is a constant over time, then the above equation can be approximated by the following simplification:

$$P_A = \frac{Y_t}{r}$$

which is the basis for the example given in the text.

For some assets, bonds, for example, Y_t is simply expected money income. For an asset like real estate, however, Y_t is the sum of any net money income (rent, for example) and the value of the housing services enjoyed by the owner of the real estate. Even if Y_t consists entirely of nonmoney income, it can be reduced by any phenomenon, like noise pollution, that lowers the value of the housing services from a real estate property in a given location. The loss from noise pollution is a real loss, as can be established by observing that if the owner rented out his house instead of living in it himself, the noise pollution problem would force down the rents he could successfully charge potential tenants. The money equivalent of the noise pollution loss must be subtracted from the initial value of Y_t to obtain the post-pollution value. Then, by the above formula for the market valuation of an asset, the income loss is said to be *capitalized* in a corresponding change in the capital value of the real estate. In reality, the extent of capitalization will depend upon such factors as the degree of uncertainty about the actual effect of noise pollution and in various, specific real estate market circumstances in Jetportville.

the airline industry. The latter indirect losses may take the form of lay-offs of pilots and skilled mechanics, who can find no comparable employment opportunities in other industries, even if the labor force is fully employed.[6] These unfortunate individuals and their families are likely to judge the redistributional effects of the noise pollution program as arbitrary horizontal redistributions of income, and a violation of our horizontal equity criterion.

The points raised thus far in this discussion are difficult to generalize because the redistributional effects of various environmental programs will vary greatly according to the circumstances special to any given environmental problem. We can observe, however, that often and, perhaps, in a majority of cases, a conflict will arise between the efficiency and equity criteria that should guide government environmental policies. An environmental program that passes a benefit-cost efficiency test is likely to violate both of our equity criteria. First, the redistributional effects of many environmental programs may be regressive or favor the rich because the benefits will be more highly skewed towards upper income classes than the tax burdens that finance such programs. Our basis for this speculation is that many environmental goods—air and water quality, peace and quiet, and natural recreation facilities—are apparently highly income elastic goods, yet the total tax structure of all governments taken together in the United States is, at best, very mildly progressive. If environmental programs are financed at the state or local level of government, the net regressivity of benefits and taxes will be even more pronounced because the slight progressivity of all taxes is the net effect of the modest progressivity of federal government taxes and the regressivity of state and local tax structures.

Two factors, not yet mentioned, complicate the above analysis. First, if the mechanism for improving environmental quality is effluent charges rather than government expenditures, we would have to know the distributional impact of a general system of effluent charges rather than the distributional effects of marginal changes in the existing tax structure. In the absence of evidence to the contrary, we would take the neutral position that effluent charges are similar in their distributional effects to a proportional tax on consumption. But because consumption declines as a percentage of income at higher levels of income, it is likely that such a tax is slightly regressive. Thus, we see no reason on this count to alter our analysis substantially. On the other hand, the existing burden of some kinds of pollution costs may fall very unevenly on the

---

[6] In an economy of fully flexible prices and wages, the adjustment would take place through a general fall in wages for skilled airline employees. In the real world of wages that are downwardly sticky, however, some unemployment is the more likely occurrence.

poor. In particular, the worst air quality is generally to be found in central cities. So, under some circumstances, antipollution measures may well have an important effect in equalizing the real incomes of rich and poor. The above point does not contradict our original hypothesis that the rich are willing to spend a greater fraction of their income on environmental quality than the poor, but it does substantially modify our generalizations about the distributional effects of environmental programs in a world in which existing pollution costs are currently distributed unequally.

Second, the largely horizontal redistributional effects of many government environmental programs will inevitably impose arbitrary losses on people who are no more to blame (in an ethical sense) for pollution problems than the general public. Many of the gains apparently accruing to firms and individuals from using scarce air, water, and land bodies as free waste disposal resources are almost entirely illusory because the cost savings from such polluting activities are, by this late date, largely capitalized and incorporated into the economy's relative price structure. The typical individual who owns some small fraction of a firm that pollutes the air paid a price for his shares of stock in the company that fully reflected the cost advantages to the firm from using the air as a free waste disposal resource. Any government program that takes away the assumed air pollution rights of the company will cause a reduction in profits and in the value of the common stock of the company. In addition, as observed in our previous example, environmental programs that force industries to bear explicit costs for the use of environmental resources lead to a contraction of the output of the industries, with indirect losses consequently borne by specialized labor and other resources.[7] None of these losses can be justified on the grounds of the moral responsibility of the affected individuals for the state of environmental quality. For the most part, the original sinners responsible for our current environmental pollution problems have gone to their graves completely unaware of their guilt in a simpler age before the existence of such problems was even recognized.[8]

How can the government balance off efficiency and equity considerations? Does potentially more for everybody justify actual, severe losses for minorities and a possible widening of the economic welfare gap between the rich and the poor? No general answer can be given to these

[7] On the basis of our analysis, we hypothesize that labor and management will join together in the 1970s to fight many environmental programs, especially those that make use of effluent charges or direct regulation of emissions.

[8] This point does not apply, of course, to new industries that attempt to claim rights to the use of scarce environmental resources. For example, it does not sanction the redistributional effects of the proposed supersonic transport (SST) program.

crucial questions. The relative weights assigned to efficiency and equity goals differ from individual to individual, and it is difficult to generalize about the aggregation of such sharply disparate views.[9] Efficiency and equity tradeoffs differ from program to program and indeed, in easy cases, no tradeoff need exist as all criteria point to the same answer. Compensation for losses suffered from the implementation of environmental programs should be considered on a case by case basis, subject to the proviso of feasibility. In general, equity considerations should not be slighted by government officials in favor of the deceptively simple and relatively uncontroversial criteria for economic efficiency.

C. EVALUATION OF GOVERNMENT ECONOMIC PERFORMANCE

Thus far in the book, we have paid a great deal of attention to the economic reasons for *market failure* with respect to environmental problems. We have argued that, even under otherwise ideal circumstances, the private market system fails to allocate environmental resources efficiently because of the pervasiveness of pollution costs external to the system. This chapter has carried the basic argument one step further to show that environmental quality is an important example of a class of goods appropriately termed *public goods,* the extreme case of externalities in which private market failure is most complete. Granted these arguments, the goal of economic efficiency in environmental resource allocation calls for collective action through some form of government intervention. But even if we leave aside consideration of the difficult equity issues discussed in the previous section, we still must face the issue of the efficiency of government in its role as a producer of environmental quality. Is it realistic to expect that any government can increase efficiency of environmental resource allocation for a society by its intervention in private markets? If so, what are the appropriate limits, if any, on the degree of public intervention?

Our discussion of these questions proceeds in the following order: First, we examine the role of voting as a mechanism for determining the public interest in environmental issues. That is, how good a substitute for the private market system is voting in providing basic information about individual valuations of different environmental alternatives? Second, given the outcome of voting and the determinations of the public interest

---

[9] The equity-efficiency tradeoff problem becomes even more complicated when we attempt to take into account the balance of the welfare of the current generation and the welfare of future generations.

in environmental problems, how well do government agencies function in achieving agreed-upon objectives? In other words, how good a substitute is the typical bureaucratic government agency for the typical profit-maximizing firm in the private market? Finally, we briefly examine the issue of the appropriate balance between the public and private sectors of the economy in the provision of environmental quality.

Voting and Efficiency

Economists often observe that consumers in a private market system vote with dollars instead of ballots. Under ideal conditions—an acceptable distribution of income (or dollar votes) and perfect competition— the market is the most sensitive of electoral mechanisms. The consumer is said to be sovereign because each dollar vote in the market has equal weight in its claim upon scarce resources. Of particular importance is the fact that the system gives the dollar votes of minorities equal weight with the dollar votes of the majority. The interests of the majority prevail, but not at the expense of minorities. In Chapter 2, we formally showed how, under ideal conditions, such a system of market voting led to a state of maximum social welfare.

For a public good like environmental quality, however, the market system of dollar voting breaks down as an efficient social resource allocation mechanism. The government must take responsibility for the provision of public goods, and, inevitably, the decisions of government officials, guided in a democratic system more or less by the wishes of the electorate, replace the decisions of the market.

Voting becomes the mechanism for revealing individual preferences about alternative allocations of environmental resources. Remember that efficiency, in the economic sense of the word, is not just an engineering concept; it is defined in relation to individual preferences. Therefore, we take up the issue of how well the mechanism of voting serves the cause of economic efficiency in comparison to a private market system of dollar voting.

The political process, as it exists today, gives public officials only the loosest set of guidelines to the true aggregation of individual preferences about environmental alternatives. Not all potential consumers of environmental quality are eligible to vote and even the eligible voters often do not participate in elections. Those individuals who do vote do not participate in numerous referenda on individual issues but, instead, generally select one of two candidates, each of whom embodies an intentionally vague stance on a wide variety of issues. Furthermore, voters do not choose candidates solely on the basis of rationality or self-interest, but are also influenced by such irrelevant considerations as the television personalities of the candidates and often also by their race, religion, and even the sexual attributes of their spouses. Minority votes do not stand on an equal footing with majority votes in determining the allocation of resources. The refusal to vote does not convey an important and unambiguous message in politics as does a refusal to spend on consumption goods in the private market system. Finally, in general, individual votes differ fundamentally from market dollar votes in that the former do not directly reveal the *intensity* of individual preferences for alternatives. Intensity of preferences can only be expressed outside the polling place by a variety of activities of varying effectiveness.[10]

Without belaboring the point any further, it should be obvious that the present political system is not a sensitive mechanism for translating individual preferences into economically efficient social decisions, especially not on issues as narrow as those that arise in the provision of environmental quality. At best, the existing political process places some broad constraints on elected public officials by not allowing them to deviate too far from the majority views of their constituencies on any particular set of issues. Even granted that this ultimate veto on unpopular decisions by government officials does exist and does operate effectively, the burden of formulating public interest about economic efficiency in the provision of environmental quality largely must reside with the relevant elected and appointed government officials.

On a more abstract level, majority voting is often said to be deficient as a mechanism for articulating the public interest even under ideal circumstances. Suppose that a society consisted of as few as three individuals, each of whom had unambiguous preferences between any two of as few as three alternatives states of the world. Would majority voting generally lead to an unambiguous collective ranking of the three alternatives? In a classic study of this and related issues, Kenneth Arrow has demonstrated that the general answer to this question is *no;* unambiguous collective rankings of the alternatives do not necessarily result from the majority vote aggregation of unambiguous individual rankings.[11] Thus, majority voting cannot be counted on as a mechanism for determining the public interest in the environmental area even if we could ignore all the practical problems of our present political system. More complex voting systems might be devised to give better, less ambiguous results in principle, but this qualification to the general Arrow argument is of little, or no, relevance to present day environmental concerns.

[10] For example, groups like the Sierra Club and Audubon Society help express the intensity of the feelings of environmentalists through lobbying and educational activities.

[11] Kenneth J. Arrow, *Social Choice and Individual Values* (2nd ed.). (New York: John Wiley & Sons, 1963).

In summary, some very difficult practical and conceptual problems arise in attempting to relate voting to the concept of economic efficiency. The issues in this area of political economy are deep and cannot be treated adequately in this book. But the reader should understand the basic point that voting does not necessarily lead to a clear articulation of the public interest in environmental issues.

Government Bureaucracy and Economic Efficiency

Let us now take as given the broad environmental decisions of the legislature, which, hopefully, reflect the preferences of the general public. To be more concrete, suppose that the Congress has appropriated funds to some agency for the administration of various environmental programs specified in previous legislation. How well can the bureaucracy of the agency be expected to function according to the criteria of economic efficiency? Will the allocation of society's resources really be improved relative to the private market as a result of the agency's activities?

Only general answers can be given to these important questions despite the existence of a huge noneconomic literature on the characteristics and performance of bureaucracies. Economists, typically, approach the problem of the functioning of bureaucracies—either private or governmental—by observing that, in general, bureaucrats should be expected to pursue their own self-interest (maximize their utility) in their jobs, very much like workers and entrepreneurs in the private sector. This presumption about individual bureaucratic behavior is neutral and is not biased towards the view that bureaucrats are either any better (more altruistic) or any worse (more selfish) than people in nonhierarchical positions.[12] The reader will recall that the self-interest of individual firms and households in the private sector is coordinated by the checks and balances of the market system, and that the invisible hand of the market will, under ideal circumstances, make the sum of individual self-interest lead to maximum social welfare. Analogously, we may ask whether a similar mechanism operates in bureaucratic structures to coordinate the self-interested behavior of individuals to produce socially desirable results.

The answer depends on whether the perceived private benefits and

---

[12] We specifically exempt the short-run performance of new agencies from our discussion. Much evidence exists that some new agencies perform well above the average because they attract enthusiastic and committed volunteers and because they are relatively free of the inertia that seems to develop inevitably over time in well-established agencies. The Peace Corps and the Office of Economic Opportunity in the 1960s and 1970s are two good examples of such deviant short-run performance immediately after birth, with a gradual development into normal bureaucratic behavior.

costs of a bureaucrat's activities correspond to *social* benefits and costs in some kind of normal, or equilibrium, state. (The analogous question for the private market is, of course, whether equilibrium market prices correspond to social benefits and costs.) Unfortunately, there are strong presumptions for believing that bureaucratic incentive structures do not foster economic efficiency. Specifically, the major incentive facing a bureaucrat usually is to increase his agency's budget appropriation. Toward this end, he will concentrate above all on the avoidance of fiscal scandal or some similar malfeasance in office.[13] In contrast to this goal, achieving efficiency of resource allocation for society is only vaguely understood and poorly motivated. Unfortunately, the social costs of the use of scarce bureaucratic time and effort to achieve these goals is likely to be vastly different from the perceived individual costs of the average bureaucrat. However abhorrent on moral grounds, individual dishonesty in the use of government funds, or failure to observe strictly directives from superiors, generally involves trivial social costs, but the costs of a severe misallocation of society's resources can be enormous.

We can summarize this complex subject with the generalization that the incentives facing government bureaucrats today do not, in general, promote socially optimal behavior according to economic efficiency criteria. The bureaucratic structure of rewards and penalties does not correspond to market prices in an ideal market system, and, therefore, no mechanism analogous to the invisible hand of the market operates to assure efficiency in the allocation of society's resources. The efficiency problem inherent in bureaucratic structures has been recognized by government administrators and valiant first attempts were begun in the late 1960s to develop *Planning, Programming, Budgeting Systems* (PPBS) in federal government agencies. The basic goal of PPBS is to promote economic efficiency by inducing each government agency to subject its own activities to a systematic analysis of the relationship of resources expended to program aims. Only if such analyses are carried out in comparable form by each agency can the executive use the government budget to coordinate the activities of all agencies toward some unified ends with reasonable efficiency. At this date, it is too early to pass judgment on the probable long-run success of PPBS or some alternative scheme to push the federal bureaucracy into more concern with economic efficiency. For the time being, however, we should expect the government structure to continue to function much as in the past, with economic efficiency in the broad social sense subject to relative neglect.

---

[13] James A. Wilson, "The Bureaucracy Problem," *The Public Interest*, No. 6 (Winter, 1967), 3–9.

The Optimal Balance of Private and Public Economic Activity

The arguments of this section are intended to dispel any illusions that the solution to all instances of private market failure is government intervention. Just as a perfect private market system is a textbook ideal, so is the kind of government activity outlined in Chapter 4, in which the divergence between the private and social costs of some market activity is perfectly offset by a scientifically calculated effluent charge. We have indicated that government economic intervention may be quite imperfect, in general, for two reasons:

1. Individual preferences are likely to be weighted incorrectly, or even overridden altogether in the process of formulating the public interest at the administrative and legislative levels of government. The prevailing system of majority voting is not an adequate substitute for dollar voting in an ideal private market for the purpose of economic efficiency.

2. Once the public interest is determined by the government, however accurate the weighting of individual preferences, the bureaucratic agencies of government that are entrusted the task of carrying out policies are not engines of economic efficiency, whatever their other merits may be. The problem of efficiency in government primarily is concerned with the optimal allocation of scarce resources relative to social economic goals, and not just the avoidance of waste of government funds or cost minimization within an agency. The structure of bureaucratic incentives inevitably pushes government agencies towards the cost minimization goals at the cost of neglecting the optimal allocation goal.

The foregoing points have lead some economists to suggest the concept of *government failure* as an analogy to the concept of *market failure*. Government failure, like market failure, is not total, but rather a matter of degree, and it does not necessarily extend to other important dimensions of government beyond the attainment of economic efficiency. But it is a key concept because it correctly implies that not all government intervention is an improvement on the private market—at least on efficiency grounds—in cases where market failure is apparent. In our imperfect world, this means that society must somehow choose in each specific case between the better of two less than ideal solutions to the allocation of resources, or perhaps more accurately, between the lesser of two evils. The specific form of government intervention to deal with any environmental problem is also an important issue. The government may be much more effective in dealing with pollution problems through one kind of intervention than with some alternative measures.

Our discussion in this section may help to clarify the reasons for what Marshall Goldman has called *the convergence of environmental disruption* in societies as different in their economic structure as the United States and the Soviet Union.[14] Why should environmental problems exist in the centralized Russian economy in which externalities in private markets surely cannot be blamed for the failure of the economic system to account for all pollution costs? Because the Soviet government owns all the important property rights, it would seem that it would allocate environmental resources efficiently by balancing all marginal productivity gains against all marginal pollution costs. But, as Goldman makes vividly clear, such is not the case. Russian environmental problems appear to match those in the much more decentralized American economy, despite the large discrepancy between the levels of total output in the two countries. Russian bureaucrats appear to pay little more attention to broad issues of economic efficiency than do American bureaucrats. The Russian environment suffers from the results of the monument-building mentality of Soviet government officials just as the American environment often suffers from the single-minded activities of the U. S. Army Corps of Engineers and the Bureau of Reclamation. The message of this discussion should be the disillusionment of any notion that government intervention *automatically* provides a solution to environmental problems.

The foregoing discussion is narrow in focus in that it assumes implicitly no ideological preferences for either the private sector or the public sector. Many economists fervently believe that there is always a strong presumption in favor of the private sector over the public sector on the grounds that greater government economic activity always results in a curtailment of precious individual freedoms. Other economists argue just the opposite position, and contend that the conception of *freedom*, in the arguments of the private market advocates, is naive and overly narrow. Such noneconomic considerations obviously will play an important role in society's choice of how best to deal with environmental problems in the absence of any clearcut presumption that either the private or public sector is a superior mechanism for attaining an efficient allocation of resources.

D. SUMMARY AND CONCLUSIONS

This chapter concludes our presentation in Part II of the book of the economic theory relevant to environmental problems.

---

[14] Marshall I. Goldman, "The Convergence of Environmental Disruption," *Science*, CLXX, No. 3953 (October 2, 1970).

In Chapter 2, we began with a discussion of the concept of economic efficiency and its relationship to the private market system, first under ideal, and then under less than ideal, conditions. Chapter 3 added one technologically realistic complication to the basic model of Chapter 2—the pervasive presence of external effects of production and consumption and the resulting environmental problems in a modern, industrial society—and showed how externalities led to private market failure according to the efficiency criterion of Chapter 2. Chapter 4 extended the analysis of Chapter 3 by demonstrating two logically equivalent ideal solutions to the environmental problems created by the presence of externalities; one, simply by means of an extension of private markets to internalize externalities, and the other, by means of an ideal system of effluent charges to make relative market prices readjust to reflect full social costs and benefits instead of just private costs and benefits.

The intended role of this chapter has been to round off the analysis of the previous chapters in three major respects. First, the concept of a public good was developed and applied to the problem of environmental quality in order to clarify the efficiency aspects of government intervention in the environmental area. We argued that a major problem arises in estimating the true value of a public good like environmental quality. Demand curves for environmental quality can be defined conceptually, but no obvious method is available to the government for obtaining the information necessary for estimating the true demand functions.

The second major point developed in this chapter is that the complex redistributional effects of government environmental programs must be recognized and given some weight, together with pure efficiency considerations, in the formulation of government environmental policy. Hard cases inevitably arise in which efficiency and distributional equity criteria clash, and society must then be prepared to make tradeoffs between goals that are not easily commensurable.

Finally, some very simple points about the workings of government reveal the sobering and not surprising conclusion that government intervention in the environmental area is not a panacea for private market deficiencies. The problems of defining the public interest through the mechanism of majority voting and of achieving agreed-upon goals efficiently through the actions of bureaucratic agencies are of comparable importance to the problems of market failure, suggesting the analogous concept of government failure. The realistic choice society faces, in meeting its environmental problems, is between two quite imperfect mechanisms for achieving efficiency, and it does not follow that, in every instance of private market failure, government intervention in any form results in a net social gain.

QUESTIONS FOR DISCUSSION

1. Consider a pollution problem in your own area. Indicate the methods you might use to obtain quantitative measures of the demand schedule for pollution reduction. How good are the measures you think you could obtain at reasonable costs?

2. How much are *you* willing to pay to improve air quality in your own community? Does your answer depend on how much others have to pay? Suppose that the air quality in your community were ideal. How much would the government have to pay you to obtain your permission to pollute it to its present state?

3. In our example in this chapter, the existing city of Jetportville imposes effluent charges on the airport authority for use of the *new* airport. In your opinion, are the effluent charges in this example equitable? Would your answer to this question differ if we had assumed that the airport predated the existence of Jetportville?

4. Suppose that the only factory in a small town pollutes the air in the area. To solve this externalities problem, the federal government bans all emissions of pollutants. In response, the firm shuts down and 50 percent of the town's population lose their jobs. Does the solution to the externalities problem in this example involve any externalities of its own? Does it involve any important equity issues? Is it at all relevant to the real world problem of the supersonic transport and the depressed job market in Seattle?

5. Suppose that your own local government were given funds to improve the quality of the environment. Based on what you know about its performance in providing other services, predict how well it would carry out its new environmental responsibilities. Specifically, would you expect it to improve significantly the overall efficiency of resource allocation?

SELECTED REFERENCES

ARROW, KENNETH J., *Social Choice and Individual Values* (2nd ed.). New York: John Wiley & Sons, 1963. A classic fundamental study in political economic theory. Very advanced.

BOHM, P., "An Approach to the Problem of Estimating Demand for Public Goods," *Swedish Journal of Economics,* Vol. LXX (March, 1971). Proposes a method of handling the dilemma of obtaining true valuations for public goods.

BUCHANAN, JAMES M., "Individual Choice in Voting and the Market," *Journal of Political Economy,* LXII, No. 4 (August, 1954). Discusses the relationship between voting and economic efficiency.

FREEMAN, A. M. III, "Distribution of Environmental Quality," in *Environmental Quality Analysis*, A. V. Kneese and B. T. Bower, eds. Baltimore: The Johns Hopkins Press, 1972. A treatment of distributional aspects of environmental quality with a review of some available empirical evidence.

GOLDMAN, MARSHALL I., *The Spoils of Progress: Environmental Pollution in the Soviet Union*. Cambridge: The M.I.T. Press, 1972. A fascinating account of environmental problems in the Soviet Union.

HEAD, J. G., "Public Goods and Public Policy," *Public Finance*, No. 3, 1962. A treatment of the relationship between externalities and public goods.

KRUTILLA, JOHN V., "Efficiency Goals, Market Failure, and the Substitution of Public for Private Action," *The Analysis and Evaluation of Public Expenditures: The PPB System*, Vol. I. U.S. Joint Economic Committee, Washington, D.C.: Government Printing Office, 1969. A good source on the effects of the government sector on efficient resource allocation.

MCKEAN, ROLAND N., *Public Spending*. New York: McGraw-Hill, 1968. A study of the relationship between government economic activities and efficient resource allocation.

MUSGRAVE, RICHARD A., *The Theory of Public Finance*. New York: McGraw-Hill, 1959. The best overall treatise on public finance, with good analyses of the public goods problem and the distributional effects of the government budget.

SAMUELSON, PAUL A., "Diagrammatic Exposition of a Theory of Public Expenditure," *The Review of Economics and Statistics*, XXXVII, No. 4 (November, 1955). The pioneering study of the economics of pure public goods.

STEINER, PETER O., *Public Expenditure Budgeting*. Washington, D.C.: Brookings, 1969. A survey of many of the topics covered in this chapter.

WEISBROD, BURTON A., "Collective Action and the Distribution of Income: A Conceptual Approach," *The Analysis and Evaluation of Public Expenditures: The PPBS System*, Vol. I. U.S. Joint Economic Committee. Washington, D.C.: Government Printing Office, 1969. A discussion of the income distribution issues discussed in this chapter.

PART 3

The
Economics
of
Environmental
Problems

Chapter 6

Water
Resources
and
Water
Quality

The next three chapters provide an overview of the technical, physical, and biological aspects of specific environmental problems. Emphasis is given to the *economic* significance of these technical facts of life. This chapter is concerned with the nature of water use, the existing quality of this nation's water resources, and the economic implications of different levels of water quality. Chapter 7 deals with the analogous interplay of technical and economic relationships as they apply to air quality. Finally, Chapter 8 discusses what may be termed broadly *quality of life* problems, including such varied topics as solid wastes, pesticides, noise, the supply of outdoor recreation, and other amenity issues.

Before becoming immersed in the complex details in these three chapters, the reader should have some perspective on how this material fits into the overall study of environmental economics. Part 1 of the book outlined the benefit-cost framework within which economists approach environmental problems. Part 2 discussed the concept of efficiency and pinpointed externalities—the divergence between private and social costs or benefits—as the common thread linking a wide variety of environmental issues. We demonstrated that externalities were the cause of inefficient allocation of environmental resources, even in an otherwise ideal market system, and outlined the theory of how government policy could cope with the efficiency problems associated with externalities. If we now wish to use the theoretical framework constructed in these earlier chapters not only to understand the causes of environmental deterioration but also to deal effectively with real world environmental problems, we must provide empirical content to such concepts as benefits, costs, and externalities. This is the purpose of Part 3.

The common theme, therefore, in the next three chapters is an attempt to identify the causes of divergence between private and social costs with respect to different environmental media and to assess the quantitative significance of these externalities. In order to do this properly, we must, first, identify the physical or biological factors responsible for the deterioration of environmental resources; trace these factors back to their sources in the economy; then, quantify the relationship between each source of pollution and the environmental damage associated with it; and, finally, translate the physical or biological effects in each case into dollar measures of economic damage.

With such a measure of environmental damage, we could then use the benefit-cost framework of Chapter 1 to evaluate the net social gains to be derived from preventing environmental damage in any particular case. Unfortunately, as we shall soon see, measures of damage for most environmental problems are elusive because the empirical basis of environmental economics is still in a rudimentary state. Without such information, much of which must be provided by the research of physical and biological scientists, it is impossible to give precise operational content to the concepts of benefits and costs, and environmental policies must operate in an empirical void. Nonetheless, we shall survey what empirical knowledge is available as of this date and at least make a beginning towards a fuller, more satisfactory treatment of this subject.

This chapter covers the economics of water use. Section A surveys the quantitative dimensions of water quality problems in the United States and reports on the extent of pollution in the nation's water resources. Section B analyzes the nature of the water cycle and considers alternative definitions of the term *water use*. Section C then classifies and describes the major types of pollutants found in water resources, concentrating on the physical characteristics of these pollutants and their impact on water quality. Section D examines the economic effects of deteriorating water quality. Section E provides an overview of current water policy in the United States. Finally, Section F summarizes the key points of the chapter.

A. THE QUALITY OF WATER RESOURCES IN THE UNITED STATES

The United States has enjoyed significant and, on average, steady economic growth throughout its history. Since 1910, our national product has grown at a 3 percent average annual compound rate of growth. Real GNP rose from $203.6 billion in 1929 to $724.1 billion in 1970 (stated in 1958 prices). Economic growth has been accompanied by increasing demands on the nation's natural resources, including an ever growing utilization of water resources.[1] The role of water in economic activity is apparent from casual observations. Besides its obvious uses for household consumption, water is a vital input in almost every industrial and manufacturing activity, in agriculture and mining, and in the generation of electrical energy. In addition to these uses directly related to production, substantial uses of water are associated with the enormous growth in outdoor recreation activities. This upsurge of recreational activities is also a byproduct of economic growth, as a wealthier population begins to take increasing proportions of productivity and real income gains in the form of leisure time and leisure activities.

Table 6–1 provides estimates of recent and projected water withdrawals for different purposes in the United States. The magnitude of the projected increases is noteworthy. Total water withdrawals are expected to more than double between now and the year 2000 with the major increases attributable to self-supplied industrial needs, steam-electric utilities, and publicly supplied municipal uses of water. It should be noted that projections of water withdrawal requirements are not independent of economic factors. Changes in production techniques and the relative cost of water may significantly affect the amount of future water withdrawals. Nevertheless, the data in Table 6–1 do demonstrate the relationship between economic activity and water use.

When water is withdrawn from a water source for a given purpose and used, it may escape from the control of man. For example, a steel plant may use water to cool burning coke and, in the process, convert the water into steam. In this situation, the steam escaping into the atmosphere would represent a *consumptive* use of water as it is no longer directly available for subsequent uses. If, however, some water is returned to the water source and remains available for subsequent uses, then the amount of water withdrawals can exceed the amount of *consumptive water use* as the same water can be reused for several purposes. However, as water may be used or lost in this obvious quantitative sense, it may also be lost or used qualitatively. Section B will pay particular attention to the

---

[1] The relationship of economic growth to environmental problems is treated in detail in Chapter 14.

TABLE 6–1   ESTIMATED WATER WITHDRAWALS AND PROJECTED REQUIREMENTS, UNITED STATES * (million gallons daily)

Type of Use	Used	Projected Requirements		
	1965	1980	2000	2020
	Withdrawals			
Rural domestic	2,351	2,474	2,852	3,334
Municipal (public-supplied) ..	23,745	33,596	50,724	74,256
Industrial (self-supplied)	46,405	75,026	127,365	210,767
Steam-electric power:				
Fresh	62,738	133,963	259,208	410,553
Saline	21,800	59,340	211,240	503,540
Agriculture:				
Irrigation	110,852	135,852	149,824	160,978
Livestock	1,726	2,375	3,397	4,660
Total	269,617	442,626	804,610	1,368,088

* Source: *The Nation's Water Resources,* Water Resource Council, Washington, 1968, p. 4–1.

economic implications of this distinction. The existence of this important quality dimension with respect to water use gives rise to general concerns of water quality and the relationship of water quality to economic activity. In many instances, the uses of water listed in Table 6–1 involve certain quality effects. For example, some uses raise the water temperature and other uses result in the discharge of organic wastes, toxins, inorganic substances, pesticides, and other pollutants into the water. This deterioration in water quality may reduce, or entirely preclude, further uses of the water, or it may necessitate substantial treatment costs before the water can be reused.

Because the issue of water quality deterioration is the central theme of this chapter, some indications of the magnitude of the problem will be useful. The projected growth of organic wastes created by municipal uses of water is of the order of about 300 percent for the U.S. as a whole between 1970 and 2020.[2] In addition to the wastes associated with domestic and municipal water uses, even larger amounts of organic wastes are generated by various industrial water users. In particular, the food processing, chemical, and paper industries are major sources of organic wastes, contributing approximately 90 percent of all organic wastes created in manufacturing. Agricultural wastes from feedlot runoffs are a further source of organic wastes.

[2] We shall treat the technical aspects of organic wastes in detail in Section C.

However, the level of organic wastes in the nation's waters is by no means the complete picture of present and future water quality problems. Although some rough national estimates of organic wastes exist, there is no comprehensive national inventory of the extent of inorganic substances entering water supplies. Yet we know industrial and agricultural uses of water add many inorganic substances to water resources. For example, a recent magazine article provided a *partial* list of substances found in a cup of water dipped from the Ohio River near the city of Cincinniti.[3] In addition to organic wastes, this water was found to contain ammonia, arsenic, barium, boron, cadmium, chloride, copper, fluoride, iron, lead, magnese nitrates, phosphorous, selenium, silver, sulfate, zinc, organic chemicals, and radioactive substances. In various degrees, these materials and others are present in many major water systems in the country. The diffuse presence of such substances in water discharges involves further considerable water quality problems. We shall treat these issues in more detail in Sections B and C.

Recently, the Environmental Protection Agency (EPA) has attempted to survey the extent of water quality deterioration in the entire nation. In 1970, the EPA reported that 27 percent of the nation's waters were polluted. In 1971, the relevant figure was 29 percent; a slight increase over the year despite a decade of extensive social policy aimed at water quality control and the expenditure of billions of dollars.

Data from this EPA survey of water pollution in the major U.S. drainage basins are shown in Table 6–2. The first column lists the total stream or shore miles in the basin. The next six columns report the number and percent of polluted miles in 1970 and 1971 and the change between the two years. It should be noted that some of these changes can be traced to EPA reporting and coverage procedures rather than actual water quality changes.[4]

The next to last column in Table 6–2 provides the EPA's duration-intensity factor which measures the degree of existing water quality deterioration. The preceding mileage figures simply indicate whether or not the stream was polluted. The duration factor relates the intensity of the pollution to the designated federal-state water quality standards for the particular water body. This factor increases as the pollution increases within any given stretch of stream mileage. Multiplying the mileage of polluted waters in 1971 by this factor yields the Prevalence-

---

[3] See *Fortune Magazine*, February, 1970, p. 102.

[4] For example, the 1971 survey covered more of the Ohio basin mileage than did the 1970 inventory. The additional miles included also happened to be polluted and this is reflected in the large increase in polluted miles reported. The water, however, was as polluted in 1970 as in 1971; it just went unreported in 1970.

TABLE 6-2 WATER POLLUTION SURVEY OF MAJOR DRAINAGE BASINS *

Watershed	Stream Miles	Polluted Miles						1971 Duration Intensity Factor	P.D.I.
		1970	%	1971	%	Change	% Change		
Ohio	28,992	9,869	.34	24,031	.83	+13,746	+.49	.42	10,093
Southeast	11,726	3,109	.26	4,490	.38	+1,381	+.12	.74	3,322
Great Lakes	21,374	6,580	.31	8,771	.41	+2,191	+.10	.45	3,947
Northeast	32,431	11,895	.37	5,823	.18	−6,072	−.19	.61	3,552
Middle Atlantic	31,914	4,620	.14	5,627	.18	+869	+.04	.47	2,645
California	28,277	5,359	.19	8,429	.30	+2,499	+.11	.27	2,276
Gulf	64,719	16,605	.26	11,604	.18	−5,001	−.08	.35	4,061
Missouri	10,448	4,259	.41	1,839	.18	−2,420	−.23	.31	570
Columbia	30,443	7,443	.24	5,685	.19	−1,758	−.05	.12	682
U.S.	260,324	69,739	.27	76,299	.29	+5,435	+.02	.41	31,282
U.S. (less Ohio)	231,332	59,870	.26	52,268	.23	−8,311	−.03	.40	20,907

* Source: Environmental Protection Agency, *The Cost of Clean Water*, 1972.

Duration-Intensity index (PDI) which is a measure of how badly the water is polluted. This PDI is reported in the final column of Table 6–2.

The overall picture of water quality derived from these data is not encouraging. Although there has been a measure of progress in some watersheds, the conclusion is that for the United States as a whole, water quality, at best, is only holding at former levels in the major drainage basins of the country.

What are the economic implications of the water quality deterioration evidenced by this brief review? Because property rights and property law with respect to assigning the full costs or benefits of the use of water are imperfect, significant external diseconomies result from the many competing uses of water.[5] These externalities, together with the extensive role of water in economic activity, imply that important efficiency and equity issues are involved in the use of the nation's water resources.

B. TECHNICAL ASPECTS OF WATER USE

Before we can analyze the specific environmental consequences associated with the use of water resources, it is necessary to discuss certain technical aspects of the nature of water supplies and the alternative uses of water. A complete investigation of water and water supplies would involve many complex issues in the physical, biological, and engineering sciences beyond the scope of this book. Our purpose in this section is to present an overview of certain physical phenomena associated with water in order to provide a basis for understanding the economic problems arising from water use.

Water is continually in movement, flowing over land, evaporating from water bodies, transpiring from vegetation, or moving in cloud and vapor form in the atmosphere. This movement is a continuous flow and forms the basis of what hydrologists call the *water cycle*. The intuitive aspects of this concept are fairly straightforward. If the water cycle is entered at a given point, for example, when rains fall on the earth's surface, we can trace this water through various routes that lead back into the atmosphere. Some of the routes will afford possibilities for man's withdrawal of water from the natural water cycle. One avenue for this water is quick reevaporation back into the atmosphere from the land surface or water bodies on which it falls. Alternatively, the water may enter the soil and percolate into underground water supplies or be taken

---

[5] Water law is discussed in the Appendix to this chapter.

into vegetation and transpired back into the atmosphere. The water may run off land surfaces into surface bodies of water. Finally, water may fall in solid snow form and be stored as ice to await melting before re-entering the cycle. When water is in liquid form in fresh water bodies or in underground storage, man is able to withdraw it for various uses before it returns to the oceans or atmosphere.

The United States, as a whole, has a relatively plentiful supply of water with an average annual precipitation of thirty inches over the forty-eight continental states. However, this rainfall is not equally distributed. The amount of water in surface sources (streams, lakes, rivers) is relatively small compared to the amount available in underground storage areas (acquifiers), but withdrawals from surface sources represent about 67 percent of total water withdrawals in the United States. Groundwater sources account for only 22 percent of water withdrawals.[6] Rough estimates of the extent of groundwater indicates that it surpasses the amount of water in all the Great Lakes. The current low percentage of use of groundwater supplies is, in part, due to the location of the acquifiers relative to the location of the users of water and the currently lower relative costs of surface sources. This relatively unused source of available water is a valuable national asset and one which will be increasingly used in the future. Obviously, the proper management of groundwater sources is an important policy concern and considerable caution is required to avoid the relatively easy degradation of water in underground sources.[7]

While water is in rivers, streams, lakes, and underground reservoirs, it becomes economically feasible for man to withdraw water and put it to his uses. The notion of the *use* of water may appear to be an intuitive and simple concept. However, we shall see that a careful definition of this concept is necessary in order to obtain a proper understanding of our basic concern, the economics of water quality. Hydrologists speak, in a technical sense, of the consumptive use of water occurring when water escapes from the land phase of the water cycle into the sea or atmosphere and is no longer physically available for further use. From this technical definition, a nonconsumptive use of water would imply water that not only is used in a given activity but also physically remains in the land phase of the water cycle and, hence, is available for further uses.

---

[6] We have omitted the ocean as a withdrawal source. However, at present, 11 percent of withdrawals are saline in nature and, with advancing desalting technology, the ocean can be expected to increase in relative importance as a water source.

[7] For example, local legislation in the city of Akron, Ohio has prohibited the use of hard detergents in this community entirely dependent on well water supplies. See *New York Times*, Dec. 13, 1970. Similar policies have recently been implemented in a number of other localities.

This technical distinction between consumptive and nonconsumptive water use is incomplete for our purposes. The essential economic implication of the term *use* is that the water is no longer suitable for subsequent desirable uses. Costs must be incurred before the water can be used again. Whether the water does or does not remain in the liquid-land phase of the water cycle is not necessarily the crucial distinction in defining an economic use of water. If we consider a quality dimension to water use within the land phase of the water cycle, it is then possible to have economic uses of water even though the water remains quantitatively the same in terms of physical availability. Once subsequent uses of water are hindered by a given preceding use of water, the water has been used, or partially used, in an economic sense. For example, if stream water is used for waste disposal purposes, then downstream uses of the water for recreation purposes may be impaired. Alternatively, if a river is to be devoted to trout fishing, it cannot be readily used as a disposal site for toxic waste or as a source of cooling water because both of these uses would destroy, or greatly reduce, the trout population (in the absence of incurring costs to remove the toxins from the discharged water or to lower the temperature of the returned cooling water).

If one use of a water supply creates quality deterioration that partially or wholly precludes another potential use of the water then the water has been used consumptively in an economic sense. Only at some costs can the water be rendered fit for various other uses. This definition of water use presents the familiar economic problem of choosing between the alternative uses of a scarce resource.

An important aspect of this problem, as it concerns water use compared to many other economic resources, is that water has a wide quality dimension and various qualities of water are called upon for various uses.[8] For example, recreational use of water requires certain biological purity characteristics; waste disposal draws on the assimilative capacity of water and the size and flow characteristics of the water body, and use of water for cooling purposes relies on the heat absorption property of water. We could extend this list to include many other uses and their associated quality demands on water. Most uses of water for purposes such as those described above are competitive and therefore the decision to use a water resource in any given use implies that some other potentially valuable uses of water must be wholly or partially foregone. Alternatively, treatment costs will have to be incurred before the water can be used for these other purposes.

---

[8] Of course, other economic resources also have quality dimensions. Unskilled labor and skilled labor are not perfect substitutes in production, and degrees of labor skill may vary just as widely as the quality of different water requirements.

Once the nature of the economic use of water is understood, then it follows that *pollution* can take the form of any action that impairs the necessary water qualities needed for subsequent and/or competing uses of the water. Given this definition, pollution, at times, can become an extremely elusive concept. For example, suppose an upriver industrial plant uses a river flow for cooling purposes and restores the water to the river without adding any type of waste discharge. However, the water temperature of the downstream flow of the river is raised, on average, by five degrees. Does this represent pollution? Is this an economic use of water? To answer these questions, we need considerably more information than the fact that the average river temperature has increased, that is, the plant has *used* some of the heat absorption capacity of the river. Suppose this particular river is the site of a considerable annual salmon run that affords both extensive commercial and sports fishing opportunities. If the increase in water temperature lowers the oxygen level in the stream sufficiently to prevent the salmon from using this river, or at least decreases their number and hence reduces fishing on the river, then there is an economic use of the water. The physical nature of the quality impairment of the water can be called thermal (or heat) pollution.

The point to be emphasized is that the issue of whether there has been an economic use of water depends on whether there are actual or potential subsequent uses of the water and if these subsequent uses have been impaired. Suppose the river was not a salmon fishing river but flowed past a downstream city and then into the ocean. The increased temperature of the river did not affect the city's use of the water for domestic and industrial purposes nor did it damage the ecological system of the river or preclude any fishing opportunities. In this situation, no economic use of the river water results from the water being used in the upstream plant. Does thermal pollution exist in this case? In a physical and not very meaningful sense, yes, because the river's water is heated to the same extent as before and, accordingly, the heat absorption capacity of the river is reduced. In the more meaningful economic sense, however, no pollution has occurred because no other uses of the water are precluded.[9] Thus, it is not always true that changes in the physical characteristics of water imply an economic use of the water. We must ask whether other potential uses are prevented by the use of water

[9] In fact, consider a third case, where the increased water temperature stimulates bacterial action and provides in this instance a *beneficial* effect on fish population and hence on fishing activity. Has pollution occurred here? The water is physically identical to the other situations, that is, a five degree increase in temperature, but here a *beneficial* effect is associated with thermal "pollution."

qualities in question. If they are, then problems of external costs arise together with the associated problems of the efficient use of the water resource.

Before we further examine the implications of the economic use of water in Section D, we shall give a brief survey of the major causes of water quality deterioration. In terms of the above discusion, we shall treat pollution in the physical sense of the factors that adversely affect water quality.

C. POLLUTANTS: AN OVERVIEW

The technical aspects of the deterioration of the physical characteristics of water are numerous and complex. This section surveys some broad classifications of the physical agents responsible for water quality deterioration.

1. Degradable Pollutants

As an initial distinction, pollutants can be categorized as either *degradable* or *nondegradable*. The term degradable implies materials that are organic in nature and undergo physical changes through the chemical and biological processes occurring in water. The most common component of degradable wastes is the sewage associated with domestic uses of water. In addition to domestic sewage, however, numerous industries, particularly paper, food processing, oil refining, and chemical plants produce large amounts of organic waste materials that are discharged, in various stages of treatment, into water bodies. When organic wastes are deposited in a river or stream, the bacteria present in the water begin to break down the unstable organic waste into stable inorganic elements, primarily phosphates, nitrates, and sulfates. Through this process, water bodies are said to have a *self-cleansing* quality whereby they convert organic wastes into more stable components.

In a clean water body, the bacterial degradation of organic wastes will occur with the use of the oxygen dissolved in the water. The process whereby bacteria utilize the free oxygen dissolved in the stream to break down organic wastes is called an *aerobic* process. An indication of the extent of the organic waste in any water body is found in the amount of dissolved oxygen used by bacteria. The higher the given level of organic waste load, the more dissolved oxygen will be needed. The oxygen requirement of bacteria needed to break down the organic wastes is called the *biochemical oxygen demand* (or BOD). As the amounts of organic wastes discharged into water increase, the BOD will also increase. In addition to the amount of the organic waste load, BOD is also affected by the temperature of the water. Because warmer water temperatures stimulate bacterial processes, BOD increases with the temperature of the water for any given waste load. Warm water temperatures are also associated with lower levels of dissolved oxygen due to the lowered capabilities of warmer waters to assimilate oxygen. The result is that in periods of warm weather, oxygen in the water is drawn up more rapidly from a base that is already relatively low. If the BOD in such conditions is sufficiently great, the level of dissolved oxygen in the water falls to extremely low levels for a considerable length of time. When this occurs, many forms of fish life in the water may be destroyed. In addition, if the BOD is so large that the dissolved oxygen level approaches zero, then bacterial degradation continues without the use of free oxygen, that is, it occurs *anaerobically*. As a result, a series of gases are given off by the water (hydrogen sulfide and methane) and the water has both a disagreeable look and a noxious smell. Water bodies with extreme organic waste loads and subsequent consistent anaerobic conditions are reduced to the simple functions associated with a sewage depository.

As noted above, the aerobic action of bacteria on organic wastes produces inorganic components, primarily, nitrates and phosphates. These byproducts of bacterial degradation form a base of plant nutrients in the water and stimulate algae growth. Although some algae growth may be desirable for fish life, excessive growths of algae, resulting from abnormal plant nutrient levels, alter the taste and odor of water and may prove toxic to fish life, obstruct navigation, and hinder recreation activities.

Due to the relatively low water circulation rates, the problems of organic waste loads in lakes and other standing bodies of water are, in some respects, more severe than those involving flowing rivers and streams. The excessive growth of algae from the abnormal levels of nutrients created by high amounts of BOD combined with large amounts of detergent-related phosphates can remove much of the dissolved oxygen from a lake. Indeed, in extreme forms lakes become devoid of oxygen over large areas. This accelerated reduction in the dissolved oxygen content of a lake represents artificial aging of the lake, or what is called *eutrophication*. Lake Erie has become the unfortunate showcase example of the problems associated with high levels of organic waste loads and the subsequent severe problems of low dissolved oxygen levels, excessive algae growth, and accelerated eutrophication. The other Great Lakes are threatened by the same series of events. Recently this problem has been the subject of extensive technical research efforts spurred on by deep concern on the part of government and private conservation groups.

2. Nondegradable Pollutants

The second major group of pollutants are those classified as nondegradable. These are substances that are not changed by the bacterial processes in water. Many industrial wastes such as various metals, metallic salts, chlorides, and toxins of various kinds are nondegradable pollutants. These substances are dispersed and diluted, but are not physically altered by natural processes in water. Another related group of pollutants that are not strictly nondegradable can be called *persistent pollutants*. These substances, though organic in nature,—DDT, and synthetic detergents are two well-known examples—deteriorate very slowly over time. Certain insecticides, herbicides, and phenols from oil products are persistent and resist both treatment processes and natural bacterial action. Radioactive wastes represent an extreme form of persistent pollutants.

D. WATER POLLUTANTS AND THEIR ECONOMIC EFFECTS

Examples of severe water pollution abound throughout the United States. Perhaps one of the most dramatic occurred in the summer of 1970, when the Cuyahoga River, flowing through industrial Cleveland, actually caught fire. Used as a receptacle for numerous industrial and municipal discharges, the wastes in the Cuyahoga burst into flames and the resulting floating fire threatened several bridges. Witnesses to this event were confronted by the incredible sight of fire control efforts directed at a river!

The destruction of once large and commercially valuable fish populations in the estuaries and rivers of the Potomac, Delaware, Hudson, Connecticut, and other East Coast rivers provide ready examples of the ecological disruptions of water pollution.

Although the Great Lakes are the largest surface source of fresh water in the world, they are being increasingly degraded by human and industrial wastes. Pollution in Lake Erie has worsened to such a degree that not only is swimming prohibited by many shore communities, but typhoid inoculations are required for persons desiring to boat on the lake for protection against the unhappy prospect of falling in!

New York City draws its water supply from a complicated upstate reservoir system while the polluted Hudson, one of the largest rivers in the United States, flows directly past the largest city in the country.

We could easily extend this chronicle of noteworthy pollution problems for many pages. The essential point, however, has been made. Water pollution is pervasive throughout the country, from rural Maine through the industrialized middle Atlantic area to the rivers of Washington and

Oregon. We turn now to a systematic evaluation of the economic effects of water pollution.

1. Health Effects

A once common effect of organic pollutants in water was the threat to public health. Disease-causing bacteria are present in domestic sewage and other organic wastes. Outbreaks of dysentery and typhoid associated with organically polluted water supplies were, in the past, common occurrences in this and other Western countries. In fact, even today the problem is not completely eliminated in the United States. The U.S. Public Health Service recorded almost twenty-six thousand cases of waterborne disease in the United States from 1946 to 1960. However, over half of the disease outbreaks were associated with untreated surface or ground water sources, and public water systems are now relatively secure from this problem.

In less-developed countries, the disease menace to public health remains a real danger. The extensive spread of cholera through various Middle and Far East countries in the summer of 1970 is an example of public health problems in less-developed countries related to water pollution. Water supplies destined for domestic use that contain unsafe coliform counts—the index conventionally used to indicate the presence of wastes from the human intestine—are treated with chlorine to destroy bacteria and prevent disease epidemics. The use of chlorine treatment in this country has successfully eliminated the major epidemic dangers of organic pollutants in public water supplies. Obviously, chlorine treatment is not costless and the economic effects of bacterial pollutants are reflected in the costs of treatment incurred to avoid the vast potential dangers associated with epidemic bacterial diseases.

Inorganic toxins and persistent organic toxins also present significant dangers to public health, and water containing these substances requires treatment to established tolerance levels. The immediate dangers in terms of mortality are known for the conventional poisons and inorganic toxins. Tolerance levels for domestic water supplies accordingly reflect significant safety margins for these pollutants. However, conventional water treatment processes are often unable to remove many inorganic pollutants, pesticides, and other complex compounds. In fact, surveys by the Public Health Service in 1969 found significant amounts of such substances in the water systems of numerous communities throughout the country. As in the case of bacterial pollutants, when treatment is undertaken, the costs incurred to control the levels of these inorganic pollutants in domestic water supplies represent another economic cost of their initial discharge into water sources.

Much less easily measured are the welfare damage costs of inorganic pollutants in terms of human health; that is, the consequences of the human ingestion of these substances following the failure of treatment methods to remove them from the water supply. Medical science has the difficult problem of determining the long-run health effects of continued human ingestion of low, *safe* levels of inorganic toxins, other inorganic pollutants, and the growing number of synthetically produced organic substances that also end up in water. The recent concern about the discovery of significant levels of mercury in certain fish and other wildlife is an example of the widespread scientific concern with the potential long-run dangers that may exist from continued use of water resources to dispose of toxins. The ability of commonly used toxins, such as mercury, to enter the foodchain via the medium of water presents unknown, and potentially significant, dangers to human health. Identifying the complex reactions of these substances with the human body processes over extended lengths of time is an enormous but critically important problem for toxicology and the biochemical sciences. The potential human health costs of these effects threaten to be of enormous magnitude.

In addition to treatment methods designed to eliminate the threats to public health associated with bacterial diseases, viruses, and various toxins, domestic water supplies are also treated to provide acceptable taste, odor, and other aesthetic characteristics. The costs of this treatment must also be included as part of the social costs resulting from the introduction of pollutants into water sources in addition to the welfare costs of water that still tastes poor, even after treatment, or *because of* treatment.

Federal government studies have estimated that almost $19 billion of capital expenditure is necessary to provide acceptable waste treatment for domestic and municipal uses of water. This would involve the upgrading of existing treatment facilities and the construction of new facilities to complement population growth and provide water treatment services where none currently exist. The normal treatment level implied by this estimate is secondary treatment, meaning an 85 percent BOD and solids reduction. The $19 billion is only a short term projection made from 1971 to 1980. Additional operating expenditures estimated at $23.6 billion will also be required during the decade and this total of $42.6 billion implies a considerable economic burden on states and local communities responsible for part of these costs.

2. Industrial Effects

Manufacturing uses of water are numerous and differ widely with respect to the necessary quality characteristics of water. However, corrosion damages resulting from a natural high mineral content of water are common in many industrial uses of water. The presence of additional inorganic substances introduced by man, such as chlorides and manganese, increase this type of damage. Water that meets the quality standards for domestic uses may require treatment for certain industrial uses in order to remove such economically damaging characteristics as hardness, acidity, alkalinity, or salinity. For example, water used in high pressure boilers, a common industrial use, should be essentially free of corrosive materials such as manganese and iron, although these minerals are tolerated or even favored in public water supplies. Alternatively, the quality of water used in paper production can be low in terms of human consumption standards but should also contain only small concentrations of corrosive elements. A measure of the pollution costs associated with these effects can be given by the expenses undertaken to avoid these industrial damages plus the damages that can actually be attributed to these pollutants.

3. Recreational Effects

Beyond the effects of water pollutants on domestic and industrial uses, we can identify a category of effects related to recreation, esthetics, and conservation. The rapid growth of public participation in outdoor recreation activities in this country is a well-documented phenomenon. Table 6–3 presents some data and projections for participation in several popular water-based recreational activities. Swimming is, by far, the most popular outdoor recreation activity and is projected to be almost three times its 1965 level by the end of this century. The other water-based activities also have large projected rates of growth, with the total of all water-based sports indicating a growth from 2.8 to 7.7 billions of activity days by the year 2000. In addition to these obviously water-oriented pursuits, many other recreational activities—camping, picnicking, sightseeing—also, at times, require the use of water resources. Thus, it is obvious that if these projections are to be realized, sufficient amounts of water, and water of appropriately high qualities, will be necessary to support society's demands for recreation.

Of the water-oriented outdoor activities listed in Table 6–3, swimming obviously requires a relatively high level of water purity in terms of coliform count. Fishing requires various levels of dissolved oxygen and relative freedom from toxins, depending on the species. Although boating has relatively low biological water quality requirements, a lack of corrosive materials and certain esthetic qualities of water—lack of odor, turbidity, and suspended solids—significantly increase its enjoyment.

Section C has already discussed the effects of organic wastes on the dissolved oxygen levels of lakes and streams. At low levels of dis-

TABLE 6–3   PROJECTED PARTICIPATION IN MAJOR
WATER-BASED RECREATION ACTIVITIES
(millions of activity days)

Activity	1965	1980	2000
Swimming	1,615	2,676	4,697
Fishing	577	738	1,020
Boating (all types)	456	774	1,353
Water skiing	73	146	296
Ice skating	108	183	325
Total of major water-based activities	2,838	4,517	7,691
Total of 25 recreation activities including the above	12,288	18,342	29,774
Water-based as a % of total	23%	25%	26%

Source: *The Nation's Water Resources*, p. 451.

solved oxygen (DO), water bodies become incapable of supporting fish life. The minimum DO level necessary to sustain fish life varies over types of fish (for example, trout, bass, and other sport fish require higher DO levels than rough fish such as carp and suckers), but all fish species are damaged or destroyed when certain minimum dissolved oxygen levels are reached. Excessive levels of inorganic and persistent toxins also eliminate fish life and preclude fishing. Thermal water effects created by industry operations, primarily in the generation of electrical energy and also by cooling processes in many industries, lower the dissolved oxygen levels in water and may have adverse effects on fish populations.

The heavy algae growths associated with high BOD levels also may hinder swimming and fishing. Unpleasant anaerobic conditions may deter various types of recreational boating in addition to eliminating fishing and swimming opportunities. Further, these anaerobic characteristics reduce the amount or the quality of other recreational activities that occur near water areas.

The value of the resulting reduction in outdoor recreation activity is a pollution damage cost that must be attributed to those pollutants responsible for the deterioration of the water quality. Given the large numbers measuring the extent of recreational activities that involve water, it is evident that the implicit economic costs of pollutants that deter or destroy recreational opportunities are quite significant.[10]

Finally, substantial economic losses in commercial fishing activity have occurred as a result of both organic and inorganic pollutants. For

---

[10] Additional considerations in this area would involve the loss due to water pollutants of unique, irreproducible, natural water environments (such as wilderness rivers). We will discuss this and similar issues in Chapter 8.

example, commercial fish catches in Lake Erie have declined from over twenty-six million pounds in 1955 to nine million pounds in 1970. This decline is general for several other Great Lakes and many other inland waters. The virtual elimination of a once substantial shad fishery in East Coast rivers is a further example of this effect of pollutants on commercial fishing. A more recent extension of the same phenomenon is the closing of many shellfish beds in East Coast estuaries and tidal areas. Even some open ocean fishing activities may be threatened by the mercury concentrations discovered in ocean fish.

We have now discussed a number of the potential effects of deteriorating water quality on human and economic activity. All of these effects impose pollution prevention costs, pollution damage avoidance costs or actual pollution damage costs on society. However, the potential magnitude of the various costs differ considerably.

A number of studies of specific industries indicate that production costs are inelastic with respect to relatively large changes in water quality.[11] This conclusion implies that relatively small cost savings for industry would be realized with improved water quality. As a result, only minor amounts of the expenditures on water pollution abatement programs can be justified by the pollution damage costs saved by industry. Similarly, other studies indicate that, in general, relatively little of the costs of water quality improvement can be matched by the resulting cost savings in public water treatment. However, this conclusion does not account for the potentially enormous, long-run health perils associated with the ingestion of a variety of inorganic substances in *safe, potable* domestic water supplies.

Nevertheless, it appears that the burden of justifying the bulk of water pollution control costs falls on the recreational and esthetic values associated with high water quality. In terms of the analysis in Part 2 of the book, this implies that the major part of the external costs caused by water pollution are associated with foregone recreation, esthetic, and ecological values. Moreover, several studies have indicated that the magnitude of the value of high water quality oriented recreation is quite capable of equaling the expenditures needed to achieve and maintain such high quality water. We shall treat the problems of systematically evaluating the dollar benefits of programs to improve and protect environmental quality in Chapter 11. At present we tentatively can conclude that, in the specific case of water resources, it is essentially the recreational and esthetic values of water that are highly sensitive to improve-

---

[11] In part, the conclusion represents the fact that a large amount of industrial water is used for cooling purposes and this use requires water of relatively low quality. Therefore, improving water quality will not significantly lower the costs of the major use of water in industry.

ments in water quality rather than the use of water in production activities or for household consumption.

E. U.S. WATER POLICY

The decade of the 1960s witnessed a growing anxiety over the quality of the nation's water resources. This concern was manifested in a number of federal and state actions designed to improve and protect water quality. The Water Quality Act of 1965 is the current basis of federal involvement in water quality control. It aims at reducing effluents from both municipal and industrial sources. Accordingly, the legislation provides for federal subsidies of up to 55 percent of the construction costs of municipal water treatment facilities. In addition, the act mandates the establishment and enforcement of *state water quality standards.*

In general, water quality standards set minimum or maximum allowable levels for numerous water quality measures—dissolved oxygen, coliform count, chloride concentration, and so on. In operation, the procedure has been for states to determine the specific uses of bodies of water within their boundaries—industrial, recreation, supporting wildlife populations, and so on—and then to establish the compatible water quality standards consistent with the proposed uses.[12] The standards, along with an implementation plan, are reviewed for approval by the EPA. Upon approval, enforcement becomes a state responsibility.

The actual performance of this legislation has been somewhat of a disappointment. Despite considerable expenditures on municipal water treatment facilities, only small improvements in water quality have occurred. The reduction achieved in municipal BOD waste loads has been more than matched by the increase in industrial water pollutants. As a result, the quality of the nation's water resources has little to show for the substantial sums spent for treatment facilities over the last decade.

In addition, the success of state water quality standards to control industrial pollutants has been relatively limited. An obvious difficulty is determining the actual level of the various quality standards. Ideally, with perfect knowledge of all the relevant damage costs of deteriorating water quality, the standards would be set in the context of the economic efficiency criteria of Parts 1 and 2—that is, the benefits of avoiding of pollution damages versus the pollution prevention costs of waste reduction. However, as we have seen, present knowledge, particularly on the damages side, is quite imperfect. Thus, only by random chance will the

---

[12] Recall that EPA's duration-intensity factor in Table 6–2 is measured in relation to these quality standards and the specified uses of the particular water body.

quality standards coincide with the appropriate efficiency criteria that should be implicit in such standards.

Nevertheless, state water quality standards have emerged from a complex social decision-making process involving political, economic, and technological considerations. It is the *enforcement*, rather than the formulation of the standards, that has proven most difficult. In large part, this problem arises from the fact that the standards apply to the water body as a whole rather than the individual sources of the pollutants. Proof, therefore, is necessary to establish the relationship between the type and amount of wastes emitted by any given waste source and the existing quality measure of the water. This becomes a complex task when there are numerous sources discharging many types of wastes into the same water. The legal proceedings brought by the EPA, although successful at times, are cumbersome and lengthy. The overall result has been sporadic enforcement of the standards and relatively minor improvements in water quality even in the presence of a detailed, carefully developed, and approved set of water quality standards.

In light of this experience, a number of other approaches have been suggested or attempted. At various times, Congress has received, but not enacted, proposals to establish a system of effluent charges designed to provide economic incentives to industry to reduce waste discharges. Another approach has resurrected an old, previously unused law, The Refuse Act of 1899. In its original form, this act prohibited any waste discharge into navigable waters unless a permit was obtained from the Corps of Engineers. Reincarnated, The Refuse Act has been a means of limiting the discharges from individual waste sources and, thereby, implicitly enforcing the state water quality standards. As might be expected, a great deal of confusion has accompanied the revival and enforcement of this legislation. However, the idea of a general permit system establishing effluent standards on the specific waste source—rather than water quality standards for the entire water body—has generated considerable interest in the Congress, the EPA, and many states.

At the time of this writing, Congress has enacted broad new legislation aimed at water quality improvement. The legislation increases the subsidization of municipal sewage facilities to 70 percent. The legislation calls for an end to discharges into navigable waters by 1985. This *no discharge* goal is to be reached in steps, with a water quality consistent with fish and wildlife populations achieved by 1981. The EPA is given broad powers to establish effluent limits for each individual waste source and this supersedes the authority of the Refuse Act.

The legislation does considerable violence to economic efficiency criteria. It calls for the EPA to insure that waste discharges will be controlled by "the best practicable control technology currently available" by 1976 and at "reasonable cost" by 1981. For all new industries, control of discharges will be achieved by "the best available technology" within a year of initial operation. Obviously, the interpretation of such language poses considerable problems. In addition, with an estimated forty thousand sources emitting water pollutants, the use of an effluent standard system to limit wastes imposes a staggering information and administration problem on the EPA.

The legislation ignores effluent charges as a possible alternative vehicle to improve water quality. Instead, the legislation ultimately relies on regulation of each individual discharger. This follows a tradition of federal regulatory efforts in other areas of the economy. In light of the mixed experience of regulation in general, a water quality program founded on massive regulation must be viewed somewhat pessimistically.

F. SUMMARY AND CONCLUSIONS

This chapter surveys the technical aspects of water resource problems and emphasizes the link between water use and economic activity. The incomplete ownership rights of water and the extensive and multipurpose uses of water in the economy combine to generate considerable externalities associated with water use. These externalities are an important illustration of the general problem of externalities discussed in detail in Chapters 3 and 4. A brief overview of the dimensions of water use indicates the vital role of water resources in the economic growth process. The major conclusion from available data is the strength of the relation between economic activity and the demands on the water resources of the nation.

Because water resources serve such varied economic functions, it is important to understand the quality dimensions of water. Different uses of water depend on differing qualities of water. A given use may, by destroying or damaging a particular quality characteristic, preclude subsequent uses of the water. This important distinction forms the basis of a careful definition of the *economic use* of water and provides a precise clarification of the economic meaning of water quality.

With this definition of water use, we survey the technical aspects of some major factors that affect water quality. A broad distinction is made between *degradable* and *nondegradable* pollutants. Both kinds of pollutants have important impacts on water quality. Pollutants of water can be related to particular water uses and to the economic effects of various water quality conditions. Some cost estimates associated with water quality provide a basis for assessing the social significance of water quality problems.

Current U.S. water policy centers on a regulatory approach. Subsidization of local public water treatment facilities and the use of water quality standards are the major features of federal participation in water quality improvement. This legislation's relatively poor record of success has led to other proposals to increase the regulatory role of the government in this area through the power of the EPA to set effluent standards for specific waste sources. Federal subsidization of treatment facilities will also be increased.

APPENDIX: Water Law

In Chapters 4 and 5, we emphasized the relationship between property rights and the existence of externalities. Property rights themselves are established by law and its interpretation over time. Accordingly, the legal foundations of environmental property rights are an important consideration for the study of externalities. The purpose of this appendix is to extend our general treatment of property rights to a specific example of the economic implications of water law and water property rights.[1]

The commerce clause of the Constitution has been interpreted to provide the federal government with jurisdiction over all navigable waters in the United States. This has resulted in extensive federal activity in hydropower, irrigation, flood control, and other far-ranging water projects. In addition, the proprietary power of the Constitution has allowed federal control of waters on public lands.

Our present concern, however, is not centered on the role of the federal government in water resource development. Of immediate relevance is the patchwork of state water law that forms the economic basis for the use, purchase, and transfer of water rights. These laws are supposedly designed to complement federal water powers, although problems of jurisdiction have arisen. As might be expected, the sovereignty of each state has created a complicated maze of water law. Nevertheless, we can isolate several general characteristics from this body of law and provide an evaluation of their economic implications.

State water law separates roughly into two categories that approximate the east-west geographic division of the country. The development of this differential water law parallels the division between the relatively water abundant eastern states and the water shortage areas of the West. The doctrine of *riparian* water law is primarily associated with the eastern states and provides the owner of the land adjoining a water body the right to withdraw *reasonable* amounts of water from the water source. A central aspect of riparian water law is that the property right to the water is inherent in the property right to

---

[1] This appendix draws heavily on the excellent treatment of water law by J. Hirschleifer, F. DeHaven and J. Milliman, *Water Supply, Economics, Technology and Policy.* Chicago: University of Chicago Press, 1972.

the adjoining land.[2] Moreover, in general, the two rights are not separable, thus preventing the possibilities of a transfer (sale) of the riparian right by the land owner to other parties. This restriction on the transfer of the riparian right without including the land hinders the economic efficiency of water resource allocation.

Beyond this problem is the obvious issue as to what constitutes a *reasonable* amount of water withdrawal. Riparian rights are not specifically stated in quantity or quality terms, and it is left to the courts to determine the particular dimensions of *reasonable* in individual situations. In addition, riparian law treats all owners identically in the sense that no seniority of ownership exists. Accordingly, present riparian owners may be required to adjust water withdrawals for any new owners, upstream or down, if the new owners meet the *reasonable* requirement of the law. For example, suppose your land holding adjoins a stream and currently you do not exercise the riparian rights, although other land owners along this stream do. You then proceed to sell the land to a new owner who automatically obtains the riparian rights. This new owner, however, desires to utilize the stream water. The other riparian owners may, therefore, be forced to adjust their water withdrawals if the water use of the new owner is deemed legally *reasonable.*

From this brief outline, it should be obvious that riparian water law is a poor device to facilitate the efficient allocation of water resources. Explicitly defined property rights are essential for the success of market transactions. The *reasonable* basis of riparian law leaves the quantity of water inherent in riparian ownership to the discretion of the courts. Riparian rights are uncertain in terms of the precise extent of the property to which the owner is entitled. Any established water quantity can be altered over time as court definitions of *reasonable use* change and new land owners exercise previously idle riparian rights. In terms of the environmental aspects of riparian rights, the qualitative dimensions of water use also are not explicit but are determined via legal procedures within the framework of the *reasonable* criterion and by federal and state regulation.

Appropriative water rights, existing in some western states, represent a contrasting form of water law. Unlike the riparian doctrine, appropriative rights are specifically defined in terms of the allowable quantity of water. Frequently, they also specify the timing of the withdrawal and even the method of diversion. The rights are granted by the state for specific purposes according to established priorities of use. Once granted, the eldest right acquires seniority over subsequent ones. In the event of drought conditions, the senior rights have withdrawal precedence over all junior rights. The specific nature of appropriative rights would seem to encourage efficient market allocations. Senior rights command higher prices than junior rights and the specified quantities and timing of the rights also help determine the value of the right. In times of water shortage, the priority of use is well established and legally binding. In addition, the rights are not linked necessarily to ownership of the adjoining land.

However, important restrictions have been imposed on appropriative rights to control their transfer via any market mechanism. Some states, for example, actually prohibit the transfer of appropriative rights from the use for which they were originally granted. In the absence of prohibition, most

---

[2] Riparian rights also apply to ground water supplies, and, to some extent, to percolating water.

states exercise some controls, usually through state water commissions, over the transfer of appropriative rights. Furthermore, appropriative rights can be lost through nonuse. Thus, unlike more conventional forms of property, unused appropriative water rights can revert to the state because of the failure of individual owners to protect the right by use.

Our short review of the two basic forms of law is now complete. The riparian doctrine relies on judicial processes to determine both equity and efficiency issues in water use. As several authorities have noted, the courts are likely to be a competent vehicle for equity judgments but are not well suited to make efficient allocation decisions.[3] The uncertainty inherent in riparian rights, in both quantitative and qualitative dimensions, makes them ill-suited as instruments for efficient allocation of water resources. In contrast, carefully spelled out appropriative rights have desirable features that could facilitate market transactions. However, this is counteracted by institutional rigidities. In fact, the trend of water law, under both riparian and appropriative doctrines, is in the general direction of more control and further regulation rather than toward changes in water laws designed to encourage private market transactions. This trend is not based on any convincing evidence of the economic efficiency of the decisions forthcoming from the courts and the various state water commissions.

An alternative means of water allocation would be to alter the structure of property rights. This might involve a movement away from riparian law toward even clearer definitions of appropriative rights. At the same time, qualitative dimensions could be built into appropriative water rights to reflect the existence of externalities in water use. Elimination of both the restrictions on transfers and the forfeiture by nonuse provisions of appropriative water law would be necessary. Such developments and the ensuing allocative effects of a market in water rights are likely to be superior to the allocation results stemming from the regulatory process. The avenue of developing a market allocative mechanism for water use is largely unexplored and is likely to remain so. Nonetheless, the important point is that the property rights governing water use are not immutable but represent policy instruments that can be altered and restructured to improve the economic efficiency of water allocation.

QUESTIONS FOR DISCUSSION

1. Refer to Question 1 at the end of Chapter 1. Do you have a different (better) answer to it now?

2. "Water pollution can be solved very simply. Just put an effluent charge on the emission of water pollutants." Comment critically.

3. Suppose that a given body of water can be used for two purposes only: (a) as a cooling agent for industrial firms or (b) as a fishing resource. Fishing does not affect the use of water by industry. Unfortunately, industrial use of the water destroys all the fish. Do these

---

[3] Hirschleifer, DeHaven, Milliman, *Water Supply.*

assumptions imply anything about the most efficient allocation of the water resource? Explain.

4. "The use of water by industry is vital to the economic health of the country. Recreational uses of water are just luxuries. Therefore, when industrial and recreational uses of a given water resource conflict, government should generally give preference to industry." Evaluate this statement critically.

5. Current water quality policy relies on specific water quality standards for a variety of pollutants. What are the economic issues involved in determining the levels of these standards?

SELECTED REFERENCES

DAVIS, R. K., *The Range of Choice in Water Management: A Study of Dissolved Oxygen in the Potomac Estuary.* Baltimore: Johns Hopkins Press, 1968. A sophisticated synthesis of economics and engineering in a case study of the Potomac.

ECKSTEIN, O., *Water Resource Development.* Cambridge: Harvard University Press, 1958. A discussion of benefit-cost analysis as applied to water investments.

Federal Water Pollution Control Administration, *Delaware Estuary Comprehensive Study.* Washington, D.C., 1966. An example of computer simulation techniques of stream flow, waste loads, and water quality.

HIRSCHLEIFER, J., F. DeHAVEN, AND J. MILLIMAN, *Water Supply, Economics, Technology and Policy.* Chicago: University of Chicago Press, 1972. A detailed treatment of the economic considerations in water supply. Provides a useful overview of both the technical and economic problems of water use. The basis of the discussion in Section B.

KNEESE, A. V., AND B. T. BOWER, *Managing Water Quality: Economics, Technology, and Institutions.* Baltimore: Johns Hopkins Press, 1968. A most comprehensive study of the economics of water. Emphasis is given to the evaluation of policy alternatives. The study also provides extensive references to applied water studies.

Water Resources Council, *The Nation's Water Resources*, Washington, D.C., 1968. A useful presentation of the current status of the supply, quality, and uses of water in the United States.

Water Resources Scientific Information Center, *Selected Water Resources Abstracts*, Office of Water Resources Research, National Technical Information Service, Dept. of Commerce, Washington, D.C. The vast water literature from many disciplines is summarized in this semimonthly publication of abstracts of relevant water articles. The abstracts are classified by several categories: nature of water, water cycle, water supply augmentation and conservation, water quantity management and control, water quality management and protection, water resources planning, and others. A ready and valuable source for pursuing detailed investigations into specific areas of water research.

Chapter 7

The Problem of Air Quality

The atmosphere is the life blanket of the earth, the essential ingredient for all living things. Air covers every part of the 200 million square miles of the earth's surface. In the course of a day, a single person breathes between thirty and thirty-five pounds of air in a constant automatic response to extract life-giving oxygen. The atmosphere extends upward from the earth's surface for hundreds of miles although it thins rapidly and man can breathe with ease only within the first ten thousand feet. The air is composed of nitrogen (78 percent), oxygen (21 percent), and various other gases: argon, carbon dioxide, helium, hydrogen, krypton, neon, and xenon. The supply of air in the atmosphere is estimated to be six quadrillion tons and is constantly in movement about the earth's surface in both horizontal and vertical directions.

These facts suggest that the atmosphere is, truly, the closest man can come to possession of an effectively infinite and free resource. Over long periods of time, the atmosphere was, in fact, a free good, and human and economic activities proceeded essentially unconstrained by air quality considerations. It is true there were, even before modern times, references to the poor air conditions over such places as London in the fifteenth century due to the emissions of thousands of home and trade fires burning at once. Also, instances of natural air pollution from volcanic action, thermal inversions, dust storms, and other natural phenomena did (and still do) occur and, at times disrupted economic activity. In fact, long before the advent of industrialized society, the automobile, and mass electric power generation, thermal inversions and natural pollutants created the Indian summer conditions well known in certain sections of this country. The haze of Indian summer weather is the result of a cold, stagnant, high-pressure air mass lying beneath warm air. This condition is an inversion of the normal weather patterns and results in the trapping of particulate matter, dust, and smoke from combustion processes in the area. This natural atmospheric event, by itself, does not cause air quality deterioration. However, when combined with heavy industrial and domestic discharges, thermal inversions have led to human fatalities and widespread illness in several air pollution catastrophies. In less severe forms, eye-stinging and lung-irritating conditions accompany thermal inversions in urban areas as man's activities greatly aggravate a situation of natural air pollution potential.

Increasing industrialization and urbanization have created growing demands to use the atmosphere, whether consciously or not, as a waste disposal medium. Thus, in certain areas at certain times, the accumulation of waste gases and particles from combustion, production, and other economic activities exceeds the natural dispersion capacity of the atmosphere. When air movements are unable to disperse wastes at a rate equal to or exceeding the rate they enter the atmosphere, air quality begins to deteriorate. At such times, the seemingly infinite supply of air becomes used up by man over broad areas.

Conditions of deteriorating air quality have grown more severe as urbanization and mass consumption become standard ways of life throughout large parts of the world. Economic growth—generating more products, greater demands for power to run the economy, and, ultimately, more wastes—is the underlying factor behind the emergence of serious air pollution problems. The decline in air quality in megalopolis areas throughout the world signals the end of free air resources. Although use of the air largely remains free to each individual disposing wastes into the atmosphere, the social costs of poor air quality in the form of dangers to human health, agricultural damages, property destruction, and many other (including presently unknown) effects are considerable for society as a whole.

The purpose of this chapter is to detail the factors responsible for air quality deterioration and to indicate the economic consequences of air pollution. Section A provides a survey of specific air pollutants and estimates the quantitative dimensions of the air pollution problem in the United States. Section B reviews the evidence concerning the effects of air pollutants on human health, agriculture, property, safety, work efficiency, and climate. Emphasis is given to established research findings and, where possible, estimates of the dollar costs of air pollution are provided. Section C briefly outlines current air quality policies in the U.S. Section D summarizes the important points of the chapter.

A. THE NATURE AND SOURCE OF AIR POLLUTANTS

Primary Pollutants

Particulate matter suspended in the air is one of the most noticeable of air pollutants and consists of chemically stable substances such as dust, soot, ash, and smoke. These pollutants are classified as *primary pollutants,* indicating that they do not change form after entering the atmosphere. Primary pollutants are dispersed and diffused by natural air movements but remain structurally unaltered within the air.

At one time, particulate matter was the most common form of air pollution in this country. It remains a large factor in some sections of the United States and in many industrialized areas of Europe. The incomplete combustion of coal is a major source of primary pollutants and home heating by coal, formerly the predominant type of domestic heating in this country, once was the single largest cause of primary pollutants. In addition, extensive industrial use of coal, as in the steel and electrical power industries, presently contributes significant amounts of particulate matter to the atmosphere. Technological changes have introduced liquid and natural gas fuels and, essentially, have replaced coal as the primary home-heating fuel. This substitution has contributed to a decrease in the amount of particulate pollutants and the United States, as a whole, has experienced a decline in the tonnage of particulate matter in the atmosphere. Part of this decline can also be attributed to the use of particulate pollution abatement devices in heavy metal industries and power plants that continue to consume large, and growing, quantities of coal.

Secondary Pollutants

Although the general decline in the level of primary pollutants is an encouraging development in itself, the switch to liquid and gas fuels has not led to an overall decline in the level of air pollution. Instead, new gaseous pollutants, of a more complex nature in terms of their structure, stability, identifiability, and effects have emerged with the basic changes in both fuel and transportation technologies. The new pollutants, called *secondary pollutants,* cause considerably more difficult control problems and pose perhaps even greater health and economic dangers than primary pollutants.

The emission of an array of gases from a large number of sources is the main basis of the air quality problem in the United States. As in the case of water pollutants, almost all air pollutant emissions are directly related to economic activity and the high mass consumption standards of the economy. In particular, millions of motor vehicles, industrial production, and electric power generation are the major sources of gaseous pollutants. Later in this chapter, we shall examine the relative quantitative contributions of these sources to the air quality problem. First, however, it is useful to describe, briefly, the general nature of these secondary pollutants.

Hydrocarbons are organic gases composed of carbon and hydrogen. Inefficient combustion in motor vehicles is the major source of hydrocarbon emissions. Hydrocarbons, by themselves, are nontoxic gases and do not pose immediate health hazards unless absorbed in extreme concentrations. The major problem with hydrocarbons is their ability to unite with nitrogen oxide via a photochemical reaction in sunlight to produce that well-known phenomenon *smog.* Visibility problems and breathing difficulties are the two major results of smog. In combination with carbon monoxide emissions—again, primarily from motor vehicles—trapped particulate matter, and other gases, smog poses serious health hazards.

Discharges of nitrogen combine with oxygen in the atmosphere to create *nitrogen oxides.* As in the case of hydrocarbons, nitrogen oxide is primarily the result of the incomplete burning of gas and oil fuels and, once again, the motor vehicle is the major source. These oxides of nitrogen make up the other gaseous component that contributes to smog formation. In addition, organic substances in the atmosphere combine photochemically with nitrogen oxides to create *ozone,* a bluish gas that has devastating effects on vegetation, causes rubber to deteriorate, and is responsible for significant amounts of other property damage.

Sulfur oxides form another major pollutant. To various degrees, fossil fuels all contain sulfur. When these fuels are burned, the sulfur produces sulfur dioxide and sulfur trioxide. Both of these gases have serious health effects. In addition, sulfur trioxide combines with water in the atmosphere to create sulfuric acid. At times, in certain areas, it has literally rained sulfuric acid, which corrodes, deteriorates and weakens structures, and results in considerable property damage. The major source of sulfur oxide emissions is electrical power generation dependent on the combustion of large quantities of coal.

Finally, *carbon monoxide,* a colorless and odorless gas produced by the inefficient combustion of carbon fuels, is a serious health problem. It is highly toxic at significant levels of concentration and can cause decreased human efficiency in low but chronic doses. Although motor vehicles are the major source of carbon monoxide emissions, other economic activities are also responsible for significant contributions of this pollutant.

Quantitative measures of the extent of air pollution in the United States are perversely impressive. Table 7–1 provides an estimate of the

TABLE 7–1   TOTAL AIR POLLUTANT EMISSIONS BY TYPE (1970)

Type	In Millions of Tons	Percent
Carbon monoxide	147.2	55.77
Sulfur oxides	33.9	12.85
Hydrocarbons	34.7	13.15
Particulates	25.4	9.62
Nitrogen oxides	22.7	8.60
Total	263.9	100.00

Source: Environmental Protection Agency.

total tonnage of various pollutants entering the atmosphere in 1970. An estimated 263.9 million tons is the sum of the discharges of millions of motor vehicles, hundreds of thousands of industrial plants, thousands of large and small power generating plants, and numerous refuse disposals, individual heating systems, and a miscellaneous collection of combustion and production activities. The data indicate that carbon monoxide represents approximately 56 percent of the total pollutant emissions, and sulfur oxides and hydrocarbons together contribute approximately 26 percent more. These three gases, therefore, compose over 80 percent of the total emissions of major air pollutants.

The relative contribution of pollutants by source is indicated in Table 7–2. Corresponding to the large share of carbon monoxide in total emissions it follows that transportation, and, in particular, the automobile, is the single largest source (54.5 percent) of air pollutants. Stationary fuel combustion is responsible for an additional 16.9 percent of total emissions. This reflects electric power operations using coal as the basic power-generating fuel. Industrial processes and refuse disposal combine for approximately 18 percent, and miscellaneous activities (primarily residential heating) are the source of 10.6 percent of total emissions.

TABLE 7–2   AIR POLLUTANT EMISSIONS BY SOURCE (1970)
(in millions of tons per year)

	Quantity	Percent
Transportation	143.9	54.53
Stationary fuel combustion	44.7	16.94
Industrial processes	36.2	13.72
Refuse disposal	11.1	4.21
Miscellaneous	28.0	10.61
Total	263.9	100.00

Source: Environmental Protection Agency.

The relative contributions of air pollution sources by type of pollutant appear in Table 7–3. Transportation is the source of 75.4 percent

TABLE 7–3   AIR POLLUTANT EMISSIONS BY TYPE AND
SOURCE (1970)
(in millions of tons per year)

Type	Carbon Monoxide	Sulfur Oxides	Hydro-carbons	Partic-ulates	Nitrogen Oxides
Source					
Transportation	111.0	1.0	19.5	0.7	11.7
Stationary fuel	.8	26.5	.6	6.8	10.0
Industrial processes	11.4	6.0	5.5	13.1	.2
Refuse disposal	7.2	.1	2.0	1.4	.4
Miscellaneous	16.8	.3	7.1	3.4	.4
Total	147.2	33.9	34.7	25.4	22.7
Percent					
Transportation	75.41	2.95	56.20	2.76	51.54
Stationary fuel	.06	78.17	1.73	26.77	44.05
Industrial processes	7.74	17.70	15.85	51.57	.09
Refuse disposal	4.89	.30	5.76	5.51	1.80
Miscellaneous	11.41	.88	20.46	13.39	1.80
Total	100.00	100.00	100.00	100.00	100.00

Source: Environmental Protection Agency.

of total carbon monoxide emissions, 56.2 percent of hydrocarbons and 51.5 percent of nitrogen oxides, and makes only minor contributions to sulfur oxides and particulates. In contrast, power generation (stationary fuel combustion) is a major factor in both of these latter categories (responsible for 78.2 percent of sulfur oxides, and 26.8 percent of the particulate emissions). Power generation is also a large source of nitrogen oxides (44 percent), and, together with transportation, is responsible for over 95 percent of this pollutant. Industrial processes are a significant source of sulfur oxide and particulate emissions (17.7 and 51.6 percent), reflecting self-supplied industrial power generation capabilities in addition to the discharges associated with regular production activities.

This brief summary of pollutant sources and types suggests the diversity of air quality problems. Some cities, relying on motor vehicles for the bulk of daily commuting transportation and offering few public mass transportation facilities (for example, Los Angeles) suffer from extreme carbon monoxide and other transportation related emissions. This major air quality problem arises despite stringent controls on particulate matter emissions and stationary combustion processes. In contrast, a city such as New York is more troubled by sulfur dioxide problems from electrical power and heating activities than from carbon monoxide and auto related pollutants. This diversity of pollutants and their sources suggests that a uniform national air quality policy may be exceedingly difficult to formulate and enforce.

Widespread private ownership of motor vehicles has traditionally been the symbol of American affluence and today almost 80 percent of all U.S. households own at least one car. Mass ownership of the auto, combined with an extensive public highway system, makes the American public the most mobile in the world. However, the dominance of the auto in the United States has not been an unmixed benefit to the society. As we have seen, transportation sources are responsible for the creation of significant amounts of pollutants from the incomplete combustion of motor vehicle fuel. Ideally, a perfectly operating engine would create only water and carbon dioxide discharges. However, real world conditions of imperfect engines, improper fuel grades, lack of regular maintenance, and the physical aging of machinery insure that motor vehicle combustion is far from ideal. The result is carbon monoxide, hydrocarbons, and nitrogen oxide emissions escaping from the exhaust system and engine parts of the vehicle. Incomplete fuel combustion combined with the vast number of motor vehicles of all ages, types, and conditions being operated in the United States is responsible for a major share of the air pollutant data in Tables 7–1 through 7–3 and for the atmospheric conditions we observe in everyday life in our auto-dominated urban environments.

Registrations of motor vehicles have increased from 49 million in 1950 to 112 million in 1971 for a 3.5 percent compound average annual growth rate. The time may not be too distant when motor vehicle registrations equal the population of the United States. Along with the increase in the number of vehicles, estimates indicate that motor vehicles are being used more extensively and operated somewhat less efficiently. Data indicate the average miles per vehicle and average gallons of fuel consumed per vehicle have increased in the last three decades. However, the average mileage per gallon of fuel consumed has declined.

The magnitude of the increase in the level of fuel consumption and total number of motor vehicles obviously results in increases in auto pollutant emissions. The decrease in the efficiency of fuel combustion and the rise in miles travelled per vehicle further compound the problem.

Recent concern about motor vehicle air pollution has resulted in the imposition of stringent federal emission controls on auto manufacturers. This legislation and the movement to less-polluting motor fuels is likely to help the air pollution problem. We shall discuss the particulars of auto emission standards and some general air quality policies in Section C of this chapter. However, at present, we can note a number of factors that may counteract improvements resulting from auto emission standards and the increasing use of nonpollutant motor fuels. First, and most obvious, is the steady growth in the number of motor vehicles being operated in the United States. If each vehicle contributes less pollutants but there are more vehicles each year, it is clearly possible to have deteriorating air quality levels. Thus, some of the reduction in motor vehicle related air pollutants due to the federal emission standards may be offset by continued growth in the number of vehicles and the increase in travel miles and fuel consumption.

In addition, the age structure of vehicles means that many vehicles in the 1970s will be operating altogether without emission controls. For example, in 1969, an estimated 38 percent of operating autos and almost 50 percent of trucks were over five years old. Moreover, the fact that new vehicles must meet the federal standards in 1976 does not insure that these same vehicles will comply with the standards five years, or three years, or even one year later. Proper and regular maintenance stimulated by periodic local enforcement must accompany these broad-based federal standards. The installation of antipollution devices cannot be a once-and-for-all policy. As vehicles age, the engines, the exhaust system, and the emission control equipment of the vehicle must be serviced regularly to preserve the effectiveness of the emission controls. Unless incentives exist to promote regular servicing of antipollutant equipment, the federal controls are not likely to be as effective in the long run as intended.

Finally, there has been considerable government and private research aimed at the development of alternative engines that are relatively pollutant-free. This research promises potential major changes in motor vehicle manufacturing and a vast reduction in motor vehicle emissions. The obvious question is the relative costs of new engine designs compared to the costs of the conventional vehicle engines. However, this benefit-cost comparison should reflect not only the relative production costs of new and standard engines but should also include the net environmental costs caused by conventional engines.

Another major source of air pollution stems from stationary fuel combustion in the generation of electrical power. Like the auto, electrical power is a basic ingredient in the mass consumption standard of living U.S. economy. Table 7–4 presents energy use data for the recent past

TABLE 7–4   UTILITY ELECTRIC ENERGY USE, 1960
TO 1968 AND PROJECTED REQUIREMENTS,
1970 TO 1990

Year	Energy Use (billions of kilowatt hours)
1960	764
1965	1,060
1966	1,150
1967	1,220
1968	1,334
1970	1,527
1975	2,194
1980	3,086
1985	4,263
1990	5,852

Source: Federal Power Commission; news release No. 16323.

and projections to 1990 of what the Federal Power Commission (FPC) calls *energy requirements*. The 100 percent increase in electrical energy use from 1960 to 1970 is impressive but is dwarfed by the projected electrical use in 1990, when almost 6000 billion kilowatt hours will be consumed (compared to the 764 billion used in 1960). Furthermore, Table 7–5 indicates that most of the electrical energy produced in this country

TABLE 7–5   ELECTRICAL ENERGY PRODUCTION
BY FUEL BASE (1969)

Source of Energy	Percent
Coal	50.0
Oil	9.5
Gas	23.1
Hydro	17.3
Total production 1,552 (billion of kilowatt hours)	

Source: Federal Power Commission; press release No. 16634.

results from the combustion of fuel (82.6 percent) rather than from hydropower sources. Thus, most of the electrical energy generated by utilities is accomplished by the burning of fossil fuels and the largest fuel source is coal (50 percent of the total). The growth in total coal consumption for electric generation from 51 thousand short tons in 1940 to 310 thousand short tons in 1969 represents a 14.7 percent average annual increase. Although the percentage of coal used of total coal equivalents has decreased (as oil, gas, and hydropower have increased their relative fuel shares), the magnitude of the absolute increase in coal consumption has significant implications for air quality. As we observed in Table 7–3, the combustion of coal in electric generation and industrial processes results in considerable sulfur oxide, nitrogen oxide, and particulate matter emissions. The projected growth in electrical energy use and the predominant use of coal as the fuel for power generation makes this area another prime concern for public policy.

The enormous projections of energy consumption, shown in Table 7–4, imply corresponding increases in the capacity and number of power generating plants. Recently, the location of new power plants has become a major environmental issue. Typically, new plants are built on rural sites although the generated power is transmitted hundreds of miles away for use in urban-suburban regions. The result is air quality deterioration in relatively unspoiled natural areas with damaging esthetic and ecological effects. This pattern is justified on the basis that the pollution damages would be much higher if the plants were located near, or actually in, the more populous using areas.

Some environmentalists and economists have argued that the FPC and similar projections of energy requirements and the need for ever more power plants are grossly overstated. Energy consumption levels are not fixed absolutes but are dependent on economic incentives. Because the price of electricity does not reflect the true social costs of energy generation due to the existence of external costs caused by air quality deteriorioration, the quantity of energy demanded exceeds the efficient level of energy production for the society. Further, not only is the price of energy below its social costs, but the conventional practice of utilities offering *lower* rates to large industrial and commercial users encourages the use of electricity far beyond the efficient level. These discounts to large users should be eliminated on economic efficiency grounds. Ending these discounts would create direct incentives to use less electricity. The results would be a substantial decline in the *energy requirements* of Table 7–4. The overall effect would be improved air quality as the efficient pricing of energy reduces the quantity demanded and results in fewer pollutants discharged into the atmosphere.

This summarizes the main point of the environmentalist's view of the energy problem, although it should be recognized that a final result of implementing such policies would be higher prices and lower production levels for goods requiring significant energy inputs. This result would be consistent, however, with pricing goods at their full social costs of production and represents a direct example of the theory presented in Chapter 3.

Industrial sources represent a considerable component of air pollutants and reflect the discharges of self-supplied electric power generation (97 percent of which was done via fossil fuels in 1968) in addition to the discharges from daily production activities. Once again, this particular component of the air pollution problem is an intrinsic part of economic activity.

Finally, the burning of refuse represents another aspect of air pollution. The increasing production of goods, the relatively low levels of recycling of materials, and the law of the conservation of matter combine to result in increasing amounts of junk and solid wastes. Estimates are that the United States generates over five pounds per day per person of solid wastes. Some of this waste material is disposed of by burning, which contributes to air pollution problems. Refuse, junk, and other solid wastes are obviously not high-grade fuels and, when burned, burn inefficiently. The result is a discharge of a variety of pollutants. Economic growth promises even greater amounts of goods in the future and, if increasing reliance is made on the burning of waste material, then, quite naturally, we can expect a rise in the contribution of refuse disposal to air pollution.[1]

In summary, the obvious lesson from the discussion of the sources of air pollution is that the problem of deteriorating air quality is inherent in economic activity and has a broad base in terms of the direct or indirect contribution of each individual in the society. Driving a car, heating a home, running an air conditioner, and, generally, sharing in the high standard of living in the United States are the basic causes of poor air quality. Next, we turn to the problem of what poor air quality means in terms of damages to human life and economic activity.

B. THE CONSEQUENCES OF DETERIORATING AIR QUALITY

This section presents some of the major identifiable economic effects of poor air quality and singles out the specific air-polluting agents responsible for these effects.

---

[1] We shall discuss the details of the solid waste disposal problem in Chapter 8. It should be noted that technological advances in solid waste combustion techniques promise to reduce the air quality problems associated with refuse disposal.

1. Human Health Effects

Spectacular catastrophes stemming from poor air quality conditions have been infrequent but, unfortunately, real events. Incidents of poor air quality leading directly to human fatalities warn us of the potentially devastating health impact of air quality deterioration. For example, in early December, 1930, a stationary air mass together with dense fog engulfed the Meuse Valley of Belgium. This thermal inversion trapped normally heavy amounts of industrial emissions in the air over the valley and inhibited natural dispersion processes. Industrial discharges of particulate matter and sulfur dioxide in conjunction with the thermal inversion resulted in poisonous air conditions. During the five days of the inversion, sixty-three deaths were directly attributable to the poor air and thousands of other individuals became ill.

Another thermal inversion accompanied by fog trapped the industrial town of Donora, Pennsylvania on the Monongahela River in a killer air mass in October, 1948. Stagnant high pressure, again in combination with substantial particulate and sulfur dioxide industrial discharges, killed twenty people and made nearly six thousand others ill.

London, England has a legendary history of fogs and misty low ceilings. These atmospheric conditions have not always contributed to the colorful history of the city. A thermal inversion in early December, 1952, together with the coal smoke discharges of millions of household furnaces created disastrous air quality conditions. Estimates indicate that the resulting smog caused nearly four thousand deaths above the normal rate for an equivalent winter period and countless other individuals were made ill. Essentially the same ingredients combined again in December, 1962, to kill an estimated three hundred Londoners. Both of these episodes occurred during winter months when widespread home heating with coal resulted in heavy smoke discharges that were then trapped by thermal inversions.

As alarming as these events are, evidence suggests that more widespread, and ultimately more damaging, effects may accompany persistent human exposure to poor air quality over long time periods. The connection between air quality and respiratory diseases has received increasing attention. Although medical evidence has established that a general relation exists between air quality and human health, an important problem is to quantify this relation and to adjust for the multitude of other factors that determine human health. Empirical research efforts have attempted to isolate the relation between air quality and such specific diseases as bronchitis, asthma, lung cancer, and emphysema, in addition to general mortality and morbidity rates. The overall weight of this evidence leaves

little doubt that widespread and adverse human health effects are associated with poor air quality. Rough estimates of the dollar costs of these
health effects are that over $2 billion of savings in health costs would
accompany a 50 percent reduction in air pollution levels in major urban
U.S. areas.

A number of medical studies have investigated the relationship between bronchitis mortality and air quality. The disease of bronchitis
manifests itself in breathing difficulties and increased susceptibility to
infection that may lead to death. Studies done in Great Britain suggest
that a strong association exists between bronchitis mortality and various
air quality indices. A correlation analysis across county boroughs in
England and Wales indicates a statistically significant and direct relation between bronchitis deaths (for male and female subgroups) and
air pollution and smoke indices. The effect of air quality on the incidence
of bronchitis seemed to be independent of the sex of the subgroups. A
similar type of study of geographic areas in the Buffalo, New York,
region indicated that for white males between fifty and sixty-nine years
of age, the mortality rates from asthma, bronchitis, and emphysema increase by 100 percent with significant increases in an associated air
quality index. Alternatively, estimates from these studies indicate that
decreases of 25 to 50 percent in bronchitis mortality rates can be realized
if air quality is improved to levels reflected by the conditions in the
highest air quality areas included in the samples.

Lung cancer in this country is annually responsible for over fifty
thousand deaths. Recent intensive investigations have demonstrated the
association between lung cancer incidence and smoking habits. However,
a number of further studies, controlling for the personal smoking factor,
indicate, in addition, that a significant difference exists for lung cancer
death rates between individuals living in urban versus rural areas. The
weight of this evidence is considerable and suggests the association of
poor air quality conditions in urban areas with increases in deaths attributable to lung cancer (even after adjusting for smoking habits).

Other studies have pointed to an association of nonrespiratory can-
cers with air quality indices and/or urban versus rural residency.[2] There
is further, but less extensive, evidence relating cardiovascular diseases to
air pollution. Various infant mortality rates, total mortality rates, emphysema, pneumonia, and pulmonary tuberculosis diseases also show increases with higher levels of air pollution and/or urban residence. Fi-

---

[2] Urban residence is taken as a proxy for poor air quality because, in fact, urban areas
do have lower air quality conditions than rural areas. However, a problem of interpretation in
this kind of social science research is to separate the effect on health of poor air in urban areas
versus all other urban factors affecting health.

nally, several studies indicate that work absences are significantly higher when atmospheric conditions reflect poor air quality than when the air is relatively clean.

The type of air quality measures used in many of these studies reflect the amount of sulfates, particulate matter, carbon monoxide, and hydrocarbons in the air. Combining the various air quality measures into an index number poses complex technical problems but the evidence is enough to suggest that, even for several definitions of air quality, the incidence of a variety of serious diseases increases markedly as the indices reflect progressively deteriorating air conditions.

Further qualifications to these studies would cite the possible need to control for a variety of other circumstances in addition to age and smoking habits before attempting to isolate air quality effects on human health. Such factors as the individual's general health condition, exercise habits, diet, or psychological strain also may enter systematically into a statistical association with overall health and disease incidence. Although this is a valid caveat, the results of the entire body of health studies are too one-sided to suggest that only a spurious relation has been uncovered between air quality and disease.

We have indicated that estimates of over $2 billion in health costs could be saved by a 50 percent reduction in the air pollution levels in major U.S. urban areas. As large as is this estimate of the external costs of air pollution, it is certainly a vast underestimate, because it includes only foregone income and direct health treatment costs. Therefore, these figures are just the lower bound of individuals' true willingness to pay to reduce disease incidence and mortality. There is considerable evidence to indicate the presence of a very high willingness to pay (above any foregone income values) to prolong or sustain human life and to minimize pain in the face of debilitating diseases. Furthermore, remember that economists argue that willingness to pay is itself a *lower bound* to the proper measure of the economic value of avoiding an external diseconomy. As suggested in Chapter 5, an *upper bound* would be the amount that individuals would require in payment for giving up their good health; that is, their asking price rather than their bid price. In the case of good health, the asking price of most individuals is likely to be infinite. These considerations suggest that measures centered on foregone income and treatment costs alone are, at best, minimum indications of the external costs associated with poor air quality.

Further health effects of poor air quality elude the $2 billion estimate altogether. Loss of efficiency on the job due to air pollution related health effects is obviously a difficult item to measure, although it is well established, for example, that carbon monoxide reduces response time of the nervous system. Sickness induced by air pollution may not be recognized as responsible for work days lost or above normal absentee-ism. Some on-the-job injuries and industrial accidents also may be attributable to air pollution although they are not recorded as such. In addition, there may be significant human health effects of persistent exposure to what is now believed to be safe levels of air pollutants. Ideally, all of these items should be included in any dollar measure of the costs of air quality deterioration. Therefore, present estimates of these costs, however large they seem, must be accepted as only a rough under-estimate of the true human health costs of air pollution.

2. Agriculture and Air Quality

Agricultural damage to crops and livestock is a second major effect asso-ciated with poor air quality. The total extent of agricultural damage caused by air pollution in this country is unknown but already there is considerable evidence to suggest that it is extensive. Biological studies have isolated the effects on vegetation of a variety of pollutants such as ozone, sulfur dioxide, and fluorides.

Ozone, for example, affects plant cells beneath the surface of the leaf and ultimately damages or destroys the plant. Studies have demon-strated that extensive ozone damage to agricultural crops exists in several industrialized states. *Sulfur dioxide* in the atmosphere is taken into plants through the respiratory process and, in combination with water naturally contained within the plant, becomes toxic to plant cells. Basic cereal crops, such as wheat and barley, are severely attacked by sulfur dioxide. Damages from sulfur dioxide can be extensive enough to result in a total destruction of the entire market value of a crop. Sulfur dioxide also adversely affects trees and there have been recent instances of damages to forested areas resulting from power plant discharges of sulfur dioxide.[3]

Fluorides adversely affect the photosynthesis of plants when ab-sorbed through the plant's leaves. For fruit trees, fluoride damage results in losses in the number and in the weight of fruit produced. Fluorides that become stored in forage foods also have devastating effects on live-stock. The consumption of forage containing heavy concentrations of fluorides results in fluorosis, causing deteriorating health, reduction in growth, loss of weight, immobility, and, ultimately, the death of the animal. An extensive case of fluoride damages occurred in Polk County, Florida, in the 1950s and 1960s, when increases in phosphate fertilizer manufacturing created widespread and, at times, devastating damage to citrus and beef cattle activities in the area.

---

[3] For example, the Virginia Electric and Power Company generating plant at Mount Storm, West Virginia, has been accused of destroying a nearby thriving Christmas tree industry as a result of sulfur dioxide discharges.

Considerable scientific evidence exists to demonstrate the causal relationship between poor air quality and deteriorating agricultural performance. However, it is not always a simple task to establish this relationship in a legal sense in any given instance of air pollution. Numerous court cases where affected parties have attempted to recover damages have met with frustration. Private companies or utilities responsible for the emission of pollutants and subsequent air quality deterioriation have readily found *expert* witnesses to testify that many factors could have caused the Christmas trees to yellow, the citrus crop to fail, or the cattle to sicken and waste away. The complex and myriad factors determining plant, animal, and, of course, human health make successful legal proceedings for the recovery of air pollutant damages an involved, costly, and often frustrating experience. This difficulty is largely a result of the current structure of property rights and the law rather than a true questioning of the causal relation between a pollutant and, for example, plant damage.

In summary, air pollutants have direct harmful effects on agricultural activities. Their damages probably involve millions of dollars annually for the U.S. economy. Available studies indicate an estimated $18 million annual air pollutant loss in field and vegetable crops on the eastern seaboard. Another study estimates a 50 percent loss in citrus fruits in California in addition to substantial losses in other crops totalling $132 million. Although no systematic estimate of the aggregate national effects of agricultural damage has yet been attempted, one advantage in this area is that market prices of agricultural products provide an indication of the agricultural costs of air quality effects.[4]

3. Property Damages

Air pollutants are also responsible for extensive damages to property. Ready examples of this type of damage would be the emission of particulate matter that soils clothes, autos, homes, and buildings. The blackened facades of buildings in urban centers are obvious testimony to particulate, hydrocarbon, and sulfur pollutants. This soiling causes cleaning expenditures considerably in excess of those that normally would be undertaken. Beyond this apparent soiling effect, air pollutants corrode, crack, and weaken materials. Ozone, for example, in addition to its damaging agricultural effects, cracks and breaks rubber. In urban areas, there is extensive ozone damage to auto tires and telephone and electrical wires. Sulfur dioxide emissions also result in substantial property damages, ad-

---

[4] Some adjustment of actual agricultural prices may be required to account for government support programs and other market imperfections in order to arrive at the true social value of lost production.

versely affecting a wide variety of property from the hardest of materials (iron and steel) to domestic furniture, synthetic fabrics, and clothing. Sulfuric acids, formed from a combination of emissions of sulfur oxides and water, weaken and wear building surfaces.

Statistical studies also indicate that air pollutants have a systematic and negative impact on residential property values. Studies have related the sale or rental prices of residences to variables such as family income, number of rooms, age and condition of the property, distance from center city, and other socioeconomic variables. Even after including these variables, statistically significant and negative correlations were found between sales or rental prices and two indices of air pollution. In part, the observed reduction in property values may represent market reaction to the adverse health and general amenity effects of air pollutants rather than actual physical property damages. It also may reflect general market responses to a mix of unmeasured urban ills. Whatever the reason, the loss in residential property value that can be attributable directly to air pollutants is a real economic cost to the owners of homes and buildings and properly should be included as part of total air pollution damage. Dollar estimates of residential property losses for eighty-five U.S. cities due to sulfur oxide and particulate matter damages total over $600 million. As in the case of agriculture, the actual market prices of residential houses and property provide reasonable indicators for the costs of air pollution damages. Once again, the main research problem in this area is to identify and quantify the actual extent of air pollution property damages. Crude estimates put the total annual costs of air pollutants to all types of property in the United States at a figure of $13 billion.

4. Safety and Amenity Effects of Air Pollution

Air pollutants may be responsible for a number of auto, air, and industrial accidents. Decreased visibility due to smog and smoke conditions contributes to the frequency of highway accidents. Smog-related poor visibility is a common condition in urban freeway driving. There have been a number of smog-induced chain car highway accidents on high speed turnpikes in recent years. The costs of these auto accidents in terms of lives, injuries, and property should be included as an additional cost of air pollution. In addition to auto accidents, Civil Aeronautic Board studies indicate that a sizeable number of air accidents are caused by situations involving adverse weather conditions. Although the extent of the responsibility of air pollution in air accidents is unknown, some of these weather-related accidents may be the result of pollutant-induced smog or haze that further complicates air navigation in existing natural weather difficulties.

Finally, we have already indicated that some on-the-job industrial accidents may be the result of poor air quality conditions. High levels of carbon monoxide, for example, inhibit the response time of the nervous system, reduce coordination ability and alertness, and, accordingly, may contribute to increasing the incidence of on-the-job industrial accidents. These same factors may result in the loss of efficiency in urban office workers. At the present time, measurement of the total costs of air pollutant-induced accidents and dollar losses in terms of worker efficiency is only a speculative exercise. However, these costs, whatever the magnitude, are a real component of the costs of air pollutants and there is a considerable need for research efforts to identify the exact role of air pollutants in the areas of travel, safety, and work efficiency.

Above and beyond the health, agricultural, property, and safety effects, further damages of air pollutants exist in the form of general amenity costs. The unpleasantness of foul odors, the dreariness of daily views of soot-dirtied buildings, and the overall disagreeability of poor air quality, as perceived by individuals, are all added costs of air pollution. Although accurate measurement of these costs are probably the most difficult of all, the willingness of individuals to pay for the avoidance of the general disamenities of air pollutants should properly be included as another cost.

5. Long Run Consequences of Changes in Air Quality

Finally, a long-run problem of air quality involves the effect of potential changes in the overall composition of the atmosphere on climate and weather. Evidence indicates that there has been an increase in carbon dioxide (CO_2) levels in the atmosphere. This rise in CO_2 is due to the growing combustion of fossil fuels necessary to meet spectacularly rising world demands for power, heating, and production. Estimates indicate that if fossil fuel consumption continues to increase with economic growth, then the CO_2 level in the atmosphere will increase 50 percent by the year 2000. The effects of this increase are unknown but potentially enormous in their implications for human existence and the environment. Small but consistent temperature changes that may result from CO_2 accumulation will affect climate, agricultural activities, ocean levels, and, essentially, all aspects of the human environment. The unknown climatic effects of increases in atmospheric CO_2 levels pose an obvious and crucial research need in this area. The result of such studies may, for example, indicate that it is necessary to change basic modes of energy generation. Worldwide coordination and enforcement of such a change is likely to prove difficult, but the alternative of drastic climatic upheavals may leave man with little choice.

The above discussion illustrates the potential danger to mankind of supposedly safe environmental quality changes—CO_2 itself is a harmless gas. Unfortunately, scientists can do little but speculate about these dangers as of this date. This situation is similar to the long-run human health problems associated with chronic exposure to low levels of known air and water pollutants. That is, we suspect the costs to be of enormous magnitude but we cannot confirm this suspicion without a great deal more scientific investigation.

C. CURRENT AIR QUALITY POLICY IN THE UNITED STATES

The Clean Air Act of 1970 as amended is the central legislation underlying federal efforts to improve air quality. It relies entirely on regulation to control air pollution and is directed at both mobile and stationary sources of air pollutants.

A major provision of the legislation requires motor vehicle manufacturers to meet emission standards for hydrocarbons, carbon monoxide, nitrogen oxides, and particulate discharges by the 1976 model year.[5] Moreover, these standards must be met on a continuous basis for five years or 50,000 miles, and this is to be stipulated in the vehicle's warranty. A considerable discussion has ensued between the federal government and the manufacturers over the technical feasibility, the timing, and the testing of the auto emission controls. Nevertheless, certain general results of the emission standards are obvious. First, the costs of new vehicles will increase—by an estimated $300 per vehicle at the proposed standards. Second, if the standards are met, significant reductions in motor vehicle emissions will be achieved in time as vehicles with emission control technology compose larger and larger portions of the total stock of operating vehicles. Finally, as we have indicated earlier, despite the reading of any warranty, there is a clear need for continued enforcement to insure the ongoing effectiveness of the emission control equipment.[6] Including an emissions test in the commonly used state vehicle

---

[5] For automobiles, the standards for hydrocarbons are set at .5 grams per milliliter (gm/mi) by 1975—down from 4.6 gm/mi in 1970; for hydrocarbons 11 gm/mi by 1975—down from 47 gm/mi in 1970, and .9 gm/mi for nitrogen oxides and .1 gm/mi for particulate matter—both of the latter two categories having no standard in 1970. Thus, the emission limits for hydrocarbons and carbon monoxide are reduced by approximately 90 percent and 80 percent, respectively. As this book goes to press, Congress is considering changing some of these standards.

[6] In part, this need is simply due to the aging of machinery and the resulting maintenance requirements. It also will help to keep the substantial number of autos without emission control devices in good operating condition by at least requiring regular engine tuneups. In addition, it will deter individuals from tampering with the emission control equipment in hopes of lowering the costs of vehicle operation.

inspection process would seem an ideal means of doing this. One state, New Jersey, has adopted such a procedure, and several others are considering similar action.

Control of air pollution from stationary sources—power plants, industrial production activities, and others—centers on the adoption and enforcement of air quality standards. These standards, like those of the Water Quality Act, apply to concentrations of the various pollutants existing in the environmental medium—in this case, the atmosphere— and do not establish specific limits for individual waste discharges. National standards have been set for sulfur oxides, hydrocarbons, carbon monoxide, nitrogen oxide, oxidants, and particulate matter. Each standard has two levels. *Primary* standards are to be achieved by 1975 and reflect pollution levels that will result in no detrimental human health effects. More severe *secondary standards* reflect an additional safety margin for preventing damage to vegetation and property. These secondary standards are to be met in a *reasonable* time period after 1975.

The National Air Pollution Control Administration (NAPCA) of the EPA is the principal administering agency. NAPCA has designated 298 air quality control regions covering all major urban areas in the country with populations of 25,000 or more. These regions represent the administrative units of air quality control. Individual states are responsible for formulating and implementing procedures to achieve the primary national air standards by 1975. The procedures are subject to approval by the EPA and involve setting actual limits for pollutants on specific waste-discharging sources. Enforcement of these emission limits is the responsibility of the state, although federal enforcement will occur when states fail to achieve compliance with the national standards.

In summary, the Clean Air Act follows the basic regulatory pattern of federal efforts in the area of water quality. The regulation of motor vehicle manufacturers represents an overt federal involvement with a major and specific source of air pollutants. However, the use of national air quality standards is a much more diffuse approach to air quality control. The diversity of air pollution sources, the administrative complexities of large scale regulation, the difficulty of relating air quality levels to specific pollution sources, and the reliance on state enforcement of the national air standards are all significant obstacles to the success of the Clean Air Act.

D. SUMMARY AND CONCLUSIONS

Unrestricted use of the atmosphere as a disposal medium has made the previously unlimited supply of air a scarce economic resource. This scarcity is manifested in deteriorating air quality conditions in many areas of the United States. Deterioration of air quality is the result of the continual injection into the atmosphere of enormous amounts of particulate matter, sulfur oxides, hydrocarbons, nitrogen oxides, and a myriad of other gases and substances. Unfortunately, these undesired pollutants are the byproducts of a desired high mass consumption standard of living and are traceable to certain broadly based sources such as transportation and power generation.

They have adverse human health effects and have been consistently associated with increases in the incidence of numerous respiratory diseases and the general mortality rate. In addition, considerable agricultural and property damages can be directly attributable to poor air quality conditions. Safety, work efficiency, esthetic reactions, and long-run weather effects are other areas of air pollution concern.

Present federal air quality control policy relies on a regulatory approach embodied in the Clean Air Act. National air quality standards have been established for major air pollutants and the individual states are charged with implementing procedures to comply with the standards. Additional and more direct federal regulation is aimed at motor vehicle pollution by requiring manufacturers to meet minimum emission standards for all new vehicles by the model year 1976.

The large (if imprecisely estimated) magnitude of air pollution damages and the promise of steady growth in air pollutants create an obvious need for air quality control policies. Essentially, the job of public policy is to internalize, to each user, all the social costs of discharging pollutants into the atmosphere. If this task is accomplished, it would represent a marked change from the historically costless and unrestricted use of the atmosphere as a disposal medium.

QUESTIONS FOR DISCUSSION

1. What are the most important differences between air and water resources from the standpoint of the economic problems associated with the quality of each? Which do you judge to be the more difficult problem for society, and why?

2. Many of the air quality problems facing this country today are due to the combustion of gas and oil fuels. Would it help solve the problem of air quality if we switched back to coal or perhaps accelerated the switch to nuclear power as alternative sources of energy?

3. "Most of our air quality problems would vanish if the government would just force the big automobile manufacturers to produce perfectly clean engines immediately." Evaluate this assertion critically.

4. What are the fundamental difficulties involved in estimating the dollar value of the welfare damage costs of air pollution? Can you conceive of ideal experiments that would enable a researcher to resolve these difficulties?

5. "The United States is running out of oil and gas and soon will face an energy crisis." Evaluate this statement critically.

SELECTED REFERENCES

ANDERSON, R. J. AND CROCKER, T. D., "Air Pollution and Residential Property Values," *Urban Studies, No. 8,* (October, 1971). An empirical study of the negative impact of air pollution on property values.

CARR, D. E., *The Breath of Life.* New York: W. W. Norton, 1965. An interestingly written layman's overview of air quality problems.

Environmental Protection Agency, *The Clean Air Act,* 92d Congress, 1st Sess., Document 92-6, Washington, D.C.: Government Printing Office, March, 1971. A detailed economic analysis of the effects of air pollutants and the development of the air quality standards of the Clean Air Act.

LAVE, L. S., "Air Pollution Damage: Some Difficulties in Estimating the Value of Abatement" in *Environmental Quality Analysis,* eds. A. V. Kneese and B. T. Bower. Baltimore: Johns Hopkins Press, 1972. Highlights the thorny problems of benefit measurements of air pollution control.

LAVE, L. AND R. SESKIN, "Air Pollution and Human Health," *Science,* Vol. CLXIV, (August, 1970). A review of research on the association between air pollutants and human health. Contains extensive footnoting of health studies.

RIDKER, R. B., *Economic Costs of Air Pollution.* New York: F. A. Praeger, 1967. An overview of the economic issues of evaluating air quality control.

STERN, A. C. ed., *Air Pollution,* (2nd ed.) New York: Academic Press, 1968. A comprehensive treatment of the technical basis of air quality in three volumes. Provides an excellent bibliography for numerous air quality topics.

Chapter 8

The Quality of Life and Other Environmental Problems

The problems of air and water quality listed in the previous two chapters have attracted considerable public attention and resources. Unfortunately, environmental deterioration is not confined exclusively to situations involving poor air and water quality. The emphasis on pollution of water and air reflects their pervasive presence and the relatively advanced technical knowledge we possess concerning these problems. Other environmental problems may involve social costs of equivalent magnitude. Thus far, these other problems have received little attention because of their more subtle nature and the paucity of information concerning their long-run environmental effects (for example, pesticides, toxic substances, solid wastes, noise). In addition, environmental concerns extend beyond the effects associated with particular types of effluents. Orderly land use, preservation of unique natural environments, and ample opportunities for outdoor recreation are all important elements involved in maintaining the quality of life.

This chapter provides a brief overview of a variety of these other environmental problems. The problems are diverse and, therefore, difficult to discuss within a common framework. Our objective in the treatment of each is to give the reader a basic understanding of an important aspect of the wide scope of environmental deterioration.

Section A presents the difficult and alarming problems of pesticide use. The end result of a high mass consumption society, solid wastes, are treated as another environmental problem in Section B. Section C discusses the largely unexplored area of noise and its effects. Finally, Section D extends the scope of our analysis to include land use problems, the supply of outdoor recreation opportunities, and the general issue of conservation. Section E is a brief summary of the chapter.

A. PESTICIDES

In the long-run perspective of history, the development and extensive use of effective pesticides have made a major contribution to human welfare. Pesticides are responsible for enormous increases in agricultural yields and for the control of once widespread and debilitating diseases. However, to balance attention given to the benefits of pesticides, recent concern has focused on their adverse effects on other aspects of human health and fish and wildlife populations. Pesticide research findings again reveal the recurring theme of environmental problems—a difficult, benefit-cost type of decision: whether, and to what degree, to continue pesticide use and gain protection of crop yields and lower incidences of some human diseases at the cost of considerable damages to environmental conditions and increased risks to human health.

Pesticide use stems from the natural competition between man and insect. Insect pests destroy crops, transmit disease to humans and animals, and, in general, plague human existence. Man and his technology have fought these pests with increasingly sophisticated devices, moving from the soap, lye, kerosene, nicotine, and arsenic applications of the nineteenth century to the complex chlorinated hydrocarbons and organic phosphate compounds of the present.

Unfortunately, in this war against pests, it is not always easy to isolate and destroy only the problem-causing pest and to contain the effects of this destruction within known and narrow limits. Most insects are not harmful to humans and, in fact, many have beneficial effects. In addition, all insect life is intimately related to a natural ecological equilibrium. Recent research has uncovered exceedingly complex environmental ramifications associated with man's attempts to eradicate or control certain forms of insects. This new knowledge has resulted in a redirection of thinking into what were previously regarded as *safe* pesticides and generated further research to develop alternative forms of pest control.

Meanwhile, as this research goes on, the production and use of pesticides increase in both the United States and the world. For some time, pesticide use was dominated by the chlorinated hydrocarbon pesticides —DDT and related compounds. Recently, however, there has been a decline in the use of chlorinated hydrocarbons and a subsequent increase in the use of organophosphates and other pesticides. We shall discuss both the chlorinated hydrocarbons and organophosphates in greater detail below. Herbicides are compounds used to combat weeds and control undesirable plant growth and are another significant and growing component of pesticide production. Weed control has always been vital for many agricultural crops, but there are additional, growing uses of herbicides associated with maintaining roadways and other public property.[1] Fungicides combat those plants that are parasites or saprophytes on living or dead organic material. Fungi are responsible for damage to wood and structures, and some types of parasitic fungi cause disease in man, animals, and certain plants (cereal crops and fruit being particularly susceptible).

Most careful studies into the question of pesticide use acknowledge the necessity of the agricultural protection afforded by pesticides. Department of Agriculture estimates indicate that a 25 to 30 percent decrease in U.S. crop and livestock yields would follow a ban on the use of all pesticides. The U.N. Food and Agricultural Organization projection of the sources of additional world food supply requirements relies on a 20 to 30 percent contribution to crop yields from controlling pest-related food losses. The implication of this estimate is that without the use of pesticides, starvation would threaten many poor countries.

Today, over 60,000 pesticides are registered for sale in the U.S. One of the most important single groups in this vast number are the chlorinated hydrocarbons (for example, DDT, DDE, TDE, dieldrin, endrin, benzaine, aldrin, chlordone, methohexachloride). This group is the prime example of the pesticide dilemma. The foremost among them, DDT, once was regarded as an ideal pesticide. DDT first was used extensively for insect control during the Second World War although the compound was known as early as 1874. The initial use of DDT was directed at control of typhus, malaria, and other diseases. The use of DDT for these purposes was a great success. Countless lives were saved, the war effort improved, and all without any observable adverse effects. DDT

---

[1] In addition, much of the recent herbicide production increase was due to their use during the Vietnam War.

administered in low concentrations was found to be deadly to insect life and had persistent toxic effects over a considerable time period. The success of DDT in disease control encouraged its use for agricultural purposes and here again it was successful in increasing the yields of many crops. This record, combined with relatively low costs, resulted in the extensive use of DDT and other chlorinated hydrocarbon pesticides. In the 1950s, however, growing evidence of severe environmental effects generated concern over the widespread use of DDT and its former *safe and harmless* reputation came under attack.

Chlorinated hydrocarbon pesticides are persistent compounds that retain their toxicity in soil and marine sediments over long time periods. They are absorbed by natural life processes into the food chain and become stored in the tissues of living creatures, concentrating principally in the organs containing fatty substances. The effects of this concentration became distressingly apparent when research traced a series of spectacular and extensive fish and wildlife kills to the use of chlorinated hydrocarbon pesticides.

A now-famous example of the deadly food chain effects of pesticides occurred in Clear Lake, California.[2] Located in the mountains to the north of San Francisco, Clear Lake is a popular recreation area that, unfortunately, harbors a large gnat population. In 1949, an effort was made to control the gnat population by a careful application of DDD (a DDT related substance, but less toxic to fish). The dosage of DDD used was not thought to be particularly excessive and, given the volume of water in the lake, the DDD amounted, on the average, to only .015 parts per million. Once applied, the DDD sank to the lake bottom and, as planned, destroyed the gnat larvae. In 1949, and again in 1950, the gnat population was negligible and the control program seemed to be successful with no apparent lasting ill effects on wildlife and fish. However, by 1954, there were large-scale deaths of the lake's waterfowl. The cause of the decimation of the waterfowl population was not immediately understood. Meanwhile, the gnat population again boomed, and further applications of DDD were made, subsequently followed by further bird deaths. After considerable puzzling over the possible causes of the bird deaths, an examination of bird fat tissues revealed deadly concentrations of DDD in excess of 1000 parts per million (ppm). Incredibly, what began as an initial .015 ppm application of DDD to the lake ended up in enormously greater concentrations in the fat tissues of the birds. The path of the DDD led from the lake bottom to absorption by the plankton life of the lake in the amount of 5 ppm. Plankton, the basic

---

[2] Rachel Carson's *The Silent Spring* dramatized the devastating effects of hydrocarbons on fish and wildlife. The Clear Lake case is eloquently presented in her book.

food supply of the ecosystem, passed on the DDD to small fish and other aquatic life, up to 400 ppm. Larger predator fish had even higher concentrations of the DDD and, ultimately, the bird life dependent on the lake's fish population for food became subject to toxic concentrations of DDD. Thus, the food chain of life from plankton to large predators increasingly concentrated the DDD pesticide.

Once understood, other examples of this deadly food chain effect were uncovered. Different types of bird species were fatally affected after feeding on insects, soil life, or seed treated with chlorinated hydrocarbons. Hydrocarbon concentrations were found to impair and, at times, eliminate breeding in many species, including robins, eagles, and certain fish. Residues of DDT showed up in milk from cows fed on pesticide-dressed forage. Human fat tissues revealed alarming concentrations of about 8 ppm of DDT in the body of an average American. Research evidence suggests a relation between some pesticide levels and the incidence of degenerative diseases such as cancer, birth defects, and other genetic damage. However, the implications of chronic DDT exposure for human health are largely unknown. Finally, pesticides were found in animal life in areas of the world, such as the Arctic and Antarctic, where no pesticides had ever been applied, indicating the persistent properties of the chlorinated hydrocarbons and their ability to invade almost all life forms.

In response to considerable public outcry and legislation resulting from the concern over environmental consequences of the chlorinated hydrocarbons, some substitutions were made, using organophosphates and other pesticides. In general, the substituted pesticides are less persistent and break down into harmless components relatively rapidly. Being less persistent, repeated applications are often necessary with the result that the use of organophosphates is generally relatively expensive. Organophosphate pesticides are, however, extremely toxic. Parathion and TEPP, for example, are highly poisonous and a number of human fatalities occur annually due to their improper handling and use. Of course, this toxicity also applies to wildlife, although the relatively nonpersistent nature of these pesticides means that they do not have the severe food chain concentration effects of the chlorinated hydrocarbons.

An additional problem with pesticides in general is the ability of insects to develop immunity to pesticide compounds. For example, there is considerable evidence of the mosquito's adaption and resistance to a wide range of pesticides. This experience characterizes geographically diverse ecological systems from the Central Valley of California to tropical areas.[3] Insect immunity results from the fecundity of the life cycles

---

[3] See, for example, R. Garcia, "The Control of Malaria," *Environment*, Vol. XIV, (June, 1972).

of most insects. Resistance to pesticides may lessen considerably the effectiveness of a given application. Stronger pesticides, in terms of toxicity or persistence, must then be used to achieve the desired degree of protection. The resulting implications for soil life and higher order life forms, therefore, are likely to be more severe than those associated with the initial pesticide administered in its original dosage although the degree of insect protection has not been improved. The implication of a treadmill race between new pesticide development and resistant insect populations casts doubt on the continued reliance on pesticides for insect control.

Human health hazards and the other deleterious environmental effects of pesticides have led to the federal government's funding a great deal of research. Much of this research is aimed at isolating the long-term human effects of chronic exposure to pesticides, uncovering the ecological ramifications associated with specific pesticide use, and the development of alternative means of pest control. A number of federal agencies are involved in these research activities: the Department of Health, Education and Welfare; the Bureau of Sports Fisheries and Wildlife; the Federal Water Pollution Control Administration; and the Department of Agriculture. This considerable research effort hopefully will be the source of the technical information necessary to design proper pesticide policies.

Pesticide policy is in a state of flux although all the present and proposed policies rely on methods of prohibition and regulation. Pesticides moving in interstate commerce must be registered with the Environmental Protection Agency. The EPA can cancel a registration if there is improper labeling of the pesticide. It also has suspension powers to halt interstate shipments when an *imminent hazard* exists. Other proposed legislation develops a classification scheme of pesticides by uses covering pesticides suitable for *general use, restricted use,* or *use by permit only.* Pesticides would be registered by the EPA according to category, and application of the pesticide would require increasing technical supervision over the three classifications.

The EPA has used its powers to cancel the registration of DDT and effectively eliminate the use of this pesticide in the U.S. This decision represents a landmark in pesticide policy and follows extensive hearings on the benefits and dangers of DDT use. The prohibition ruling was based on the evidence of DDT's persistent toxic effects to wildlife and its long-run dangers to human health. The costs of this prohibition are likely to be increases in insect damage to crops and in insect-control costs as more expensive pesticides are used more frequently to achieve the protection once provided by DDT.

Because approximately 80 percent of the pesticides are directed toward the control of only about a hundred pests, additional research efforts have concentrated on the development of nonchemical pest controls. For example, alternative methods rely on destruction by natural predators and diseases, sexual sterilization of the insect population, the use of attracting and destroying devices, and different crop culture practices. Further research is directed at producing pest- and disease-resistant crops. Stringent quarantine laws exist and are tightly enforced in an attempt to control the imports of products that might contain pests (over 120 of the several hundred major pest species in the U.S. are "imports"). Finally, the Food and Drug Administration establishes limits for pesticide residues on both human and animal foods in interstate commerce.

No policies involving the use of economic incentives have yet been employed in pesticide control. However, possibilities do exist for their use. One major problem in pesticide policy is the present low cost of the various pesticides relative to nonpesticide control methods. Government taxation and subsidy policies could be devised to encourage the use of less damaging pesticides. For example, assume that a number of possible pesticides are available for a specified use and that all are capable of providing essentially the same degree of protection. Furthermore, assume that the pesticides vary in price and also in their estimated environmental impact but that none is deemed dangerous enough to warrant a total ban or suspension of use. Given enough information on the respective environmental effects and costs, appropriate use of tax or subsidy policies could create economic incentives favoring those pesticides with less damaging environmental consequences.

However, the realistic outlook in pesticide control is for continuation of policies stressing government regulation. This regulation will rely on prohibition and tight control over specific pesticides with respect to extent of use, location, and purpose. Heavy government research expenditures in pesticide problems are likely to continue. At least for the time being, therefore, sophisticated economic policies, in the form of taxes and subsidies, are likely to make only minimal contributions to efficient use of pesticides.

B. SOLID WASTES

The relationship between economic prosperity and environmental problems is probably most evident in the area of solid wastes. In 1970, national trash collections amounted, on average, to one ton of solid wastes per person. Readers can visualize the dimensions of this problem by considering the volume of trash generated by each of their households in a single week and multiplying by 50 million. All the bottles, cans, paper, and plastics used as containers for consumption goods are discarded regularly by the average household and end up as refuse. Some scattered data indicate the magnitude of the waste disposal problem. New York City generates a daily solid waste load of 30,000 tons. Paper consumption in the United States is estimated at 576 pounds annually per person. Estimates of 1969 per capita consumption of plastics show a 759 percent increase over 1950 levels. These wastes, and others, place great burdens on the generally antiquated solid waste collection and disposal systems of the United States.

Solid wastes consist of agricultural, industrial, mineral, and residential, commercial, and institutional wastes. Table 8–1 indicates the magnitude and components of the solid waste problem in the country. Although agriculture is the single largest source of waste (53 percent), the wastes from industrial, residential, commercial and institutional sources pose the largest social dangers. These nonagricultural wastes are usually generated, collected, and disposed of in populous areas and, consequently, have the potential to affect large numbers of people.[4]

TABLE 8–1   SOLID WASTES OF U.S.—1969

Category	Millions of Tons	Typical Components
Residential, commercial, and institutional wastes	250	
Collected	190	Paper, plastic, rubber, food wastes, bottles
* Uncollected	60	
Industrial wastes	110	Glass, paper, metals, rags
Mineral wastes	1700	Mineral byproducts (slag, mill tailings)
Agricultural wastes	2280	Manure and other organic wastes
Total	4340	

* Wastes not collected by organized public or private means.
Source: Council on Environmental Quality, First Annual Report, 1970.

The collection of solid wastes is the obvious initial problem for waste management, and in areas where refuse collection has been halted for some reason—strikes or natural disasters—the need for prompt col-

---

[4] This does not imply that the costs of agricultural solid wastes are negligible. Polluted ground water supplies, eutrophication of surface waters, and health hazards are some of the effects often associated with agricultural solid wastes.

lection has been dramatically apparent. In such situations, the rapid deterioration of sanitary conditions creates considerable human health hazards. Waste collection is undoubtedly a vital service in our urbanized society. Although some technical progress has occurred in collection techniques (for example, the compactor truck), refuse collection in the United States relies almost entirely on costly hand pickups of wastes from individual waste sources.

Once the collection of solid wastes is accomplished, disposal becomes the next problem. In the United States, disposal usually means depositing the wastes in open dumps. Over three-fourths of the estimated 190 million tons of residential, commercial, and institutional wastes collected in 1969 ended up in open dumps. An additional 8 percent was incinerated, frequently leading to air quality problems, and 13 percent more went into sanitary landfills. The remaining 2 percent was either dumped at sea, salvaged, or composted. Expenditures on the collection and disposal of solid wastes were about $3.5 billion in 1969.

The principal method of waste disposal, open dumping, often creates health hazards and scenic eyesores. Dump fires occur regularly and add to air quality deterioration, particularly in urban areas. In 1970, the EPA initiated a program to eliminate 5,000 of the 15,000 open dumps in the U.S. and to substitute properly designed landfill disposal outlets. A few progressive localities have developed advanced waste management techniques and have turned solid wastes into new land areas, parks, and open spaces.[5] Waste management of this type offers exciting possibilities of creating public benefits from sources previously considered to be only costly problems.

Waste disposal by incineration often creates adverse air quality effects. Although there are some promising technical advances in incineration techniques, the types of incinerators commonly in use combined with the relatively low fuel grades inherent in solid wastes mean that air quality problems will continue to accompany the estimated 8 percent of wastes that are disposed of via burning. Disposal of wastes at sea is only a small fraction of the total disposal (26,000 tons in 1969). The ecological implications of this dumping, like other ocean dumping, are largely unknown but are believed to have potentially significant social costs. In 1970, the Council on Environmental Quality recommended a prohibition be imposed on new solid waste ocean dumping and a gradual elimination of existing ocean dumping.

Finally, reuse of waste material, or *recycling*, is a viable disposal

---

[5] For example, a ski mountain has been built in DuPage County, Illinois, out of garbage and trash. The hill, nicknamed Mount Trashmore, features public facilities for winter recreation sports.

method that can be directly influenced by economic policies. In the case of some waste materials, particularly within the mineral and industrial classifications, the amount of recycling is already considerable. Substantial amounts of lead and copper are recycled into productive processes. However, for most wastes, recycling is currently economically unattractive and is negligible in amount. The problem is basically economic. Federal tax laws, for example, provide economic incentives to producers to find and use virgin supplies of natural resources. In many situations, therefore, it is more costly to recycle materials than to use new raw materials. This situation gives little private profit incentive to develop recycling technology, and the present, relatively primitive, recycling technology insures the continued unattractiveness of recycling as an input source. In addition to the implications for the solid waste problem, the incentive to use raw materials over recycled ones has considerable ramifications in terms of land use, open spaces, fish and wildlife populations, and other environmental amenities. For example, of 58.3 million tons of paper consumed in the U.S. in 1969, almost 40 million tons ended up as wastes (that is, were not recycled). Beyond the collection and disposal costs associated with waste paper, are the effects of relying primarily on new raw materials for paper production. These effects might include diminished forest land, loss of recreational opportunities, deterioration of water quality (the paper pulp industry is a large source of organic wastes), and poor air quality as some of the discarded paper is disposed of by burning.

The nature of the solid wastes in this country, particularly those generated by residential, commercial, and institutional sources, creates certain technological problems for recycling. In almost all cases, the collected wastes arrive at the disposal site as mixed refuse. Plastics, glass, metals, paper, rubber, and other materials all are thrown together. Efficient separation of the wastes into various elements and categories is obviously required. Hand sorting of wastes is an expensive and cumbersome method given the magnitude and diversity of waste loads. Considerable research efforts are underway to develop mechanical waste separators that will solve this problem. Obviously, any separation technology will have a cost and the difficulty (costliness) associated with the separation of wastes is now a considerable economic deterrent to the recycling of a number of materials. Another possible answer to the sorting problem is to separate wastes into some basic divisions at the waste source. This might involve a public-spirited appeal at the household and commercial level. Another possibility is local legislation requiring the sorting of wastes before collection occurs. Alternatively, another policy might be to provide economic tax and subsidy incentives to waste sources to separate their wastes.

Economic policies can be designed to encourage the use of re-cycled material. The distinction between *resource* and *junk* is not abso-lute. It depends on existing technology and market conditions. These, in turn, depend on existing economic incentives. As noted in Chapter 1, developments in basic science point to a future in which many productive processes will not require specific inputs but simply some source of energy and mass. Changes in economic incentives, therefore, can affect both technology and prevailing market conditions to transform what was once considered *junk* into valuable *resources*.

For example, the income tax incentives now incorporated in de-pletion allowances could be weakened, eliminated, or even reversed by higher extractive or severance taxes, thereby encouraging the develop-ment of alternative sources of raw materials and energy. Another policy, already in effect, is for the federal government to direct its purchasing policies towards products made of recycled inputs. In 1970, the General Services Administration required all paper bought for federal govern-ment uses to contain a certain percentage of recycled paper. This policy creates considerable economic encouragement for recycled paper produc-tion because of the large amount of government purchases of this particular item. Similar policies could be implemented at other levels of government and for other types of material. Taxes on disposable con-tainers, bottles, and cans could be levied on purchasers of such items to stimulate the production of reusable items. Such taxes have been imple-mented in some areas (for example, Oregon has a five-cent deposit tax on all regular-size beer and soft drink containers) and many states are considering similar legislation or actual prohibition of nonreturnable con-tainers. Beyond the imposition of user taxes on specific items such as beverage bottles or containers, more broad-based taxes could be im-plemented at the production level on materials that contribute greatly to waste loads. These taxes, in addition to creating recycling incentives, would seek to reduce the solid waste problem by lowering the amount of wastes generated or by changing their composition. In 1970, Congress received a proposal for a *national disposal fee* to be set on all final manu-facturing at a penny per pound. The purpose of this fee, based solely on weight for simplicity in assessment, would be to create a source of fund-ing to improve local solid waste collection and disposal. It would also, obviously, serve as an incentive towards lighter products.

This discussion does not mean to imply that some or all of the above policies should be immediately implemented. Careful study is necessary to determine all the relative costs of alternative disposal and recycling methods before an overall waste management policy is formed. However, in the face of continued economic growth and rising consumption levels, we can expect sharply increasing social costs if the present archaic waste management techniques continue in use. Policies making use of economic incentives, therefore, have an important role in solid waste management. Properly designed tax and subsidy policies are appropriate mechanisms for encouraging improved recycling technology, changing the nature of the input base, altering the components of solid wastes, and, ultimately, reducing the overall social costs of solid wastes.

C. NOISE

Everyday life in urban areas is exceedingly, and some times intolerably, noisy. Horn honking, demolition work, jet aircraft landing and taking off are just a few instances of what one writer has called *decibel madness*. The immediate causes of noise are often painfully obvious but the under-lying source is, again, economic growth and the resulting desire by people for increased mobility, more consumption goods, and greater convenience.

The amount of noise generated, like GNP, is often a rough yardstick of economic progress. However, for many, the cliché of the *hustle and bustle* of city life no longer invokes the image of an area of thriving, throbbing, economic activity but rather, an earshattering, nerve bending, assaulting cacophony of sounds. The problem of noise is not confined to the downtown areas of major cities. Excessive noise is extensive through-out sprawling metropolitan regions and even invades formerly quiet rural areas.

Table 8–2 gives decibel ratings for a variety of sounds encountered in everyday activity. The decibel unit measures relative sound and a reading of zero represents the threshold of audible sound for normal human hearing. The decibel scale is measured in logarithms and indicates that although the sound level at 10 decibels is 10 times that at zero deci-bels, it is 100 times as intense at 20 decibels. Experts agree that prolonged exposure to levels of sound in excess of 85 to 90 decibels results in per-manent hearing damage. Unfortunately, as Table 8–2 indicates, many ordinary daily sounds are considerably above this level.

Industrial activity, quite naturally, is one large source of excessive noise. The construction industry in particular is experiencing a long-run boom that is expected to continue as population, urbanization, and eco-nomic activity increase. Some estimates indicate that world-wide urban building construction in the next fifty years will exceed the total of all existing structures. The necessary increase in the use of jack hammers, air compressors, bulldozers, cement mixers, pneumatic rock drills, cranes, and so on, is not a pleasant prospect for individuals living or working near these construction sites.

TABLE 8–2   WEIGHTED SOUND LEVELS AND HUMAN RESPONSE

Sound Source	dB(A) *	Response Criteria
	—150	
Carrier deck jet operation—140		
		Painfully loud
	—130	Limit amplified speech
Jet takeoff (200 feet)	—120	
Discotheque		Maximum vocal effort
Auto horn (3 feet)		
Riveting machine	—110	
Jet takeoff (2000 feet)		
Shout (0.5 feet)	—100	
N. Y. subway station		Very annoying
Heavy truck (50 feet)	— 90	Hearing damage (8 hours)
Pneumatic drill (50 feet)		
	— 80	Annoying
Freight train (50 feet)		
Freeway traffic (50 feet)	— 70	Telephone use difficult
		Intrusive
Air conditioning unit (20′)— 60		
Light auto traffic (50 ft.)		
	— 50	Quiet
Living room		
Bedroom	— 40	
Library		
Soft whisper (15 feet)	— 30	Very quiet
Broadcasting studio	— 20	
	— 10	Just audible
	— 0	Threshold of hearing

* Typical A—Weighted sound levels taken with a sound-level meter and expressed as decibels on the scale. The "A" scale approximates the frequency response of the human ear.
Source: Department of Transportation.

Another major source of noise is transportation. Motor vehicle noise can be a frightening experience, as anyone who has been unexpectedly overtaken by a ten-ton truck on a superhighway is well aware. If we recall the data in Chapter 7 indicating that over 100 million motor vehicles are in operation in the United States and that this number will increase greatly in the future, the potential noise problem from this source is apparent. Moreover, the widespread ownership of autos makes noise control a difficult problem. Individuals may desire the right to peace and quiet in their home and neighborhood at the same time they desire to move about quicker, farther, and more easily in their cars. These two wants often coexist without a realization that they conflict. Further, the interrelationships between the auto, air pollution, noise, congestion, and land use make the motor vehicle issue a most pressing and complex environmental problem.

Finally, as imposing as the auto traffic, construction, and industrial noise problems are, they are dwarfed by the projected levels of air travel and the accompanying din. Air travel has boomed in this country with domestic schedule airlines flying almost 133.7 billion passenger miles in 1971, up from 30 billion only twelve years previously. Over 10,000 airports now service this demand for travel and the projections of airline use are enormous (266 billion passenger miles by 1977, 458 billion by 1982). Certain airports, such as O'Hare and Los Angeles International, average a takeoff or landing every minute. The magnitudes of the projections for air travel necessarily imply that increasing numbers of people will be exposed to jet noise. Bigger aircraft with increased passenger capacity are the result of technological progress but they often mean longer landing approaches and more people subject to jet noise. A study of Kennedy International Airport in New York reported that a twenty-three-square-mile area containing 108,000 people was exposed to high noise levels. Estimates of similar areas include 106,000 people at O'Hare and 129,000 at Los Angeles International.

Supersonic commercial jet planes have been developed in an attempt to exploit further the economic advantages of bigger and faster modes of air travel. The Concorde, developed by French and British efforts, is aimed at what its sponsors see as a potentially extensive commercial supersonic jet market. Supersonic commercial planes and many military aircraft feature an ability to fly faster than the speed of sound. Conventional commercial aircraft may also, at times, fly faster than sound. The result is sonic booms—loud, sudden, thunderlike sounds, affecting wide land areas. The fad aspects of sonic booms have long ago worn off on the U.S. public and have been replaced by irate damage claims. Significant government research expenditure, therefore, has been undertaken in the area of aircraft design and noise control of jet engines. However, research in this area faces a pressing race with the projected increases in air traffic.

All these facts point to the depressing conclusion that the United States will probably become an even noisier place to live in the future. Identification and evaluation of the social effects of this flood of noise become of growing importance. Presently, we know very little about the economic effects of noise, but what we do know is alarming. Occupationally caused loss of hearing has long been a serious problem in industrial societies. The Council on Evironmental Quality estimates that sixteen million individuals in the United States are subject to on-the-job noise levels capable of inflicting hearing damage. Federal government estimates show a potential cost of $450 million in claims awards if only 10 percent of the eligible workers were to file for hearing loss. Beyond the dollar figures are the unmeasured costs of personal psychic losses associated with hearing deficiencies.

Noise is also a contributing cause of industrial and domestic accidents because it often masks warning signals and distracts attention. A study by the Department of the Interior estimates noise-induced property and structure damages at between $35 and $85 million annually. Numerous noise suits from individuals living near airports are continually in the courts. In 1970, for example, because of growing complaints about intolerable noise levels, the city of Los Angeles was forced to buy almost two thousand homes near Los Angeles airport. The ultimate taxpayer cost of this project is estimated to be over $200 million. Many of the purchased homes were simply demolished. The project included the incredible spectacle of the purchase of a $97,000 home by the city and the subsequent payment by the city of an additional $360 to a wrecking company to destroy it. Studies show considerably more residential areas equally affected by noise in the Los Angeles area not included in the purchase program. Home owners in these areas are forced to absorb the noise pollution damage costs of jet noise in terms of lower real estate values, frayed nerves, and unknown other physical and psychological problems. The long and bitter fight in the 1960s over the location of a fourth jet airport in the New York area exemplifies the extent of public resistance to jet noise and disturbance.

Less obvious effects of noise include the possible relation between physiological stress and cardiovascular disease. The role of noise as a causal factor of cardiovascular disease has not been scientifically established. However, it is known that noise creates emotional stress that, in turn, constricts the flow of blood circulation by reducing the diameter of blood vessels. This is the basic cause of noise-induced hearing loss, as hearing cells die from blood deprivation. Scientists have suggested that a similar phenomenon may exist in the case of cardiovascular disease and chronic exposure to high noise levels. Emotional stress has also been linked with other physical ills but the relationship is only tentatively established. In fact, the entire relationship between emotions and physical illness is still largely unexplored. The contribution of noise to emotional stress is now only a challenging research problem for the medical sciences. The social costs of noise, in terms of health and productivity losses, may prove to be considerable.

Noise obviously disturbs sleep and rest. Sleep loss due to noise has direct economic effects in terms of work productivity although no estimates exist of the magnitude of this effect. In addition, noise is often simply an irritating invasion of privacy.

Although the growth of noise in our society is undeniable and there are clear indications that significant social costs may be involved, noise abatement presents difficult policy problems. Modern technology is linked to economic progress and, although antinoise laws and regulations exist throughout the country, enforcement is often extremely difficult. For example, New York City's model antinoise ordinance essentially boils down to prohibition of any sound without *social utility*. Accordingly, a socially useful activity such as daytime construction is usually exempted from the antinoise regulations. Moreover, locally disturbing noises such as horn blowing and dog barking are nearly impossible to prosecute under public nuisance laws, although Chicago, for example, uses a cruising mobile decibel-measuring team that locates and tickets violators. This type of enforcement, although novel, probably is not a realistic general noise control enforcement procedure.

Zoning laws are a possible device for noise protection and for resolving the basic conflict between economic activity and noise abatement. However, the tradeoff between economic activity and lower noise levels presents the familiar benefit-cost dilemma inherent in environmental issues. For example, should trucks be denied the use of certain highways at night? Should a plant located near a residential area be prohibited from operating a third shift? Should the federal government require noise control devices on industrial and construction machinery similar to the emission control requirements for motor vehicles? Should these controls be national in scope or apply only in populous urban areas? Should certain highways be rerouted or, perhaps, not even built because of the increase in noise exposure to large numbers of people? The economic implications of these questions suggest the difficulties involved in evaluating noise abatement programs.

Some states (California, Connecticut, and New York) have enacted legislation that establishes maximum noise levels for motor vehicles. In addition, most states require mufflers on motor vehicles and these are usually checked during the routine state inspection process.

In a related policy area, the federal government controls air traffic and aircraft noise limits. Furthermore, laws exist to enable injured parties to recover the value of noise-created damages. However, court rulings have established that air space over private property is *part of the public domain*. The burden of proof concerning damages from noise rests on the plaintiff. Court proceedings initiated to recover damages are often lengthy, costly, and frustrating. As suggested in Chapter 5, changes in the legal framework could have immense impact on the severity of many environmental problems.

Any effective noise reduction, of course, involves an opportunity cost. Soundproofing, designing new noise-controlled industrial equipment, building different types of highways, and controlling jet engine noise all will cost somebody money. We have previously noted that there has been a considerable amount of government expense aimed at noise control in jet aircraft. The auto industry is experimenting with the de-

velopment of reduced-noise vehicles and industrial equipment manufacturers are increasing their research into noise abatement devices. In
addition to zoning and noise control laws, some economic incentive
programs have been proposed for noise control. For example, one proposal calls for a one dollar antinoise tax to be levied on each passenger
and cargo ton using Los Angeles airport, with the tax revenue earmarked
to defray the soundproofing costs in nearby residential sections. In
England, the government offers a subsidy of up to one-half of the cost
of soundproofing three rooms for houses within twelve miles of London's
Heathrow Airport. The Environmental Protection Agency has been given
authority to determine noise emission standards in construction and transportation. This form of noise control by regulation would be analogous
to similar EPA policies that set air and water quality standards.

However, in general, the use of economic incentives in noise abatement programs seems to be limited. Laws, regulations, and zoning techniques have been the major instruments of noise control and these policies
have been largely ineffective. The basic causes of this failure are the
diffuse and broad-based nature of noise sources, the growth in these
sources, the difficulty of enforcing legal remedies, and the conflict of
noise control with economic activity and modern urban life. In many
situations, noise is a relative problem and although both my neighbor
and I may fight vociferously for a local prohibition of trucks from our
residential streets, we may disagree considerably on the proper volume
of my stereo, the all-night running of his air conditioner, the use of my
son's minibike, or the barking of his dog.

In summary, noise control is one of the most difficult environmental
problems. Reliance on self-imposed industrial noise abatement is unrealistic. Expanded, tighter government controls may prove the only
effective remedy. Perhaps development of new technology someday will
permit the use of economic incentives for noise abatement in the form
of noise emission charges. A large amount of research remains to be done,
first to identify, and then to quantify, the extent and incidence of the
social costs of noise. Additional research is needed to estimate the costs
and effectiveness of various noise abatement programs.

D. OUTDOOR RECREATION, LAND USE, AND CONSERVATION

Unlike the previous environmental problems we have considered, outdoor
recreation and land use practices are not associated with a particular
group of effluents, production processes, or economic activities. Nevertheless, adequate outdoor recreation opportunities and the protection of

natural environments are becoming increasingly important aspects of the quality of life.

1. Outdoor Recreation and Land Use

A major national growth trend of the past two decades has been public participation in outdoor recreation. Since the end of World War II, this country has turned increasingly to the outdoors for its recreational and leisure time pursuits. New recreational activities like snowmobiling have emerged and become popular, and traditional outdoor sports such as swimming, camping, and fishing have boomed. Rough projections of recreation activity days for twenty-five outdoor activities estimate an increase from 12.2 billion days in 1965 to 29.8 billion days by the end of this century. National Park system attendance has increased from 33 million visits in 1950 to 200 million in 1971.[6] Such statistics and everyday observation confirm the fact that the American public is engaging in outdoor recreation in large and growing numbers.

The roots of this upsurge in outdoor recreation are many. Steady population growth is an obvious reason, but changes in the age distribution, migration patterns, and mobility of the population are probably just as fundamental demographic causes of the popularity of recreation activity. In addition, continued economic growth has resulted in decreases in the length of the workweek and increased leisure time. Paid vacations are now commonplace and their length has tended to increase. A downward trend in retirement age combined with an increase in longevity has added to leisure time. Most important, however, is the steady growth of per capita real income—from $2,342 in 1950 to $3,572 in 1971, in 1958 prices. All available evidence indicates that outdoor recreation is *income elastic,* in other words, as incomes increase, the purchase of outdoor recreation increases *more* than proportionally. Higher income levels have led to increased demands for leisure time and a major share of this increase in leisure is devoted to outdoor recreation activities. Thus, the substantial increase in income in the postwar period has been a major factor in the observed growth in outdoor recreation participation.

The seemingly immutable rise in the number of automobiles and their travel miles along with the completion of an extensive interstate highway system has meant easier accessibility to recreation areas. The diversity of license plates at the national parks during summer vacation time is a ready indication of the mobility of the population.

---

[6] This rise in attendance has forced radical policy changes in some of the parks. For example, Yellowstone National Park has restricted the use of private autos due to extreme congestion.

An obvious question accompanies this mushrooming national pursuit of outdoor recreation: Are adequate facilities available to accommodate the present and future demand? And, more important, how can the government efficiently plan expenditures to manage outdoor recreation demand? The economic issues involved are exceedingly complex. Recent federal attention to outdoor recreation problems has resulted in considerable activity in this area by a diverse group of agencies. The Bureau of Outdoor Recreation, the Bureau of Sports Fisheries and Wildlife, the Forest Service, the Bureau of Land Management, the National Park Service, the Corps of Engineers, and the Environmental Protection Agency are some of the agencies involved in outdoor recreation planning. In addition, state and local governments have various departments engaged in outdoor recreation management. The coordination of planning, budgets, and jurisdiction between these agencies and levels of government presents some complex administrative problems in addition to the fundamental economic question of resource allocation.

The basic economic dilemma in outdoor recreation is just one facet of the well-recognized failure of private markets to provide sufficient amounts of public goods. Social and economic changes have spurred large increases in the population's demand for outdoor recreation. The private market has responded efficiently in providing all the necessary equipment for recreation activity, from surfboards to forty-foot houseboats. The difficulty arises in the market's response in supplying the basic outdoor recreational facilities and opportunities. Beaches, wetlands, clean water and clean air, open spaces, and natural environments are obviously necessary for the proper enjoyment of many outdoor recreation activities. However, the success of the private market in providing for the immense diversity of recreational equipment is matched by its failure to supply adequately the natural areas necessary for outdoor recreation. As explained in Chapter 5, the nature of recreational facilities as a public good is the cause of this imbalance.

Private markets have been quick to develop extensive resort communities in numerous locations throughout the country. The initial attraction that spurs these resort developments is often the recreational and environmental amenities available nearby. However, the ability of private profit interests to develop a resort area frequently leads rapidly to a reduction or destruction of the very environmental amenities that provided the initial attraction! The familiar syndrome of congestion, solid wastes, water quality deterioration, and elimination of fish and game populations is a common problem in many resort areas in the United States. Basically, the problem is one of land use. Although private markets work reasonably well to develop rural areas into suburbs, shopping centers, industrial sites, sources of raw materials, and even resort communities, they fail to preserve the natural integrity of water, air, and land resources for their public recreational, esthetic, and ecological values.

There are a number of reasons underlying this failure. In Part 2 of this book, we explained how the common property basis of air and water resources is a principal cause of externalities. This common ownership of air and water resources leads directly to problems of *exclusion*. In terms of the pollutants caused by production and consumption, we have seen that it is often not possible to charge individuals and firms the full social costs of their economic activities. However, this also implies that individuals and firms are unable to collect the entire social value of protecting the quality of air and water resources. Just as they cannot be charged the full social costs of environmental deterioration, they also cannot fully exclude others from the benefits of any action to maintain environmental quality. It is this inability to capture the full benefits of protecting environmental quality that lies behind the failure of private markets.[7]

A further cause of the undersupply of outdoor recreational opportunities and natural amenities is often the capacity of such sites to accommodate large numbers of people at any given time. Therefore, the marginal costs of additional use of the site are near zero and average costs decline over wide ranges of use. Profit-maximizing behavior, following the socially efficient rule of price equals marginal cost, would result in economic losses. Private interests would not operate in such a situation or, at best, would undersupply the amount of outdoor recreation and natural amenities relative to the socially efficient quantity. Accordingly, the value of recreational and ecological uses of the environment has only imperfect market outlets for expression. The incentive for *free rider* behavior on the part of individuals valuing environmental amenities compounds this problem even further. It is these public good characteristics of recreational activities and ecological values that warrant government intervention to protect and augment the supply of environmental amenities.

Considerable research effort has been undertaken to provide economic guidance for government's role in outdoor recreation. The objective of this research is to estimate the social benefits associated with a given *free* recreation site or natural area. This is a thorny problem be-

___

[7] Of course, the ability to exclude individuals from the benefits of environmental amenities varies considerably. It is probably most difficult in the case of air quality. On the other hand, the owner of land surrounding a lake can quite readily exclude individuals from its use and, therefore, charge a fee to fishermen, and so on. Such privately supplied recreation opportunities are numerous. However, exclusion becomes much more difficult, if not impossible, when we are dealing with a river system, an entire coastline, or a scenic canyon area of hundreds of square miles.

cause no market provides information on the demand price for each recreational facility. However, if it can be solved, then a rational comparison can be made between recreation benefits and the opportunity costs of alternative uses of the land. Various attempts aimed at quantifying recreation benefits have met with mixed success. Initial efforts used travel distance from the recreation site as an indication of the individual's valuation of a recreation visit. When summed over all users of a recreational site, this figure provided a measure of the total benefits of recreation for that particular site. The argument is that the individual would not incur the travel costs to the site if he did not value the recreation experience at least as much. As travel costs increase with distance from the site, then the number of recreation visits decrease. Thus, a demand curve can be derived from the relation between the implicit price, the travel cost, and the number of recreation visits. The area under this curve is a measure of the total benefits of the recreation activity and can be compared with the costs of providing the recreation opportunity and/or the benefits of the site in alternative uses.

Extensions of this method incorporate other determinants of an individual's desire to engage in recreation activity in addition to travel cost (the proxy for the price of recreation). Such variables as income, socioeconomic status, and available leisure time can be added in order to obtain a more valid price-recreation quantity demand relationship.

Other attempts to estimate recreation benefits use ingeniously devised questionnaire techniques to elicit willingness-to-pay responses from recreation seekers and then translate the sample responses to aggregate populations. This method is a costly one in terms of research effort. As explained in Chapter 5, it can also be misleading because numerous pitfalls exist in attempting to obtain such information from questionnaires. However, carefully designed surveys can provide some of the information about the demand for public recreation activities that private markets generate for conventional goods.

Thus far, we have treated outdoor recreation as a single group of activities and described how economists attempt to calculate the economic benefits of outdoor recreation. However, outdoor recreation is not a homogeneous group of activities. The National Recreation Survey of 1965, for example, questioned respondents in terms of twenty-five different and carefully defined outdoor activities ranging from *remote wilderness camping* to *playing outdoor games and sports*. The diversity of outdoor recreation activities often implies conflict between activities that compete for the same sites or resources. Familiar examples of this situation are the general incompatibility between waterskiing and fishing or between remote camping and what is called general, or developed, camping. In the first case, waterskiing and fishing may occur with basically the same type of resource, namely, a relatively clean body of water; and the difficult question, given their incompatibility, is one of the relative social values of the water in each use.[8] In the second case, not only are the two types of camping in conflict, but they require considerably different resource bases with correspondingly different costs. It is also easy to visualize the general conflict between popular recreation activities and fragile ecological systems. Again, we face the familiar benefit-cost evaluation problem in the environmental area; this time, however, the comparison is between different recreational uses of natural resources.

2. The Economic Defense of Conservation

Preservation of natural areas and environmental quality has developed into an important national political issue. Ultimately, however, an economic rationale must be clearly demonstrated in favor of conservation if its aims are to succeed against more conventional forms of economic development. A general version of the economic argument for conservation is that although the demand for recreation activity and unspoiled natural areas is increasing, the supply opportunities are constantly shrinking, creating a steady rise in the implicit price or social value of natural environments.[9] Further, many conventional types of economic development automatically foreclose future options because the development process of a natural environment is largely irreversible. The damming of a free-flowing river, the draining of wetlands, or the use of open land for a housing community are examples of natural environments irrevocably changed by development. This irreversibility and necessary loss of future options to use these sites as unspoiled recreational or unique ecological resources create a persuasive rationale for a careful development policy.

Maintaining future options of land use for natural unspoiled areas has economic value. This value will increase over time, due to the continued upward trend in recreation demand and also because more individuals currently enjoying the amenities of natural environments pass on the skills, attitudes, and appreciation of outdoor activities to future users and, thus, spur recreation demand even higher. The thrust of this argument is that the present population's experience with outdoor recreation results in an increase in future recreation demands. This interdependence of demand over time creates difficult research problems and may greatly complicate benefit-cost analyses of resource preservation programs.

[8] In order to isolate this problem, we can assume that no other uses of the lake exist and that there is a definite incompatibility in the activities. One possible solution, for example, might have zoned areas within the lake, with certain boundaries defining exclusive waterskiing zones, leaving other areas for more passive water sports.

[9] This argument draws heavily on the economic reasoning of J. V. Krutilla, in "Conservation Reconsidered," *American Economic Review*, LVII, No. 4, September, 1967.

A further economic justification for preservation is that many individuals receive satisfaction from just knowing, for example, that a wild river flows, untamed and unspoiled, through a remote and spectacular wilderness even though they have absolutely no *current* desire to *float* the river themselves and whose entire contact with water, in fact, may be presently limited to the community swimming pool. This *option demand*, as it is called, has legitimate economic value and should be properly included as a social benefit of preservation and natural areas. However, individuals cannot readily express their option demands in private markets. The recent growth of interest and membership in such groups as the Sierra Club, Wilderness Society, National Wildlife Federation, and Audubon Society suggests the validity of this preservation argument. Indeed, some private organizations have attempted on a small scale to formalize the values of option demand and preservation by actual purchases of natural areas for conservation purposes.[10]

A final economic rationale for conservation also centers on the option demand argument but involves the relation of basic research to the existence of natural biota. The natural biological environment is an ecological system of plants and animals that form a genetic pool. From this natural genetic bank has come a great variety of discoveries resulting in advances in basic scientific knowledge, development of new drugs, agricultural innovations, and so on. If this pool is diminished by the loss of a species, many future research possibilities may be foreclosed. Economic value should be assigned to the maintenance of the entirety of the natural gene pool. In addition, the research potential of the geophysical sciences is also conditional on having available the widest possible range of natural phenomena.

Considerable effort has been made to provide orderly land use and preservation of natural areas. The Wilderness Act of 1964 established a program of maintaining unspoiled natural areas, and ten million acres are currently under its protection. Additions to the National Park system also have been made. Various wildlife protection measures have gained support (for example, endangered species protection, programs to reduce or eliminate the incentives of predator control, and restrictions on pesticide uses). The Land and Water Conservation Fund provides revenues to purchase natural areas. These revenues come, in part, from taxes on motorboat fuel and user fees collected in federal recreation sites (that is, from sources using the environmental amenities associated with out-

---

[10] This development represents an extension of the market solution of externalities presented in Chapter 4. However, all the organizational, free rider, and coordination problems discussed in Chapter 5 are relevant to this situation and, therefore, this kind of extension of the market is, at best, an imperfect and limited expression of social values.

door recreation). In 1971, more than half of this fund of $200 million went to state and local governments on a matching basis for the purchase and development of outdoor recreation sites. The remainder is to be used for federal land acquisition. The sale of hunting stamps (for waterfowl hunting) has generated considerable revenues for additions to the thirty million acre National Wildlife Refuge System.

Finally, current reviews of federal land management practices may bring a change in emphasis away from land development values and towards preservation and esthetic considerations. The National Environmental Protection Act requires all federal agencies to report on the environmental impact of any proposed projects. Although the impact statements do not contain the authority to halt or forbid any particular project, they do call for additional information that can result in the delay of project construction and raise the further possibility of executive action. This was the situation in 1971, when an executive order by President Nixon stopped the completion of the Cross-Florida Barge Canal of the Corp of Engineers. Conservation interests have also achieved delays in the development of the Tocks Island Dam on the upper Delaware River and the much publicized and fought over Alaskan pipeline.

In summary, society's growing desire for the amenities associated with open spaces and outdoor activities will result in an increasing social valuation of protecting the natural integrity of land and water areas. However, uses of land and other natural resources for their environmental values compete with more conventional land development interests. One distinct advantage favoring development over preservation is the relatively more complete market expressions of the value of the natural resource in its private development uses. Proper land use policy attempts to provide a more orderly use of land and natural resources by explicitly measuring the economic values of the resource in its natural state. The obvious problem arises of measuring the public recreational and esthetic values of resources preserved in their natural state relative to the opportunity costs of lost raw materials, suburban housing, plant sites, or any of the other potential private uses of the resource.

E. SUMMARY AND CONCLUSIONS

This chapter has attempted to provide a broad view of various environmental problems. The social costs of pesticides, solid wastes, and noise are significant additions to the more widely recognized water and air quality problems of Chapters 6 and 7.

The potential damages of pesticides relative to the social benefits of pesticide use pose difficulties for both research and policy. Solid wastes are intimately related to economic growth, and economic policies have a major role to play in determining the direction of waste management in this country. Noise and its chronic human effects present formidable research challenges to the medical sciences and are a potentially large source of external costs associated with modern urban life. Finally, preservation of natural environments, wildlife populations, emphasis on scenic and esthetic values, and conservation of open spaces face the constant pressure of effluent discharges and private market land development. Economic analysis suggests that there is an increasing social value to preserving natural environments and their amenities. Government intervention is required to insure the protection of the public interest in land uses.

Our survey of major environmental problems in Part 3 has covered a wide range of closely related problems. The one recurring theme of our discussion has been the enormous complexity of contemporary pollution problems and the amorphousness of the concept of environmental quality. Environmental problems are multidimensional, encompassing interdependent physical, chemical, biological, economic, and sociopolitical phenomena. Unfortunately, the single most important lesson to be gleaned out of this mass of complex details is that no one easy solution exists to environmental problems. Given the relatively primitive state of knowledge today about the fundamental nature of many environmental problems, optimal risk-averting social policy may call for a mix of various antipollution measures, including some cases of outright prohibitions of certain kinds of emissions. Furthermore, because many environmental problems are physically and economically interrelated, any partial equilibrium solutions aimed at individual pollution sources must somehow be centrally coordinated in an overall environmental policy. With these important considerations in mind, we next turn, in Part 4, to a more detailed evaluation of the general policy instruments available to improve and protect environmental quality.

QUESTIONS FOR DISCUSSION

1. In your judgment, are the various problems discussed in this chapter of equal importance to the air and water quality problems covered in the previous two chapters? What is the basis for your answer?

2. Some agricultural experts have argued that a ban on the use of DDT could not withstand a careful benefit-cost analysis. Identify the main benefits and costs that would enter into such an analysis and indicate the difficulties involved in estimating the proper dollar amounts.

3. Suppose that your local government passed a law requiring every household and firm to separate its trash carefully, prior to collection. Set up a benefit-cost analysis of this law. Can you think of any better alternatives available to the government?

4. Why do not markets exist for noise abatement? Can the government provide a workable *effluent charge* solution for the externalities of excessive noise? Why or why not? Should the federal government impose maximum noise standards for new vehicles?

5. What are the difficulties involved in estimating a demand schedule for the conservation of a wilderness area? How does your answer relate to our previous analysis of public goods? How should the government allow for the interests of future generations in making decisions about investments in wilderness areas?

SELECTED REFERENCES

Pesticides

CARSON, R., *Silent Spring*. New York: Houghton Mifflin Co., 1962. An eloquent treatment of the effects of pesticides on man and wildlife. The initial source of widespread public concern over the consequences of pesticides.

HEADLEY, J. C., and J. W. LEWIS, *The Pesticide Problem: An Economic Approach to Public Policy*. Baltimore: The Johns Hopkins Press, for Resources for the Future, 1967. A discussion of the basic economics behind evaluating the benefits and costs of pesticide use.

LANGHAM, M. R., J. C. HEADLEY, and W. F. EDWARDS, "Agricultural Pesticides: Productivity and Externalities," in *Environmental Quality Analysis*, ed. A. V. Kneese and B. T. Bower, Baltimore: The Johns Hopkins Press, 1972. A study evaluating the externalities associated with pesticide use.

MELLANBY, K., *Pesticides and Pollution*. London: Collins Press, 1967. A useful description of individual pesticides and their environmental consequences.

PIMENTAL, D., *Ecological Effects of Pesticides on Non-Target Species*. Washington, D.C.: Government Printing Office, 1971. A technical presentation of the effects of pesticides on wildlife and other natural populations. Contains an extensive bibliography.

Report of the Secretary's Commission on Pesticides and their Relationship to Environmental Health, Parts I and II, Washington, D.C.: Government Printing Office, 1969. A comprehensive treatment of all facets of the pesticide problem. Has an excellent bibliography.

Solid Wastes

Council on Environmental Quality, *Toxic Substances*. Washington, D.C.: Government Printing Office, 1971. A broad view of toxic substances in the environment. Surveys sources, extent, and effects of various materials entering the environment.

Council on Environmental Quality, *Environmental Quality, The First Annual Report of the Council on Environmental Quality.* Washington, D.C.: Government Printing Office, 1970. Provides a brief treatment of the solid waste and noise problems among other specific environmental concerns.

Council on Environmental Quality, *Ocean Dumping, A National Policy.* Washington, D.C.: Government Printing Office, 1970. Treats the waste disposal problems of ocean dumping for a variety of waste types (in addition to solid wastes).

LEONTIEF, W., "Environmental Repercussions and the Economic Structure: An Input-Output Approach," *The Review of Economics and Statistics,* LII, No. 3, (August 1970). Uses input-output analysis to evaluate the relationship between production levels and waste discharges.

Noise

BARON, R. A., *The Tyranny of Noise.* New York: St. Martins Press, 1970. An articulate description of the sources and effects of the noise problem. Also contains a policy section on current attempts at noise control.

BERLAND, T., *The Fight for Quiet.* Englewood Cliffs, N.J.: Prentice-Hall, Inc. 1970. A survey of the noise problem containing a good bibliography.

STEVENSON, G. M., *The Politics of Airport Noise.* Belmont: Duxbury Press, 1972. A survey of aircraft noise problems with a comprehensive treatment of the legal experience with noise damage claims.

STILL, H., *In Quest of Quiet.* Harrisburg: Stackpole Books, 1970. Another descriptive account of the noise problem in the U.S.

Outdoor Recreation

CICCHETTI, C. J., J. J. SENECA, and P. DAVIDSON, *The Demand and Supply of Outdoor Recreation.* Washington: Bureau of Outdoor Recreation, 1969. An empirical study attempting to quantify the demand factors and supply responses influencing individual recreation activities.

CLAWSON, M., and J. L. KNETSCH, *Outdoor Recreation.* Baltimore: Johns Hopkins Press for Resources for the Future, 1966. A comprehensive treatment of the economic issues of outdoor recreation backed by quantitative descriptions of the problem.

KNETSCH, J. L., and R. K. DAVIS, "Comparisons of Methods for Recreation Evaluation," in *Water Research,* ed. A. V. Kneese and S. C. Smith. Baltimore: Johns Hopkins Press, 1966. A useful summary of the benefit estimation problem for outdoor recreation with an interesting comparison of the travel cost and willingness to pay solutions.

KRUTILLA, J. V., "Conservation Reconsidered," *American Economic Review,* LVIII, No. 4 (September, 1967). The classic presentation of the economic reasoning for the preservation of natural environments.

KRUTILLA, J. V., editor, *Natural Environments, Studies in Theoretical and Applied Analysis.* Baltimore: Johns Hopkins Press, 1972. A selection of studies concerned with natural resource issues.

Outdoor Recreation Review Commission, *Outdoor Recreation Review Commission Reports 1–26,* Washington, D.C.: Government Printing Office, 1960. An overview of the dimensions of outdoor activities in the U.S.

The Vehicles of Collective Environmental Action

Chapter 9

Regulation
and
Prohibition

Part 4 of the book, consisting of this and the next two chapters, analyzes the main alternative strategies available to society in its efforts to improve environmental quality. Part 2 of the book was limited almost entirely to pure economic theory, and Part 3 concentrated on the technical biological and physical aspects of the major environmental problems facing our nation today. Part 4, in turn, is intended to survey the major issues in government environmental policies, with a preponderance of facts and institutional details over abstract theory. Each of the chapters of Part 4 covers one of the three broad classes of government proenvironmental actions. The present chapter analyzes the economics of government regulations and prohibitions. Next, Chapter 10 discusses government fiscal measures affecting polluters: taxes, including effluent charges, and subsidies. Finally, Chapter 11 takes up the issues involved in direct government provision of environmental services.

PUBLIC POLICY AND THE ENVIRONMENT

The theme common to this and the previous parts of the book is the notion that the fundamental factor underlying most environmental problems is the failure of the private market system to allocate resources efficiently because of pervasive external spillover effects of production and consumption. Given this premise, it follows that the main justification for government intervention in the private market system for environmental purposes should be to deal, directly or indirectly, with these external effects—to somehow *internalize* for society those effects that are *external* to individual firms and households. It is relatively simple to spell out theoretically how an enlightened, efficiency-oriented government agency should behave in a world where full information is available at very low cost in order to improve the workings of the private market system. We have already stressed the point in Chapter 5, however, that the phenomenon of government failure parallels the concept of private market failure, and we shall attempt, therefore, to make some realistic assessments of the potential for *effective* government actions in the following discussion.

Some preliminary distinctions between the various classes of government action may be useful to the reader as part of an introduction to our discussion of social environmental policies. We confine ourselves to a consideration of (1) regulation and prohibition, (2) fiscal incentives and disincentives, and (3) direct government production of environmental services. We specifically do *not* discuss a government policy that consists merely of exhortation to better behavior by individual polluters. The authors doubt that such exhortations are effective in altering mass tastes and behavior in the long run unless they are backed up by more concrete economic policies.

Regulation in the United States conventionally means some degree of control by regulatory commissions over the services provided and the per unit rates charged by firms. Regulatory commissions are the creation of the legislative branch of government, but commissioners are appointed by the executive and their activities are subject to judicial review. As a rough generalization, the commissions allow regulated firms to make the great majority of decisions involving their own business affairs, subject only to pricing and service guidelines set down by the commissions in attempting to implement their conception of the public interest. More generally, regulation could mean any government directive controlling or limiting the actions of firms or households in the private sector.

In contrast, government *prohibition* means outright legislative bans on various activities. Congress, state, and local legislatures pass laws forbidding a specified activity, and the laws are subsequently enforced by the police and the judicial system of the state.

Government *fiscal measures*—taxes and subsidies—also are implemented through laws passed by the legislative branch of government. Such measures do not directly control or prohibit private economic activities. They may, however, entail an addition to, or subtraction from, the benefits (costs) of conducting private market activities in specific ways.

Government production of environmental services involves transactions between the agencies of the state and the private owners of productive resources. The government pays the firms and households that own certain resources a mutually agreeable price or, in certain cases, uses its overriding legal right of eminent domain to compel sale at the government's price. Even in the latter case, however, the government must, in our society, pay *fair market value* for the property, with the price subject to judicial review. It then uses these resources to produce a variety of environmental services, very much as private firms hire resources to produce private sector goods and services.

The distinctions between these various classes of government intervention are clear enough in principle, but in certain borderline cases it may be difficult to place a particular government action in just one or another category. Regulation and prohibition are the most difficult to distinguish, because regulation, as practiced in this country, consists essentially of piecemeal prohibitory measures by quasi-legislative agencies. That is, the regulatory commission generally sets a *maximum* rate of return and prescribes certain *minimum* standards of service for a regulated utility. The firm may then conduct its business as it sees fit, subject to the limitation that it is *prohibited* from charging rates above the regulated maximum and from allowing the quality of its service standards to fall below the regulated minimums.

Even the contrast between a tax and a prohibition is not as clear as it may seem on first encounter. A tax of t per unit on a pollutant, P, may seem to differ in kind from a prohibition against the emission of any units of P, for example, but, in fact, the effect of both measures is to raise the cost of conducting a business in such a way as to allow the emission of P. The tax per unit of P adds directly to the firm's unit or average costs by a determinate amount, $(= \$\left(\dfrac{X}{Q}\right) \cdot t)$ where $\dfrac{X}{Q}$ is the number of units of P emitted per unit of output Q, but a prohibition adds to the firm's costs only indirectly. If the firm is prohibited from emitting P, it must either switch to another, more expensive technique of production [1] or ignore the prohibition and continue to emit P, thereby accepting

---

[1] If an alternative technique of production were *not* more expensive, presumably the firm would have used it in the first place in order to minimize costs of production and thereby maximize profits. Admittedly, the passage of the prohibition on the emission of P may have the effect of causing the firm's management to seek cheaper techniques of production that do not involve the emission of pollutants.

the legal penalties for doing so. The latter alternative is by no means farfetched in the common situation in this society in which environmental law enforcement is erratic and the penalty for breaking the law may be small relative to the firm's total costs of production. In a probabilistic sense, the firm may thus consider that a law forbidding the emission of P is equivalent to a tax of a given amount per unit of P emitted, subject to the proviso that violation of the law involves a perhaps significant moral onus in addition to pecuniary considerations. Abundant evidence exists that laws regulating, or even forbidding, various forms of pollution in the United States have been openly disobeyed.

In addition, note the close relation between a regulated maximum rate on the firm's sales of its output and a tax per unit of output. Both measures may have roughly comparable effects in reducing the firm's actual revenues below potential maximum levels.

Finally, government production entailing the use of privately owned resources may be considered as an ultimate form of prohibition on the private use of property within the private market system. Instead of taxing or prohibiting a specific use of land, for example, the government may attempt to effect the socially optimal use of the land by purchasing it and thereby removing it entirely from the vagaries of the private market system.

Preview of this Chapter

The most frequent response by the average layman who perceives the seriousness of environmental problems is to urge that the legislature pass a law forbidding polluting activities. This response is in keeping with a long American tradition of attempting to solve complex social problems through prohibitory legislation. A good analogy is the antitrust legislation of the turn of the century that attempted to prohibit certain practices by giant corporate monopolies. Also, the reader may recall the Prohibition Amendment as a typically American reaction to the perceived threat of internal pollution by alcohol. In contrast, most economists argue that prohibition and regulation are inefficient mechanisms of collective action relative to the alternative of various fiscal incentive and disincentive techniques. This chapter spells out the economic argument behind this negative attitude towards legalistic solutions to environmental problems, but also indicates those special circumstances in which the prohibitory strategy makes good sense.

Section A of the chapter discusses the role of regulation in a national environmental policy. It considers, first, the possibility of extending the scope of the authority of the existing regulatory commissions and, second, the prospects for the regulatory measures of some agency like the

Environmental Protection Agency. Section B then examines the role of prohibitions. It presents the benefit-cost approach to the economic effects of prohibitions and considers the specific case of a possible prohibition on the use of automobiles. Section C discusses a special and important form of regulation and prohibition, zoning. A final Section D gives a brief summary of the chapter.

A. REGULATION

The Present Regulatory Commissions

Regulatory commissions currently operate in the United States at both the state and federal levels of government. Many of the industries regulated by these commissions are public utilities, including mainly the various transportation, communications, and power industries. Public utilities may be characterized roughly as *natural monopolies,* or industries in which only one or a very small number of firms can operate efficiently in a single market because of large fixed costs of production. The telephone industry is a good example of a public utility according to the above characterization. Enormous fixed costs are required to build up a basic network of transmission facilities in order to provide telephone services between any two points, but once such costs have been absorbed, additional services can be provided to consumers at only small marginal costs. From society's standpoint, competition in the telephone industry would be wasteful in that it would necessitate the costly duplication of the basic network of transmission facilities. Society therefore tolerates and even demands monopolistic control of the industry, but at the same time establishes regulatory commissions as watchdogs over the monopolistic firm in order to forestall possible abuse of monopoly power.[2]

The five federal regulatory commissions in the United States whose activities may be relevant to environmental quality include the Interstate Commerce Commission (ICC), the Federal Power Commission (FPC), the Federal Communications Commission (FCC), the Civil Aeronautics Board (CAB), and the Atomic Energy Commission (AEC). The ICC has jurisdiction over interstate transportation and oil pipelines; the FPC, over power projects and interstate transmission of electricity and natural gas; the FCC, over telephone, telegraph, radio, and television transmission; the CAB, over civil aviation, and the AEC, over nuclear energy.

---

[2] Not every regulated industry falls as neatly into the public utility-natural monopoly niche as does the telephone industry, which is to say that all regulation, as it is practiced today in the United States, cannot be justified by the rationale given in the text.

Various state commissions have roughly corresponding jurisdictions with the ICC, FCC, and FPC within individual states.

Regulatory commissions have, in the past, been mainly concerned with regulating the rates charged by regulated firms, but they have also had the responsibility of maintaining the quantity and quality of services provided, including the public safety aspects of quality. Control over rates is obviously not sufficient to prevent potential abuses of monopoly power, because a regulated firm could, in the absence of other controls, circumvent maximum rate schedules and earn monopoly profits by cutting costs through allowing deterioration in the quality of its services. For our purposes, it is of interest to note that the commissions also exert some pressures on regulated firms to provide services to all consumers at a uniform price even if the firm incurs higher costs for some customers than for others. In effect, the firm, under such circumstances, can earn a competitive rate of return only by charging its relatively low-cost customers a price high enough to subsidize the provision of services to marginal or relatively high-cost consumers. The beneficiaries of such hidden subsidies are often the residents of communities off the main grid of a transportation or communications network. These implicit subsidies could be interpreted as a social judgment that isolated communities should not be deprived of the services of public utilities on the basis of the private sector profit and loss criterion. A theoretical justification for such subsidies could be that the whole society receives external benefits (or avoids external costs) from the preservation of existing communities.

The Environmental Policy Role of the Present Regulating Commissions

What role, if any, can the existing regulatory commissions play in an overall environmental policy? Some of the most serious environmental problems of our society can be traced directly to the various effluents produced by regulated public utilities, in particular the gas and electric power companies regulated by the FPC and by state and municipal commissions. For example, a federal government agency has estimated that about half of the total sulfur oxide pollutants, one-fourth of the particulate, and one-fourth of the nitrogen oxide emissions in the United States can be attributed to the discharge of fossil-fueled electric plants. One important part of a national environmental policy could entail consciously extending the activities of the regulatory commissions to include a major concern with the environmental problems traceable to regulated firms.

The regulatory commissions already have become involved in environmental policy, due to mounting public protests over the location of new power plants and to various other activities of regulated firms. But the environmental role of the commissions could be greatly increased either within their present mandates or under new authority granted them by Congress. The FPC, for example, might redefine quality of service to include the negative outputs of power generation, and enforce its new quality standards by setting maximum permissible levels for each effluent for regulated firms. The ICC might take into account the environmental consequences of different modes of transportation and their impacts on land uses, in setting its rate schedules; the FCC might concern itself directly with the aesthetic external costs imposed on society by existing transmission lines and force consideration of possible alternatives; and the CAB might impose more rigid noise controls at various airports. The AEC already attempts to insure human safety from nuclear energy uses and might pursue these activities more vigorously. The state regulatory commissions could undertake similar steps within their own jurisdictions. Ideally, all these activities and more could, if undertaken, enhance the quality of the environment in our society.

Yet few economists would express much enthusiasm for greatly extending the activities of the regulatory commissions into the environmental policy sphere. Even granted that such activities could succeed in helping to alleviate serious problems of pollution, the real issue is whether the benefits of the *solution* would be worth the costs. In part, the economist's doubts about the potential environmental role of the regulatory commission follow from his general bias against social economizing through prohibition. In addition, however, economists fear that environmental regulation through the commission mechanism would compound the social wastes inherent in social control through prohibition. If a commission prohibits an activity by a regulated public utility that apparently harms the environment, the result will almost certainly be to add to the costs of providing the regulated service. These additional costs likely then will be passed directly on *in full,* in the form of a higher price for consumers, because the commission will almost certainly not deny allowing the costs it has mandated on the firm to be added to the cost base for the regulated rate schedule. Unfortunately, however, the regulatory mechanism provides no incentive to the regulated firm to minimize its costs of production. In contrast, prohibition under conditions of market competition still leaves incentives to minimize the costs of pollution abatement unimpaired.

To elaborate on this basic point, let us suppose that a state public utilities commission bars the burning of dirty (high sulfur content) fuel for the generators of electric power companies. The regulated firms will respond to this directive by replacing the dirty fuel with more expensive clean fuel. The resulting increase in the costs of providing electric power will then be the basis of requests for higher consumer charges for electricity, requests that, as we have already observed, can hardly be denied by the state commission. In evaluating the net social outcome of this environmental *solution* by regulation, the following points should be stressed.

Most regulatory commissions in the United States have, in the past, been notoriously sympathetic to the interests of the firms they are supposed to regulate. An innocent observer from another planet might legitimately infer from the behavior of most commissions that they have perceived their major task as guaranteeing an adequate rate of return on the invested capital of regulated public utilities. On the basis of the historical record, most economists would predict that the commissions will, in general, be reluctant to enforce any antipollution measures that the regulated firms strongly oppose and accede all too readily to any requests for rate increases to compensate firms fully for the increased costs of any such measures that cannot be avoided. Such a prediction might, of course, turn out to be incorrect if the new conservation movement is successful in putting countervailing political pressures on the regulatory commissions.

As noted above, the additional costs of any genuine antipollution measures imposed on regulated firms are likely to be passed on in full to consumers without the usual corresponding market pressures on firms to reduce such costs over time by the adoption of advanced technology. In our example, the firm responds to the clean fuel directive of the commission by purchasing cleaner fuel at whatever price obtains on the market and charging its customers a correspondingly higher price for electricity. Unlike an unregulated firm, it has virtually no profit incentive to seek more efficient alternatives as, for example, more efficient combustion technology or emission control devices that would reduce a large proportion of the sulfur emissions. The profit motive fails to operate if the firm has unexploited monopoly power *and* if the commission allows the firm to use the costs of new antipollution regulations to take advantage of this monopoly power.

Under the circumstances assumed in this example, the regulated firm has virtually unlimited market power in its efforts to bid clean fuel away from unregulated competitive users. As it knows it can pass on the higher costs of clean fuel to its customers, it can bid the price of the fuel to whatever level is necessary to force previous users to switch to the relatively cheaper dirty fuel or to do without fuel entirely. In addition, the general inelasticity of demand for energy insures that quantity demanded will not decline sharply. Under these conditions, there can be no presumption of social efficiency in the allocation of different grades of fuel between competitive users by the market system, because as observed above, the high bid price of the regulated firm merely reflects its protected monopoly position and not the relatively high value of the fuel to the customers it serves. The displaced users of clean fuel now will be forced to switch to the consumption of dirty fuel and pollution problems will tend to be transferred from the regulated to the unregulated sector of the economy, with no presumption of any improvement in the total environment. Such ambiguous environmental outcomes of regulation are possible under the circumstances assumed above whenever substitution of polluting substances is technically feasible between the regulated and unregulated sectors of the economy.

One beneficial consequence of the regulation in our example should be added to round out a full analysis. The regulation will, as noted already, shift demand away from dirty fuel towards clean fuel. This demand shift will cause the relative price of clean fuel to rise, which will, in turn, induce a supply response of relatively more clean fuel production. Because it takes time to adjust production techniques and to complete investment in new capital equipment, the supply response could be expected to be of greater magnitude in the long run than in the short run. Thus, the regulation does seem to be of long-run value to society in helping to internalize the external costs of burning dirty fuel. But the real issue is whether or not society could engineer the same relative price changes and supply responses by alternative techniques that do not involve the inefficiencies of the regulatory process.

Regulation by an Environmental Protection Commission

Regulation of polluting activities need not, of course, take place within the existing regulatory commission framework. Indeed, the United States Environmental Protection Agency (EPA), acting through the states, has already entered in an important way into the list of regulatory agencies. The EPA has a great advantage over the present regulatory commissions in that it can provide a broad overview of the interrelatedness of all environmental problems. In contrast, an agency like the FPC can deal only with one narrow aspect of the environment. Furthermore, the EPA has only environmental quality as its responsibility and can devote full attention to it without being diverted by the more immediate public utility concerns of the existing regulatory commissions. We shall not attempt to describe the way the EPA *actually* operates today, or will operate in the future, as we deal with this subject elsewhere in the book. We shall instead imagine the existence of an idealized regulatory agency attempting to deal with the environmental problems confronting any modern, industrialized economy. To distinguish this *hypothetical* regulatory agency from the *actual* EPA, we shall call it the *Environmental Protection Commission,* or EPC. We shall assume that the EPC is given jurisdiction over all private sector activities that may adversely affect environmental quality and is granted far-ranging enforcement powers. As most environmental problems spill over city and state boundaries, the EPC logically would be a federal agency, and state and local EPCs, if needed at all, would play only a minor role in an overall national environmental program. Let us now run through the problems facing the EPC.

ENVIRONMENTAL QUALITY STANDARDS. Presumably the EPC would begin its operations by attempting to determine specific environmental quality goals. Experts from different disciplines could suggest broad guidelines to the EPC in the process of determining appropriate quality standards for different dimensions of water and air quality. If the EPC is dedicated to promoting the public interest, it must attempt to approximate some relevant segments on the social demand or marginal social benefit functions for each aspect of environmental quality (as defined in Chapters 1 and 5). The final decisions on quality standards therefore ideally would reflect the workings of the democratic political process or some more direct appeal to individual tastes—as, for example, carefully designed public opinion surveys.

IMPOSITION OF CONTROLS. Once the EPC has determined more or less appropriate quality standards for any environmental medium, it must then attempt to promulgate a set of regulatory controls consistent with these standards. Suppose that the level of a pollutant, P, in the air in a given area exceeds the quality standard determined for that area by an amount X. The task of the EPC would be to reduce the level of P by X units by imposing quantitative controls on the amount of permissible P emissions by each current emitter of P. It should be evident, first, that any initial set of regulatory controls will be consistent with the quality standards for P only with great luck. The relationship between current emission flows of any pollutant and the equilibrium level of that pollutant in the environment will have to be discovered by a trial-and-error process in most cases, with the EPC jiggling its regulations up and down incrementally as it searches for achievement of the desired quality goals. Second, the EPC will have to be aware of all relevant ecological interrelationships if its several environmental quality standards are to be achieved simultaneously. Regulatory controls over one pollutant emitted into one environmental medium may result in firms and households switching to other activities that cause some other pollutant to be emitted into the same, or into some other, medium. The EPC's regulations must, therefore, be comprehensive and consistent with simultaneous control over all environmental media.

THE PROBLEM OF ALLOCATION. Assuming that the EPC could deal with both of the above complexities, it must still determine how to *allocate* the necessary total reduction in P among the different demanders for air disposal rights for P in the target area. The crux of the regulatory problem is that no obvious, generally equitable, *and* efficient solution to this allocation problem can be specified.

One possible regulatory allocation of the air disposal rights for P is first to determine how much P each firm and household emits before controls are initiated and then to force each polluter to make the same percentage reduction in emission of P. Economists can provide some fundamental objections to any such scheme. Although an equal percentage reduction in pollution emissions for all is appealing superficially on equity grounds, it is not economically efficient. Some firms and households will find it extremely expensive and even impossible financially to comply with the new regulations, but other firms and households will be able to comply at much smaller expense. As the reader should recall from Chapter 2 of this book, such differentials in the marginal costs of producing any good—less pollution, in this instance—imply social inefficiency in its production. Until marginal costs are equalized for all firms, society could produce the same amount of the good at less total cost by shifting production from high-cost firms to low-cost firms.[3] Because not all producers of reductions in emission of P will be equally efficient, it follows that the equal marginal cost principle will not, in general, be met under uniform reductions in emission levels.[4] The EPC could, of course, attempt to depart from uniform reductions in the name of efficiency, but to do so would invite lawsuits and other manifestations of deep unrest about the alleged inequity of differential standards. In addition, it could only estimate roughly the differences in costs for all regulated firms and households, unless it invested substantial sums in gathering the necessary data.

Once any firm or household has complied with EPC regulations, it has little economic incentive to invest in research and development for the purpose of reducing the cost of the productive input of air disposal rights for P. Before the regulations are imposed, any firm regards the air disposal rights for P as a free input service. After the regulations go into effect, the air disposal rights remain a free input service up to the regulated level imposed on the firm and then become, in effect, an unac-

[3] Under the unlikely condition that it is technologically and economically feasible to transport P from one site to another, a black market may result from the imposition of uniform regulatory controls. Firms that find it relatively inexpensive to dispose of P within the regulation may discover that other firms and households are willing to pay it substantial sums to dispose of their P, with mutual gains available to both parties through voluntary agreements.

[4] The relation of a regulation policy and effluent charges in terms of efficiency implications will be treated in more detail in Chapter 10.

ceptably expensive input service beyond that level, assuming strict enforcement. Unlike normal input services such as labor or capital services, air disposal rights do not have an explicit price attached to their use and so do not enter into the firm's cost calculations. Thus, the profit incentive for technological advance in economizing on the use of this input will not exist as it does for other, normal input services. In contrast to the static efficiency considerations discussed previously, this latter problem is dynamic in that its effects extend into the future and are of fundamental importance in the process of economic growth and in the secular improvement of environmental quality.

The EPC might attempt to deal with this problem, however, by providing a *time schedule* of regulations. Such a time schedule would set increasingly more stringent standards over a period of time; say, 1,000 units of effluent A permitted for a firm in 1974; 970 units, in 1975; 940 units, in 1976; and so forth. Variable standards of this kind are analogous to a pricing scheme for factors of production that includes a built-in rate of inflation as, for example, a typical multiyear management-union labor contract. Standards that are known to become tougher over time would clearly encourage firms to invest in techniques to reduce pollution. Unfortunately, variable standards involve more difficult problems of administration than do fixed standards. How much should standards be tightened over time with respect to pollutant A relative to a completely different pollutant B? If economic efficiency considerations call for faster tightening of standards with respect to A than with respect to B, could the EPC act accordingly without inviting a rash of lawsuits? Such problems might plague the EPC if it once departs from completely fixed standards.

ENFORCEMENT. Any allocation scheme determined by the EPC must be enforced if the regulations are to have their desired effect in enhancing environmental quality. At best, enforcement will be a difficult and expensive process. Thousands of major polluters may exist even in a small area and the emissions of each one may have to be monitored continually. A schedule of penalties for violations must be established and the EPC must be prepared with a battery of lawyers to meet appeals of its decisions in the courts. In addition, the EPC will not only have to identify and regulate existing emitters of P but will also have to deal with the complex dynamic problem of potential *new* polluters. Every year, new firms and households may request the right to emit P. Should the EPC afford new firms equal treatment with existing firms and households or should it force them to adopt the latest and best techniques for minimizing pollution? In a growing economy, provision for new polluters in a regulation scheme implies rising levels of pollution unless regulatory controls become progressively more stringent on existing firms. Every time regulatory standards are revised, the issue of interfirm equity arises again. In addition, the EPC will surely be the object of enormous political pressures, as regulated firms seek special treatment. Historical experience with regulatory agencies suggests strongly that the EPC may be heavily influenced by the firms that have the largest stake in the establishment and enforcement of pollution standards.

To summarize this discussion, pollution control through a regulatory agency like the EPC is not a promising prospect for several reasons. Detailed control of private activities through regulatory commissions is not an activity that governments in the United States have performed satisfactorily in the past, and there are no solid grounds for believing that the EPC will perform any better in the long run once its initial reforming impulse runs its natural course. Furthermore, as we have argued, even the best conceivable regulatory commission could not control pollution levels both equitably and efficiently.

B. PROHIBITION

The economic case against prohibition as an environmental policy instrument has already been made implicitly in the elementary benefit-cost analysis presented in Chapter 1. A ban on polluting activity may or may not be preferable to a continuation of some existing level of pollution, but, in general, society need not be forced to choose one extreme alternative or the other. Instead, society, in effect, can trade off some potential gains in environmental quality in return for more than compensating gains in the production and consumption of goods and services.

Figure 9–1 illustrates the choices open to any society in determining environmental policy. As in Figure 1–1, the MSB and MSC schedules are drawn in reference to the units of pollution abatement for some hypothetical pollutant. The schedules represent the marginal social benefits and marginal social costs, respectively, associated with each level of pollution abatement and the corresponding level of environmental quality. As demonstrated in Chapter 1, OA is the optimal level of *output* of pollution abatement within the framework of benefit-cost analysis. For all the reasons given in Chapter 1, the exact level OA is extremely difficult for the government to determine, but this complexity is not, in general, a valid argument for a ban on all polluting activity. Rigidly enforced prohibitions may move society along the horizontal axis as far as OB; that is, to absolute purity, which people do not value and may not even be able to perceive. As drawn in Figure 9–1, the marginal social cost of achieving perfect purity may be extremely large, as it could

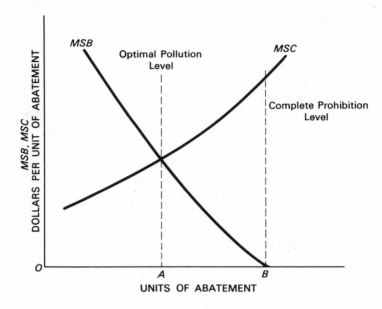

FIGURE 9–1. Analysis of Prohibition.

involve the complete shutdown of some industrial firms or public utili-ties. Economists observe, moreover, that the costs of achieving environ-mental quality will, in general, be widely shared throughout the whole society. Despite the claims of some popular journalists, the burden of the costs of any prohibitions on polluters will not be limited to just a few firms or individuals.

Thus the economist's benefit-cost analysis provides a strong argu-ment against prohibition as a general environmental policy instrument. Nonsystematic, piecemeal prohibitions are open to much the same ob-jections as regulation, on the grounds of the difficulty and inefficiency of effective enforcement. In general, alternative policy measures can reduce pollution levels to an acceptable degree and do it more efficiently than prohibition.

However strong the general efficiency case against prohibition, it may still be the best of several less than ideal alternatives available to society in specific circumstances. First, alternative environmental policy measures, such as regulation and effluent charges, must rely on the monitoring and measurement of emission flows. In contrast, prohibi-tion requires only the determination of *on or off* for potential polluters. It is at least conceivable that the administrative costs of measuring effluent flows to the necessary degree of precision may be too high relative to the environmental benefits derived from the abatement of pollution levels. If such is the case, society will then have to face the all or nothing choice between inaction and complete prohibition. The reader should be aware, however, that prohibitions do not enforce themselves. If the potential gains to violators of pollution bans are sufficiently high, the laws will not stop polluters. Extremely high statutory penalties for violations are not necessarily a sufficient deterrent, for as the history of the prohibition of marijuana in the United States has recently demonstrated, judges, juries, and the police are most reluctant to act against wrongdoers if penalties appear to be out of proportion relative to the social consensus about the seriousness of the offense.

Second, prohibition could possibly be justified in special circumstances on equity grounds. Suppose, for example, that the optimal use of some environmental resource calls for a very high price to ration its use among only a few consumers. Assume that naturalists determine that only one hundred visitors a year can visit a wilderness area without inflicting irreparable damage to its fragile ecology. The price system could be used to ration entry to the appropriate number by setting the entry fee high enough to exclude all but the very wealthiest nature lovers. Justice in such a circumstance is not necessarily best served by reliance on the price system, however, even if intensity of desire to visit the wilderness area is accepted as the criterion of equity. Willingness to pay a high entry fee reflects *both* intensity of desire to enter the wilderness area and the distribution of wealth. If society judges that wealth should not, in fairness, count in the allocation of some scarce resource, it must opt for an alternative rationing device in preference to a price system. In this specific example, entry into the wilderness area could perhaps be made a prize, to be awarded by a carefully selected panel of distinguished citizens for meritorious social service in conservation. Otherwise, entry would be prohibited. In general, however, such nonprice allocative mechanisms are cumbersome, inefficient, and prone to fall under political influence leading to discriminatory practices perhaps more inequitable than the workings of a price system.

Finally, prohibitions make sense under extreme circumstances when potential environmental damage is so large that the marginal reasoning underlying benefit-cost analysis cannot legitimately be applied. If emission of some pollutant threatens widespread loss of life or catastrophic disruption of ecological systems, marginal tradeoffs between environmental quality and consumption of other goods and services are not meaningful. Under some circumstances, the emission of certain pollutants threaten the entire ecological balance supporting human life. At the present state of knowledge, *uncertainty* about the complex long-run effects of different concentrations of such pollutants makes nonsense of any attempts to determine an optimal balance between the marginal benefits and costs of different hypothetical levels of pollution. Complete prohibition (at least in populated areas), strictly enforced, is the only rational social policy.

The reader should be cautioned, however, that arguments for prohibition based on this reasoning can be pushed to ridiculous extremes. Almost every industrial process involves the emission of substances whose long-run effects are not yet fully understood and that may conceivably be a threat to human health and to present and future ecosystems. To live is to take risks, and it is fatuous to argue that man should attempt to purify his environment at all costs just because our knowledge is incomplete. The cost of achieving complete environmental purity and eliminating uncertainty about all long-run consequences of pollution is the abandonment of our industrial civilization. The alternative is to limit prohibitions to those cases in which serious danger is imminent and simultaneously to pursue research on the long-run effects of various pollutants and to encourage the development of the technology required to deal with environmental problems.

Ban the Automobile?

The automobile appears to be a most important focus of the emerging political struggle between the new conservationists and their opponents. On the one hand, the automobile is a major villain of the scenario of environmental degradation portrayed by the conservationist movement. More than half of all the air pollution in the United States can be traced to the emissions of the automobile's exhaust system. Urban sprawl, urban blight, and the general lack of amenity in our cities are also partly blamed on the automobile and the highway networks that must be built to serve it. As a final aesthetic insult, scrapped automobiles pile up as unsightly, rusting junk to ruin the beauty of the countryside. On the other hand, the automobile is viewed traditionally as the hallmark of our industrial civilization. The automobile, according to the arguments of the traditionalists, has significantly enhanced the quality of life of the average American by making possible unprecedented mass mobility in a cheap and convenient form. As evidence, they cite the many surveys of Americans that point to the contribution of ownership of an automobile to the conception of the good life, and to similar surveys of foreigners that find widespread envy of the mass ownership of the automobile in this country. The importance of the automobile as a consumption good is matched by its position in our industrial structure. The automobile industry has become one of the largest and most technically progressive industries in the United States. Many other large industries, such as rubber and steel, are heavily dependent on it, and the production of the automobile, directly or indirectly, provides employment for millions of workers.

The battle lines are clearly drawn, and the economist is forced to contribute what little he can to the dispute. The first observation any economist would make on this issue is that an immediate ban on automobiles would involve immense, unacceptable costs to society. No economy can adjust to the tremendous disruption that would ensue from the shutting down of a large segment of its total industry. Whatever policy measures must be undertaken with respect to the automobile for environmental reasons should be implemented gradually if economic chaos is to be avoided, and prohibitions are poor policy instruments for the purpose of effecting gradual changes.

Supporters of a ban on automobiles need to make their ultimate objectives clear. If the environmental harm associated with automobiles is only air pollution, then environmental policy should be concerned directly with the quality of the air. Chapter 7 discussed the federal emission standards mandated by the Clean Air Act. In addition, some states are implementing emissions tests to insure the continued effectiveness of these controls. Furthermore, there is extensive and promising research to develop alternative auto engine designs relatively free of emissions problems.

The case for banning the automobile would seem to rest, then, on the issue of congestion, and more generally, the quality of life in urban areas. The use of acceptable, low-pollution engines in automobiles in nonurban areas does not involve these problems. Any proposed ban on the automobile on these grounds should be confined to specific urban areas only. (Although even in nonurban areas, a good argument can be made that the private costs of using an automobile often fall short of total social costs, including congestion, land use, and aesthetic costs.) The argument for such partial bans rests on the technical circumstance that, as yet, we have no feasible mechanism available for levying a system of charges on the use of automobiles on particular streets at particular times. If society determines that the quality of life in a given area suffers because of the intrusion of the automobile, it therefore faces the all or nothing alternatives, posited in the previous section, of no action or complete prohibition.

Limited experiments, banning the use of automobiles on certain streets for restricted time periods, have been attempted with uncertain success in Manhattan. Such laws have been extremely popular with some people but have run into vociferous objections from some merchants and residents in the affected areas and from the American Automobile Association. Benefits and costs of such partial laws are difficult even to approximate, and they are distributed very unevenly throughout the general population. Thus, a satisfactory economic evaluation of these experiments does not appear feasible at this time. At present, there seems to be little presumption that longer-run prohibitions of the automobile can be sustained, even in Manhattan, probably the most feasible site in this country for such a policy because of its small area and highly developed system of public transportation. But this conclusion holds only in the context of accepting the present urban transportation system as given, which means poor available substitutes for automobiles and a system of commerce based on the existing motor vehicle-dominated transportation mix. We shall discuss further the problem of urban congestion and the role of transportation systems in determining the amenity of urban life in Chapter 13.

C. THE ECONOMICS OF ZONING

Zoning is the most important of the various governmental controls exercised over the use of land in the United States. Traditionally, the power to zone land—that is, to classify sites according to permissible uses and to *prohibit* all other uses—has been delegated by the states to local governments. The federal government has extensive land holdings of its own but has traditionally had little influence over private land use. In addition to zoning ordinances, other governmental regulations, such as subdivision controls, sewer and water permits, and the use of the power of eminent domain (the acquisition of privately owned land) are employed to exercise social control over the workings of the private market in the development of land and its allocation among alternative uses. For our purposes here, however, we shall lump these various measures used in social planning for the use of land under the general rubric of *zoning*.

The Economic Rationale for Zoning

For an economist, zoning can be justified, in principle, as a necessary means of internalizing for a community the potential external costs that might follow from unregulated private development of land. In the absence of zoning, each site would tend to be devoted to a use that maximized the profit of the individual owner, but the aggregate of such individual maximizing behavior would not result in the most efficient use of all sites because of the importance of external costs in land development. For example, if land in a pleasant residential neighborhood were not zoned strictly for residential use, the owner of a slaughterhouse might find it profitable to move his plant into the area or at least threaten to do so and then allow himself to be dissuaded by a sufficiently large bribe paid by the threatened homeowners. In general, zoning is an essential component of an overall social planning process that attempts to take into account the proper balance between amenity and economic development. Ideally, the zoning process would allocate large tracts of land among well-coordinated residential, industrial, commercial, and recreational uses and then permit the private market system to allocate individual sites *within* each of the zoned tracts. Thus, proper social planning would prevent the occurrence of the most serious external costs of unplanned development but would allow the market mechanism scope for achieving allocational efficiency within the regulated framework.

Problems of Zoning

Unfortunately, zoning does not always work well in practice to foster the amenity of urban life while promoting orderly economic development. First, zoning inherently involves some degree of allocational inefficiency in the absence of costless perfect information. In the process of avoiding external costs of land development, zoning boards necessarily bar socially advantageous uses of land as well. To illustrate this point, suppose that, in the absence of zoning, a retail store could profitably locate in a residential neighborhood even after paying full compensation for all external costs it imposes on homeowners in the area. (Of course, no compensation for externalities would be paid, which means that the private gains to the firm from locating in the area would exceed net social gains by the amount of the uncompensated external costs.) Zoning prevents such socially profitable uses of land from taking place and, therefore, inevitably involves some efficiency losses as well as efficiency gains. As the example above also indicates, it clearly involves significant *distributional* considerations as well; zoning, in the hypothetical case outlined above, yields welfare gains to the owners of homes in the area but imposes large opportunity losses on the retail merchant.

Local Politics and Zoning Policy

Probably because of the importance of its distributional effects, zoning in this country has been an intensely *political* subject at local levels of government. Considerations of economic efficiency—especially with respect to environmental quality—are too often distinctly subordinate to the issue of the distribution of potential gains and losses among competing groups and individuals. The typical zoning board in urbanized areas is heavily influenced by the dominant political forces within its jurisdiction in making decisions concerning zoning ordinances. Business and real estate interests, in particular, can threaten any one community with loss of valuable taxable properties if they move to another community with less restrictive zoning regulations. They can play one community off against another because of the heavy fiscal dependence of local governments on industrial and commercial properties and, as a result, can often succeed in obtaining variances from any existing ordinance that prohibits the desired development of some site.

The discussion, thus far, has been limited to the effects of zoning within a single, small community, but the more important problem is the net social outcome of zoning at the community level. Within a large metropolitan area, zoning by each of a great number of independent communities will not, in general, promote environmental quality. Zoning, at best, internalizes the external costs of land development within a given jurisdiction and any such costs spilling over from one area into another tend to be ignored. Zoning, at the local government level, tends to result in small clusters of industrial and commercial property, whereas optimal land use from society's standpoint may call for more centralization of such properties across jurisdictional lines. Similarly, each community is likely to have its own small park and recreational areas whereas, without political fragmentation, economies of scale considerations might make large parks and playgrounds socially preferable. State and national parks partly substitute for the lack of large-scale recreational areas in some communities. Unfortunately, the distribution of these facilities is unsatisfactory. Most national parks, in particular, are remote from the average urban dweller in the East and Midwest. In general, the fragmented structure of local government results in uncoordinated planning concerning social environmental quality. The apparent solution to this problem is for the states to reallocate zoning power from local communities to area-wide planning agencies.

Centralization of zoning power is a most unlikely political development in the short run, however, because the distributional aspects of zoning dominate the efficiency aspects. Relatively well-off communities use the zoning power as an effective but apparently impersonal and non-discriminatory mechanism for excluding the poor. The common device employed by wealthy suburban communities in urban areas is minimum acreage requirements for construction of new single-family houses and a prohibition on the construction of multifamily dwellings. In recent years, these restrictive practices have sometimes been defended on "environmental" grounds. Zoning ordinances have contributed to the isolation of the poor in the older, urban core areas and have been instrumental in prohibiting the movement of racial minorities in suburban communities. Civil rights organizations have increasingly attacked extreme zoning ordinances in the courts, but the distribution of political power suggests that current practices will be hard to change.

D. SUMMARY AND CONCLUSIONS

This is the first of three chapters on the public policy aspects of environmental economics. The chapter begins by introducing and defining several alternative strategies available to the government for internalizing the various externalities that produce environmental problems. These alternatives include regulation and prohibition, fiscal measures, including various kinds of taxes and subsidies, and government production of environmental services. These strategies pose clear alternatives for the main thrust of government environmental policy.

Regulation may be considered in two contexts. First, it is possible to conceive of extending the activities of existing federal and state regulatory commissions, especially with respect to the environmental problems associated with public utilities generating electric power. The benefits available from extension of traditional regulatory techniques in this area seem to be inadequate to balance the costs. This conclusion rests, in part, on economic efficiency arguments and, in part, on the observed behavior of the various regulatory agencies in the past—behavior that is heavily influenced by political traditions that are most difficult to modify.

Regulation may also be considered in the more promising context of a hypothetical regulatory agency, the *Environmental Protection Commission* or EPC, that has extensive powers to deal specifically and directly with all environmental problems. Our analysis of the EPC leads again to pessimistic conclusions. Economic efficiency, equity, and administrative problems make the regulatory solutions, even under an EPC, an unattractive environmental policy approach to most problems.

Outright legislative prohibitions on polluting activity are another environmental policy alternative. A benefit-cost analysis of the prohibition strategy demonstrates that it is, in general, economically inefficient, in that it ignores possible tradeoffs between different levels of environmental quality and other valued goods and services. On the other hand, prohibition makes sense either if administrative problems do not permit the adoption of other policy alternatives or under conditions in which benefits and costs are not continuous and tradeoffs are not meaningful. The latter situation would appear to be pertinent, for example, under circumstances of extreme uncertainty about the effects of growing concentrations of some pollutants on human health.

A possible ban on automobiles is considered as a special case of the general policy of prohibition and compared with alternative policies. Such a prohibition appears to make economic sense within the framework of the existing transportation system only in a few highly atypical situations.

The economics of zoning and planning of land use is then examined as another special case of both prohibition and regulation. Our discussion centers on how zoning actually works in the United States today as a policy for fostering urban amenity. The discussion of zoning concludes that it produces disappointingly little environmental benefit largely because its administration at local levels of government is preoccupied with the distribution of income and wealth.

QUESTIONS FOR DISCUSSION

1. Some writers have suggested that regulations and prohibitions would place the subject of environmental quality outside the scope of petty economic considerations. Do you agree or disagree, and why?

2. Suppose that it was already agreed to lower emission levels of a certain pollutant in a given area by a total of 10 percent. If you were an economic consultant to the responsible regulatory commission, what guidelines would you give the commissioners to help them in allocating the total emission reduction among all different firms and households?

3. "The same economic logic that favors effluent charges over prohibitions in the case of pollution should also favor excise taxes on heroin over the present prohibitory policy." Do you agree or disagree, and why?

4. The Water Pollution Control Act of 1972 states that all water pollutant discharges will be controlled "by the best available technology" by 1985. What are the equity and efficiency implications of this statement? Would you anticipate any difficulties in defining and enforcing this requirement? Why?

5. Some wealthy communities in rural New Jersey have recently established one-acre or even two-acre minimum lot sizes for new single-family houses and have prohibited the construction of multifamily dwelling units. One rationale for such zoning practices is to preserve the amenity of the areas and to prevent ecological disruption. Why do you think these zoning regulations have been challenged in the courts? Do you favor such regulations?

SELECTED REFERENCES

DAVIS, OTTO A., "Economic Elements in Municipal Zoning Decisions," *Land Economics,* XXXIX, No. 4 (November, 1963). An economic analysis of zoning.

Energy Policy Staff, Office of Science and Technology, *Electric Power and the Environment*, Washington, D.C.: Government Printing Office, 1970. A discussion of the environmental problems associated with electrical power generation.

GOLDMAN, M. I., "Pollution: The Mess Around Us," in *Ecology and Economics: Controlling Pollution in the 70s*, ed. M. I. Goldman. Englewood Cliffs, N.J.: Prentice-Hall Inc., 1972. An introductory survey of environmental policy alternatives.

MISHAN, E. J., *Technology and Growth, The Price We Pay*. New York: Praeger Publishers, 1969. A lively and skillful discussion of zoning policy applications to environmental problems.

RUFF, LARRY, "The Economic Common Sense of Pollution," *Public Interest*, No. 19 (Spring, 1970). Another introductory survey of environmental policy alternatives from a somewhat different point of view than the Goldman treatment.

WILCOX, CLAIR, *Public Policies Toward Business*, (3rd Ed.). Homewood, Ill.: Irwin, 1966. An introduction to the economics of the existing regulatory commissions.

Other relevant references are given at the end of Chapter 10.

Chapter 10

Taxes, Subsidies, and Effluent Charges

This chapter continues our discussion of the alternative broad policy instruments available to a government attempting to improve or protect environmental quality. The previous chapter presented the strategy of regulation and prohibition, which makes use of the fiat authority of government to restrict private property rights pertaining to the use of water, air, and other environmental resources. This chapter covers the alternative strategy of using various taxes and subsidies designed to encourage private economic behavior conducive to improved environmental quality. The ultimate objective of these broad policy strategies is exactly the same, and the real issue is which of the two is a more effective means to the common end. The choice between them involves many complex considerations: their relative allocational efficiency, as measured by the ratio of total social benefits to total social costs; the differential demands they make on hard-to-obtain technical information; the differences in enforcement problems associated with each; and their relative political acceptability. Economists can make a valuable contribution to resolving at least the first of these issues.

Government tax, subsidy, and expenditure policies play a number of important roles in influencing economic activity. On the macro level, they are the stabilization weapons of fiscal policies that attempt to move the economy to a full-employment level of output. Taxes, subsidies (transfer payments), and expenditures providing free collective services are also major social instruments for redistributing income. These same fiscal instruments allocate resources between the public and private sectors of the economy. Finally, and most important for our present purposes, taxes and subsidies can be used to reallocate resources *within* the private sector. Specifically, these fiscal weapons can internalize the externalities underlying environmental problems and thus cause changes in both consumer and firm behavior to take full account of the total social costs and benefits of their activities. In this way, the government can redirect private sector behavior to produce beneficial effects on the quality of the environment.

This chapter analyzes aspects of the fiscal approach to environmental policy. Section A discusses the theoretical foundations of tax and subsidy policy, and contrasts this policy with the regulation and prohibition alternative. It also demonstrates the symmetry between taxes and subsidies. We define effluent charges to be the particular form of tax policy most directly applicable to environmental problems, and contrast the incentive and income distribution effects of effluent charges and subsidies. Section B discusses some of the institutional obstacles to the implementation of systems of effluent charges in the United States. It goes on to chronicle examples of domestic and foreign experience with various fiscal incentives to improve environmental quality. Section C outlines the desirable characteristics of a comprehensive effluent charge system and Section D provides a brief summary of the chapter.

A. EFFICIENCY ASPECTS OF TAX AND SUBSIDY POLICIES

Review

Chapter 4 discussed the use of an output tax to eliminate the difference between the marginal social cost and marginal private cost schedules of a firm responsible for an external diseconomy. The tax, when correctly set, internalized the full external costs of production to the firm. This induced the firm to decrease output, which led, in turn, to a cleaner stream, and also implied increased production of other goods. Moreover, this adjustment was made in response to straightforward economic in-

centives and did not require extensive government supervision or enforcement.

We can conceive of this rudimentary example of the use of tax
policy to correct for environmental externalities as a benefit-cost problem.
Initially, the price of textiles, the particular good in our example, is
below the full marginal costs of production, that is, the costs inclusive
of the externalities associated with textile production. Equivalently, the
benefit of textile consumption, as given in the price willingly paid by
consumers, is less than the marginal social costs of textile production.
This imbalance between benefits and costs indicates an oversupply of
textiles. Imposition of the output tax forces the firm to consider the full
marginal costs of production and, when extended to an industry level,
the output tax on all textile firms reduces total quantity supplied and
increases price.

Chapter 4 further demonstrated that the quantity adjustment results
in a *reallocation* of resources from textile production to the production of
all other goods, thereby restoring the maximum social welfare result of a
private market system. By a symmetrical analysis, we recall that in
situations involving an external economy, proper subsidy policies will
reallocate resources in favor of that activity, and also restore the marginal benefit-cost equality condition.

Effluent Charges as a Special Case of Tax Policy

In general, properly designed tax and subsidy schemes are viable
methods of influencing resource allocation and environmental quality.
They rely on creating economic incentives that, in conjunction with
profit motives, alter economic activity. The potential targets of taxes as
a general fiscal weapon are varied and could include such items as
specific products, factors of production, incomes, or effluents. Any specific
tax acts as an economic penalty and a deterrent not only to the taxed
activity but to related ones as well.

Within this general category of tax weapons, effluent charges are
the particular form of taxation having the most direct application to the
problems of environmental quality. A per unit tax on effluent discharges
removes the zero price tag associated with the use of air and water resources for waste disposal purposes, and thereby narrows the unrestricted
property rights implicit in the free use of the environmental media. With
a policy of effluent charges, the government formally establishes its
property rights to air and water resources and determines the price that
must be paid for their use. Firms and individuals are thereby forced to
consider effluent charges as another cost of doing business (that is, they

must lease the rights granting them use of the waste disposal media).
An effluent charge, therefore, creates an incentive for firms to evaluate
the alternative costs associated with avoiding the tax. Profit motives
operate to induce the waste discharger eventually to adopt a minimum
cost solution. This solution may involve a combination of waste treatment, output reduction, and payment of the effluent charge.

Figure 10–1 depicts the familiar example of the effluent charge

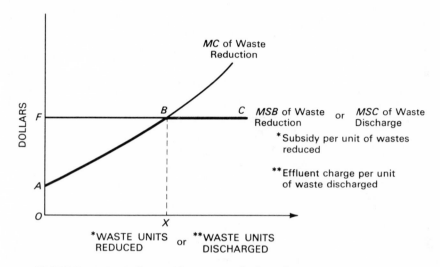

FIGURE 10–1.   Effluent Charge or Subsidy Policy.

system presented in Chapter 4. The firm's marginal cost schedule of
avoiding the discharge of wastes into the environment reflects the least
cost combination of presently available methods. With an effluent charge
of *OF* dollars per unit of waste discharged, the firm takes action to not
discharge its first *OX* waste units, saving *AFB* dollars relative to paying
the effluent charge for discharging this amount of wastes. To the right of
point *B*, the firm will pay the effluent charge and discharge wastes rather
than incur the higher costs of not discharging. Thus, the firm acts along
the heavily shaded line *ABC*, taking internal actions to avoid waste
discharges from *A* to *B* (that is, the first *OX* waste units) and if the
waste load exceeds *OX* units, electing to pay the *OF* per unit effluent
charge on the remainder. Changes in waste treatment technology, factor
costs, and prices of final output will shift the marginal cost curve and
the interested reader can trace through these effects on the analysis.

Subsidies Compared to Effluent Charges

In Chapter 4, we noted that an offer by the party (or parties) affected by the externality of OF dollars per unit of waste *not* discharged would achieve the identical result. We argued, however, that real world conditions favored the effluent charge system over an attempt to create a private market for avoidance of pollutants.[1] Nevertheless, the basic approach of an offer not to discharge pollutants need not be confined to a private market correction for externalities. Equivalently, the government could offer a *subsidy* of OF dollars per unit of waste not discharged. This policy would be symmetrical to the effluent charge policy in terms of waste reduction. The firm would reduce wastes up to OX units because it is profitable to do so, earning a net profit of AFB dollars on the OX units of wastes treated.

However, a fundamental difference in economic incentives exists between the subsidy and the effluent charge methods. In the case of an effluent charge, the firm reacts to the potential economic penalty of a tax per unit of waste discharged into the environment. The firm takes action to minimize the net revenue effect of this tax by avoiding waste discharges if it can do so for less than the OF dollars per unit and paying the tax for all other waste units. An ultimate effect of the effluent charge is to increase the overall costs of operation and thereby reduce the quantity of final output offered at each price. If the effluent charge is applied throughout the industry, the final result is to increase the market price of its product and to reduce the quantity sold. Thus, the improvement in environmental quality is paid for by the consumer of the product via higher prices and by the society, in general, through a decrease in output.

On the other hand, a government offer of a subsidy of OF dollars acts as a *bribe not to discharge wastes*. The subsidy is an opportunity cost in terms of foregone revenue and also has the effect of internalizing the social costs of waste discharges. A subsidy scheme implies a markedly different structure of property rights in the air and water media from that of an effluent charge policy. With a subsidy offer, the property rights of discharging wastes into the environment implicitly accrue to the polluter. The government, in effect, offers a payment to the polluter not to exercise this right. Therefore, the polluter treats waste reduction as another potentially *marketable* good (that is, the selling of rights to discharge waste) and attempts to maximize profits when given the government offer. Normal profit incentives will operate as in any other

---

[1] These reasons involved the unwieldy and costly nature of multiple contractual arrangements when the incidence of the externality was widespread and uneven. The *free rider* problem, discussed in Chapter 5, is also a considerable deterrent to the feasibility of this approach.

market, and the more efficient the firm is in its waste reduction, the greater the profit opportunities. We can conceive of the firm selling its pollutant rights for the first OX units in Figure 10–1 at $\$OF$ per unit and not discharging these wastes untreated into the environment. Beyond X units of wastes, the firm will utilize its implicit rights to discharge wastes rather than sell them because the selling price is less than the per unit costs of treatment.

One objection to a subsidy policy such as the one outlined above is that it creates incentives to generate wastes if the costs of reducing or treating wastes are less than the per unit waste subsidy. Some firms may go into the *waste-making business* in response to the perfectly elastic demand schedule for treated waste created by the government's offer of a flat per unit subsidy.[2] The distinct possibility of this type of behavior is an obviously unwanted perversion of the original intention of the subsidy policy and a strong argument against its implementation. However, waiving this objection to a subsidy policy, a comparison of a government effluent charge policy with a policy of a subsidy per waste unit avoided yields several conclusions. First, both methods provide the same amount of waste treatment, ignoring the possibility of blackmail behavior, discussed above. Second, the *distributional* differences between the two methods are profound. The effluent charge method directly increases the costs of polluters, and this increase in costs is passed on throughout the industry in the form of higher prices and lower quantities sold and consumed. In the subsidy scheme, government expenditures to purchase the implicitly owned pollution rights of the waste discharger must be offset by increased taxes and/or reduced government purchases in other areas. The incidence of the costs of obtaining the same level of waste treatment (OX units) is thus likely to be more diffuse throughout the economy with a subsidy policy than with effluent charges. Finally, with an effluent charge policy, the government formally establishes its ownership of the property rights in the environmental media, but a subsidy scheme implicitly creates producers' property rights to use the media for waste disposal.

Imperfect Knowledge, Fiscal Incentives, and Regulation

Thus far, we have tacitly assumed that the informational problems associated with either environmental policy are of manageable proportions. This assumption is highly unrealistic, particularly with respect to ascertaining the marginal benefit curve of waste reduction. The informational

---

[2] The reader may recognize some striking analogies of similar perverse effects of certain government agricultural subsidy policies.

requirements necessary to determine such benefit functions are exceedingly complex in the situation of externalities that affect large numbers of firms and individuals. The considerable environmental research problems discussed in Part 3 provide some perspective on the difficulties of isolating and quantifying the full social costs of various pollutants. Moreover, portrayal of a constant benefit function in Figure 10–1 is also unrealistic and it is more likely that such a function would exhibit a downward slope, indicating decreasing damages as the level of waste treatment rises.[3] The informational difficulties associated with establishing this curve have important implications for the efficiency effects of a tax or subsidy policy.

   Suppose, for example, in Figure 10–2, that the downward sloping

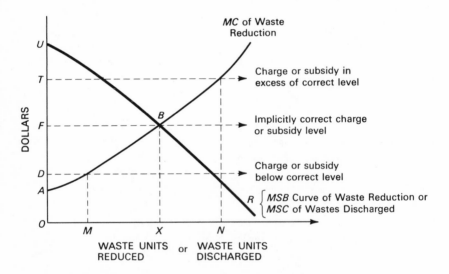

FIGURE 10–2.   Realistic Marginal Benefit Curve.

line UR is the *true* benefit function per unit of treated waste. However, because of research difficulties stemming from the complex nature of the effects of this particular pollutant, the effluent charge (or waste reduction subsidy) is set lower at OD dollars than the implicitly correct value of OF dollars. The result, under either policy, will not be socially optimal, that is, *less* than OX units of wastes are treated (OM units). Alternatively, if the charge (or subsidy) is set in excess of the

---

[3] The argument here is that the demand curve for environmental quality (waste reduction) has, like other demand relationships, an inverse relation between price and quantity.

true marginal benefit function (for example, at OT dollars) then too much waste reduction will occur (ON units). In general, the difficulty of obtaining the proper marginal benefit function raises the distinct possibility of either of these above situations. In the case of *full* information about the marginal benefit and cost functions, this problem would not arise and the efficient setting of the OF tax on each unit of waste discharged or as a subsidy per unit of waste *not* discharged could be made.

In fact, with an assumption of full knowledge of the marginal benefit and cost functions, either a tax or subsidy scheme would be identical in allocational effects to a policy of regulation. Knowing the benefits of avoiding wastes and the costs of waste reduction, the government could readily set OX units as the waste treatment quota for the firm represented in Figures 10–1 and 10–2. The firm, facing a legally enforceable requirement to treat OX units of wastes, incurs the same cost as in the effluent charge or subsidy method ($OABX$). The effects on final output price and quantity will also be identical to that of the effluent charge scheme. A regulation policy such as this formally appropriates for the government the waste disposal rights inherent in the first OX units of wastes. Thus, with perfect knowledge, regulation becomes an attractive policy and can achieve the identical efficiency results of a correctly set subsidy or effluent charge.

To be realistic, accurate knowledge of the relevant benefit and cost functions is unlikely. In addition, once we move away from the case of a single firm and recognize that numerous pollution sources are likely to exist, then a regulation scheme rapidly becomes unwieldy. Chapter 9 discussed the general efficiency aspects of regulations but we can now explore these in more detail as they relate to policies of effluent charges and subsidies. Let us take, for example, a simple case of only two firms, each emitting the same effluent and each having differing waste reduction costs. This situation is portrayed in Figure 10–3, where the horizontal axes measure an identical treatment level for identical types of wastes for each firm. Suppose, for simplicity, that these are the only two firms located in this river basin and that the local government has instituted a regulation policy which sets a target of a waste reduction of X lbs. of BOD equivalent for the river.

The first problem that arises is how the total amount of waste reduction should be allocated between the two firms. Equity criteria might suggest that each firm share the targeted reduction equally and thus each firm would be required to reduce wastes by $\frac{1}{2}(X)$. This equal reduction quota is what J. H. Dales calls an *across-the-board policy*, implying each and every waste source must reduce wastes by the same amount (or same percent) regardless of any underlying cost differentials. In Figure 10–3, an across-the-board policy would mean an equal quota

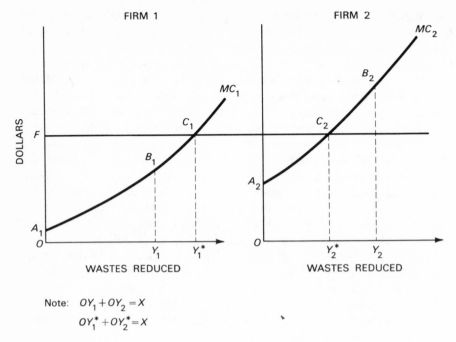

FIGURE 10–3.   Interfirm Efficiency and Equity.

of OY units of wastes to be reduced by each firm (assume $OY_1 + OY_2 =$ the overall target of X). Accordingly, Firm 1 incurs a cost of $OA_1B_1Y_1$ to meet its quota, and Firm 2 has a cost of $OA_2B_2Y_2$. An obvious result is that the costs of reducing the X units via this across-the-board scheme are not the minimum possible costs of avoiding the discharge of this amount of wastes.

With full knowledge of the relevant cost functions, the across-the-board quota could be altered into what Dales refers to as a *point-to-point* scheme, which assigns separate waste quotas to each waste source. The objective of individual quotas would be to correct for the inefficiency implicit in an across-the-board scheme when waste reduction cost functions differ between sources. Thus, in Figure 10–3, costs would be minimized if Firm 1 would increase its level of waste reduction above OY_1 units and Firm 2 lower its amounts below OY_2 units until the marginal costs of each firm are equal, recognizing the constraint that the X target must be maintained. This occurs at a level of $OY_1{}^*$ units for Firm 1 and $OY_2{}^*$ units for Firm 2. The costs associated with this distribution of waste quotas are minimal with respect to any other division of the X target between the firms (that is, $OA_1C_1Y_1{}^* + OA_2C_2Y_2{}^*$). Therefore, individually assigned quotas can restore efficiency to a regulatory policy. However, the obvious difficulty of achieving this least-cost solution is that complete information is required for each cost function. In our example, this would mean obtaining the technical cost information for the two sources of wastes. As we expand the number of waste sources beyond two, the required information for an efficient point-to-point regulation policy increases. This has obvious implications in terms of the costs of gathering and analyzing such data, the required bureaucratic machinery to administer individual quotas, the necessary monitoring of compliance, and, of course, the subsequent use of enforcement procedures if necessary. Such considerations tend to make a point-to-point regulatory policy extremely cumbersome and costly. Accordingly, the efficiency gains of moving from an across-the-board policy of equal waste reduction to individually assigned waste quotas may be offset by the enormous increase in costs associated with formulating and implementing a point-to-point regulatory policy.

A Workable Environmental Policy

Thus far, our analysis of the various environmental policies has been somewhat pessimistic. Complex informational difficulties exist when we attempt to measure the true marginal benefit and cost functions, and this mitigates against the likelihood of selecting the socially optimal effluent charge or waste reduction subsidy. Within the choice between a tax or subsidy policy, the perverse economic incentives inherent in setting a flat subsidy per unit waste reduction work against the implementation of this type of environmental policy. Moreover, the fiscal ramifications of such a subsidy policy create significant obstacles in addition to the equity and political implications of rewarding polluters. Regulations, on the other hand, offer a theoretically identical solution to effluent charges in the presence of perfect knowledge of the cost and benefit functions. In the likely absence of this information, an across-the-board equal reduction quota aimed at some overall target of waste reduction will be inefficient once we admit the real world conditions of many polluters with differing costs of waste reduction.[4] An attempted correction of this condition by assigning waste quotas to specific sources encounters nearly intractable information and administration problems.

What then remains in terms of obtaining a viable environmental policy? Precise measurements of the social benefits of a comprehensive waste reduction program involving a variety of waste types are likely to remain elusive for some time despite the energetic efforts of research-

---

[4] Indeed, not only will costs differ, but the benefits of waste reduction will differ over geographic area, type of effluent, timing of discharge, and so on.

ers in the physical, biological, and social sciences. A synthesis of waste treatment and waste reduction cost data, although more manageable, poses additional formidable research problems. This information represents a crucial missing link for the design of a socially optimal environmental policy—be it taxes, subsidies or regulations—in terms of the resource allocation criteria presented in Chapters 2 and 3.

If, however, a social agreement can be reached on some overall target of environmental quality and, hence, a rough idea of the required reduction in wastes can be obtained, then a viable policy can be put together. Suppose we return to Figure 10–3 and now assume that there exists a socially determined objective of reducing wastes by X units, recognizing that this target is unlikely to reflect the optimal waste reduction implicit with full knowledge of all the relevant cost and benefit schedules. We know that an across-the-board enforcement of regulations to meet this objective will be inefficient, but a point-to-point policy presents insurmountable practical difficulties. A further possible solution is to subsidize polluting sources up to the amount necessary to achieve the stated across-the-board reduction. This will eliminate some of the costs inherent in a policy of a flat subsidy per waste unit reduced and prevent some of the perverse economic incentives of this policy previously discussed. It will still be inefficient, however, and in addition, it may not fully eliminate the incentives for polluters to overstate their waste reduction costs even with a fixed target for each waste source.

Probably a more efficient policy approach, given the goal of a waste reduction of OX units, is to implement an effluent charge. The important difference between this effluent charge policy and our previous discussion concerns the awareness that the effluent charge is now being levied to achieve the environmental quality target and not an unknown MXSW or *Pareto optimal level* waste reduction. All the advantages of an effluent charge policy will remain with respect to economic incentives, efficiency, and distributional implications. Returning to our simple example in Figure 10–3, an effluent charge levied at OF will bring about the efficient reduction of X units of wastes between the two firms. This will occur without the government having to obtain detailed cost data for each waste source. Of course, it is unlikely that the OF charge will be set correctly on the first attempt. Suppose, for example that the charge was initially levied greater than OF. This would result in a combined waste reduction of greater than OX units and an environmental quality level in excess of the targeted condition. In such a situation, the signal will be to lower the charge. Conversely, if the initial charge is set below OF then the achieved waste reduction will fall short of the desired amount and this should indicate an increase in the charge is necessary. Thus, by adjustment of the effluent charge, an efficient least-cost solution will be obtained consistent with the desired waste reduction target.

Distributional Impacts

Distributional considerations may modify the above policy prescription that is based solely on efficiency criteria. Price increases in final products would of course, follow the effluent charge policy and make some consumers worse off. Moreover, firms and waste sources with relatively efficient treatment facilities could reduce wastes more cheaply than inefficient ones and, in some cases, force them out of business. Thus, equity considerations may be important in assessing the desirability of implementing effluent charges. However, in general, it is hard to see why the costs of using environmental resources should, in the long run, be treated any differently from the costs of using other resources. Subsidization of the costs of waste disposal resources is not called for any more than the subsidization of the wages that firms have to pay their workers.

Implementation of effluent charges would force waste sources with costly reduction techniques to pay relatively high effluent charges and would not allow them to escape the economic penalties of their inefficiency. The revenues generated from such charges might be used to subsidize research on waste treatment technology and the implementation of more efficient waste reduction techniques. The eventual replacement of costly waste reduction methods could result in lower effluent charges and hence lower costs to the initial least-cost firms because more of the burden would be taken up by the previously inefficient waste treatment sources.

Prohibition Reconsidered

One final task in our comparisons of alternative environmental policy actions is to relate the tax and subsidy approach to the most severe regulation policy available; the limiting case of prohibition. A complete ban on all effluent discharges is certainly a possible policy alternative. As noted in Chapter 9, prohibition is a drastic measure in the sense that it automatically forecloses alternative courses of action. It should be obvious to the reader that a generalized prohibition policy covering all categories of effluents in all areas would be grossly inefficient, socially undesirable, and, probably, politically impossible. Nevertheless, selective use of prohibition policies may be economically justifiable and consistent with the outcome that would follow a socially optimal tax or subsidy policies.

The essential economic issue concerning prohibition as an environmental policy alternative is one of the level of social costs involved and the availability of close substitutes. Suppose that the social costs of a particular effluent are clearly known to be of enormous magnitude (nuclear wastes, for example). In such a situation, any effluent charge on nuclear waste should properly be set so high that no discharges of wastes would occur. In our example in Figure 10-1, the OX treated waste units forthcoming from a OF charge should exceed any level of wastes actually possible in current conditions. Therefore, the effluent charge becomes redundant and would not be used. The simple solution in such a situation is to prohibit any discharge of this particular type of waste.

Although prohibition policy is obviously desirable with respect to nuclear wastes, the decision is not nearly as clear-cut for such items as DDT or phosphate detergents (two products where prohibition policies have also been used). Here, the crucial issue is the level of private and social costs and the availability of close substitutes (that is, equally effective, but readily degradable, pesticides or nonphosphate cleansing agents). If, at one extreme, an identical substitute does exist and is available at no additional private cost and considerably lowers or eliminates external costs, then a prohibition policy makes economic sense. On the other extreme, if no close substitutes exist to satisfy the above conditions, then a prohibition policy is inefficient. Situations lying between these extremes necessitate a return to our policy menu involving modified forms of regulation, subsidy, and/or effluent charges.

Our analysis of the economic issues involved in alternative environmental policies is now complete. The general conclusion is that an effluent charge policy is a flexible, efficient method to deal with a broad variety of environmental problems but recognizing, of course, that the specifics of individual situations (for example, geographic area, type of wastes, incidence and extent of social costs) should influence the details of any final environmental policy. However, recent environmental policy experience in this country has not been in the direction of effluent charges and instead has relied on combinations of regulatory and subsidization policies. In the next section, we attempt to explain why this has occurred in terms of institutional obstacles to effluent charges. We also provide some background by detailing the limited examples of effluent charge policies that have been implemented or proposed in the United States and supplement this information with an example of a comprehensive foreign experience with a similar program.

B. INSTITUTIONAL OBSTACLES AND SOME EFFLUENT CHARGE EXPERIENCES

Barriers to Effluent Charges

Most professional economists strongly endorse effluent charges as a general environmental policy. However, as we recall from our brief surveys in Part 3 of existing environmental policies, the arguments for effluent charges have not yet had any substantial impact on environmental policies in the United States. Why such a divergence between the views of economists and the actions of government, especially in an age when economists have seen their policies put into effect in other areas of practical application? The question is a complex one and many factors contribute to a full explanation.

The first, somewhat surprising reason is the considerable opposition to effluent charges voiced by various conservation societies and groups devoted to environmental protection. In the 1960s, environmental interests opposed effluent charges with arguments based on emotional slogans such as "they are nothing more than a license to pollute," or "the environment is not for sale." In effect, these groups were saying that the value of environmental resources was infinite. The extent of this opposition may be exaggerated and its role in deterring a national effluent charge policy is moot. Nevertheless, it is interesting to note that this resistance stemmed from the very people most concerned with improving environmental quality and essentially involved a basic misunderstanding of the economic implications of effluent charges. Environmentalists, at one time, were inclined to rely completely on strict legal enforcement of prohibition policies or stringent regulations. By the early 1970s, however, major environmental action groups, in part motivated by the poor success of the regulatory policies of the 1960s and also due to the growing awareness of the fundamental economic roots of environmental problems, began to swing their support behind the idea of effluent charges.

Although the initial resistance of environmentalists is an interesting case study in economic literacy, the politically weighty opposition of influential business spokesmen is probably the major continuing deterrent to effluent charges. In large part, business resistance derives from the obvious distributional impact of effluent charges. Our analysis in Section A indicated that under a regime of effluent charges, firms' costs will increase as a result either of actions taken to avoid the tax or of actual payment of the charge or some combination of both. Cost increases endanger profit margins, create upward pressures on price, and reduce final output. They may also raise the danger, in certain extreme cases, of outright business failure. For these cogent reasons, it should not be surprising that business opposition to effluent charges has been strong and virtually unanimous. Businessmen recognize that the days of the complete absence of an environmental policy are over. However, when forced to some position, business spokesmen opt for the weakest possible regulatory schemes backed by heavy subsidy policies.[5] As we have already

---

[5] By weakest, we mean the lowest environmental quality standards with as many exceptions as possible. Our description of the environmental policies of business conflicts with the glowing descriptions found in annual reports and advertising statements. The reader is free to draw his own conclusion on this issue.

seen, such policies are likely to be more costly and less effective than an effluent charge policy targeted at the same level of environmental quality. Business's adherence to these more costly policies is due simply to the fact that they offer an avenue of avoiding the direct costs of environmental improvement and thus minimize immediate fiscal effects on their own operations.

Reinforcing these straightforward distributional reasons behind industry opposition are more elemental arguments concerning the ownership of property rights. We have argued previously that effluent charges formally establish the issuing authority's rights—be it federal, state, or local government—to the environmental media. This represents a drastic change from the previously existing *de facto* ownership of rights to the waste disposal capacities of air and water resources. Although public sovereignty over these resources may have long been a matter of law, the historical absence of any overt assertion or, more importantly, *enforcement*, of the rights to use the ambient environmental resources effectively created a situation where these rights reverted by default to individual ownership. Not surprisingly, industry exercised its *de facto* rights and, as observed in Chapter 5, the rights to dispose of wastes in publically owned media became traditionally costless to the firm and embodied in its capital structure. The imposition of an effluent charge would create an abrupt change in this situation, with a sudden reappropriation of environmental rights by the government at the expense of private interests. If firms desire continued use of the waste assimilative capacity of the environment they will have to pay a fee based on the economic consequences of the desired use. The prospect of this course of events creates considerable resistance, exactly comparable to the resistance that would arise should the government threaten to appropriate *any* form of wealth previously considered private property.

From a more detached historical perspective, an effluent charge policy does not represent a radical departure from conventional fiscal experience. In fact, it is a member of the quite well known and frequently used family of excise taxes. It is true that effluent charges are a form of excise taxes extended to a new target and a target long considered as improper, or not even conceived of as a target at all. Thus, it is the novelty of an effluent charge policy and the unexpected nature of its aims rather than any radically different fiscal features that creates the resistance to its adoption.[6] It may be useful to recall, at this stage, that the origin of the federal income tax is relatively recent (1913). Certainly, at that time, a tax on income represented a radical departure for a federal fiscal system previously dependent on excise and customs taxes for its

---

[6] In fact, excise taxes have the longest history of any taxes in this country.

revenues. Thus, the resistance to the federal income tax was long and bitter.

However, the familiar cliché concerning the certainty of death and income taxes and the implicit acceptance of the inherent truth in this saying suggests that income taxes, once implemented, lost their radical nature and became part of the accepted rules and boundaries of economic activity. A similar situation existed with the corporation income tax, which was first initiated in 1909. Memories of its *radical socialist aspects* have been short-lived, and it, too, has become readily accepted as part of the costs of doing business. Obtaining new taxes on previously untaxed items will be much more difficult to achieve than raising already existing taxes. In the case of effluent charges, therefore, the hardest problem is the initial implementation. Once this substantial hurdle is cleared, effluent charges simply will become another cost of doing business and part of the existing structure of economic incentives. This does not mean, of course, that the level of the charge, particular adjustments, the degree of comprehensiveness, and so on, are minor problems. However, just as numerous changes to the federal personal and business income taxes have occurred, the details and alterations that will be necessary over time in any effluent charge scheme can also be worked out.

A final objection by business to effluent charges is that they are unnecessary and redundant, once environmental quality standards have been imposed. The argument is that the legally enforceable nature of laws establishing quality standards for air and water will be sufficient to insure compliance. Therefore, imposing fees in addition to these standards represents an unneeded *overkill* solution to the problem. Although this argument has a certain logical appeal and may be a significant force against implementation of a policy of effluent fees, it is largely fallacious. Relying on legal enforcement proceedings means undue amounts of delay in achieving the ultimate objective of improved environmental quality. The road through the courts is a long and tortuous one, often extending years before final decisions are reached. Delays of five years and even longer, in terms of ultimate court decisions, are not uncommon in environmental cases, and one or two year proceedings are normal. In addition, a natural bureaucratic inertia operates counter to bringing court actions against established, successful, and prominent businesses and businessmen.[7] Finally, as our discussion in Section A indicated, using a regulatory approach to achieve these standards will require masses of costly information and, in the likely absence of these data, the environ-

---

[7] This aversion to instituting legal proceedings is characterized by the statement of one highly placed government official who indicated "we are dealing with top officials in industry and you just don't go around treating people like that." *Audubon*, March, 1971, p. 8.

mental standards will operate inefficiently at best. Effluent charges there-fore offer a direct, equitable method to achieve the objective quickly and efficiently. They are not redundant in the presence of environmental standards, but act to insure their achievement.

Up to this point, our discussion has rested primarily on the re-sistance of business to effluent charges on the basis of some very funda-mental and obvious economic arguments. Related to the strength and origins of this resistance is the final obstacle to an effluent fee policy, legislative action. A national effluent charge program must originate with the Congress and, in fact, a number of such proposals have come before the Congress in recent years. Like all general tax policies, any effluent charge program would be subject to partisan politics, political pressures from lobbyists, and the give-and-take compromise committee procedure that characterizes legislation. We can expect that, because effluent charges are elementally against the basic interests of business, and, especially, very powerful industries (oil, autos, steel, paper, and so on), substantial political pressures will be brought against a comprehensive and strong effluent charge proposal. In addition, Congress is also susceptible to the type of "logic" which initially characterized conservation groups when presented with the idea of effluent charges.

Although these political obstacles are most formidable, increasing awareness of the attractiveness of effluent charge schemes has been able to overcome some of these legislative barriers and political aversions. Pioneering and continued efforts by economists such as Allen V. Kneese of Resources for the Future and others who have championed effluent charges over a considerable time period, are beginning to make inroads in terms of influencing the direction of national environmental policy. We can now turn to some examples of this trend.

Effluent Charge Experience

Although no national effluent charge policy has been legislated in any broadly defined area of environmental concern, numerous proposals abound, and in some isolated local and state situations, effluent charge policies of various types have been implemented. Not all of the policy proposals we shall discuss fit precisely into the definition of a fee placed on the extent of discharged effluents or an output tax levied to reflect the implicit environmental costs associated with a particular product or product group. Nevertheless, a central aspect of these policy proposals is the reliance on fiscal measures to create profit incentives that result in improved environmental quality. Before we begin this discussion of effluent charge proposals and actually implemented policies, it is impor-tant to note that we are excluding those policies that involve fines for noncompliance with regulated environmental standards. Much existing

national and state legislation establishes legally enforceable environmental quality standards and is armed with fines and penalties. Although
the existence of fines obviously creates economic incentives for improved
waste treatment, a system of legal penalties does not represent a proper
example of an effluent charge policy. Fines imposed for not meeting certain environmental objectives, when set on a daily basis rather than as
a single lump sum, tend to merge with a policy of effluent charges. However, such fines are conceptually distinct from effluent charges in that
they do not involve the formal extension of public property rights for
the use of the resources of air and water and the accompanying determination of a price for purchasing these rights.

1. THE PURE AIR TAX ACT PROPOSAL.   In 1972, the Nixon administration submitted the Pure Air Tax proposal to Congress. This bill provides for a national effluent charge levied on sulfur oxide emissions. As
explained in Chapter 7, sulfur oxides are a major air pollutant and cause
significant health, property, and agricultural damages. Sulfur oxides primarily are emitted from stationary sources of combustion of fossil fuels
—electric power generation, industrial power, and home heating. The
proposed tax would commence in 1976 and would be implemented on a
regional basis. The Clean Air Act, also discussed in Chapter 7, requires
air regions to meet primary air quality standards by 1975 (a primary
standard reflects levels of air quality consistent with human health) and
the tax is designed to create incentives for compliance with the national
air quality standards. In regions not meeting the primary standard for
sulfur oxides in 1975, the tax would be set at fifteen cents per pound of
sulfur discharged from all sources within the region. If the region meets
the primary standard but not the more restrictive secondary standard,
the tax would be ten cents per pound. If there is compliance with both
standards, no tax would be levied. The assessment of the tax within a
region poses some problems. As envisaged in the proposed Pure Air Tax,
there would be regular monitoring of known, large sources of sulfur
oxide emissions (power plants, industrial sites). Smaller sources would
pay the tax based directly on the sulfur content of their purchased fuel.
Thus, the Pure Air Tax represents the first seriously considered
national effluent charge. It is designed to complement the national air
quality standards and provide the economic incentives to comply with
the air quality targets of the Clean Air Act. The immediate effects of
the sulfur tax would be to encourage firms to install antipollutant technology and, at the same time, to move towards lower sulfur content fuels.

2. OTHER EFFLUENT CHARGES PROPOSED TO THE CONGRESS.   Another proposal that has received some attention, and that is similar to
the sulfur tax, is for a tax on lead in gasolines. This tax would be based

on the extent of the lead content in gasoline and is designed ultimately to reduce lead emissions.

Both the above proposals would apply nationwide and would be implemented by Congressional action. The details would be administered by the Environmental Protection Agency. Various other national effluent charge proposals also exist. In Chapter 8, we mentioned a proposal that Congress received for a national disposal fee, set at a penny per pound, and levied on the final stage of production. This policy would be an output tax whose sole criterion is weight. It is designed to make producers aware of the implicit waste disposal costs of their products and to create incentives toward types of products that make less of a demand on the environment when their useful life is over. Congress has also considered a similar proposal for a tax on packaging material.

3. THE MILLS PROPOSAL. A variation of the single-criterion, national waste disposal fee based on weight is a more generalized materials disposal fee, suggested in an unpublished paper by economist E. S. Mills. He argues for a fee structure that would vary over particular types of material inputs, with the fees being greater for those materials whose ultimate environmental disposal costs are relatively high. As an example, Mills sets a differential fee structure between degradable and nondegradable materials and proposes that refunds would be granted based on the type of disposal process used for each group of materials. The refund would increase with disposal methods creating the least environmental damages. The plan would offer tax credit provisions for avoiding discharges of wastes in their most socially injurious form. The fees would be imposed at the level of production with the revenues made available to local authorities for waste treatment purposes. The amount of the revenue payment would be based on the extent of treatment and/or recycling undertaken. Variable fees over types of material, and variable refund rates over the quality of the waste treatment or extent of recycling, would create private economic incentives consistent with the social interests of improved environmental quality. Of course, the informational requirements for this generalized materials fee policy would be much greater than the simple, penny-a-pound proposal mentioned above.

4. THE PROXMIRE PROPOSAL. Water pollution has long been a primary environmental concern, and it is not surprising that discussions of effluent charge policies initially developed in the context of the problem of water quality. In fact, there has been extensive foreign experience with effluent charges in terms of achieving water quality improvement. Despite considerable favorable testimony in Congress and much official discussion, effluent charges have not yet been implemented on emissions

into water resources. Numerous proposals have been forthcoming, however, and Senator Proxmire introduced an effluent charge scheme based on the amount of biochemical oxygen demand (BOD) in water-borne waste.[8] Reduction of organic waste loads would be the aim of this legislation and the proposed fee set at a flat ten cents per pound of BOD.

5. Regulatory Activities of the Environmental Protection Agency. The use of the 1899 Refuse Act, which mandates obtaining a permit for any industrial discharge into navigable waterways, formalized the government's property rights to the waste-assimilative capacities of these waters. Under this legislation and the recent Water Pollution Control Act of 1972, any firm or individual desiring to dispose of wastes in navigable waters must obtain a permit. The application for a permit requires technical information concerning the type of wastes, the quantity of wastes, where the discharge will occur, when, and so on. The environmental consequences of these permits are evaluated either by the Environmental Protection Agency or the equivalent state agencies, and the authorities decide either to grant or to deny the application, or recommend particular treatment levels. It is interesting to note the date of the original law providing this power and to speculate on the lack of enforcement of it for over seventy years. It is also worth observing that there has been an enormous flood of applications to discharge wastes since this law was resurrected. The information and data evaluation problems facing the EPA and state agencies are enormous and point to the cumbersome nature of this regulatory approach to environmental problems. The permits are not allocated by a pricing (effluent charge) scheme and, therefore, do not properly represent an example of the fiscal weapons implicit in an effluent charge policy. Nevertheless, given the existence of this law, its belated enforcement, and the public property right nature of a permit system in general, a relatively simple extension would be to price these permits. The price could vary with type and amount of waste, the location, the time of year, and so on. This extension would embody all the salient characteristics of a classical effluent charge solution to environmental quality.

As an example of the potential effectiveness of such an approach, Oregon has used a permit system in combination with the threat of daily fines to achieve impressive improvements in the water quality of the Willamette River. Each year, all municipalities and industries are granted a quota of permits establishing precisely how much waste they can legally discharge. Over time, as waste sources increase, the quotas are

---

[8] See S.3181, *Congressional Record*, 91st Congress, 1st Sess., November 25, 1969. (Washington, D.C.: Government Printing Office.)

reduced by lowering the allowable pollution per permit. The daily fine acts as an incentive for discharges to remain within the assigned pollution quotas and the Willamette is now supporting major autumn salmon runs and extensive fishing activity for the first time in many years.

6. STATE EFFLUENT CHARGES. At the state level, we can cite several actual instances of effluent fees and output taxes. Oregon has enacted legislation that establishes a requirement for a five cent deposit on regular-sized bottles and beverage cans and a two cent deposit on the smaller size of beer bottles. These deposits revive the once-common practice of offering refunds when beverage containers are returned to the seller. This policy is, in effect, an excise tax on a particular product and is similar in its underlying economic incentives to the proposed national disposal fee. In Vermont, the Water Resources Board has the authority to levy an effluent charge on any waste source that does not comply with the state's water quality standards.[9] Michigan has given similar powers to its Water Resources Commission by requiring all waste dischargers to pay a fee "for the cost of surveillance of industrial and commercial discharges and receiving waters." Thus, the fee can range from a simple minimum associated with monitoring the waste source to a possible maximum of $9000 for each waste source *in compliance* with the Michigan standards. No limit is set on the possible fee for any discharges not meeting the standards. Maryland's Environmental Service Act allows similar open-ended effluent fees that can be determined by the social costs of waste discharges.

7. SEWAGE TREATMENT FEES. The Council on Environmental Quality, in its *Second Annual Report,* endorsed the policy of charges and fees to achieve the efficient obtainment of given environmental quality objectives.[10] The Council cites two examples of sewage charges to illustrate the potency of the fee approach. In Springfield, Mo., a $1400 monthly sewage processing fee, based on waste loads, was levied on a packaging plant using the municipal facilities. Within a short time, the firm took various waste reducing actions that lowered this fee to $225. In a similar case, an overloaded municipal sewage treatment plant in Otsego, Michigan, placed a waste charge on an industrial firm that previously had sent 1500 pounds of BOD daily to the municipal facility. Within a month after the charge was imposed, the waste load was down to a 900 pound aver-

[9] Again, although not precisely a classic effluent charge policy, this method represents an enforcement of the state's water quality standards based on a tax *per unit* of effluent in *excess* of the standards.

[10] *Second Annual Report of the Council on Environmental Quality,* Washington, D.C., Government Printing Office, August, 1971, pp. 136–139.

age, and after ninety days, it fell to 500 pounds. Both examples illustrate the dramatic effects of the economic incentives contained in the effluent charge system. Confronting a full pricing system for waste treatment services, both firms quickly explored alternative waste reduction techniques in order to minimize the costs incurred by paying the waste treatment fees. These examples reflect firms' reactions to full cost pricing for waste treatment. We would expect similar rapid waste reduction responses to follow a general policy of charges based on the extent of effluents emitted into the environment.

8. THE GERMAN EXPERIENCE. Although the experience of the United States with effluent charges has not been extensive, the highly organized river basin authorities in Germany have developed a sophisticated institutional structure to control water pollution in one of the world's most industrialized countries. Our interest in discussing this system concerns its use of effluent charges to allocate the costs of waste treatment among the firms and municipalities.[11] The German approach of a coordinating river basin authority is not a recent phenomena but dates as early as 1904. The general term for the river basin organizations is *Genossenshaften,* which, in translation, means cooperative associations. These institutions are numerous throughout Germany and derive their authority from broadly worded legislation. In some cases, they have only a single purpose (for example, land drainage) but in others, they have jurisdiction over all aspects of water quality. Our particular interest centers on the *Genossenshaften* of the Ruhr Valley, where a comprehensive and successful water quality management system has evolved.

The engineering details of the Ruhr *Genossenshaften* are complex but are not of primary interest here. Our basic concern is the use of effluent charges as one method of achieving a least-cost solution to water quality management. The Ruhr Valley area is heavily industrialized with concentrations of iron, steel, and related production activities, all of which have heavy waste-producing technologies. The population of the area exceeds eight million and the river system is a relatively small one by American standards with a combined flow measure for all five rivers in the Ruhr system significantly less than the flow in such U.S. rivers as the Delaware and Potomac. Nevertheless, this river system carries an enormous waste load while providing a water supply for domestic and industrial uses. In addition, it is a substantial source of recreational opportunities. The key element responsible for this success is the approach

---

[11] A comprehensive treatment of the German experiences, from which we draw heavily, appears in A. V. Kneese and B. T. Bower, *Managing Water Quality,* Chap. 12. See the Selected References of this chapter.

to water quality management taken by the *Genossenshaften*. By treating the river basin as a whole, the authorities have been able to take advantage of the many economies of scale in waste treatment technology. Numerous waste sources of differing types have funneled their wastes to central treatment facilities. Certain portions of rivers have been zoned for recreational and amenity purposes; other rivers are used solely for waste discharges. The *Genossenshaften* have also been instrumental in altering the location decisions of industries when the effects of the location were deemed undesirable for water quality. Many specialized waste treatment techniques have been practiced when consistent with least-cost achievement of water quality objectives. In the case of one authority, a technical relation expresses all effluents in terms of their effect on fish life, and both treatment levels and costs are allocated on the basis of this formula.

Of vital interest to our discussion is the use of direct effluent charges based on the type and quantity of the waste. The *Genossenshaften* have employed this policy in coordination with their overall water quality management decisions to achieve waste reduction through increased waste treatment and changes in production processes. Industrial activity is the largest source of wastes in the Ruhr Valley and effluent charges have achieved significant reductions in discharged waste loads. The underlying philosophy of the authorities has been to allocate the costs of waste disposal to the sources of wastes. This basic decision, in combination with a sophisticated systems management operation, has resulted in a river system capable of supporting the needs of large-scale heavy industry and the water requirements of a population of eight million. At the same time, areas within the river basin offer water quality levels capable of affording significant recreational and esthetic benefits.

The lesson of the German experience points to the desirability of a systems management approach to environmental problems and a reliance on the basic principle of seeking an efficient allocation of costs. The experience of effluent charges in assessing these costs based on the contribution to total wastes has been particularly successful.

C. AN EFFLUENT CHARGE PROPOSAL

From our comparison of regulation, prohibition, taxation, and subsidy policies, we conclude that taxation of effluents is the most desirable single weapon to use in establishing a broad-based environmental policy. This section outlines the necessary components for a workable effluent charge policy in the United States.

The production identity between the extent of input material and subsequent residuals provides the initial requirement for tax policy design.[12] We have argued that decisions about the form of various waste residuals—liquid, solid, gas—are a function of the existing technology and economic incentives. Proper environmental policy should be structured so that the differences in the social costs associated with each waste form would be automatically included in this decision. Furthermore, piecemeal policies, aimed at particular environmental problems, must be avoided where direct tradeoffs can occur between possible forms of pollutants. For example, in 1971, U.S. Steel Corporation in Clairton, Pa., was faced with stringent water quality standards for waste discharges into the Monongahela River. As an alternative to discharging its process water, which contained phenols, ammonia, cyanide, and other chemicals, and the subsequent risk of being found in violation of the existing water quality standards, the firm elected to use the waste water to cool off burning coke from its coke ovens. In this *quenching* process, the waste water is boiled off and the very same pollutants, which were previously waterborne, are discharged into the atmosphere in the form of steam. Consequently, U.S. Steel ran afoul of the air quality standards of the county and lengthy court proceedings followed. Although this one case was the result of a single firm's reaction to environmental quality standards, the lesson is equally applicable to effluent charge policy. The dramatic example of a firm switching forms of residual discharges (that is, from water to gas) highlights the potential ineffectiveness of any *partial* environmental policy. In fact, placing a tax on waterborne effluents, for example, and not taking any policy actions with respect to air quality or solid waste discharges would, in situations such as the above, create economic incentives to exploit these other forms of waste residuals. Accordingly, careful coordination of effluent charges among all the relevant residual forms is required to achieve overall environmental improvement.

In the case of tax policy, this means a system of effluent fees based on technical information identifying those situations where residual tradeoffs are likely in addition to any data on the social cost differentials across possible residual forms. This latter information could be used to structure differing taxes for different types of waste, penalizing most those waste forms associated with relatively injurious social effects.[13] The informational difficulties of this policy are formidable but the essential point is

[12] Recall the discussion in Chapter 3 of the conservation of matter and energy as it effects environmental quality through the materials balance between inputs and residuals.

[13] This is similar to the differential materials fee proposal of E. S. Mills discussed in Section B, except that the materials tax is placed on inputs and an effluent charge applies to residuals.

to avoid structuring isolated environmental policies targeted only at specific pollutants. A minimum policy, therefore, would be to impose similar effluent fees on all those waste forms subject to residual tradeoffs, leaving a differential tax structure to situations in which the required information on social costs is readily available. Thus, a systems tax policy approach is required as a counterpart to the basic interrelated systems nature of residuals in the production and consumption processes.

A second major aspect of tax policy design concerns the geographic dimensions of effluent charges. Essentially, the issue is whether to structure policy on the basis of differential or identical tax rates over geographic areas of the country. On the one hand, economic theory indicates that an ideal tax system should embody any geographic differences in the social costs of effluents. This would mean, for example, that a given effluent would be taxed differently, depending on the location of the discharge. Thus, effluent taxes in rural areas or otherwise relatively pollution-free regions would be set lower than the fees on identical effluents discharged in more heavily populated sections in order to reflect the implicitly higher social costs of the latter. This differential approach to environmental taxes would be consistent with the resource allocation theory of Chapters 2 and 3. However, an obvious defect in this scheme is the informational problems associated with establishing an effluent tax structure based on geographic differences in social costs. In fact, this problem is the equivalent of the argument used against a point-to-point regulatory policy. In addition to this informational problem, the effects of effluents within their relevant air, water, and land sheds unfortunately do not conform to political boundaries. Therefore, existing political institutions would not provide for easy administration of a tax structure that would necessarily traverse state and municipal jurisdictions.

A final consideration concerns the allocative effects of a regional effluent charge policy. At the margin, lower effluent taxes in one area will function as economic incentives to attract industry away from areas with higher effluent fees. Because the higher fee regions have relatively lower environmental quality conditions initially, the locational attractions of differential effluent fees will act to distribute waste loads more evenly over the country. A redistribution of pollutants may be undesirable, given an objective of maintaining high environmental quality in certain areas to protect the unique amenities associated with rural space and natural ecological systems, rather than having all areas equally clean or, equivalently, equally polluted. Accordingly, a *neutral* effluent charge policy would impose identical charges throughout the country on identical effluents and avoid the relocation incentives inherent in a variable tax system. In fact, in order to preserve the environmental integrity of existing clean regions, effluent charges might be set higher in areas that are presently pollution-free! [14]

The many difficulties of variable effluent fees indicate that a national setting is required to formulate and administer environmental tax policy. The Environmental Protection Agency provides a suitable administrative framework to conduct the necessary research and serve as a vehicle for tax determination and administration. Some coordination with the Treasury and the Internal Revenue Service will be necessary. In addition, the federal government should recognize explicitly its responsibility to counteract any employment effects of environmental taxes. The problem of unemployment resulting from effluent charges is equivalent in its effects to other causes of unemployment (for example, the shift from a war to a peace economy, the effects of adverse balance of payments positions, insufficient aggregate demand, and discrimination and educational disadvantages). Appropriate governmental policies exist to cope with unemployment and the labor force effects of environmental policies should properly receive the direct attention of monetary, fiscal, and special manpower and retraining programs.

As a final point, we should note that the technical research required for an environmental tax policy has been under way for some time in the EPA and other governmental agencies. This research involves the determination of environmental standards for the multitude of pollutants. An effluent charge policy acts as a substitute for the reliance on regulation and subsidies to achieve these standards. Accordingly, no massive redirection of basic environmental research is needed but simply a change to a more efficient, effective, and equitable policy of implementation.

D. SUMMARY AND CONCLUSIONS

Once a social consensus is reached to "do something about pollution," a number of possible public policy strategies exist to achieve improvements in environmental quality. The first two chapters in Part 3 have evaluated the public policies of prohibition, regulation, and fiscal actions. The outcome of this comparison suggests the overall attraction of effluent charges as a general environmental policy. The use of tax instruments like effluent charges avoids the enormous informational requirements of an efficient point-to-point regulatory policy. In the absence of this information, an across-the-board regulation policy is grossly inefficient.

Effluent charges rely on the basic profit-maximizing behavior of

---

[14] **Note that the Pure Air Tax, however, proposes lower charges in the cleaner air regions.**

firms to obtain the desired level of environmental improvement. Once implemented, taxes represent flexible instruments that can be altered according to changes in environmental objectives. In terms of equity criteria, effluent fees internalize external costs directly to the producers and consumers of products responsible for environmental deterioration. As a fiscal alternative, a subsidy program rewards pollution sources by offering to purchase the implicit environmental property rights of the polluter. In addition, per unit subsidies actually may create profit incentives to generate pollutants.

In certain situations when the social costs of a pollutant are clearly unacceptable, the effects of a prohibition policy will coincide with an optimally determined effluent charge. However, where a range of product substitutes exists and the social and private costs of these relevant products differ significantly, prohibition is not economically efficient.

Although the U.S. experience with effluent charges has been limited, several actual instances of environmental taxation policy have met with remarkable success. In addition, a growing amount of support for effluent fees has been voiced by professional economists, environmental groups, leading research organizations in the environmental field, and the Council on Environmental Quality. The showcase success of effluent charges by the *Genossenshaften* of Germany in the context of a sophisticated water quality management system also reinforces the attraction of this method of environmental control.

Nevertheless, we realistically recognize that even in light of the appealing efficiency and equity aspects of effluent fees, significant business opposition exists to any environmental taxation policy. The roots of this opposition are, fundamentally, the distributional results of effluent charges and involve a decline in output, higher prices, losses of property rights, and potential decreases in profits. The nature of the legislative process in combination with the political weight of industry pose further obstacles to the implementation of a generalized effluent charge policy.

If an effluent charge policy is implemented, it should take a systems approach to reflect the systems nature of the production process with respect to the generation of waste residuals. In addition, the use of regional tax rates versus geographically homogeneous charges raises important practical problems. The degree of the locational incentives for industry that may result from a differential effluent charge structure should be carefully evaluated. As a concluding but important point, it is crucial for the federal government to recognize its responsibilities for correcting any adverse employment effects of environmental policies.

QUESTIONS FOR DISCUSSION

1. "The government already gives substantial subsidies to farmers, oil companies, and others. Therefore, it would be fairer to subsidize firms to control pollution emissions than to impose effluent charges on them." Do you agree or disagree, and why?

2. Should effluent charges be set higher for new firms than for existing firms, on the ground that the former would otherwise have an unfair advantage over the latter in being able to reduce emission levels at relatively low costs by adoption of the latest antipollution technology?

3. "Once economists admit the vast uncertainty that prevails about the nature and extent of environmental costs and benefits in the real world, they have to acknowledge, in all honesty, that there is no theoretical presumption for effluent charges over alternative environmental policies." Discuss critically.

4. If you were the president and principal stockholder of a sulfur mining company, what would be your position on the proposed Pure Air Tax? Why?

5. One river in the Ruhr Valley, the Emscher, serves exclusively as a waste conduit and has even been completely lined with concrete. Does this fact lead you to reconsider the favorable evaluation of the Ruhr *Genossenshaften* in the text? Why or why not?

SELECTED REFERENCES

BAUMOL, W. J., "On Taxation and the Control of Externalities," *American Economic Review*, LXIII, No. 3 (June, 1972). An analysis of the difficulties of designing tax policies consistent with *Pareto* efficient resource allocation conditions.

BOWER, B. T. and A. V. KNEESE, *Managing Water Quality*. Baltimore, Maryland: Johns Hopkins Press, 1968. A thorough discussion of effluent changes and standards. Contains chapters on the water quality management of the Ruhr Valley authorities and several river basin planning experiences in the United States.

DAVIS, O. A. and M. I. KAMIEN, "Externalities, Information and Alternative Collective Action," *The Analysis and Evaluation of Public Expenditures: The PPB System*, Joint Economic Committee, 91st Congress, 1st Sess. Washington, D.C.: Government Printing Office, 1969. A survey of alternative public policy possibilities.

ETHRIDGE, D. "User Charges as a Means for Pollution Control," *Bell Journal of Economics and Management Science*, III, No. 1 (Spring, 1972). An empirical study of firm reaction to sewer charges.

MILLS, E. S., "User Fees and the Quality of the Environment," unpublished, Princeton, N.J., 1971. A survey of alternative environmental policies. Argues in favor of a taxation approach to environmental quality and suggests a differential materials fee structure.

SCHULTZE, CHARLES L., "The Role of Incentives, Penalties and Rewards in Attaining Effective Policy," *The Analysis and Evaluation of Public Expenditures: The PPB System,* Joint Economic Committee, 91st Congress, 1st Sess. Washington, D.C.: Government Printing Office, 1969. A general discussion of economic incentives in public policy with examples drawn from various federal programs.

TYBOUT, R. A. "Pricing Pollution and Other Negative Externalities," *Bell Journal of Economics and Management Science,* III, No. 1, (Spring, 1972). A discussion of the controversy concerning the symmetry of subsidies and charges.

Chapter 11

Governmental
Production
of
Environmental
Services

A third broad environmental policy alternative available to the government is to produce environmental services itself. The prohibition and
regulation measures of Chapter 9 alter the rules delimiting the scope of
private market actions, and the fiscal measures of Chapter 10 change
the nature of the profit incentives influencing private firm behavior. But
both of these two alternatives leave the production of goods and services
to the private sector. Production of environmental services in the public
sector is thus a third clear alternative for the government. This chapter
discusses the efficiency and equity problems that arise once the government makes a decision to adopt this most direct form of intervention in
environmental problems.

The U.S. economy of the 1970s is best characterized neither as
capitalistic nor socialistic, but rather as *mixed*. Most economic activity
is carried out in the private sector in response to the profit motive, but
the public sector is large and its relative size has been increasing. The

federal government is the single largest employer and purchaser of goods and services in the economy and its spending in recent years amounts to about 20 percent of gross national product. State and local governments also have substantial budgets and provide numerous services within their political jurisdictions. The treatment of sewage and collection of trash are typical of the environmental clean-up programs that are important responsibilities of local government in the United States. All levels of government provide services directly or indirectly affecting environmental quality, and the list of additional environmental services they have been asked to provide by the new conservation movement is a long and expensive one.

The classic case of government ownership and production of services is the Tennessee Valley Authority (TVA). The TVA supplies electrical power to a wide area of the South and, at the same time, its lakes are major outdoor recreation resources. Another example of government ownership and production is the Atomic Energy Commission, which, in its role as producer and regulator of energy, has profound potential effects on the quality of our environment. The federal government has long had an extensive role in water resource development, with far-reaching implications for the quality of water resources and the supply of recreational sites. In addition, over 70 percent of the water supply systems in the United States are municipally owned and operated. National parks, seashores, and forests are further examples of government ownership and operation of outdoor recreational resources. More generally, the policies governing the disposition and use of 760 million acres of federal government land are of crucial importance for the quality of the environment.

The examples of current government activities in the previous paragraph suggest the important role public sector ownership and production already play with respect to environmental quality. The many proposals for new environmental programs would greatly expand this role. Note, in particular, that government provision of environmental services goes beyond the narrow objective of controlling effluents and waste residuals and encompasses far broader objectives. Specifically, the primary concern of this form of government intervention is with the *expansion* and *enhancement* of recreational resources and amenity, rather than simply with the preservation of existing environmental resources.

This chapter treats the topic of government provision of environmental services within an expanded and more sophisticated discussion of benefit-cost analysis, and is organized according to the following outline: Part A reexamines the technique of benefit-cost analysis and discusses its role in establishing criteria for general public expenditure programs. Part B attempts to give a more rounded view of benefit-cost analysis by detailing some of its major conceptual and operational problems. Part C adds another practical complexity, with a discussion of the possible role of benefit-cost analysis in the political process underlying public expenditure decision making in the federal government. Part D then examines the use of benefit-cost analysis in the specific environmental policy context of water resource development. Part E follows with another relevant application of benefit-cost analysis to public land policy. Part F provides a brief summary of the chapter.

A. PUBLIC EXPENDITURES AND BENEFIT-COST ANALYSIS

Government expenditures have many dimensions. The amount and timing of public spending has significant impacts on aggregate output and employment. At full employment, the level of public expenditure directly determines the overall mix between public and private output. Moreover, given a fixed amount of public expenditure, the composition of public output becomes an important social question. Finally, government expenditures raise implicit distributional issues because the incidence of benefits is likely to differ from the incidence of costs (the costs being primarily paid from federal personal and business income tax revenues).

In Chapter 2, we discussed how private markets, under certain ideal conditions, allocated resources efficiently. The maximizing calculus underlying each decision by producers and consumers results in an efficient allocation of resources or a maximization of social welfare. However, as Chapter 5 indicated, certain goods such as environmental amenities are not produced, or are underproduced, by private markets. Consequently, government provision of these goods becomes necessary. Unfortunately, the basic problem of the efficient utilization of resources does not disappear simply because there is a need for public production of a good or service. Government production involves opportunity costs. With a fixed public budget, any decision to proceed with any one project means other possible undertakings are foreclosed. Obviously, as a first criterion, it would be useful to ascertain if the project in question generates benefits in excess of its costs to society. Simply, does the project add more output to society than it takes away? If the project passes this test, a further question immediately arises; namely, how does this project compare to all others that also meet the initial efficiency test? In other words, on what basis can we rationally choose between many worthwhile outlets for public expenditure?

Benefit-cost analysis is a method increasingly used to answer these questions. Chapter 1 introduced the basic idea of this technique of evaluating and ranking potential public projects. Our purpose now is to explore it in more detail. In a general sense, benefit-cost analysis attempts to proxy the criteria of private markets as they would extend to public expenditures. It involves a systematic evaluation of the social benefits generated by a given project relative to the social costs of the undertaking. Both costs and benefits are measured in dollars and are supposed to reflect the economic values of the inputs and outputs of the project. In Chapter 3, we argued that private markets fail, in certain instances, to account for the full costs or benefits of production or consumption decisions because of the pervasive nature of externalities and, therefore, resource allocation becomes inefficient. The identical problem awaits us in benefit-cost analysis. The measures of costs and benefits must be inclusive of all relevant social values if the analysis is to avoid the pitfall of inefficient public resource allocation. For example, a water quality improvement project in a river basin may bestow benefits in the form of decreased water treatment costs for municipalities and industries. In addition, however, it may provide a net increase in the resources available for public recreation activity. The total benefits of such a project would be the sum of decreased treatment costs plus the incremental recreation benefits generated by the project.

Symmetrically, all input costs must also be accounted for because they are resources used by the project and are no longer available for alternative uses. Furthermore, any additional external costs also should be included. For example, environmental costs created by the project (natural habitat disruptions, waste discharges, and so on) properly belong in the cost total. Thus, benefit-cost analysis seeks to estimate the entire extent of a project's benefits and costs.

A benefit-cost study ultimately reduces to a ratio where the numerator expresses the total present value of all benefits and the denominator measures the total present value of all costs. If this ratio exceeds unity, the project passes the first efficiency test. That is, the project promises to make a net contribution to society's economic welfare in the sense that the output produced has a greater value than the resources used for the project would have in the private sector.

The concept of *present value* is of central importance in benefit-cost analysis. Many public projects have long lives and are characterized by substantial initial construction costs followed by recurring, but relatively low, annual operating costs. Benefits, on the other hand, tend to be distributed more evenly over the life of the project. Thus, the bulk of a project's costs often occur early in its life, but the benefits are spaced over a considerable following period.

Obviously, the decision to undertake a project must be made in the present. The problem is to express a future, uneven stream of costs and benefits in terms of its value today, or, in other words, to reduce all the costs and benefits occurring in future time periods to a common present day value. The necessity of taking time into account centers on a basic economic tenet that a dollar received at a specified future time is not as valuable as the receipt of that dollar today. Equivalently, a dollar today returns more than a dollar in the future when it is lent at interest. Exactly how much more a dollar will be worth at the end of a specified number of years will depend on the interest rate. Obviously, the higher the rate of interest, the more a dollar will return at the end of the time period. The logic can also be reversed. If an expected amount of dollar benefits is forthcoming at a known future time and the interest rate is given, we can compute the present value of those benefits today. Precisely how much would have to be lent out at the given interest rate in order to generate that particular sum of benefits at the specified future time? Formally, the relation between present and future values can be expressed as;

$$PV = \frac{B_t}{(1+i)^t}$$

where PV is present value, B indicates dollar benefits, i is the interest rate and t is the time period in which the benefits accrue. The expression can be solved for PV given values of i, t, and B. If benefits occur over a series of years and in differing amounts, then the present value of this series of benefits, PVB, is obtained by summing the PV of each component of the benefit stream as computed by the above formula. We can express this summation process,

$$(PVB) = \sum_{t=1}^{T} \frac{B_t}{(1+i)^t}$$

where the summation covers the life of the project (T years). By identical reasoning, the costs of the project should also be expressed on a present value basis. However, one segment of costs, the capital outlays, occurs in the initial year of the project. Accordingly, the present value of the capital construction costs is stated by their full dollar value. Recurring, or annual operating, costs are spent over the life of the project and it is necessary to compute the present value of these costs. The present value of costs (PVC), therefore, can be given by

$$(PVC) = K + \sum_{t=1}^{T} \frac{RC_t}{(1+i)^t}$$

where K indicates the capital costs incurred in the initial year of the project and RC indicates recurring, or operating, costs.

The benefit-cost ratio (BCR) is computed as

$$(BCR) = \frac{PVB}{PVC} = \frac{\sum\limits_{t=1}^{T} \dfrac{B_t}{(1+i)^t}}{K + \sum\limits_{t=1}^{T} \dfrac{RC_t}{(1+i)^t}}$$

This ratio determines whether the present value of the estimated benefits of the project exceeds, falls short of, or equals the present value of the costs. It answers the efficiency question implicitly posed by public expenditures. Moreover, projects can be ranked according to their benefit-cost ratio. The technique can also be used to determine the efficient size of a project by computing the marginal benefit-cost ratio as project size changes and selecting the size where the benefit-cost ratio is at a maximum.

At first glance, benefit-cost analysis is an appealing tool of social accounting. If carefully done, it offers useful information to public decision making. The systematic evaluation of the full extent of benefits and costs provides a sound basis for rational public investment decisions and, thus, an efficient allocation of society's resources. However, before we are completely won over by this elegant tool, it is important to point out a number of its theoretical and practical difficulties.

B. ISSUES IN BENEFIT-COST ANALYSIS

Determination of the Social Discount Rate

The role of the interest rate in benefit-cost analysis is a crucial one. It is not surprising that it has been the center of a considerable controversy in the professional literature of economics. The simple mechanics of the benefit-cost formula reveal that the higher the interest rate, the lower will be the present value of costs and benefits. Table 11–1 indicates the sensitivity of the present value of benefit and cost totals to the interest rate. As higher interest rates are used, the present values decrease. Moreover, because, in many cases, costs are concentrated in the beginning of the period but benefits are either spread more evenly over time or predominate later in the project's life, the benefit-cost ratio is also sensitive to the choice of interest rate. The example in Table 11–1 gives hypothetical benefit and cost values for a project over an eleven-year period. Initial costs of $20,000 are followed by much lower annual operating costs of $500. Benefits, however, gradually build from $1,000 per year to $5,000 per year. The three columns below this benefit and cost listing portray the sensitivity of the benefit-cost ratio to the interest rate. In this example, a project efficient at a rate of 3 percent, or even 6 percent, turns inefficient between 9 and 12 percent. In general, more projects will become worthwhile as lower interest rates are used. Lower rates will also favor long-lived projects over short-lived ones. Accordingly, the selection of the interest rate or *social discount rate*, as it is commonly termed, is crucial because it may determine whether a project is deemed efficient or not.

Current practices by many federal agencies call for the use of discount rates that are considered too low by many economists. If this is a valid criticism, then the discount rates actually overstate the true social value of projects and may make inefficient or marginal projects appear worthwhile. The argument against using a social discount rate lower than the current market rate can be summarized as follows.

TABLE 11–1   THE SENSITIVITY OF THE BENEFIT-COST RATIO

Year	Benefits	Costs
0	—	20,000
1	1000	500
2	2000	500
3	3000	500
4	4000	500
5	5000	500
6	5000	500
7	5000	500
8	5000	500
9	5000	500
10	5000	500
Total	40,000	25,000

Social Discount Rate	(PVB)	(PVC)	(BCR)
0	40,000.00	25,000.00	1.6
3	33,220.54	24,265.02	1.369
6	27,640.07	23,679.70	1.167
9	23,651.02	23,209.86	1.09
12	20,246.50	22,828.83	.8868

Private markets represent an alternative use of the resources required by public projects. Therefore, the return that resources are earning in private pursuits is the social opportunity cost of using resources in public undertakings. Accordingly, this private rate of return is the true opportunity cost of public investment and, hence, the relevant discount rate. This position would employ discount rates over twice the size of the ones used in many federal studies. The obvious result would be fewer projects yielding a benefit-cost ratio in excess of one.

An alternative argument claims that private investment decisions account only for private benefits and costs. The result is market failure with respect to the allocation of investment funds yielding nonappropriable social benefits. Accordingly, this position argues that a rate below the prevailing private market rate is the appropriate social discount rate choice and will correct for private investment market failure.[1]

Comprehensive Measurement of Benefits and Costs

A further issue is the importance of making the cost and benefit measures as all-inclusive and as accurate as possible. This point needs to be stressed because it is central to the justification of public investments. In many instances, attempts to measure the full benefits of public investment encounter significant problems. A major difficulty is the absence of equivalent, or nearly equivalent, outputs or products in the private sector. Market prices cannot serve as measures of the benefits of many public outputs. Numerous ingenious attempts have been made to obtain benefit measures in such instances. Benefit-cost analysts must be wary of all the problems of evaluating public output discussed in Chapter 5; namely, the impossibility, or difficulty, of exclusion, the free-rider aspect of public goods, and the subsequent effects on willingness to pay.

Even where similar private products and prices do exist, distortions in the structure and operation of private markets may imply that market prices are not true indicators of the social value of the goods. Cost measures are subject to the same difficulties. Chapters 3 and 4 argued that many private production processes generate substantial external costs and, therefore, involve a misallocation of resources. If public investments involve the equivalent of external costs (that is, costs not included in the cost measures), then, by the same argument, benefit-cost analysis is guilty of the identical resource misallocation charges made against private market processes characterized by externalities. That is, it may be responsible for exactly the same failures of the private markets

---

[1] It is important to note that economists are not in agreement on this issue and that many counterarguments exist. The Haveman reference at the end of this chapter provides a useful review of the various positions.

that government programs purport to correct. Therefore, considerable effort must be made to identify and evaluate all the costs associated with public investment, inclusive of any external costs imposed by the project, that is, costs beyond the market costs for factor inputs, materials, and so on.

Income Distribution and Pricing

A final set of issues in benefit-cost analysis concerns the distribution of the benefits and costs of public investment. Thus far, we have treated the objective of benefit-cost analysis in terms of efficiency criteria only; that is, whether a public investment has a positive net return to the society. Implicit in the analysis has been the assumption that the dollar benefit and/or cost total is independent of the incidence of benefits or costs. Equivalently, the value of the project to society would not be altered if there were a change in the composition of the beneficiaries and/or those who pay the cost. This assumption says, in effect, that a dollar of benefits or costs is worth the same regardless of who receives or pays it and permits a comparison of total benefits and costs without having to be concerned with the identity and circumstances of those who benefit from the public investment and those who bear its costs.

If we admit, however, that the role of public investment may extend beyond efficiency criteria to include changes in income distribution, then the identity of those who benefit and those who pay becomes an important matter. If a more equitable income distribution is a valid social objective, costs and benefits could be assigned varying weights. The weights would be chosen to reflect the social worth of benefits and costs according to the identity of individuals receiving the benefits or paying the costs. Suppose, for example, that a project confers benefits of $10,000 on individuals with annual incomes in the upper 5 percent of the income distribution. If a government objective is a more egalitarian distribution of income, then $10,000 is not a true benefit measure but rather $W \times$ $10,000$ where $W < 1.0$. The weight value W indicates a dollar's worth of benefits accruing to individuals in the upper reaches of the income distribution is not equivalent to a dollar's worth of social benefits. Rather, it is less than a dollar and exactly how much less depends on the value assigned to W. An equivalent argument could be applied to the cost side, weighing less those costs borne by wealthier segments of the society and weighing more those costs paid by low-income groups. The result of such weighting would be an entirely new benefit-cost ratio for any given project.

The idea of assigning varying weights to dollar costs and benefits has met heavy resistance from many economists. It requires benefit-cost analysts to identify precisely all the distributional impacts of public investment. A further and more considerable difficulty is the question of who determines the weights and by what process. These latter problems are likely to prove formidable in practice. Thus, the conclusion among many economists is that tax and direct income transfer programs rather than public investment should accomplish the income redistribution goals of the society.

A somewhat related issue concerns the determination of the price for public outputs. If the price of publicly provided goods is set at zero, for whatever reason, then all costs of the public good are paid via the incidence of the tax structure.

There are several valid reasons for pricing public goods at zero. In many situations, exclusion is either impossible or very costly. In addition, society often decides, on equity criteria, that some public goods should be equally available to everyone, or, at least, not allocated by price and willingness to pay; that is, not on the basis of the underlying income distribution. An alternative policy is to extend the role that price plays in private markets to situations involving public goods. Private markets are constantly allocating goods and services on the basis of price. Willingness to pay the market price determines who receives the product. Consequently, with rational behavior attributed to consumers, goods are allocated to those who value them the most. In those public good situations that lack a strong social judgment favoring equal availability and where exclusion is a practical possibility, an overt pricing policy may be desirable.

Assigning a price to public output serves several functions. First, the question of who pays for public goods is now answered precisely. The costs of the public good, in whole or in part, are paid by the individuals actually using the good or service rather than being widely distributed among users and nonusers alike through the incidence of the tax structure. In addition, equity considerations would seem to favor this solution in the sense that those who benefit from the good, public or private, bear the cost. Second, pricing public goods will yield a more efficient allocation of the available public output. Because there is a great deal of evidence that the demand curves for most goods slope downward, it should not be surprising that public goods available at zero prices are quickly depleted. In the presence of capacity constraints, zero pricing leads to overuse, congestion, and quality deterioration. Examples of public highways and free recreational facilities quickly come to mind. Pricing offers a means of reducing congestion costs and maintaining the quality of the public good by reducing the quantity demanded. At the same time, it provides a measure of demand at nonzero prices and avoids a tendency to overexpand public outputs on the basis of justifying the expansion by the size of the demand at the zero price!

Effluent charges can be reexamined in this broader context of the pricing of public goods. Effluents, or waste residuals, involve the use of a public resource, namely, the waste-absorbing services of the environment. We have argued that this use should be paid for by those responsible, instead of distributing the costs more generally throughout the society via the incidence of the externalities created by the pollutants or the tax costs of subsidizing pollution treatment. Effluent charges result in less use of the public good compared to a situation where the environment's assimilative capacity is available at a zero price. The outcome will be a more efficient allocation of resources.

Application of Benefit-Cost Analysis to Environmental Problems

Benefit-cost analysis provides the general framework for evaluating all potential public expenditures and it can serve as the major vehicle of an active government policy to provide and protect environmental amenities. Carefully planned public investment decisions should not cause the same environmental problems often encountered in private markets. There is little question, however, that some actual or proposed public projects can cause adverse environmental impacts, often with the same intensity as private, profit-oriented market activities. The abortive Cross-Florida Canal project, the proposed Tocks Island Dam on the Delaware River, the SST, and lumbering and extractive activities in national forests are ready examples of government expenditure and subsidy programs involving considerable harmful environmental consequences.

The National Environmental Policy Act (NEPA) requires an explicit statement of the environmental impacts of all proposed federal projects. The impact statements are conventionally given in physical terms. However, a properly executed benefit-cost analysis would embody an estimate of the dollar costs and benefits of the environmental effects of any project. The NEPA requirement strengthens the well-established, but not necessarily well-heeded, rule of including the entire range of benefits and costs in the calculation of the benefit-cost ratio. Careful adherence to proper methodology would eliminate many projects with considerable environmental damages by raising the estimated present value of costs and, hence, lowering the benefit-cost ratio.

On a more positive note, benefit-cost analysis can be redirected towards evaluations of public programs for resource protection and improvement. In the framework of J. V. Krutilla's defense of conservation, as summarized in Chapter 8, a highly industrialized society with a continually growing GNP will place increasing value over time on open space, natural environments, and environmental amenities. A vigorous environmental policy program would attempt to capture these values in a systematic context in order to justify the preservation of remaining natural amenities. Programs designed to augment and protect environmental quality can be the subject of benefit-cost analyses in the same manner as more conventional resource development programs. Examples of positive environmental projects would be air and water quality clean-up programs, changes in the policies establishing uses of federal lands, and increased public expenditures to expand the supply and quality of recreation land. However, before we examine several particular areas of government environmental policy, it may be useful to consider the practical political obstacles to the effective implementation of benefit-cost analysis.

C. THE INSTITUTIONAL FRAMEWORK

Thus far, we have treated benefit-cost analysis as a scientific tool of social accounting that coldly and impartially evaluates alternative public projects and steers public funds to their most socially efficient use. It would be erroneous, however, to leave the impression that public expenditure decisions are reached in the laboratory conditions of benefit-cost methodology. These decisions are deeply rooted in a complex political process. A brief description and evaluation of this process places the role of benefit-cost analysis in a considerably different perspective.

Public expenditure decisions are made in the determination of the annual federal budget. This budgetary process begins with a lengthy interchange of funding requests, arguments justifying these requests, and budget reviews between the Office of Management and Budget, the various governmental agencies, and the President and his staff. After these negotiations are completed to the President's satisfaction, a budget request is sent to Congress for actual funding. The outcome of this process reflects intense bargaining and pragmatic compromises among many competing agencies.

Congressional funding decisions involve further considerable political bargaining. Initially, the various subcommittees of the House Appropriations Committee receive the relevant budget requests from the administration. The procedures of these subcommittees conventionally include public hearings, evaluations, and the actual writing of an appropriations bill for the particular funding area in question. The subcommittee bill is then sent to the Appropriations Committee where it may be adjusted before it is sent to the full House. At this stage, the full House may ask for further revisions before passing the bill and sending it to the Senate. In the Senate, a similar process is followed until the Senate passes its own version of an appropriations bill in each of the budget areas. House-Senate conferees adjust any differences between the two versions of the bills. This adjustment may involve significant changes in controversial areas and a return of the bill to each congressional body for substantial revision. Finally, the adjusted and passed bills are signed by the President and become law.[2]

It is obvious from this brief description that budget decisions are the end result of a long and involved political process. At every stage, the budgeting process is characterized by extensive political bargaining, feedback, and subsequent adjustment before the final appropriation of funds is made. Given our previous discussion, the obvious question arises: What is the role of benefit-cost analysis in this inherently political decision-making process? Unfortunately, the answer is that, until recently, benefit-cost methods have played relatively minor and isolated roles in actual appropriations decisions. Entrenched congressional traditions, the power of seniority in committee and subcommittee chairmanships, and the natural reluctance on the part of the Congress to relinquish control over such a crucial area as appropriations are formidable obstacles to the widespread use of benefit-cost techniques to direct public expenditures. As noted in Chapter 5, in 1965, the Johnson administration made an attempt to institute a systematic evaluation of public expenditures throughout all government agencies—the Planning Programming Budgeting System, or PPBS. PPBS essentially involves the application of benefit-cost methods on a consistent basis for discretionary public expenditures in all federal agencies. A key aspect of PPBS is to identify the output provided by public expenditures and to evaluate this output in terms of its social benefits, costs, and the available alternatives. Ultimately, the purpose of PPBS is to give explicit direction to the expenditure decisions of the Congress and President.

Thus far, the overall success of PPBS has been limited. A variety of problems are responsible. Obviously, an effective PPBS would necessarily remove some of the discretionary and politically valuable powers of Congress. However, resistance to PPBS has extended beyond the understandable reluctance of Congress. At times, individual federal agencies, fearful of budget cuts stemming from a systematic evaluation of their operations, have opposed the implementation of PPBS. To repeat the points made in Chapter 5, some students of government have argued that the incentive structure in bureaucratic agencies creates desires for large budgets and increased discretionary powers. For many public

---

[2] Some theorists have characterized the process of government in terms of a behavioral theory in much the same manner that economists have used to portray the economic theory of markets. Several references are provided in the Selected References listing at the end of this chapter.

programs and agencies, these incentives may conflict with the results of properly conducted benefit-cost studies.

In conclusion, the outlook for an effectively operating PPBS concerning environmental programs is mixed. Its objectives are highly desirable, the most laudable being the ranking of potential public expenditures according to their value to society and the subsequent ability to conduct congressional expenditure decisions on a more economically rational basis. In operation, PPBS has foundered on the hard shores of congressional and bureaucratic reality. This does not imply, however, that PPBS is doomed to failure. Continued vigorous effort is necessary in order to make the PPBS an ongoing, functioning part of the process of public expenditure decision making. As a whole, therefore, PPBS is an encouraging move towards changing the institutional structure of public decision making in a manner consistent with improving the economic efficiency of public resource allocations, including those directly related to environmental quality.

D. WATER RESOURCE DEVELOPMENT

Historically, there has been extensive federal development of the water resources of the U.S. This dates from 1824, with the appropriation of $75,000 to the Corps of Engineers, providing for clear navigation of the Ohio and Mississippi rivers. In 1972, the Corps budget totaled $1.59 billion. In addition to the Corps, the Bureau of Reclamation, Department of Agriculture, the Tennessee Valley Authority, and several additional Interior Department agencies are involved in water resource projects. These projects go far beyond the initial navigation and harbor improvements of the early nineteenth century and encompass extensive flood control, hydroelectric power, water supply, recreation, irrigation, and other multipurpose objectives. Inherent in these projects are extensive environmental effects in addition to conventional efficiency and equity issues.

It is not surprising that benefit-cost techniques evolved from the continuous and significant federal involvement in water resources. The foundation of benefit-cost analysis can be traced to the River and Harbor Act of 1902, which required a review of the commercial benefits and costs of Corps of Engineer projects. This requirement was formalized by an equivalent act in 1920, and, in 1936, the Flood Control Act specified that no project would be authorized unless the benefits, "to whomsoever they may accrue," exceeded the costs. The Flood Control legislation represents the modern basis of benefit-cost practice. It is interesting to note that for all its current sophistication and dominance by economists, benefit-cost analysis began as an engineering device to evaluate water resource expenditures.

From this beginning, Corps of Engineer, and other, water projects have received increasing benefit-cost attention from economists. Gradually, a general methodology was developed and Congress became increasingly familiar with the intent, if not the operational specifics, of benefit-cost studies in the water resource area. Water development projects not meeting the benefit-cost criterion are usually not even considered for Congressional authorization.

A series of federal guidelines to benefit-cost analysis of water investment have attempted to aid the federal applications of this technique. This process has recently culminated in the *Principles and Standards for Planning Water and Related Land Resources* (referred to as the *Principles*) established by the Water Resources Council in 1971.[3] These statements have provided a basic operational guide to benefit-cost practices and, in terms of our interests, have attempted to move to a more comprehensive framework of assessing public water resource investments.

Although a long history of River Basin Committees, Bureau of Budget, and Corps of Engineer reports have documented benefit-cost practices, the adoption in 1962 of an interdepartmental report known as Senate Document 97 represents an important advance in applied benefit-cost analysis.[4] The document followed the formation of the Water Resources Council under the Kennedy Administration and was designed to provide uniformity for benefit-cost analysis of federal water resource investment. Senate Document 97 required the calculation of a benefit-cost ratio that measured national economic benefits and costs. However, goals other than economic efficiency were also recognized as part of the evaluation process. These included preservation of natural environments and income redistribution effects. Thus, any given water project, when appearing before Congress for appropriations, would usually be summarized by its benefit-cost ratio, and then, infrequently, supplemented by additional statements concerning its intangible effects and an indication of the income distribution impact of the project. In actual practice, however, the benefit-cost ratio became the primary evidence supporting the appropriations argument.

[3] U.S. Water Resource Council, *Proposed Principles and Standards for Planning Water and Related Land Resource Projects*, 92nd Congress, 1st Sess., September, 1971 (Washington, D.C.: Government Printing Office).

[4] President's Water Resources Council. *Policies, Standards and Procedures in the Formulation, Evaluation and Review of Plans for Use and Development of Water and Related Land Resources.* Senate Document 97, 87th Congress, 2d Sess., 1962. (Washington, D.C.: Government Printing Office.)

A growing concern developed in the mid-1960s over federal water investments and the benefit-cost practices employed in evaluating these projects. One basic objection was the seemingly one-sided interest of agencies like the Corps of Engineers and Bureau of Reclamation in project development. In part this stemmed from the methods of computing benefits. Discount rates in the 3 percent range were the common practice at a time when private market rates were over twice this level. This led to the criticism that the benefits of many projects simply were overestimated. If a more careful benefit estimation had been conducted at higher discount rates, then many projects that were actually authorized, funded, and constructed would have been ruled out as inefficient. This criticism was aimed directly at the efficiency aspects of benefit-cost analysis and claimed that the actual practices of benefit-cost analysis did not correctly measure the purported target of national economic efficiency.[5]

At the same time, increasing concern was focused on the cost side of the analysis. Lack of consideration of the environmental costs of water projects also led to a dominant emphasis favoring project development. For example, many of the large scale dam projects in western states, designed to provide electric power generation, irreversibly altered natural environments and involved the destruction of free-flowing rivers and the inundation of wilderness areas. The loss of unique natural environments, free-flowing water recreation, and the future option to use these resources as wilderness or white water sites were not included as opportunity costs of the construction and operation of the dams.

Conversely, some projects that improved environmental amenities—dune preservation by channel cuttings, bay protection, and so on—might not pass the benefit-cost criteria on strict economic efficiency conditions because the bulk of the benefits might not be measurable within the current state of benefit-cost methodology. Finally, there was criticism that benefit-cost analysis simply was not practiced consistently over all federal water projects.

In 1968, the Water Resources Council proposed an increase in the discount rate to 5 percent and later initiated an interagency attempt to broaden the entire evaluation procedures of Senate Document 97. The result was the adoption in 1971 of the *Principles*. This superseded Senate Document 97 and formally included a multiobjective framework for water resource development. In addition to national economic de-

---

[5] See, for example, Senator Proxmire's criticism of the Glen Elder project in Kansas, a Bureau of Reclamation project grossly overstated in benefits and underestimated in costs. U.S. *Congressional Record*, 87th Congress, 2d Sess., 1962, pp. 21325–21371. (Washington, D.C.: Government Printing Office.)

velopment, the *Principles* require an explicit listing of the impact of any project on the quality of the environment, income distribution and social well-being, and regional development. A benefit-cost ratio is still computed but its reflection of national economic efficiency is only one piece of evidence within these other objectives. A project's effects in terms of income distribution, environmental impact, and regional development will be described quantitatively where possible and qualitatively in all other cases. The explicit and mandatory inclusion of broader objectives for water resource development is designed to allow nonefficiency goals to enter the project decision process. The assumption is that most of the externalities caused by water investments will continue to be unmeasurable by benefit-cost analysis. This creates the need to account explicitly for these effects even if they cannot be measured in dollars. An alternative view is that externalities can be measured and routinely included in benefit-cost analysis, thereby permitting a consistent evaluation of the project within the framework of formal benefit-cost methodology.

The *Principles* also raise the discount rate to 7 percent but contain a *grandfather clause* allowing previously authorized, but not appropriated, projects to remain on the public investment shelf without being recalculated at the 7 percent rate.

At first glance, the *Principles* appear to be a laudable attempt to solve some of the criticism of the narrowness of benefit-cost analysis. Upon closer inspection, however, it is obvious that major problems accompany the *Principles*. The discount rate established by the *Principles* is still below current market rates. More importantly, the introduction of the multiobjective framework strengthens the possibilities for pork barrel decision making for water investments, an aspect that benefit-cost analysis has long attempted to minimize. Double counting of benefits is also likely in the national efficiency and regional accounts of the *Principles*. No consideration of the cost of alternatives to the project's objective is provided and there is no attention to the important issue of pricing public outputs.

In summary, the new *Principles*, for all their well-meaning intentions to account for environmental effects and other than efficiency implications of water investments, are not likely to improve decision making. A more complete benefit-cost analysis, including environmental and opportunity costs, would be superior. Essentially, this could involve emphasis on precise and inclusive measures of benefits and costs rather than a move in the direction of the qualitative, verbal project descriptions forthcoming under the *Principles*.

E. PUBLIC LAND POLICY

Although historically portrayed as a prime example of private enterprise, throughout its history, the U.S. economy has been characterized by extensive public ownership of land. The apex of federal land holdings occurred in 1850, when an estimated 1.2 billion acres were under federal control. Even in 1971, there were over 400 million acres of federal land in the forty-nine states, excluding Alaska, representing 21 percent of the total land area.[6] If Alaska is added, the total rises to 760 million acres or almost 33 percent of the land area of the entire fifty states. Within the contiguous forty-eight states, most federal lands are located in the western states, and, in eleven western states, federal lands constitute 47 percent of the total land area.[7]

Public lands range from extensive holdings of forests, unique natural sites, grazing areas, and offshore water rights, to the land sites of federal buildings in major urban centers. Despite the concentration of public lands in western states, every state contains some federal land. Moreover, the ownership and administration of this land is spread among numerous agencies. The National Park Service, the Bureau of Land Management, the Bureau of Reclamation, the Department of Agriculture, the military services, the Atomic Energy Commission, and the Forest Service are some of the agencies having important jurisdiction over public lands.

To a large extent, the vast federal land holdings of the early years of the United States were not the result of an overt policy to retain land in public ownership. Rather, the enormous land areas annexed by the westward expansion, in combination with the small population of the country, placed the new lands into federal ownership by default. Federal land policy, throughout the nineteenth century, was primarily concerned with the disposal of the public lands. The effects of this policy are reflected in the decline in public land acreage reported above, although this decline bottomed by 1930 and federal land holdings have been essentially stable since then.

The disposal of public lands during the last century took a number of forms. Probably the best known method was the homestead land grants to settlers. In addition, public lands were sold outright, given to states, and, at times, granted to private enterprises, as, for example, the extensive land grants to railroads.

Gradually, in the last years of the nineteenth century and then with

---

[6] Although our concern in this section is with federal lands and federal land policy, it is important to note that there are extensive land areas owned and administered by state and local governments.

[7] These states are Washington, Oregon, California, Idaho, Wyoming, Nebraska, Utah, Arizona, Colorado, New Mexico, and Montana.

more force in the twentieth century, a concern developed over this single-purpose policy of disposal of the public lands. As a result, disposal was gradually replaced with a policy commitment to retain the remaining public lands in federal ownership. One of the major reasons behind this change in policy stemmed from the private uses of the disposed public land and the aftereffects of these uses on the land itself— timber cutting, grazing, mineral extractions, and so on. The Taylor Grazing Act of 1934 replaced disposal as the dominant policy for public lands with a policy of reserving the lands in public status.

The public lands of today have many users. Although the actual sale and, hence, the outright transfer of the property rights of the land has ceased to be the prevailing policy, public lands are still used for purposes of private profit. This is accomplished by leasing the land to private individuals or business for various purposes. The primary private uses of public lands are for timber harvest, livestock grazing, and mineral extraction. Individuals and businesses purchase leases of public lands, in most cases at competitive market prices, and these leases are the exact equivalent of a lease in the private market. The government leases the property rights in the public lands for specific purposes, for stated time periods, and for certain conditions of use. In return, the government receives the revenues of the leases of public lands. In recent years, this revenue has totaled over $300 million annually. In leasing public lands for private purposes, the government is effectively acting as a supplier of factor inputs. If the prices of the leases of the public lands are determined by competitive bidding, they will equal the value of the lands in private markets.

Another major use of public land is outdoor recreation. The enormous popularity of the national park and forest system is an obvious example. We have previously indicated the dimensions of this popularity and discussed the economic implications of the burgeoning demand for outdoor recreation. At present, we can note that outdoor recreation is an important and growing source of demand for public lands. In many situations, the use of public land for recreational purposes may compete with the private uses described above. Another point worth recalling is that recreational uses of public land are often offered at zero or nominal prices. Thus, unlike a situation of competitive bidding for private leases of public lands, there is no direct, obvious measure of the value of public lands in their recreation uses.

Alternative uses of public lands do not present a land management problem until the uses begin to conflict with each other. When both the private and public demands for lands were low relative to their availability, the several demands could be met without major problems. This situation may have characterized the public lands through the first quarter of this century. However, over the last several decades, the booming recreational uses of public land increasingly have come in conflict with private uses.[8] Under such conditions, public land management becomes a much more crucial problem and requires increasing direction from economic analysis. Obviously, a desirable policy objective is to establish efficient land practices within any individual type of land use and to encourage the development of land management practices that accommodate several diverse uses on the same land area (for example, timber harvest, and recreation and watershed).

Our primary concern, however, is directed to the problem of evaluating conflicting uses of public lands. Frequent controversies have developed between environmental interests, concerned with the orderly protection of public lands, and the proponents of certain public land management policies such as clear cutting of timber in national forests, the location of the Alaskan pipeline through public lands, the lease of offshore drilling rights, and the use of public lands for livestock forage. We can expect public land policy increasingly to be confronted with the task of resolving competing demands. It is precisely this type of problem that can be treated in a benefit-cost framework.

For example, consider a benefit-cost analysis of a realistic situation involving a conflict between use of a certain tract of public land for mineral extraction and use as a recreation site. Let us assume the land has only these two mutually exclusive uses. In benefit-cost terms, an obvious measure of the benefits of using the land for mineral production would be given by either the value of the bids by private producers for the lease rights to the public land or, if the bidding is not competitive, by the value of equivalent privately owned land in mineral production. Such benefits would be measured over the time period of the lease and discounted at an appropriate interest rate. The cost measure, however, unlike the conventional treatment of costs discussed in Part A for ordinary government expenditure programs, would attempt to reflect the social value of the lost recreation opportunities and environmental amenities. In other words, the relevant cost measure is the *opportunity costs* of using the public land for timber and mineral production (the cost in terms of the foregone recreation and amenity values). An interesting aspect of treating the question of public land use in this framework is that the cost measure would not necessarily be confined to the time period of the lease. In the context of our example, suppose mineral extraction rights are leased for five years. The costs of using the land for

---

[8] Moreover, as noted in Chapter 8, conflicts are not necessarily confined to the obvious recreational or conservation vs. private uses, but also occur *within* recreational uses (for example, developed versus wilderness camping, or more generally, maintaining wilderness areas compared to their development for popular recreation activities).

mineral production, however, would be the opportunity costs of the foregone recreational values for the same five years *only* if recreation could resume in the sixth year as if the mineral extraction had not occurred. If this is not the case, then the costs should be measured for the time period over which recreational opportunities are lost and this may be considerably longer than the five-year mineral lease.[9]

Benefit-cost analysis can proceed after recognizing the necessity of the adjustment. The obvious requirement is to measure the value of the foregone recreational and environmental amenities over the appropriate time period. We have already discussed some of the difficulties of obtaining such measures in Chapter 8. Nevertheless, given necessary care, the cost measures, once developed, would be discounted and the benefit-cost ratio calculated. Studies following the outline of this hypothetical example can contribute significantly towards improving the efficiency of public land policies. An excellent example of this type of cost-benefit application is the Hells Canyon case in Idaho. The controversy centers on whether the Snake River should be impounded for electrical power or whether the area is to be retained in a wilderness state for recreational and amenity values. An ingenious and sophisticated benefit-cost study of this problem has estimated the critical values necessary to assign to recreational use in order to justify preserving Hells Canyon in its undeveloped state.[10]

In summary, we can expect the pressures of population and economic growth to increase demands for use of the public lands. Although land policy can attempt to devise technically sophisticated ways to accommodate various demands on the same land, it will also increasingly be confronted with the difficult issue of choosing between competing uses of public land. To this end, benefit-cost analysis is a useful tool for improving the economic efficiency of these inevitable public land allocation decisions. It provides the means to express the value of outdoor recreation and environmental amenities and to justify the preservation and protection of public lands. In the absence of a benefit-cost framework, achievement of this protection might be considerably more difficult because the comparison would be reduced to the unvalued and unmeasured appeals *to preserve the national heritage* versus the dollar values of public resources leased to private interests or developed as public power sources.

---

[9] Of course, any perceived increase in the value of mineral production (and hence, the value of mineral land) should be built into the estimated stream of benefits to the extent this may not be reflected in the price of the lease. We also assume that the addition or deletion of the mineral production will not appreciably affect the industry price of the particular ore in question (that is, the production from this land area is small compared to the total production).

[10] See the Fisher, et al. reference in the Selected References.

F. SUMMARY AND CONCLUSIONS

The issue of the efficient utilization of society's resources spans both the private and public sectors. Unfortunately, government investment faces the identical resource allocation problems of private markets. Benefit-cost analysis is a general method of social accounting designed to evaluate the efficiency aspects of public expenditures. Given care and thoroughness of measurement, it can help to allocate public funds efficiently among alternative outlets.

A number of difficult theoretical issues confront the benefit-cost practitioner. The choice of the discount rate directly influences the calculation of the benefit-cost ratio. Current federal practices employ discount rates considerably below private market interest rates. This discrepancy has generated significant controversy among economists. One position, arguing in favor of higher discount rates, claims that private market interest rates provide the correct measure of the opportunity cost of public investment. Alternatively, other economists argue that market rates do not reflect the social gains and costs of investment decisions. The result is private investment failure with respect to providing nonappropriable benefits for future generations. This position calls for social discount rates below market rates.

A further issue is the determination of the prices of public output. Many public projects are characterized by exclusion difficulties. Others involve a social consensus that the benefits should be equally available to all. In both of these situations, a zero or nominal price policy is usually followed in allocating the public output. However, for projects where neither condition holds, increased use of an overt pricing policy offers significant efficiency gains in the form of protection of the quality of the available public output. It also can provide much-needed information to improve benefit estimates by revealing the actual willingness to pay of the beneficiaries of public output.

Institutional obstacles pose significant practical problems to the effective use of benefit-cost analysis. Although Congress is cognizant of benefit-cost studies, other criteria than allocational efficiency heavily influence the appropriations process. Additional resistance to systematic benefit-cost analysis also stems directly from agencies fearful of resulting budget reductions.

The application of benefit-cost analysis to programs concerning the protection and production of environmental amenities is relatively new. We examined two specific areas of government ownership and production involving important environmental issues: water resource development and public land policy. Benefit-cost analysis of water resource investments represents the initial application of this technique to public expenditures. Historically, this has involved a standard comparison of the capital and discounted operating costs to the discounted measurable benefits of the project. Recent changes in institutional procedures, however, require a more explicit accounting of the environmental consequences of water resource development, although numerous major problems remain. The general movement to broader definitions of benefits and costs also carries important implications for federal land policies. Costs should not be restricted simply to development costs but should include the opportunity costs of foregone options, recreational, and environmental values. This extension of the benefit-cost framework promises to remove environmental protection projects from the weak defensive position that relies on appeals to *save our heritage*. At the same time, it should reduce the number of conventional public production programs that generate severe environmental disruptions.

QUESTIONS FOR DISCUSSION

1. Do you think that the problems inherent in benefit-cost analysis are more serious for environmental programs than for government programs in other areas, for example, defense, transportation, and education?

2. Some economists have argued that much of the benefits from public investments in environmental resources are received *now* by people who are made better off by the knowledge that their grandchildren will benefit from the availability of such resources. Does this argument make any sense to you? What is its relevance to the determination of the social discount rate in benefit-cost analysis?

3. Hydroelectric projects are justified by externalities on the benefit side of benefit-cost analysis. Could such projects also involve some externalities on the cost side? Explain how any externalities should be treated in computing the benefit-cost ratio.

4. "Charging fees for entry into national parks is wrong, because all such fees do is to keep the poor from sharing in the enjoyment of our national heritage. The national parks belong to everybody and should be available to everybody on an equal basis." Evaluate this argument.

5. "Benefit-cost analysis will never be accepted by Congress because it threatens the jobs of incumbent Congressmen." Comment critically.

SELECTED REFERENCES

BUCHANAN, J. M. and G. TULLOCK, *The Calculus of Consent*. Ann Arbor: University of Michigan Press, 1962. A presentation of developments in theories of government behavior.

CICCHETTI, C. J., *Forecasting Recreation in the United States*. Lexington: D. C. Heath and Co., 1973. A detailed treatment of projection methods for outdoor recreation activity.

CLAWSON, M., "Public and Private Interest in Public Lands," in *Land Use Policy and Problems in the United States*, ed. C. W. Ottoson. Lincoln: University of Nebraska Press, 1963. A summary of the economic aspects of public land issues. The volume also provides a series of further readings in public land policies.

Council on Environmental Quality, *102 Monitor*. Washington, D.C.: U.S. Government Printing Office. A monthly publication summarizing environmental impact statements received by the Council in response to NEPA requirements.

DAVIDSON, P., F. G. ADAMS, and J. J. SENECA, "The Social Value of Water Recreational Facilities Resulting from an Improvement in Water Quality: The Delaware Estuary," in *Water Research* ed. Kneese, A. V. and S. C. Smith. Baltimore: Johns Hopkins Press, 1966. A benefit-cost study of water based recreation and water quality in the Delaware River.

FISHER, A. C., J. V. KRUTILLA, and C. J. CICCHETTI, "The Economics of Environmental Preservation: A Theoretical and Empirical Analysis," *American Economic Review*, LXII, No. 4 (September, 1972). A technical analysis of preservation arguments in the context of the Hells Canyon case demonstrating that preservation values may exceed the development values for the proposed hydroelectric project.

HAVEMAN, R. H., "The Opportunity Cost of Displaced Private Spending and the Social Discount Rate," *Water Resources Research*, V, No. 5 (October, 1969). A brief but thorough summary of the discount rate issue.

HAVEMAN, R. H., *Water Resource Investment and the Public Interest*. Nashville: Vanderbilt University Press, 1965. A detailed treatise on the income distribution aspects of water investment decisions.

HAVEMAN, R. H., *The Economics of the Public Sector*. New York: John Wiley and Sons Inc., 1970. An introductory treatment of federal participation in economic affairs, particularly relevant are Chaps. 6, 7, and 8.

HOWE, C. W., *Benefit-Cost Analysis for Water System Planning*. Baltimore: Publication Press, 1971. An application of benefit-cost analysis providing detailed case studies in addition to discussion of general methodology.

McKEAN, R., "The Unseen Hand in Government," *American Economic Review*, LV, No. 3 (June 1965). Presents a competition argument in the context of a theory of government.

MISHAN, E. J., *Cost-Benefit Analysis, An Introduction*. New York: Praeger Publishers, 1971. A comprehensive treatment of the issues of cost-benefit analysis.

U.S. Joint Economic Committee, *The Analysis and Evaluation of Public Expenditures: The PPB System*, Vols. I-III, Washington, D.C.: U.S.

Government Printing Office, 1969. Previously cited in Chap. 4, these volumes contain discussions of a number of benefit-cost issues and descriptions of the problems and progress of the PPB System.

U.S. Joint Economic Committee, *Economic Analysis of Public Investment Decisions: Interest Rate Policy and Discount Analysis*, 90th Congress, 2nd sess., Washington, D.C.: U.S. Government Printing Office, 1968. Public hearing proceedings of discount rate policy providing coverage of the major discount rate positions.

WEISBROD, B., "Concepts of Benefits and Costs," in *Problems in Public Expenditure Analysis* ed. S. B. Chase. Washington, D.C.: The Brookings Institution, 1964. Discusses the idea of weighting benefits and costs by varying amounts according to their incidence.

PART 5

Population, Economic Growth and Environmental Quality

Chapter 12

Population
Levels
and
Environmental
Quality

This chapter discusses the role of the *level* of population in determining environmental quality. The relationship between population level and environmental quality may appear to be all too obvious to many readers who associate the densely populated city directly with the worst air and water pollution problems and with the severe disamenities that they observe every day. In the United States and most other economically developed countries, however, the environmental problems of densely populated urbanized areas cannot legitimately be attributed to *general* overpopulation. In the 1970s, crowded conditions in individual American cities coexist with a general abundance of living space per capita by international standards. In fact, the growing urbanization and concentration of population in the United States has been matched by the *depopulation* of rural expanses in the Midwest and in other scattered areas of the country. Many environmental problems are more severe in the United States than in India, for example, but the latter country is much more crowded and at the same time much less urbanized.

Environmental problems associated with urbanization are not, of course, completely independent of the overall level of population. If the United States population had grown less rapidly in the past, our cities today would almost certainly be smaller and, perhaps, also less crowded, and the localized air and water pollution problems of urban areas might also be somewhat less severe. On the whole, however, it seems appropriate to defer, as much as possible, the analysis of the environmental problems that result specifically from urbanization and population density to Chapter 13. In this chapter, we shall confine our attention to environmental problems that are the direct consequence of high levels of population *per se,* with or without modern tendencies to greater urbanization.

Government policies affecting population growth involve many vital socioeconomic issues beyond that of environmental quality. For example, achievement of a lower population growth rate through a reduction in the birth rate would mean that our society would have fewer children to educate in the future, and that pressures on public school budgets would ease. The savings in terms of educational quantities could be devoted to education quality or to other alternative uses. On the other hand, lower birth rates have another consequence that many people would not welcome—a population with a higher average age. This chapter will ignore such important issues in order to focus on the single, narrow issue of the relationship between population level and environmental quality. We also shall not discuss the crucial moral issues involved in the various birth control techniques that are the major instruments of modern population policies. These moral issues may well be of overriding importance in determining the shape of future national population policies, but we believe that they should be treated in a lengthier, more specialized monograph.

The chapter is organized as follows: Section A briefly reviews some important demographic facts to establish the necessary statistical background for population levels and trends, both in the United States and in the rest of the world. Section B then summarizes current economic thinking about the complex relationship between population levels and various aspects of environmental quality. Section C outlines a simple economic theory of fertility, and Section D utilizes this theory to specify the policy variables available to governments interested in influencing population growth rates. A final Section E summarizes the main points of the chapter.

A. POPULATION GROWTH IN PERSPECTIVE

The Basic Demographic Variables

The net population growth rate (PGR) of any society during any given time period is equal to the algebraic sum of the excess of the birth rate (BR) over the mortality rate (MR), and the net immigration rate (IR). In symbols,

$$PG = (BR - MR) + IR$$

where all rates are customarily measured as the number of births, deaths, and net immigrants per thousand of the existing population. IR can be negative, of course, if emigration exceeds immigration, and PGR can be negative if $MR > BR + IR$. The algebraic difference between BR and MR is called the *rate of natural increase*. For the world as a whole, migration results only in the redistribution of a given population among different countries, and the rate of world population growth is therefore equal to the world rate of natural increase.

Demographers distinguish between the concept natural *fecundity*, a biological measure of maximum potential reproduction, and *fertility*, the actual reproduction of a species. The fertility of man is everywhere less than his natural fecundity, even in societies that have available no effective contraceptive devices. Through various methods, including sexual abstinence, individuals and societies have been able to exercise at least crude control over the fertility of man. Fertility varies with the state of economic and cultural development of societies and involves much more than the biological nature of man. The number of births in a period of time as short as a year reflects the number of women of child-bearing age at that time and other transitory and random factors as well. Demographers, therefore, regard the (crude) birth rate—the number of live births per thousand of the total population in a society—as only the simplest measure of fertility. More comprehensive measures of fertility average the short term influences on the crude birth rate and are calculated whenever sufficiently detailed data are available.

Mortality rates in the United States and other economically developed societies are now very low, about ten per thousand of population per year, reflecting a slow and steady decline in the last few decades. Mortality rates appear to be approaching a temporary biological limit in these countries, pending possible scientific breakthroughs in the treatment of degenerative diseases. Mortality rates in the majority of the less-developed countries have fallen dramatically in recent decades, but are still far above the levels in more advanced countries. Crude mortality rates as well as crude birth rates may reflect the age distribution of the population and temporary or random factors, and age-adjusted mortality rates can be calculated to average the short-run influences of the age distribution on the crude rate.

International migration, once a major factor in redistributing world population, has become less and less important in the twentieth century, as all economically developed countries have acted to restrict the potential influx of immigrants from poor, overpopulated countries. Immigration into the United States was sharply limited just after World War I and continues today at a relatively low level. Within just the last fifty years or so, the remaining empty habitable lands on earth have vanished, and it now is clear that human population problems must be dealt with directly by national population policies.

The tremendous growth in world population, beginning just two or three centuries ago, and accelerating in the last half century, is the result of the growing control by man over his mortality at younger ages without a corresponding control over his fertility. To appreciate the environmental consequences of continued population growth at past and present rates, it is necessary to go beyond such a qualitative generalization and to review some relevant quantitative trends.

Population Developments in the United States

The population of the United States as of the 1970 census was 205 million. This figure compares with less than 4 million counted in the census of 1790, some 50 million in the 1880 census, and 106 million in the 1920 census. Table 12–1 shows data on the components of United States population growth for quinquennial averages between 1935 and 1969. Note that net population growth rates in this country have varied widely between the average 1.72 percent per year in the late 1950s to the average 0.82 percent per year in the late 1930s and the average 1.09 percent in the late 1960s. The low birth rates in the 1930s are generally attributed in part to the extraordinary economic conditions during the Great Depression. The depressed economic circumstances during the decade were especially burdensome on young workers without secure careers, and encouraged young married couples either to limit the size of their families or to postpone having children. In contrast to the 1930s are the high birth rates of the late 1940s and 1950s, the period of the so-called Baby Boom. Since 1958, birth rates have once again declined steadily to levels almost as low as those of the Depression. As the data in Table 12–1 make clear, the major difference between the net population growth rates of the country in the 1950s and the 1960s was due to differences in birth rates, as the mortality and net immigration rates remained relatively stable.

TABLE 12–1   THE COMPONENTS OF UNITED STATES
POPULATION GROWTH, 1935–1969 (rates
per 1,000 of the midyear population)

Annual Average	Population Growth Rate	Birth Rate	Mortality Rate	Net Immigration Rate
1935–39	8.2	18.8	11.0	0.4
1940–44	11.4	21.2	10.8	0.8
1945–49	15.7	24.1	10.1	1.6
1950–54	17.1	24.8	9.5	1.8
1955–59	17.2	24.8	9.4	1.8
1960–64	15.1	22.6	9.4	2.0
1965–69	10.9	18.2	9.5	2.2

Source: United States Census Bureau.

With given assumptions about future mortality and migration experience, census projections of the United States population vary widely
with different plausible assumptions about fertility rates. The range between the projections based on extreme high and low fertility assumptions is large even by the end of the century—between 300 million and
250 million. Two conclusions can be drawn from these projections: (1)
In the immediate future, population in the United States will continue
to grow steadily, barring a nuclear war or some other catastrophe of similar magnitude. Even if fertility rates fell immediately and permanently
to the level consistent with zero population growth over the long run,
the population of the country would grow by some 20 percent by the year
2000 due to the age distribution of the present population. (2) Over the
long run, relatively small differences in fertility rates will result in large
differences in the population of our country.

The fall in the crude birth rate in the United States in the 1960s
and early 1970s has led some observers to project optimistically a
leveling off of our population. A deeper look at the factors influencing
fertility trends makes most demographers more cautious. One important
factor explaining the fall in birth rates after 1958 has been the relatively
low number of women of childbearing age, especially during the first
half of the 1960s. This demographic circumstance was the result of the
low birth rates during the economically depressed 1930s—a so-called
echo effect. A second factor appears to have been a tendency to later
marriage and the postponement of children by young married couples
who intend eventually to have children. This development may be due in
part to economic difficulties resulting from the Vietnam War, such as
the adverse effect of the draft on the employment prospects of young
males, and to housing shortages. A third factor is a real decrease, of some
unknown degree, in the *true* fertility rate. The sum of these three factors

is clearly evident in actual birth rate data, but it is impossible to disentangle the effects sufficiently to be sure of the relative importance of the latter two.

Until recently, surveys of the family plans of young couples indicated that the expected number of children per completed family was, on average, about three. This level is significantly lower than that for older couples, but it is still consistent with the highest of the census population projections. Given the relatively large number of women who will be of childbearing age in the 1970s, the direct consequence of the Baby Boom of the late 1940s and early 1950s, the realization of these family plans could result in a sharp increase in the birth rate and a corresponding resurgence in net population growth. But the most recent evidence indicates that both *actual* and *expected* fertility have dropped sharply in the early 1970s to levels consistent with zero population growth. These latest developments are grounds for optimism about an easy, painless solution to population stability in our society. But we have no conclusive evidence in hand yet that fertility will permanently decline to a level consistent with eventual zero population growth under normal, peacetime, economically prosperous conditions.

Population Developments in the World

The population of the world stood at over 3.5 billion as of 1970. Estimates of world population going back more than a century are little more than inspired guesses, but it seems likely that no more than half a billion human beings lived on earth at the beginning of the seventeenth century. Just one century ago, the world population was probably only about one billion. By the year 2000, world population will reach close to 7 billion, again assuming no nuclear war or some comparable catastrophe. Thus, man is today behaving as if in response to the Biblical injunction to multiply and cover the earth. The population problems of the United States, the richest and one of the least crowded of nations, are trivial in comparison to those of much of the rest of the world.

Population growth in the United States and in other countries that are now at a relatively high stage of economic development resulted from initial sustained economic advances. Economic progress set off a complicated chain of events leading to declines first in mortality rates and then, after some time lag, to declines in fertility rates. In contrast, less-developed countries today have benefited from the importation of modern health techniques from the more developed countries and have been able to reduce their mortality rates without any prior industrial breakthrough leading to sustained economic growth. Because of this difference in the time sequence of economic growth and demographic change, we cannot predict with confidence that fertility rates in less-developed countries will follow the pattern of developed countries and begin to decline in the near future.

Table 12–2 gives estimates of rates of natural increase for different

TABLE 12–2   WORLD POPULATION GROWTH RATES, 1970–1975 (rates per 1,000 of the population)

Area	Rate of Natural Increase	Crude Birth Rate	Mortality Rate
WORLD, TOTAL	18.8	32.4	13.6
More deveolped areas	10.1	18.7	8.6
Less developed areas	22.5	38.2	15.7
South Asia	25.3	40.8	15.5
Europe	6.2	16.3	10.1
U.S.S.R.	11.9	19.0	7.1
Africa	25.6	45.1	19.5
Northern America	13.2	22.6	9.4
Latin America	29.1	38.2	9.1

Source: United Nations Department of Economic and Social Affairs.

areas in the world for the period 1970–1975. The figures in this Table show that the rate of natural increase in less-developed countries, 22.5 per thousand, is more than double the rate in developed countries, 10.1 per thousand. The disparity in population growth rates is due to the high birth rates in the less-developed countries, which more than offset the lower mortality rates in the developed countries.[1]

Table 12–3 gives estimates of the population of selected countries in the years 1920, 1950, and 1980. The clear implication of these estimates and the comparative rates of natural increase in Table 12–2 is that the combined population of the United States and other developed countries will be a much smaller fraction of the world total in the future than now or in the past. Most of the three and a half billion additional human beings in the world by the end of this century will live in countries in which the demand for rapid economic growth dominates most other concerns. The significance of this trend is that it will not be sufficient simply to double total world output levels in order to meet the demands of an expanding world population. Per capita national output of goods

[1] The low mortality rate shown for Latin America is due to the highly skewed age distribution of that continent. The crude mortality rate reflects the very young average age of the population, but age-specific mortality rates in Latin America are much higher than in developed countries.

TABLE 12–3   POPULATION ESTIMATES OF SELECTED
COUNTRIES: 1920, 1950, 1980 (population
in thousands)

Country	1920	1950	1980
Mainland China	475,000	560,000	843,000
Japan	55,391	82,900	111,064
India	250,500	359,250	682,300
France	38,750	41,736	53,250
Italy	37,006	46,603	56,400
United Kingdom	43,718	50,616	57,250
Norway	2,635	3,265	4,250
South Africa	6,842	12,447	26,800
United Arab Republic	13,277	20,448	46,750
Israel	480	1,258	3,141
United States	106,782	152,271	240,893
Brazil	27,554	52,328	123,716
Mexico	14,500	25,826	70,581
Australia-New Zealand	6,641	10,127	18,237

Source: United Nations Department of Economic and Social Affairs.

and services is over $3,000 in the United States and less than $300 in some of the poorest countries in Asia, and the American economy will surely continue to grow over the next three decades. The almost universal expectation of a higher per capita standard of living in the less-developed part of the world means that an enormous increase in the rate of world output is required to bring their living standards even close to those of the United States or of other developed countries. Even though such very high growth rates are not feasible, we can expect output levels throughout the world to rise sharply to meet the demands of the burgeoning world population. These increased output levels may place unprecedented demands on all scarce economic resources, including clean air, potable water, and the amenity elements of a life-sustaining environment.

B. POPULATION LEVELS AND ENVIRONMENTAL QUALITY

This section attempts to specify the relationship between the level of population in a society (or in the whole world) and the quality of its environment. The important policy question is to what extent a lower population growth rate in the future would ease the various threats now evident to specific environmental resources. In other words, should birth control be a weapon in the government's arsenal of antipollution measures, together with effluent charges, regulation, and direct government provision of environmental resources? If so, how important should its role be, relative to these alternative measures? The reader should remember that the following discussion concentrates on population *levels* and thus abstracts from the largely separate issue of population *concentration* in urbanized areas, which is the main topic of the next chapter. Finally, our discussion of the relationship of population level to environmental quality is most directly applicable to an advanced economy like the United States. Population growth in less-developed countries involves somewhat different issues, which we postpone for the time being.

The most obvious consequence of population growth in any society is that more babies today means more potential workers in the next generation. That is, the higher the fertility rate in a society, the higher will be the rate of growth of its potential labor force. Growth of the labor force, combined with growth in the supply of other productive factors and with improvements in technology, result in a sustained rate of growth in the level of output of an economy. But, as observed throughout the book, levels of the flow of pollutants have been a function of levels of output. Thus, growth in population levels is most directly related to deterioration of environmental quality via the link between population growth and labor supply and the relationship of labor supply to the level of output and pollution in an economy.

The quantitative importance of population growth as a factor affecting environmental quality depends on the importance of labor force growth relative to other factors that determine the rate of growth of output. In the last decade, economists have attempted to explain statistically how much labor force growth and other factors each contribute independently to the total growth rate of output. After adjusting for growth in the capital stock, including both physical capital like plant and equipment and human capital of education and training embodied in workers, surprisingly little economic growth remains to be explained by growth in labor force and population—perhaps one-fourth to one-third of the average 3 to 4 percent annual growth rate in total output. Similar studies done for other advanced economies appear to be consistent with this basic conclusion.[2] Thus, this method of estimation implies that population growth by itself is responsible for only a small fraction of the total growth rate of output or of the growth rate of effluent emissions in developed economies.

Noneconomists tend to approach this subject from a different perspective. They attempt to factor the growth of specific effluents into the separate effects of population growth and all other factors. Such dis-

[2] The authoritative source on the determinants of economic growth is Edward F. Denison, *Why Growth Rates Differ* (Washington, D.C.: The Brookings Institution, 1967).

aggregated studies are valuable because they show how population policies contribute to changes in the composition, as well as to the total level,
of effluents. For example, growth in human wastes is certainly more
directly related to population growth than is the total level of effluents.
Studies done from this perspective yield different conclusions, however,
about the relative importance of population growth as a factor in determining effluent levels. Barry Commoner, who has done some of this
work, has concluded that only between 12 and 20 percent of the total
change in his various *environmental impact* indices is due to population
growth. For example, he reports that after adjusting for the effects of
technological change and changes in per capita output, the independent
effect of population growth could account for only about 20 percent of
the environmental impact of synthetic pesticides between 1950 and
1967. Paul Ehrlich and his coworkers have disputed the work of Commoner and claim to be able to show a much more important role for
population growth in causing the growth of effluent levels.[3] Their results
are based on the notion that the impact of total consumption of some
good or resource can be factored into growth of the per capita consumption level and growth in the consuming population. This methodology
appears to make the implicit assumption that growth of output and effluents is proportional to growth of population. But as we have seen, such
an assumption is clearly refuted by the evidence. Population growth
appears to be responsible for only a fraction of growth in total effluent
levels in this and other developed economies.

The implications of the above discussion for environmental quality
are quite straightforward. If population growth were stabilized by a
permanent drop in fertility, the growth rate of total output would fall,
eventually to perhaps 75 percent of the rate that would occur under the
continuation of past fertility rates. This conclusion assumes that advanced
economies like the United States could adapt their economic and social
institutions successfully to a zero population growth rate situation. With
a slower growth rate of output, pollution problems would be correspondingly less severe, other things equal. Of course, the above analysis is not
limited to restraining population growth alone but applies equally well
to *any* measure that inhibits economic growth. Population control is
unique, however, in that it is the only one of the set of growth-inhibiting
policies that will not, in the long run, affect the growth rate of per capita
output and consumption. Expectations of improvements in per capita
economic well-being are deeply ingrained in the culture of economically

---

[3] For a debate between Commoner and Ehrlich on the relative importance of the population factor in explaining environmental problems and related issues, see *Environment,* XIV, No. 3
(April, 1972).

developed societies in the world today, and it seems most unlikely that explicit sacrifices of consumption per capita will receive much popular backing for the sake of the modern conservation cause. But a zero population growth rate policy does have the attraction of promising to lower output and effluent growth rates without a corresponding reduction in anticipated per capita consumption standards.

The discussion thus far has implicitly taken all other policies affecting the environment as given. But our analysis implies that a population policy is both a potential substitute and a potential complement of alternative environmental policy measures, such as effluent charges, that deal with environmental problems directly. Economists are generally biased in favor of specific solutions to specific problems. That is, if environmental pollution is caused fundamentally by failure to take account of external costs of production and consumption, then the straightforward solution to this problem is to take account of those externalities directly through a system of explicit charges for the use of environmental resources. In contrast, attempting to solve the problem indirectly by limiting population growth seems a clumsy, inefficient alternative. In this connection, the reader should note again that population growth per se is a relatively modest factor in contributing to the growth rate of output and, therefore, to growth in the level of emissions of pollutants.

The case of the automobile and its attendant environmental problems provides a good example of the contrast between population policies and alternative environmental measures. Some writers take the present ratio of motor vehicles to people in the United States (approximately one motor vehicle to every two people) as given and project the horrible prospect of perhaps 25 to 50 million more vehicles on the roads by the year 2000. Society can avert such a development by use of the blunt instrument of population control to control the denominator (people) of this ratio. But the government can also work on the numerator (vehicles) by more direct policies. For example, higher excise taxes on the sales of automobiles will raise their price and reduce their consumption. So will regulations requiring expensive air pollution controls, an alternative that directly alleviates the worst environmental consequences of mass automobile consumption. Higher tolls on highways and more reliance on mass transit in congested urban areas are other direct environmental measures that are alternatives to population control. All of these measures get directly at the root of the externalities associated with automobiles in contrast to reliance on the birth control solution to the problem.

As noted in the introduction to this section, our analysis is most applicable in the context of developed economies, in which consumption levels are already relatively high and the process of sustained economic growth leading to ever higher per capita consumption levels is well established. All the developed countries taken together account for less than one-third of the present total world population, and this fraction is expected to decline to about one-sixth by the year 2000. Paradoxically, it is population growth in the relatively sparsely populated, developed economies that poses the immediate threat to the *world* environment. This is the case because less than one-third of the world population, in the relatively well-off countries of Europe, North America, and Japan, accounts for more than five-sixths of the consumption of available world resources, including the waste-absorbing services of the earth's waters, land, and atmosphere for various effluents. Various pollutants, including human wastes, do pose serious health problems for some less-developed countries, but these problems are generally localized in their impact.

Every additional child born today in the United States will likely consume over his lifetime several automobiles, hundreds of consumer durables, and immense amounts of electrical energy. His counterpart born in Southeast Asia will likely live much the same life of grinding poverty his parents live today, consuming little more than a minimal amount of food and other necessities. Thus, the average American baby of 1970 may, over his lifetime, draw as much upon the scarce world resources required to absorb effluents as ten or more Malaysian children. Ironically, then, the immense problems of population growth in poor countries are largely localized (economically, if not politically), but the much less serious population problems of the affluent countries may contribute significantly to world environmental problems. Some polluting activities of developed countries may seriously hinder the development possibilities of poor countries. If water pollution destroys the world fisheries, for example, the less-developed nations will lose an important potential source of inexpensive calorie and protein supply. This could change if the less-developed countries of today perform the miracle of surmounting all their problems and succeed in achieving an economic breakthrough to Western per capita consumption standards. In solving their own domestic economic problems, however, they would likely join the ranks of developed countries as major sources of the despoilment of the earth's environment.

Let us return to the context of economically developed societies and consider a distinct, less obvious consequence of population growth for the quality of the environment. An ominous threat to environmental quality, broadly conceived, in the United States, is the overutilization of certain scarce, unique resources. These resources include the small areas of the earth that are ocean beaches, mountain lakes, and other natural facilities ideally suited for recreational purposes. Other closely related examples are the even fewer sites of surpassing natural beauty, such as the

Grand Canyon or San Francisco Bay. In addition, a few remaining wilderness areas are unique resources in that they shelter rare species whose survival depends on the preservation of their natural habitats free of the intrusion of human beings. These resources are unique because they have no good substitutes and they cannot be augmented or replaced if ever they are destroyed, however advanced the level of technology.

Unfortunately, many of the most precious unique resources in the United States are increasingly threatened by the *combination* of population growth and rising per capita income levels. Only a decade or two ago, places like Glacier Park were the preserves of a small, wealthy elite. Today they are visited by a much larger cross-section of our larger and wealthier population. Crowding of these natural resources occurs because every year a larger population with a higher per capita income level seeks to share their benefits. But the essential characteristics of these resources are such that crowding threatens to destroy their fragile ecosystems and to degrade their quality to the point where their consumption value will fall to zero for all potential consumers. Note that this kind of crowding is quite distinct from the crowding that occurs as a consequence of urbanization. Even if we could miraculously end the current degree of urbanization in the United States and spread our population evenly throughout the hinterlands, the problem of crowding in unique sites would remain, as long as population growth and the spread of affluence continue to make such sites available to ever larger numbers of pleasure seekers.

Population and affluence have already reached levels in the United States to produce crowding that threatens specific unique natural resources. Ocean beaches near large metropolitan areas are highly congested on sunny, weekend days to the point that the net pleasure of many sunbathers and surfers is moot. As Casey Stengel once observed about a popular restaurant: "It's so crowded that nobody goes there anymore." Yellowstone Park and Yosemite Canyon are fit at times only for people who enjoy bumper-to-bumper traffic and a Coney Island atmosphere. Similar population *cum* wealth pressures face the few remaining wilderness areas in this country. The very term *wilderness area* loses all meaning when the rate of utilization reaches high levels during peak tourist seasons that threaten disastrous results to fragile ecosystems. The progressive deterioriation of some of the most beautiful natural resources in the United States has occurred at a frightening pace during the 1950s and 1960s. Projections of population and income growth rates through the end of this century point to a pessimistic conclusion about the possibility of preserving the quality of these resources.

In many instances, such unique natural resources can be rationed effectively by charging a high enough entrance fee or user charge. Unfortunately, fees and charges may be expensive to administer because of the problem of enforcing exclusion. In addition, it may be politically objectionable on distributional grounds to ration these resources. What politician would care to defend the denial of entry to beaches and national parks to poor children? Another means of rationing these resources would be to limit access to them by not allowing automobiles to approach closer than, say, ten miles from the entrance to parks and beaches. Or visitors may be limited to the *capacity* of a site on a first-come, first-serve basis. It is not obvious whether such rationing schemes are fairer than a system of rationing by money prices. In any case, no rationing scheme is a panacea for the basic problem. Again, population control is both a substitute and a complement to more direct environmental policies.

C. AN ECONOMIC THEORY OF FERTILITY

Population growth is the inescapable sum of natural increase—the excess of births over deaths—and of net immigration. Government policies that would attempt to manipulate mortality in order to control population are, of course, unthinkable. As of this date in history, it is also unrealistic to expect that further restrictions on immigration into the United States will significantly affect population growth. Immigration into the United States has already been reduced by restrictive legislation to low levels. The current level of immigration today is far below what would be necessary to meet the demands for entry and any further cutback in immigration levels faces persuasive humanitarian and economic objections. Furthermore, as we have already noted, migration between nation states can no longer be an important factor in solving the *world* population problem. Thus, by a process of elimination, only birth control remains as a realistic vehicle for government intervention in the process of population growth. We present an economic theory of fertility that is intended to identify those variables affecting fertility that are subject to social control.

The point of departure in an economic theory of fertility is the presumption that the number of children born to families reflects a considerable degree of rational choice by the parents. The empirical basis for this presumption is the fact that everywhere in the civilized world, but especially in more economically developed societies, fertility is considerably less than fecundity. The presumption of rationality does not deny that a great many births are the result of irrationality or of accident, but it does assert that, on average, fertile couples tend to have close to the number of children they desire to have. We shall attempt to outline a theoretical framework within which rational family planning decisions take place.

Following the pioneer in this field, Professor Gary Becker, we can conceive of a couple's demand for children as being a demand for a unique type of consumer durable good. (We admit that any profession that thinks of the desire for children in this framework deserves to be called the *dismal science*.) That is, we shall consider the desire to have children in the same analytical framework used to analyze a family's decision to buy a durable good such as an automobile, a stereo set, or a washing machine. In common with these other consumer durables, children presumably are expected, before their acquisition, to make the con-sumers—their parents—better off or happier over an extended period of time in the future. This expected happiness may derive from a pure love of children, or from a desire to propagate the race, or from the need to assert masculinity or femininity, or in order to acquire symbols of ma-turity and respectability, or from any other motive, however noble or base. To use the terminology of economics, we say that children are expected to yield a flow of *consumption services* to their parents over time, much like the consumption services expected from other consumer durables. Some parents, especially in less-developed societies, may also expect their children eventually to help support them in their old age, and if this is the case, these direct income support payments should be added to the expected value of the consumption services of children to obtain the total benefits of children. All or some of these benefits may involve a great deal of uncertainty, but such uncertainty is a feature shared by all consumer durables that are supposed to yield net benefits to the owner over an extended period of time into the future.

Most couples expect the benefits of children to be large enough to justify the *purchase* of a limited number of them.[4] But just as most people buy only one or two automobiles, most couples have less than the maxi-mum number of children they could have. It is a straightforward economic problem to explain why people limit their purchases of auto-mobiles; in brief, limited incomes force families to ration their purchases of automobiles and of *all* desired consumer goods and services. By analogous reasoning, couples must limit their purchases of children. Families have limited incomes and the bearing and raising of children involve considerable costs. A rational couple will have one more child only if the present value of the expected lifetime stream of benefits from

---

[4] To be more precise, the theory refers only to the *demand* for children, or the number of children couples desire to have. Some couples are unable to have as many children as they desire.

the child exceeds the present value of the expected lifetime stream of costs of the child.[5] The additional cost incurred in having another child may best be thought of as an opportunity cost—the automobiles, stereos, trips to Europe, and so forth that a couple must forego once it chooses to have the child. According to this theory, all couples continually make joint decisions on their *consumption* of children and their purchases of all substitute and complementary goods and services in their total lifetime budget.

From this brief outline of the economic approach to the theory of fertility, we can hypothesize that the significant forces determining the number of children demanded by a couple are (1) its tastes for children, (2) family income, and (3) the costs of children *relative to* the prices of alternative goods and services in the family budget.

Tastes for children vary from couple to couple, but it is evident that a meaningful, if somewhat vague, norm is determined by various social pressures operative within a given socioeconomic class. For example, young, highly educated professionals in the 1970s tend to choose between having two or three children, and couples who have four or more children are definitely regarded as being somewhat eccentric. The norm varies considerably, of course, across different socioeconomic groups.

Family income, defined to include both current and expected future incomes, sets the limit or budget constraint to all lifetime consumption expenditures by any family, including its expenditures on children. Families with high lifetime incomes can afford to have more children than poorer families, just as they can afford to purchase more of every good and service. This pure income effect on fertility is very weak, however, and is generally more than offset by factors such as education level and birth control knowledge that are highly correlated with income.

The cost of a child relative to the prices of alternative goods and services affects the allocation of any given income between children and

---

[5] To be formally correct, only the prices of the goods and services a couple buys for the support of a child are fixed in the market. The quantities of these goods and services actually purchased by the couple are subject to its discretion. Thus the cost of the child (the sum of all prices x quantities) is a variable, subject to some control by the family. A given family can choose to purchase large quantities of goods and services for its child, thus producing a "high quality" child, and another family can skimp on its child and end up with a "low quality" product. The obvious analogy here is the choice between a Cadillac and a Chevrolet; a higher level of expenditure presumably yields a better product.

On the plausible ground that families in a given socioeconomic class have virtually no discretion over the "quality" child they must raise once the child is born, we shall assume for simplicity that the cost of a child is fixed for any given couple. This assumption implies that families do not choose, for example, between having either two high quality children or three low quality children. It also implies that they do not choose between having either a high quality child or a low quality child *and* a more expensive automobile.

all alternative forms of consumption. A fundamental theorem of micro-economics says that, given tastes and incomes, an increase in the relative cost of children will cause couples to purchase less children and to shift their expenditure towards more of the now relatively cheaper alternatives in order to maximize their economic well-being. The crucial empirical issue is the elasticity, or quantitative sensitivity, of this relative price response. That is, if the relative cost of children rises by 10 percent, will the number of children demanded by all families fall by 20, 10, or perhaps only .001 percent? The answer to this question may be crucial to the eventual success of government population control policies.

To return our discussion closer to the realm of practical policy applications, let us now consider, concretely, the costs of children. The total cost of a child includes both *upkeep costs* and *human capital costs*. Upkeep costs include expenditures on food, clothing, medical care, and other necessities for the child. Human capital costs, on the other hand, involve outlays on such items as schooling, private music lessons, and summer camp. The difference between the two kinds of costs rests on the usual economic distinction between current and capital expenditures. Upkeep expenditures are those necessary to maintain life for the child at some socially determined acceptable level, but human capital expenditures are intended to enhance the *value* of the child by bringing him up to the norm level of some socioeconomic class. It is largely by means of such human capital investment in children that the upper middle classes in this country are able to pass on their relatively advantageous positions in society to their offspring.

To measure the relative cost of children, the economist ideally should have available current measures of the cost of children and a corresponding index of the prices of the closest substitutes for children. Such data are not available, but it seems plausible to assume that the two most important variables in the determination of the relative cost of children are the job opportunities available to women with and without children and the relative cost of education.

A significant cost of children for most families today is the opportunity cost of the foregone earnings of the wife who must leave the labor market once she becomes a mother. The decision to have a child means the loss of valuable continuity and experience in a career and places the mother at a severe competitive disadvantage on the job market, relative both to men and to women without children. In addition, women tend to move either when they marry or when their husband moves to a new job. These two factors, combined with the reinforcing fact of pure sex discrimination so deeply rooted in our culture, result in low wages and poor career opportunities available to women. If job opportunities for most women are relatively poor, it follows that the opportunity cost of having children is relatively low in terms of the foregone earnings of married women.

If the recent movement in the United States to end sex discrimination is successful, the opportunity cost of having children will rise directly with the improvement in the relative wage rates and career opportunities of women. Reinforcing this purely economic factor, of course, will be the changed attitude of women towards their appropriate roles in society, including their roles as mothers and housewives. Any government program that successfully reduces the impact of sex discrimination, therefore, should tend to decrease fertility rates in the future. On the other hand, if the supporters of the Women's Liberation Movement are successful in their demand for government provision of free, or highly subsidized, child day care facilities, the result may be to encourage higher fertility rates. With child care centers available, new mothers would no longer have to forego labor market attachment to care for their children, and the opportunity costs of having children would largely disappear. Thus, the net effect of the recent movement towards greater sexual equality, on balance, may turn out to be either significantly pro- or antinatal, depending on the specific institutional developments of the next few years.

In the United States, elementary and secondary education is provided "free" by the government in the form of compulsory public schooling up to varying ages, but usually extending to about age sixteen in urbanized areas. For the middle classes, however, education through four years of college has now become virtually a felt necessity, and a large fraction of total college costs is borne directly by the student and his parents. The relative cost of education has apparently been rising over time in the United States, presumably because of the failure of educational institutions and other service industries to achieve productivity gains comparable to those experienced in manufacturing industries. The increase in the relative cost of education has been most evident in the rapid rise in college tuitions in the United States since World War II. Elementary and secondary school costs have also risen sharply, but these costs are somewhat masked because they are financed largely by local property taxation within individual school districts in most areas of the country.

Our economic theory of fertility predicts that the rising relative cost of education should decrease the number of children demanded, provided that the increased relative cost is fully reflected in the budgets of individual families. In most communities, increased educational costs are reflected in higher property taxes that vary only with the real estate value of a family's house, not directly with the number of children it sends to the local schools. Nonetheless, a mechanism does exist that, in an imperfect way, makes a couple take some account of the incremental educational costs of a child. A childless couple might be able to escape high real estate taxes by living in a community with poor schools. If it decides to have a first child, it can then move to a community with a good school system and incur the additional property taxes required to support the better schools. This mechanism works imperfectly, however, because of the great inequalities in average income and wealth levels across school districts, and because the psychic and pecuniary costs of moving are high relative to the benefits for many people.

The mechanism also is imperfect because it works only for the first child. If a family decides to have its first child and consequently accepts the higher tax costs of a community with good public schools, this tax cost remains invariant to the number of *additional* children it may choose to have. The decision to have a second, or higher order, child will not, in general, be influenced by the consideration of any additional public education tax costs, because its tax liability is determined solely by the value of the real estate it owns. In other words, no mechanism exists that makes families pay the additional or marginal costs of educating an extra child, and, therefore, the rising relative cost of education has probably had little effect on the number of children demanded in the post-World War II United States.

The example of education is representative of the more general phenomenon that the total social marginal costs of children exceed the private marginal costs of children for the individual family. The federal personal income tax provides a modest direct subsidy for children through the personal exemption granted the taxpayer for each dependent child. The effect of the children's exemption is to shift some of the costs of children from the individual family to the general taxpaying public. Another subsidy for children in the personal income tax allows the deduction of some child-care expenses for working mothers. This subsidy has recently been greatly expanded in response to the demands of women's rights advocates. In addition, child expenses for poor, and near-poor, families are heavily subsidized by federal, state, and local governments through welfare programs providing free school lunches and other goods and services and through various other welfare programs providing cash support varying directly with the number of children. Children from families at all income levels are provided free, or below-cost, recreational services by governments and by civic groups in local communities throughout the country. Some communities also provide subsidized medical, transportation, and other kinds of services specifically for children. All such subsidies reflect the healthy tradition in this country of broad social responsibility for the proper care and education of children. They have the unintended side effect, however, of reducing the marginal cost of additional children for the individual couple to well below the total social marginal cost per child, and, therefore, are clearly pronatal.

Even if all such subsidies were ended immediately, however, the private marginal cost of a child would still be below the total social marginal cost, because each additional child involves external costs to society in the form of more crowding. (Some people make the parallel argument that there are significant external benefits to society from more children.) No individual family will rationally take into account the additional environmental problems for society that results from its decision to have one more child. Even if a couple is fully aware of the effects of population growth on the environment, it knows that its child has a negligible effect on the total population, and it also knows that the family planning decisions of all other families are not affected by its own decision. The aggregation of all families acting according to such individually rational considerations results in a rate of population growth that may make everyone in society worse off. Thus a *perfectly contraceptive* society, in which no undesired children are born, should not be confused with a society that enjoys optimal population growth, in which the marginal social costs of children, including all external costs, are equal to the marginal social benefits. This point is just one more example to illustrate the principle of Chapter 3 that the invisible hand of the private market system will not necessarily bring about a socially desirable result if external or spillover effects cause private costs to diverge substantially from total social costs.

D. POPULATION POLICIES

The analysis of the previous section suggests that governments desiring to control population growth can attempt to manipulate one of three variables: (1) tastes for children; (2) family incomes; or (3) the relative cost of children.

Any attempt by the government to influence tastes for children would encounter strong opposition in the United States today as being unwarranted propaganda and interference in what have traditionally been private family concerns. To avert such criticism, the federal government thus far has tended to limit itself to advocacy of the concept of *family planning*, the notion that each family should be helped to have exactly the number of children that it desires. Family planning does not necessarily mean moving in the direction of lower fertility. If every couple should be able to achieve its family plans, then the government should logically help otherwise childless couples to find some means of having children, perhaps by subsidizing expensive research in the problems of sterility. At this time it seems unlikely that the government would go much further than to endorse family planning in attempting to reduce fertility.

A second strategy apparently open to the government in controlling fertility is to limit the growth rate of family incomes. As noted in the previous section of this chapter, however, virtually no public support yet exists for a policy of zero, or even of a lower, growth rate economy. Furthermore, the income effect on fertility is probably very small, quantitatively. The one variable that apparently remains as a realistic possibility for government manipulation is the relative cost of children.

The policy implication of the preceding discussion seems to be that, if the government wants to reduce fertility, it should end all subsidies directly or indirectly reducing the individual family's cost of bearing and raising children. It could even levy a child excise tax on parents (perhaps only on the third and higher order children) to force them to take account of the full social costs of children in making their family-planning decisions. Such a policy would explicitly treat the third and higher order children in a family as if they involved the same spillover costs for society as industrial effluents. To complete the analogy, an effluent charge would be required to achieve a socially desirable allocation of resources.

Professor Kenneth Boulding has suggested an ingenious solution to population control that carries the measures outlined above to the logical extreme. In order to stabilize population, he would have the government issue marketable licenses for children. In one version of his scheme, each mature female would be given, say, 2.11 child certificates. The government would demand a full certificate from each mother at the birth of a child. (Woe to the mother of triplets!) Any woman who had two or less children could sell her unused certificates on the market for such licenses to women who desired 3 or more children. The forces of supply and demand would establish the price of licenses at any time. Thus, people who wanted to have more children than the number consistent with zero population growth could have them as long as they were willing and able to pay the market price. Such a scheme is certainly a logical extension of Becker's conception of children as consumer durable goods. Unfortunately, Boulding does not address himself to the critical issue of how to enforce his plan. That is, what does the government do when a woman has a child without being able to pay for the necessary licenses in the market? The answer to this question is crucial for the workability of his scheme, but Boulding only notes in passing that its implementation would require some kind of income grants to the poor.[6]

[6] See Kenneth E. Boulding, *The Meaning of the 20th Century* (New York: Colophon Books, Harper & Row, Publishers, 1956), Chap. VI.

Even if such a proposal ever overcame its political problems, more fundamental humanitarian concerns would still persist. Any program intended to punish overly fertile parents involves the grave difficulty that it will likely result in punishing the children instead. A child excise tax or a child license scheme would reduce the spendable income of the family and force it to reduce its total consumption, but this reduction is all too likely to come at the expense of the children. The circumstance that poor families in the United States tend to have relatively large numbers of children further aggravates the problem. Poor families with many children find it difficult today to provide sufficient food and other necessities for their children even with the aid of child subsidies. The only possible evasion of this difficulty is for the government to guarantee a minimum standard of consumption for all children. Such a guarantee could be enforced either by requiring parents to prove that they provide the standard level of child support, perhaps at the cost of depriving themselves of necessities, or by taking children away from their parents and providing direct government support in institutions or through a foster-parent type of arrangement. Such drastic steps are unacceptable in the United States today, even to advocates of strict population control policies. Such currently unthinkable government interference in the most intimate of family matters would gain political support only if population problems become much more severe than they are today.

At the present time, population policy in the United States embraces much more limited programs. The federal government has only recently given tentative approval to a limited program of aid to family planning—a euphemism for birth control. In an attempt to minimize political opposition, such aid is rationalized on the basis of the traditional liberal dogma that each family should be able to implement its own plans for the number and spacing of its children. In keeping with this rationale, government programs go no further than to provide basic sex education information, including information about birth control techniques. These programs are not supposed to coerce couples to limit the size of their families. Optimistic supporters of present family-planning program nonetheless expect great benefits in the form of sharp fertility reductions in return for the very low outlays currently in the government budget. According to some estimates, about 10 percent of all children born in the United States are unwanted by their parents. Similar programs have been undertaken in some foreign countries, sometimes with limited American aid, but it is still premature to assess the general success of such programs in reducing fertility rates over the long run.

One country in which government population policies have had notable success, however, is Japan, which has greatly reduced its high pre-World War II fertility. Japan's success has been due in part to provision of cheap, legal abortions upon demand, a step that has just gained grudging acceptance in this country. But fertility reduction in Japan may also be due to widespread public acceptance for the need for population reduction in an overcrowded country with pollution problems that, in some areas, dwarf those of the United States. It should be noted in this connection that despite its unprecedented achievement of a radical reduction in birth rates, Japan expects its population to grow from a level of about 100 million in 1970 to over 120 million by the year 2000. In contrast to Japan, the population problems of the United States today appear to be relatively minor.

In conclusion, the prospects for population stabilization in the United States are most promising as of this date. The combination of present population policies and other circumstances appears to be pushing fertility rates close to the zero population growth rate level of 2.11 children per mature woman. In any event, the population growth rate is already at a very low level relative to the past and relative to other societies today, and population growth does not appear to be one of our society's most pressing problems. Fertility rates have been volatile and unpredictable in the past and circumstances may change for the worse in the future, but if they do, government population policies can adapt to the new situation. Thus, demands for more drastic population control measures for the purposes of environmental policy make little sense today. Slower rates of population growth do produce some environmental benefits but, as we have noted in this section, measures to reduce fertility also involve some substantial social costs and equity problems. Most important of all, for our topic in this book, there exist many good alternative policies that can substitute for population policies to alleviate environmental pollution.

E. SUMMARY AND CONCLUSIONS

The net population growth rate of any society is the sum of its rate of natural increase—the excess of its birth rate over its mortality rate—and the rate of net immigration. Of the three components of population growth, the largest changes in the United States in recent times have occurred in the birth rate. The crucial variable in determining United States population growth in the future will probably be the fertility rate —a measure of the birth rate that averages out the transitory factors affecting births in any short period of time.

Population growth in the United States is currently about 1 percent a year, a very low rate relative to past experience and relative to most other societies in the world today. The net growth rate fell steadily in the late 1960s and early 1970s after the end of the Baby Boom of the immediate postwar period. The most recent evidence available on fertility developments suggests that our society may be approaching a state of zero population growth, but it is still too soon to make any firm predictions about long-run population trends under normal economic and social circumstances. Population growth in other developed countries is comparable to United States experience, but growth rates in the majority of less-developed countries are much higher, reflecting high fertility and progress in reducing mortality. Thus, population growth problems are relatively minor, or even negligible, in the developed economies with widespread environmental concerns.

The environmental consequences of population growth must be distinguished from the problems of population crowding in urban areas, although the two are, of course, somewhat related. Postponing the problems of urbanization until Chapter 13, the remaining environmental problems of population growth are (1) the impetus given to total economic growth by population growth through growth in the labor force, and (2) the crowding and eventual degradation of unique natural resources, especially sites of great, but fragile, natural beauty. Both these problems involve the interaction of increases in income and output levels with a growing population. Population control is a substitute and a complement to other environmental policies, such as effluent charges, directed at the solution of these problems.

Possible government intervention to control and stabilize population can best be investigated within the framework of an economic theory of fertility. Such a theory emphasizes the role of rational choice of family size by a couple, given its tastes for children, its family income, and its perceived private cost of additional children. Various circumstances in our society combine to make the private marginal cost of an additional child to its parents diverge from its marginal social costs, including all the eventual negative effects of higher population levels on environmental quality. Because additional children involve external costs to society, the aggregation of individual family decisions does not necessarily lead to an optimum rate of population growth, even if all private costs of children were borne by the parents.

Present government programs in this country to control fertility so far have stressed only the elimination of unwanted births through the dissemination of modern birth control techniques. Although such a limited family planning policy does not guarantee success in the long run for population stabilization, present fertility developments are promising as of this date. Unless fertility rates unexpectedly turn upward again in the future, the United States may be fortunate enough to be able to achieve population stability without resorting to more drastic alternative policies toward population control.

QUESTIONS FOR DISCUSSION

1. Many writers on population problems have made the point that population growth must end someday because the available space on earth is finite. How relevant is this point for current United States population policies? (Suggestion: Look up population density estimates for different developed countries in some recent years.)

2. Suppose that the level of emissions of a particular pollutant rises from E_0 in year O to E_t after t years. During the same time period, population grows from N_0 to N_t. Also assume that per capita emission levels remain constant; that is, $E_0/N_0 = E_t/N_t$. Is this information sufficient to conclude that growth in population explains the growth in pollution emissions? Explain.

3. Human wastes may be assumed to vary proportionally with population. Does it follow that birth control is the best environmental policy to deal with pollution due to human wastes? Explain.

4. Is optimal population growth equivalent to zero population growth? Would either result if family planning policies successfully achieve a perfectly contraceptive society?

5. Suppose that Congress enacted a Boulding child license scheme and at the same time enacted a generous negative income tax program providing substantial cash transfers to all poor families? Would the negative income tax program offset the intended effects of Boulding's plan on fertility rates? Explain.

SELECTED REFERENCES

BECKER, GARY S., "An Economic Analysis of Fertility," in *Demographic and Economic Change in Developed Countries,* Universities—National Bureau for Economic Research. Princeton, New Jersey: Princeton University Press, 1960. A pioneering article in expounding the economic theory of fertility. This same volume includes other outstanding articles on various aspects of demography.

COALE, ANSLEY J., "Man and His Environment," *Science,* 170 (October 9, 1970). A lucid statement by an eminent demographer of the view that population is a negligible factor affecting environmental problems.

DAVIS, KINGSLEY, "Population Policy: Will Current Programs Succeed?" *Science,* 158 (November 10, 1967). A pessimistic assessment of existing population programs relying on family planning.

EHRLICH, PAUL R. and JOHN P. HOLDREN, "Impact of Population Growth," *Science,* 171 (March 26, 1971). Argues that population growth causes a disproportionate impact on the environment. Intended as an answer to the Coale article cited above.

FISHER, ANTHONY C., "Population and Environmental Quality," *Public Policy,* XIX, No. 1 (Winter, 1971). A readable statement by an economist about the subject of this chapter.

HAUSER, PHILIP M., ed., *The Population Dilemma,* (2nd ed.). Englewood Cliffs, N.J.: Prentice-Hall, Inc. 1969. An excellent collection of essays providing an introduction to the field of demography.

Population and the American Future, The Report of the Commission on Population Growth and the American Future. Washington: U.S. Government Printing Office, 1972. Gives a variety of views on U.S. population problems.

United Nations Department of Economic and Social Affairs, *World Population Prospects as Assessed in 1963.* New York: United Nations, 1966. A convenient source for world population data. For more recent data, see the latest edition of the annual *United Nations Statistical Yearbook.*

U.S. Bureau of the Census, *Current Population Reports,* Series P-25, various numbers, Washington: U.S. Government Printing Office, various dates. A series of publications providing basic United States population data, projections, and interpretations.

Chapter 13

Environmental
Problems
and
Urbanization

Most of the serious environmental problems the United States faces today
are concentrated in our giant urban agglomerations. The most notorious
example of air pollution is the smog of Los Angeles and its surburbs.
Water pollution is most apparent in urban areas, where concentrations
of industrial plants emit enormous, concentrated amounts of pollutants.
Problems of the quality of life, or amenity, are especially associated with
modern city life. The dirt, and noise, and hectic pace of life in cities
are contrasted by social critics with the relative peace and tranquility of
the farm and small town. Indeed, it is remarked that we need to preserve
recreation, rest, and rehabilitation areas outside the cities in order to
allow urban dwellers to survive continued exposure to the unnatural
environment of the modern city. This chapter examines these problems
of the modern urban environment. No new analytical tools will be
necessary for our discussion—urban environmental problems are essentially the same in substance as all other environmental problems. But this

chapter will approach these problems from a somewhat different perspective than we have employed previously in the book, and will provide a useful supplement to the analysis of the previous chapters.

The chapter proceeds according to the following outline. Section A first surveys the present and projected future levels of urbanization in the United States and then goes on to make some tentative generalizations about the relationship of urbanization to various environmental problems. It poses the important question of to what extent *concentration* of people and industry in urban agglomerations is a causative factor in the creation of environmental problems. The analysis in Section A is the basis for evaluating appropriate government policies towards population and industry dispersion in Section B. Section C next provides a brief economic analysis of urban congestion as an environmental problem, with special attention given to urban transportation policies. Section D then looks at environmental programs as one of a competing set of programs on the budget agenda of urban area governments. It argues that some of the shortcomings of government environmental policy are due to the fragmented structure of local government in metropolitan areas. Section E summarizes the main points of the chapter.

A. THE URBAN ENVIRONMENT: AN OVERVIEW

The Level of Urbanization in the United States

Over two-thirds of our nation's population now live in urban areas, as delimited by the Census Bureau's definition of Standard Metropolitan Statistical Areas (SMSAs). This definition of urbanization includes rural parts of partly urbanized counties and excludes small cities, but it is sufficiently precise as a measure of the concentration of population for most purposes. Urbanization has grown steadily over our nation's history. Probably only 5 percent of the population lived in urban areas prior to the nineteenth century, but well over 80 percent of the population may be included in SMSAs within a decade or so. One study projects that about 90 percent of the near-term future growth in our population will be concentrated in SMSAs, 10 percent of it in central cities and almost 80 percent in surrounding suburban areas.[1] Thus, our future population density patterns will apparently be an extension of the past. We are already a heavily urbanized society, and urban agglomerations will expand

---

[1] P. L. Hodge and P. M. Hauser, *The Challenge of America's Metropolitan Population Outlook—1960 to 1985.* The National Commission on Urban Problems, Research Report No. 3. Washington, D.C.: Government Printing Office, 1968.

still more in the future, relative to rural and small town areas. The great majority of our people now live along the coast lines of the two oceans, the Gulf of Mexico and the Great Lakes, and this pattern is expected to become still more pronounced in the new few decades. How does this large and increasing degree of urbanization relate to various environmental problems?

Water Pollution and Urbanization

Most large cities are situated next to important water resources. New York City grew up around the magnificent natural harbor at the mouth of the Hudson River. Chicago is located at the extreme southern tip of Lake Michigan; and even an apparently landlocked city like Denver is situated at the confluence of the South Platte River and Cherry Creek, formerly important waterways for the fur trade. The proximity of cities to water resources is, of course, no accident. Water transport and travel have historically been cheap relative to overland alternatives. Cities naturally developed first as *entrepots* for water-based transportation and, in many cases, later expanded as industrial centers, as well. But cities historically found adjacent bodies of water valuable resources in five additional respects: first, as sources of power (a factor of negligible importance today); second, as sources of fresh drinking water; third, as waste disposal resources—natural sewers in the case of rivers; fourth, as an input in production processes; and fifth, as recreational or amenity resources.

The waters adjacent to most major cities in the United States are currently badly polluted. The waste disposal function of water resources has been chosen by society in almost every instance that it conflicts with the recreational or amenity function. (Nevertheless recreational uses of water resources are still extremely important in many cities despite high pollution levels.) Society's choice has not been explicit in most cases. Pollution has occurred largely by default—for lack of an effective social decision to halt polluting activities. In the absence of explicit policies inhibiting emissions of water pollutants, or at least without effective enforcement of the laws governing such emissions, rising levels of economic activity in the cities inevitably caused the pollution of our most important water resources.

Without contradicting the facts given above, economists do not agree unanimously that water pollution is an *urban* environmental problem per se. In fact, some even argue that the social costs of water pollution outside urban areas are greater than the social costs of urban water pollution. This dispute cannot be fully resolved in this chapter, but we can raise the following pertinent issues.

The first point to recognize is that the social costs of water pollution in a hypothetical less-urbanized society than our own would not necessarily be less than the costs we now actually incur. Assuming a given degree of industrialization and a given level of technology, the main advantage of a less-urbanized society over our own would be the technical circumstance that the natural self-cleansing abilities of bodies of water are generally more effective if the amounts of pollutants are low relative to the amount of water in a given area. For example, little pollution may result if 100 factories emit pollutants into a river over a 200-mile stretch of water. But if the same 100 factories are all located within a one-mile length of the same stream within a city, pollution may become a serious problem. The importance of this technical point will, of course, vary greatly with the characteristics of different water resources and with the type of pollutant. We conclude that the main direct impact of urbanization within a modern industrialized society on the social costs of water pollution is the result of concentration of pollutants within a relatively small geographical area.

But this point does not settle the question at issue. On the other side are some cogent arguments that urbanization is not a fundamental cause of water pollution. First, it is not clear that a given amount of damage to water resources in urban areas involves the same degree of external costs to society as it does in rural areas. On the contrary, concentration of water pollution damage downstream in urbanized areas may result in significantly less foregone social benefits than if the damage were spread evenly throughout a whole river basin. The benefits foregone because of water pollution in urban areas seem to be limited for the most part to aesthetic considerations, or loss of amenity, and to increased travel costs. Good substitutes for the water resources immediately adjacent to cities are often available for recreation and drinking water purposes, provided that upstream (rural) water resources remain relatively unpolluted. That is, transportation costs for city people to rural recreational water resources and for rural drinking water supplies to city people may be low relative to the costs of pollution prevention or pollution damage avoidance in the cities themselves. Moreover, it may be socially more efficient to transform polluted water into safe drinking water by conventional treatment methods than to prevent the pollution in the first place. Some evidence indicates that treatment costs for municipal and industrial uses are relatively insensitive to the degree of water pollution over wide ranges of pollution concentrations. Thus, the greater concentration of pollution in urban areas may be relatively unimportant in affecting the treatment costs required to produce economically useful water. A closely related point is that if society does choose to treat water discharges into water resources, there are likely to be significant economies of scale in water treatment processes if the sources of pollution are highly concentrated in urban areas. All of these points suggest that under some circumstances, spreading a given amount of pollution evenly over a large area is *not* obviously better than concentrating it in just a few locations and leaving most of the area relatively unpolluted.

Finally, as we have already observed, some urban recreational uses of water—boating, in particular—are apparently compatible with a high degree of water pollution. Again, there is doubtlessly some unknown degree of loss of amenity when people have to swim or boat in the middle of beds of algae and industrial wastes. Treated drinking water is not necessarily the same thing aesthetically as untreated water, and this difference, too, has to be recognized in assessing the full social costs of water pollution. More generally, the fact that people have to live in close proximity to foul-smelling and filthy water clearly diminishes the amenity of urban life to some extent.

On the whole, these points suggest that water pollution as a social problem may not be primarily a result of urban agglomeration, even if the deterioriation of water resources is most evident in the vicinity of cities. On the other hand, none of these points indicate the conclusion that water resources in urban areas are sufficiently clean today. The important policy issue is, however, whether the social policy mix of water quality control measures should include any of a number of governmental measures to discourage urban agglomeration or whether government efforts should be confined to the more direct measures analyzed in Part 4 of this book. Our discussion above does suggest that policies that would intentionally disperse people and industry more widely might have little impact on the total social costs of water pollution.

Air Pollution and Urbanization

Air pollution, like water pollution, is most evident in urbanized areas. The arguments we have just gone through for the problem of water pollution indicated that this fact by itself does not suffice to identify the factor of urbanization as the fundamental cause of air pollution. Let us again perform the conceptual experiment of comparing air pollution in our economy with the same problem in a hypothetical economy that is significantly less urbanized than our own but is otherwise identical in every respect. As a first approximation, the total quantity and composition of pollutants emitted into the atmosphere could be taken to be identical in this comparison. Following our argument in the case of water resources, it seems reasonable to posit that only the relative dispersion of pollutants would be affected by the differences in the concentration of people and industry in urban agglomerations between the two economies. The social costs of air pollution are clearly greater in our own society than they would be in a hypothetical less urbanized economy.

Just as in the case of water pollution, the concentration of air pollutants is an important factor in determining how well the natural processes of the air can cleanse themselves in a given area. But, in sharp contrast to the case of water, dispersion of air pollutants is probably all-important in determining the total social costs of a given level of air pollution emissions. Unlike water pollution, air pollution in a small area results in significant social costs because man has not yet discovered any good, relatively cheap substitutes for clean air in the cities where he must live and work. Low concentrations of many gases or particulates in the atmosphere seem to have virtually no harmful consequences to man, but high or chronic concentrations can have all the insidious, economically damaging effects detailed in Chapter 7. People can avoid unclean air in cities only by the very costly expedients of commuting long distances to work, quitting their jobs, or by purchasing air filtration systems for their homes and venturing outside as little as possible. Therefore, public policies affecting population concentrations seem, on first consideration, to have a significant role to play in minimizing the net social costs of air pollution. We shall take up this issue in more depth in Section B.

Amenity and Urbanization

Urbanization necessarily involves the crowding together of people in small areas. The resulting congestion produces a special kind of external cost, which differs in one fundamental respect from the external costs of water pollution or air pollution. The latter kind of externality results from individuals or firms emitting waste products into socially owned environment media. The externality is *nonreciprocal;* the victims of air or water pollution do not inflict external costs back on the polluter. In contrast, congestion in cities involves *reciprocal* external costs. People and goods simply get in each other's way and everybody is a loser.[2] For example, when 1,000 automobiles are crowded together on a city street built to accommodate only half that number, every one of the 1,000 drivers inflicts congestion costs on the other 999. All 1,000 share responsibility for the externality equally and all bear the costs according to how much they value the time they lose waiting for the traffic jam to clear. Other external costs directly associated with congestion costs in cities include the noise, dirt, and hectic pace of modern life.

Beyond the relatively straightforward problem of congestion costs, virtually nothing of objective validity can be said about the connection between degree of urbanization and the general level of amenity in a society. High densities of population and industry in cities inevitably

---

[2] The distinction between the two kinds of externalities is due to Jerome Rothenberg, "The Economics of Congestion and Pollution: An Integrated View," *American Economic Review. Papers and Proceedings,* LX, No. 2 (May, 1970).

lead to all sorts of externalities, both good and bad. In Manhattan, for example, one man's activities impinge on another man's welfare to the maximum degree possible in this country. When Mr. X plays his radio in Manhattan, Mr. Y, in the adjacent apartment, listens whether he wants to or not. Mr. X and Mr. Y litter the streets at each other's expense and they constantly are in each other's, or somebody's, way during rush hours. Compared to Manhattan, the pace of life is slower and more relaxed in less densely populated areas, and certainly smaller towns are cleaner and quieter. Some evidence exists that the extent of mental illness in New York is astoundingly high, and some people would ascribe this fact to the disamenity of life in an overcrowded metropolis.[3] These observations tempt the authors, and perhaps the readers, to conclude that high levels of urbanization cause much of the disamenity of modern life.

The case for making urbanization the villain responsible for disamenity is not very persuasive, however. The first point to the contrary is simply that much of the evidence linking urbanization to disamenity is limited to the United States. For example, London is almost as big and densely settled as New York City, but is notably quieter, cleaner, and more relaxed. Other cities in Europe appear to manage to preserve amenity much more successfully than their American counterparts. (But recently, traffic conditions in Paris and Rome seem to have matched the worst conditions in our cities.) These observations suggest that something special in American culture, rather than urbanization per se, is the fundamental cause of urban disamenity. Second, we must recognize that tastes differ radically as to what is an external economy or an external diseconomy when it comes to questions of amenity. Very few people like dirty air or water, but some people—especially the young— like the noise, excitement, and crowds of cities. Although Mr. Y may hate living in such close proximity to Mr. X, Mr. X may love being close to Mr. Y and may dread, above all, the isolation of the farm or even of the suburbs. Given the above complications, economists can obviously make few safe generalizations about the functional relationship of urbanization and amenity.

B. POPULATION DISTRIBUTION POLICIES AND ENVIRONMENTAL QUALITY

The issue we shall analyze in this section has already been foreshadowed by our informal discussion in the preceding section. That is, should the

---

[3] See Leo Srole, et. al. *Mental Health in the Metropolis. The Midtown Manhattan Study.* (New York: McGraw-Hill Book Company, Inc., 1962.)

government consciously attempt to control growing urbanization and to redistribute population and industry more evenly throughout the country to help alleviate environmental problems. Our analysis, thus far, helps us to identify air pollution and urban congestion as the two environmental problems most directly linked to urbanization in our society and we shall therefore concentrate our attention on them. Our goal in this section is to assess the usefulness of population dispersion as an environmental policy relative to the more direct environmental policy alternatives discussed in Part 4 of the book.

Arguments for a Government Role in Population Decentralization

The case for population redistribution rests on a variant of a familiar theoretical premise—external diseconomies. In Chapters 3 and 4, we presented the theoretical case for the proposition that industries producing external diseconomies as a byproduct tend to be too big, in the sense that everybody's economic welfare could be enhanced if the output of such industries were made to go down and the output of other industries were made to go up. Some writers hold an analogous view of population concentration in cities. They argue, in effect, that high-density levels in urban areas produce external diseconomies in the form of air pollution and congestion. From this argument, they conclude that cities tend to be too big in the absence of government intervention. They call for various government policies to decentralize and disperse population and industry. Such policies might include the following specific measures: (1) special income tax allowances for people living in low-density areas, or, alternatively, special surtaxes for people living in high-density areas; (2) subsidies to industries that locate new plants in low-density areas, or alternatively, additional taxes on industries that locate new plants in high-density areas; and (3) the construction of new government installations in low-density areas, or alternatively, a ban on construction of government installations in high-density areas. By this point in the book, the reader can doubtlessly think of additional measures that would have much the same effect as the specific measures outlined above. The basic notion is simply that the government could provide positive and negative incentives for population decentralization.

Arguments for Laissez Faire in Population Distribution

Many economists strongly oppose the arguments given above, even though they accept the premise that urbanization is the cause of some external diseconomies. Their views are based on some simple economic principles of urbanization, which we must summarize briefly here to present the other side of this issue effectively.

The basic premise of urban economics is that the growth of cities is a phenomenon that cannot be ascribed either to historical chance or to government policies. Instead, they originate, persist, and grow for solid economic reasons. The high correlation between degree of urbanization and the level of economic development across societies strongly suggests that the causes of urban agglomeration are basically economic in nature. Urban economists conclude, on the basis of many different kinds of evidence, that the economic rationale for urbanization is that higher densities of people and firms make possible significant cost savings—economies of agglomeration—in the production and distribution of goods and services in a modern, highly developed economy. Economies of agglomeration come in many forms, some obvious and some more subtle. Just one example of such economies are the cost savings in communication and transportation to a business firm that locates in close proximity to its suppliers, bankers, accountants, lawyers, and customers.[4] One important piece of evidence supporting this contention is the concentration of industries in large cities despite the fact that wage levels are significantly higher in these cities than in more sparsely settled communities. If economies of agglomeration were *not* important, the forces of competition should induce firms to move operations to less densely populated areas. But the *net* movement of economic activity and people is, of course, in the opposite direction from rural areas to cities and has been for hundreds of years. The evidence is most persuasive that economies of agglomeration associated with urbanization are an important source of productivity increases and of higher real incomes in developed economies. Granted this basic point, it follows that policies designed to control the growth of dense urban centers may have the harmful side effect of making the production of goods and services less efficient and lead to lower real incomes for the population over time. In other words, such policies may involve significant social costs.

The assertion that the process of urbanization is an important factor in explaining productivity growth does not, by itself, dispose of the possibility that cities grow *too* big in the absence of government intervention because of air pollution or other similar external diseconomies of urban density. Let us analyze the relationship between air pollution and urbanization within a highly simplified framework. Suppose that total air pollution costs can be measured and that the functional relationship between such costs and urban density in a given site is known and can

[4] The reader who desires a more extensive discussion of this subject should refer to Edwin S. Mills, *Urban Economics* (Glenview, Illinois: Scott, Foresman and Company, 1972).

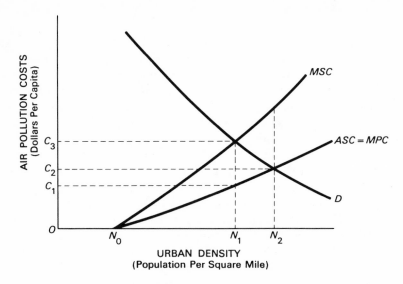

FIGURE 13–1.   Air Pollution Costs and Urban Density.

be represented by Figure 13–1. The diagram assumes, first, that up to a critical density, N_0 persons per square mile, air pollution costs in a city are zero. At densities greater than N_0, however, everyone in the city incurs the welfare costs of air pollution in different forms of damage to health and property. High density is the cause of air pollution in the sense that it is responsible for high densities of automobiles and other sources of emissions of pollutants into the air in the city. These costs are assumed to vary directly with population density, which has the important implication that the marginal social costs of air pollution, MSC, exceed the average social costs, ASC. The relationship between the MSC and ASC curves in this case of reciprocal externalities can best be explained by the use of a simple numerical example. Suppose that density level N_1 in Figure 13–1 corresponds to a population of one million persons in a given area and that C_1, the ASC corresponding to N_1, is ten dollars per capita. Let us assume that an additional person in the city raises average air pollution costs per capita along the ASC curve by one cent per capita. A potential migrant to the city could rationally ignore his own marginal contribution to average pollution in the city because one cent is negligible relative to the ten-dollar existing average cost level. In making his decision whether or not to move to the city, the potential migrant therefore takes ten dollars to be the air pollution "price" of moving to the city, which is why we state that $ASC = MPC$ in Figure 13–1; average *social* costs are equivalent to marginal *private* costs. But note that the marginal social cost C_3, at density level N_1, is greater than the average social cost C_1. Average pollution costs rise by one cent for each of the existing 1 million inhabitants of the city when the million and first person moves into the city. And one million persons times one cent per person is not a negligible marginal social cost; it equals $10,000. Thus, we see that the marginal social costs in this kind of situation can greatly exceed average social costs.

We are now in a position to give some economic content to Figure 13–1. An individual contemplating migration to an urban area with density N_1 faces a level of per capita air pollution costs of C_1, or the average air pollution cost level associated with density N_1. If he moves to the city, he will have to pay an amount C_1 (plus one cent) either in the form of pollution prevention costs—expensive and time-consuming journeys to his work, for example—or in the form of outright welfare damage to his health or property. Therefore, he will rationally migrate to the city at this density level only if a sufficiently high wage differential and other net advantages of living in the city compensate him by at least an amount C_1. But the price of C_1 he faces for moving to the city is *too low*. When he moves to the city, he inflicts marginal air pollution costs on all people already living in the city of an amount C_3. The marginal social cost C_3 is the price he should pay for moving to the city. Because the price he takes into acount, C_1, is less than C_3, the true marginal social cost, it seems that we can conclude, on the basis of our arguments in Chapters 3 and 4, that cities will grow too large in the absence of government intervention. In Figure 13–1, we can see that if we interpret the D curve to be a demand (or marginal social benefit) curve for living in the city related to its air pollution price, equilibrium city size will be N_2, where $D=ASC=C_2$. Optimal city size, however, is only N_1, where $D=MSC=C_3$.

The flaw in the above argument for policy purposes is that it implicitly assumes that the only effective antipollution measures in these circumstances is to limit population densities. But, as the reader surely knows by this point in the book, such an assumption is almost certainly wrong. If air pollution is a problem in densely populated cities, why not simply resort to some system of effluent charges on various kinds of waste emissions? Or even prohibit some kinds of emissions, if necessary? After all, for most people, it is not population density itself that is objectionable, but the side effects of population density, such as air pollution. Therefore, the most logical public policy measures are those directed squarely at the undesirable side effects. This kind of reasoning leads many economists to prefer direct antipollution measures, such as effluent charges, to indirect measures involving government interference with population distribution. Incidentally, if effluent charges are instituted, the net effect on city sizes is not clear on a priori grounds. An efficient system of effluent charges would make all city dwellers pay, directly or indirectly, the full marginal social costs of external diseconomies due to high-population density. This effect by itself would tend to make cities less densely populated, of course. On the other hand, cities will become more pleasant places to live once pollution is dealt with directly, and this factor will tend to make cities larger. The net effect of these two offsetting factors on urban densities cannot be predicted without knowledge of the relative costs of pollution abatement in areas of high density as compared to areas of low density. But urban density in itself is not an important policy target. In terms of economic efficiency, the important argument is that direct policy measures such as effluent charges are generally preferable to indirect measures, such as the population redistribution measures discussed previously. Finally, the reader should note that our arguments concerning population *redistribution* in this chapter closely parallel our arguments concerning population *levels* in Chapter 12. Economic analysis suggests some skepticism as to whether either type of population policy could pass a benefit-cost test except in circumstances of extreme population pressures and lack of feasible alternative policies.

C. THE PROBLEM OF URBAN CONGESTION

Congestion is the one disamenity problem that is uniquely urban in nature. Indeed, this must be true by definition, for what else does urbanization mean, if not high population densities and crowding? For this reason, we single it out of the large number of special disamenity problems in urban areas for a brief analysis in this chapter.

Urban congestion problems are closely linked to urban transportation policy issues. The travel of people from the home to the job and back to the home, shopping and recreational journeys, and the transportation of raw materials, intermediate products, and final goods between firms all compete for the scarce space of city streets and of other urban transportation facilities. The resulting congestion is an important source of the disamenity of urban life for many people.[5] This section briefly summarizes the economic approach to the problem of urban congestion.

Let us begin our analysis with the simplifying assumptions that the locational structure of cities and their basic transportation systems are given. That is, we assume that the nature and extent of necessary trips

---

[5] Congestion in city streets caused by too many automobiles in a limited space also aggravates urban air pollution problems, as we have already noted in Chapter 7.

both for people and goods are already virtually fixed by previous locational and capital investment decisions in order to concentrate most effectively on the demand for the facilities of an existing transportation network. With this assumption, what can we say about the social costs of urban congestion? Specifically, what is the economic sense of the term *too much congestion?*

This question can best be answered by reference to Figure 13–2,

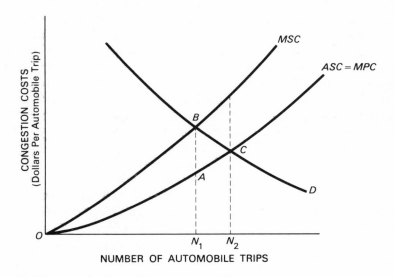

FIGURE 13–2.   Congestion Costs and Optimal Tolls.

which depicts the relationship between congestion costs and the number of automobile (or any highway vehicle) trips on the highway network of a typical urban area. Given our simplifying assumptions for this example, we may take the number of trips on the horizontal axis to be proportional to the population in the urban area. Congestion costs per automobile trip on the vertical axis include the costs of time wasted for both people and goods delayed by traffic jams and the amorphous but significant psychic costs of the frustration and discomfort individuals suffer when stalled in traffic. The average social costs of congestion per trip, ASC, in Figure 13–2, are shown to rise more than proportionally with the number of trips to reflect accurately a fact that is well documented and probably well-known to the reader. The marginal social costs of congestion, MSC, rise much more rapidly than the average social costs, and the MSC curve lies above the ASC curve at any level of trips.

The explanation of the divergence between the ASC and MSC

curves in Figure 13–2 is completely parallel in the congestion costs case to our previous explanation in the case of air pollution costs in Figure 13–1. An additional automobile on a highway raises average congestion costs, not just for the additional individual person in the automobile, but also for everyone else on the highway. The difference between the ASC and MSC curves in Figure 13–2 measures the external congestion costs an additional trip imposes on all other individuals or firms. If we interpret the D curve in Figure 13–2 as the demand for travel related to its implicit congestion cost price, we can read off the diagram that too much travel—resulting in too much congestion—will result, in the absence of any intervening government policy. Individuals take the congestion costs of their own travel into account only as it affects them as individuals, but do not concern themselves with the external congestion costs they impose on other travelers. That is, they take the congestion price of travel to be the marginal private cost of congestion, MPC, which they perceive to be equal to the average social cost. Therefore, the equilibrium level of travel in Figure 13–2 will be N_2, where $D = ASC = MPC$. The N_2 level of travel is too large for efficiency in the use of the highway network, because D, which measures the marginal social benefits of travel to individuals, lies below MSC, the marginal social cost of travel, at this point. Efficient or *optimal* congestion calls instead for a travel level N_1, where $D = MSC$. In other words, the usual efficiency criterion that the value of the last unit of anything to all consumers be equal to its marginal *social* cost will not be satisfied in the case of urban travel and transportation.

The reader should note that it is good economics to call a nonzero level of congestion efficient or optimal. Common sense can be completely misleading on this point. Zero congestion costs may be efficient in rural Kansas, but definitely would not do in midtown Manhattan! Densely urbanized areas exist because they provide great potential benefits for the interaction of people and goods. Society can *purchase* zero congestion in crowded city streets only at the cost of giving up some of these large benefits of communication and commercial transactions. Additional congestion, like any other real cost, is worth bearing by society up to the point where its marginal costs just become equal to its marginal benefits. Unfortunately, as we have just shown, the market system by itself will tend to produce too much congestion in cities to satisfy the maximum efficiency criterion.

By this point in the book, the reader can readily anticipate the policy implications of our discussion, for we are back on a very familiar track. Too much congestion is a result of the externalities of private decision making concerning travel and transportation. An *effluent congestion charge* or toll on the use of urban highways (and of other transportation facilities) should therefore be levied on the users of this scarce resource. In Figure 13–2, the optimal toll ideally should be equal to an amount AB to attain optimal travel and congestion levels at N_1. With a toll of AB, the sum of the marginal private costs (equal to the money cost of the toll AB and the nonmoney congestion costs) would just be equal to the marginal social benefits on the D curve at N_1 trips.

Economists long have advocated efficient pricing of transportation facilities and some of them have put their ingenuity to work to propose the appropriate pricing mechanisms.[6] For example, extra tolls could be levied during peak-load rush hour periods on urban highways, bridges, and tunnels; mass transit fares can also be varied according to differences in usage and congestion costs; and differential charges can be placed on alternative routes to encourage traffic to shift from highly congested to less congested roads. All the above measures are called for on the grounds of efficient resource allocation; whether they will conflict with the income distribution objectives of society will vary from case to case. Economists have to admit, however, that with the present state of technology, transportation pricing schemes face severe practical limitations. Times Square may be overcrowded, but attempting to charge motorists or pedestrians for the use of this space is not practicable. Establishing new toll booths on already overcrowded roads may create more congestion than it dispels. Thus, even if the strong political opposition to charging for the use of free city streets should miraculously vanish, it would be impossible to reduce congestion costs everywhere to optimal levels until the technology of administering congestion charges makes significant advances.

In the real world, of course, transportation facilities are not simply given, as we have assumed above, and the pricing of transportation facilities should be coordinated with public investment in new facilities. The great urban transportation policy dispute of our age is between the proponents of more urban highways, with the implied reliance on buses and private automobiles, and the advocates of more and better mass transportation. The implementation of rational pricing of *all* transportation facilities might help to narrow ideological differences on this dispute. If charges were levied on all transportation media to cover full marginal social costs, the resulting pattern of consumer demand could be taken as a more reliable guide to future public investments in urban transportation than existing demands, which are a function of haphazard pricing or zero pricing. The urban transportation pricing problem for the government is immensely difficult. Automobiles and express high-

[6] See, for example, William S. Vickrey, "Pricing in Urban and Suburban Transport," *American Economic Review, Papers and Proceedings*, LIII, No. 2 (May, 1963).

ways in cities involve additional externalities beyond congestion costs in the form of air pollution, noise, land use, and various types of disamenity, and the same is true, to some extent, for some types of mass transportation. Such externalities should be taken into full account in optimal pricing schemes in urban transportation, but nobody, as yet, pretends to be able to estimate the various external cost functions with any accuracy.

Finally, we should take note of a strong, persistent argument against urban highways and the automobile that transcends the conventional economic analysis in this section. Urban location patterns are undoubtedly a function of existing transportation systems that, in the main, were established long ago by governments that could not foresee the age of mass automobile ownership. If we acknowledge that urban location patterns and urban transportation systems are intimately interrelated, then we must leave the confortable world of marginal analysis altogether to consider urban systems as an integrated whole. Optimal pricing schemes, as investment signals for urban transportation systems, can be defended on allocational efficiency grounds only if we take as given the present locational structure of cities. But some less conventional economists and city planners argue that optimal modern cities and their transportation systems have to be built together from the ground up. Many such critics strongly believe that *New Towns* should be built entirely without access for automobiles in order to provide maximum amenity and efficiency in the use of space. Economists are generally skeptical about such grand schemes and want to be shown concrete results, but conventional marginalist analysis is not sufficient in itself to prove these ideas wrong. As the reader can see, much about the fundamentals of urban life remains an open question.

D. ENVIRONMENTAL QUALITY AND PRIORITIES IN LOCAL GOVERNMENT BUDGETS

State and local governments spend twice as much as the federal government on all nonmilitary programs. The dominance of state and local governments in the all-governments civilian budget is even greater in resource-allocation activities, as much of the federal government budget is devoted to income redistribution.[7] Expenditures related to environmental quality are today a small but growing share of state and local government budgets. The main issue we shall raise in this section concerns the appropriate role of state and local governments in a total national en-

[7] For details, see Dick Netzer, *Economics and Urban Problems*, Basic Books, New York, 1970, Chap. VII.

vironmental strategy. Specifically, we ask whether more responsibility for environmental quality should flow downwards to the local level of government or upwards to the state and federal governments.

The United States, in contrast to Western Europe, has a strong tradition of relying on local governments to provide government services unless such services clearly must be provided at higher levels of government. Ideally, strong local governments provide maximum responsiveness to the wishes of a diverse citizenry. Unfortunately for the proponents of maximum reliance on local governments, the advantages of providing government services at the local level are offset to some extent by disadvantages that have increased in importance over time. These disadvantages are in part distributional—the segregation of rich communities and poor communities to the advantage of the former. They could, in principle, be solved by equalizing grants either from the national or state governments. But the disadvantages also, in part, involve issues of allocational efficiency; local governments may be too small in some cases to take advantage of economies of scale in providing government services and they may be too small also in the sense that spillovers or externalities among political jurisdictions lead to significant inefficiencies.

One important spillover among small political jurisdictions is pollution in various forms, and the problem seems to be particularly acute in urban areas. Specifically, economists venture the generalization that local governments in urban areas will spend too little and do too little to deal with environmental problems in the absence of intervention by the state or federal governments. The basic reason for the low priority given environmental problems in local government budgets in urban areas is straightforward. The central fact of life for both central city and surrounding suburban governments in urban areas today in the United States is that they face enormous pressures both to provide more services (spend more money) and to keep tax rates down. Urban local governments all face the problem of invidious comparisons with their neighboring jurisdictions. If tax rates relative to the level of services provided get out of line in any one local jurisdiction, both people and business firms will tend to migrate out of that community to some other part of the urban area, taking valuable tax resources with them. It is relatively unimportant how strong the incentives to migrate really are in response to local fiscal incentives and disincentives; it is all-important that local government officials fear that the incentives to migrate are strong and act in response to these fears.

Such intergovernmental fiscal competition has beneficial aspects in inducing cost minimization in the provision of government services but, if spillovers are important, efficiency in resource allocation may be badly served. The case of air pollution best illustrates the nature of the problem. Air pollution within an urban area is typically most serious in the

older, heavily industrialized central city. But the central city government likely will do and spend too little in attempting to deal with the
problem unless the state or federal government intervenes. The benefits
of air pollution abatement in the central city will be shared, in general,
among residents and taxpayers of the central city and residents of surrounding suburban communities. But the benefits flowing outside the
central city will be regarded by the central city officials as external to
their decisions, because these officials respond only to the wishes of
their own taxpayers. Therefore, they will ignore such extracentral city
benefits and will spend and do too little about metropolitan-wide air
pollution. Exactly the same considerations will affect the decisions of
suburban governments, with the result that air pollution levels in the
urban area will be too high. The smaller the individual geographical
areas included in each political jurisdiction, the less will be the resources
expended on air pollution abatement.

A closely related consideration reinforces the factors outlined in
the previous paragraph. If a single local government places an effluent
change on emissions of a local industry or even prohibits some emissions,
it raises the cost of doing business in the city for that industry just as
any other tax would. The benefits of pollution abatement from an
effluent charge or a prohibition in emissions will, on the other hand,
provide few direct benefits for the affected industry because its stockholders are likely to be widely dispersed throughout the country.[8] Industries threatened by local government antipollution measures will
likely threaten, in turn, to curtail or even close down operations in the
city. Few fiscally hard presed city officials will call their bluff, especially
if the industry is vital to the local economy.

A third factor may further weaken local government antipollution
activities. The middle class and the rich can often respond to the problem
of air pollution and congestion in an urban area by moving far away
from the central city, but the poor generally do not have this option.
However, the outmigration of the well-off and the concentration of the
poor in central cities may weaken political pressures for improving
environmental quality where it is poorest. As we argued in Chapter 5,
demand for environmental quality is probably highly income elastic;
the poor have more urgent economic priorities than clean air or amenity.
For all the reasons above, we conclude that the present fragmented
structure of government in urban areas is probably inadequate to solve
various environmental problems.

A narrow concern with environmental quality would argue for an

---

[8] Pollution abatement could aid the industry indirectly if it makes the urban area a more
attractive place to live and thereby aids in the recruitment of a labor force. Business firms are
unlikely to find this kind of indirect effect on their costs persuasive, however.

obvious solution—consolidation of local governments into a metropolitan government. Such a solution ignores the cogent arguments for strong local government and it also poses the issue of where consolidation logically should end. Environmental spillovers and intergovernmental competition are not limited to sharply identifiable urban areas. If metropolitan government is good, would not elimination of *all* local governments and consolidation of government functions at the state level be even better? But the modern megalopolis spreads out over several states, so the same arguments would call for consolidation at the national level. And, recently, economists have called attention to the problems of international spillovers, with the seeming implication, by this same logic, that protection of environmental quality calls for an all-powerful international government.

Consolidation of governments at any of these levels seems a remote possibility, politically, at this time, and we must recognize the dilemma this fact presents for environmental policy. One possible alternative solution is the creation of special metropolitan, or regional, agencies whose jurisdiction is limited to narrow environmental concerns. More extensive use of regional airshed or watershed authorities, such as the existing Delaware River and Ohio River Basin Commissions, may be helpful in this regard. The political advantage of such agencies is that they leave local governments with their sovereignty unimpaired in nonenvironmental areas, but such agencies may have their political disadvantages as well. Another possible solution is voluntary agreements between governments with common environmental concerns. Unfortunately, such agreements are notoriously hard to negotiate in the first place and unstable in the long run, because local government officials are jealous of their independence. The federal government may be able to play a creative role in this area by providing generous financial support for environmental purposes but making the money available only after the creation of metropolitan environmental protection agencies or of some workable scheme of cooperation between local governments. Otherwise, the major alternative would seem to be further centralization of environmental policy measures at the federal level of government. For example, many cities today have instituted strict air codes in response to federal standards. Further intervention by the federal government may be necessary to insure effective enforcement of these codes.

E. SUMMARY AND CONCLUSIONS

Most serious environmental problems in the United States are to be found in urban areas. Some of these problems, notably air pollution and congestion, are a direct consequence of urbanization. Others, water pollution, for example, are not as clearly the result of urbanization and might be even more severe in a hypothetical industrially developed economy with more dispersion of people and industry.

Arguments for government policies to redistribute population by dispersing it more widely rest on the concept of the reciprocal externalities associated with urban crowding. The external costs of air pollution and urban congestion lead to the growth of cities that are too large for optimally efficient resource allocation. Arguments for laissez faire with respect to population distribution concede the point that reciprocal externalities in urban areas lead to too much air pollution and congestion but maintain that direct solutions to those problems are preferable to government tinkering with population distribution. Such direct solutions would include effluent charges on emissions of pollutants into the atmosphere and higher tolls on roads that are excessively congested. More drastic solutions, involving basic changes in the transportation networks of urban areas, may also be required.

The fragmented structure of local government in urban areas may result in too low a priority for environmental programs in government budgets. The basic problem is that environmental costs and benefits spill over from one local political jurisdiction to all others in urban areas. This circumstance creates a kind of political externality that must be solved, directly or indirectly, at some higher level of government. The same political spillover problem exists to some extent at the international level and may call for some form of international cooperation with regard to problems such as pollution of the oceans.

QUESTIONS FOR DISCUSSION

1. If the total amount of pollution emissions in our country is given, is it better, in general, to concentrate these emissions in just a few small geographical areas or to disperse them much more evenly?

2. How would the levying of effluent charges on air pollutant emissions affect the curves in Figure 13–1? How would the construction of mass transit facilities affect the curves in Figure 13–2?

3. Suppose that advances in technology made it feasible to impose optimal congestion tolls on the highways in large cities. Would the burden of such tolls fall more heavily on high-income or low-income groups?

4. What is the fundamental difficulty in measuring actual congestion costs of urban highways (as depicted in Figure 13–2)? Can you think of any indirect methods for measuring such costs?

5. Urban highway construction requires enormous amounts of land. When governments decide to build new highways, they measure the costs of this land as the dollar costs of acquiring it. What is wrong with such a measure? Explain how you would value such land if you were doing a full benefit-cost analysis of a proposed urban express-way.

SELECTED REFERENCES

BAUMOL, WILLIAM J., *Environmental Protection, International Spillovers and Trade.* Stockholm, Sweden: Almquist and Wiksell, 1971. A discussion of the problem of spillovers across political jurisdictions.

EDEL, MATTHEW, and JEROME ROTHENBERG, ed. *Readings in Urban Economics.* New York: The Macmillan Company, 1972. An excellent set of readings.

HENDERSON, WILLIAM L. and LARRY C. LEDEBUR, *Urban Economics: Processes and Problems.* New York: John Wiley and Sons, 1972. An elementary textbook treatment of urban economics.

MILLS, EDWIN S., "Economic Aspects of City Sizes," Commission on Population Growth and the American Future, *Population, Resources and the Environment, Research Reports,* V. Washington: U.S. Government Printing Office, 1973. The best discussion of the issues covered in Section B of this chapter.

MILLS, EDWIN S., *Urban Economics.* Glenview, Illinois: Scott, Foresman and Company, 1972. An urban economics text, more advanced than Henderson and Ledebur or Netzer.

NETZER, DICK. *Economics and Urban Problems.* New York: Basic Books, Inc., 1970. An elementary treatment of urban policy problems.

OWEN, WILFRED. *The Accessible City.* Washington: Brookings Institution, 1972. An analysis of modern urban transportation issues.

Population Growth and the American Future, The Report of the Commission on Population Growth and the American Future. Washington: U.S. Government Printing Office, 1972. Contains recent viewpoints on some of the population issues discussed in this and the previous chapter.

SUNDQUIST, JAMES L., "Where Shall They Live," *The Public Interest,* No. 18 (Winter, 1970). A succinct statement of the case for government policies to disperse population and to limit city size.

Chapter 14

Economic Growth and Environmental Quality

This is the final chapter of an introductory textbook treatment of the economics of environmental quality. Despite the length of the book, some important material remains to be covered. Previous chapters have tended to concentrate on the theory and factual evidence relevant to specific, current environmental policy issues. In this chapter, we attempt to shift gears somewhat by introducing the reader to some of the broader social issues involved in the economics of the environment. The central theme of our discussion will be the relationship between economic growth and human welfare, for it is on this question that traditional economists and their conservationist critics are beginning to differ more and more sharply.

The chapter is organized according to the following outline: Section A first presents a restatement of the traditional economic view about the relationship of economic growth and the progress of human welfare.[1] Briefly summarized, this view essentially involves a strong endorsement of continued economic growth as a *prerequisite* for the good life. Writers in the mainstream of economics tend to accept this basic precept as self-evident and generally limit their qualifications to an acknowledgement of the knotty problems of measuring economic growth accurately and making wise use of the additional output available to society. Section B then presents the essence of assorted radical critiques of the traditional economic position on this question. These critiques are radical not so much in the political as in the philosophical sense of the word, for they go to the root of matters to question the most fundamental premises of the traditional view. The critiques are diverse, but they have one theme in common; they deny that economic growth will improve the lot of man. Section C attempts what may appear to be the impossible: a (partial) reconciliation of the two fundamentally contradictory positions outlined above. It suggests the major features of a hypothetical political economy in which many of the important divergences between the two ideological camps might well disappear. Section D is an addendum to the main body of the chapter in that it sketches the nature of the research frontiers in the infant science of environmental economics. But it belongs in the main body of the chapter because some of the problems on these research frontiers are closely related to the issues raised in Sections A, B, and C. Finally, Section E is a brief summary of the chapter.

A. ECONOMIC GROWTH AND WELFARE: THE CONVENTIONAL WISDOM

Economists generally accept as self-evident the optimistic proposition that sustained economic growth in the last 200 years has increased human welfare.[2] Human welfare is a most difficult notion to quantify, and, therefore, its connection to the level of economic development in a society can never be proved to skeptics. But certain kinds of persuasive evidence may convince all but a few hard-core doubters. First, we can compare some objective circumstances of the same society at different stages of its economic development. Data about economic and social conditions prior to industrialization are scarce and unreliable, but nonetheless it is clear that life expectancies and health, in general, in all developed societies, have improved dramatically over their levels of two centuries or more

[1] We call this view of the world *traditional* for convenience, but it has dominated Western thought only in the last two or three centuries. The *no growth* or *antigrowth* views of the world are really much more traditional in a broad time perspective on human history.

[2] See, for example, the epigraph to Chapter 38 in Paul A. Samuelson, *Economics*, (9th Ed.). (New York: McGraw-Hill Book Company, 1973.)

ago. Sustained economic growth must be credited for this revolution in the human condition, both directly and indirectly; directly, through the adequate food, housing, and shelter available to the average man today but not to his great-grandfather, and indirectly, through advances in medical technology, which were part of the renaissance in all the sciences that was both a prerequisite and a byproduct of the Industrial Revolution. Economic growth has done much more than raise the levels of consumption of goods and services in the developed countries; it is also directly responsible for easing the tremendous toil required of men, women, and children alike before industrialization, just to sustain a bare existence. People in the labor force in the United States today average less than forty hours of work a week and, for the most part, they work under relatively pleasant conditions. Furthermore, they go to work only after the enforced leisure of an extended formal schooling and prior to a retirement age that is slowly but steadily declining below the traditional age of sixty-five. Even during their working years, they enjoy additional leisure during weekends, numerous holidays, and paid vacations. In brief, man today enjoys higher consumption standards at the cost of less toil over his lifetime than his ancestors. Other clear benefits to man of economic progress could be detailed, but the above are sufficient to make a strong *prima facie* case.

Similar comparisons can be made between conditions in rich and poor countries today. Most of the world still lives close to the edge of hunger in the 1970s but the privileged minority in the developed countries worry about putting on too much weight. Despite the wide diffusion of modern medical technology to the less-developed countries of the world, people in the developed countries enjoy much better health and longer lives than their counterparts in the poorer countries. Comparisons of rich and poor individuals within our own generally affluent society underscore the same basic point. Some well-off college students may conceive of poverty as romantic but the poor themselves in this country have no illusions about the advantages of material prosperity.

Most people, and especially most professional economists, conclude from such historical and international comparisons that economic growth is obviously the means to the end of greater human welfare. Probably the most eloquent statement of this conventional wisdom was given by a man considered by many to be a most unconventional economist, John Maynard Keynes. Keynes speculated, in a famous essay written in 1930, about the economic possibilities of our (his) grandchildren. He noted that *sustained* economic growth had become possible only since the Industrial Revolution but could be expected to continue indefinitely, even though it might be interrupted from time to time by short-term cyclical fluctuations, wars, or natural disasters. A sustained growth rate of output per capita of 2 percent a year—a realistic figure in a society like the United States with projected low growth rates of population— implies a doubling of output per capita every thirty-five years. Keynes therefore speculated about the economic and social consequences of a probable eightfold increase in potential output per capita over the next century.

His basic conclusion was that the successful achievement of sustained economic growth would solve the basic economic problem of man —scarcity. He greeted this possibility with enthusiasm. In his view, satisfaction of all of humanity's important material wants would finally free the creative artistic and intellectual talents of man for their fullest development. He proclaimed that once this happy day was attained —in only a century or so, by his calculation—materialism and economizing would die an unmourned death. In Keynes's view, the need to economize—to work hard, save, and strive for material prosperity—had a legitimate *social* function only in the transitional stage of rising from general poverty through scarcity to a final happy satiety. Once man achieved material satiety, the unnatural and unesthetic habits of economizing could happily be dropped, for they no longer would have any useful social function. Thus, Keynes saw economic growth as a good thing *not in itself*, but rather as a *prerequisite* for the good life for all of mankind.

Measurement Problems

The great majority of economists probably still agree with the views of Keynes, although with some philosophical qualifications of the naive optimism of a more innocent age prior to concentration camps and the widespread deployment of thermonuclear weapons. The one major economic qualification to Keynes's arguments involves the more mundane issue of accurate measurement of changes in the level of *net* economic output over time. The analytical problem is basically straightforward. Conventional measures of output, such as those implicitly referred to by Keynes, cannot be used as accurate measures of true changes in economic welfare. Many reasons can be given for this generalization, but for our purposes in this book, we shall concentrate only on the accounting issues involving environmental quality.[3] Net national product (NNP), probably the best conventional measure of economic output, is defined as the market value of gross *final* output of goods and services (gross national

---

[3] For a recent collection of critiques of the conventional national income accounts, see "The Economic Accounts of the United States: Retrospect and Prospect," Part II, *Survey of Current Business*, LI, No. 7, (July, 1971).

product) net of estimated depreciation charges against capital equipment. NNP is also defined to be equal to the sum of all the factor costs incurred to produce this output (except for depreciation charges). When most people talk about economic growth, they, either explicitly or implicitly, refer to increases in the value of *real* NNP over time; that is, increases in NNP adjusted for changes in the purchasing power of money.

Real NNP is clearly a deficient measure of net output because it does not take into account all the external costs of environmental pollution. *Pollution prevention costs* are accounted for in the national income accounts, as are *pollution damage avoidance costs*. That is, government expenditures undertaken to enforce a ban on emissions or to clean up pollutants in the atmosphere or water are appropriately part of NNP because they enhance the quality of the environment and because the resources used for such purposes are diverted from other kinds of potential collective or individual consumption.[4] However, much of the remaining portion of total pollution costs—the welfare costs of actual pollution damage—are not accounted for in NNP because they are external to the marketplace transactions that enter into the national income accounts. For this reason, NNP will be *overstated* by the amount of such welfare costs. (But, see footnote 4 for an accounting problem that tends to *understate* true NNP.) Not accounting for the welfare costs of environmental damage overstates true NNP for two distinct reasons. First, and most obvious, the flow of environmental *bads* to individuals, such as the daily breathing of polluted air, should be subtracted from gross consumption of goods and services to derive the net consumption of goods and services included in NNP. Second, to the extent that pollution reduces the economy's stock of environmental capital resources, some amount of *capital consumption allowances* should be added to the estimated depreciation of physical capital stocks in going from gross national product to net national product. In other words, it is proper national income accounting practice to measure *net* output as net of all the loss in value of an economy's capital resources, and these capital resources should logically include environmental capital resources.

All economists acknowledge the problem of accounting for environmental pollution in measuring NNP, although they may differ somewhat concerning the technical accounting details. We know very little, however, about how much difference there would be to measured growth rates of net output if we could make the desired adjustments to conven-

---

[4] Such expenditures undertaken by private business firms are incorrectly deducted from NNP as current costs instead of being treated as final outputs of capital or consumption goods. They are conceptually equivalent to government or individual expenditures to improve the environment or to counteract environmental pollution. This problem qualifies the main point developed in the text.

tional measures of NNP. As of the time this book goes to press, only one serious effort has been published concerning the *quantitative* importance of accounting for pollution in measuring growth rates. Professors William Nordhaus and James Tobin of Yale University have attempted to measure the disamenity costs of economic activity indirectly by estimating the income differential required to induce people to live in cities rather than rural areas over time—what they call *a disamenity premium.* Because urbanization has increased over time, they adjust conventionally measured NNP for the additional disamenity costs borne by city dwellers over time. Their adjustment for disamenity costs is of significant magnitude—8 percent of disposable family income in 1965. However, it does not have any effect on the measured *rate of growth* of output between 1929 and 1965, the years covered by their study. Income growth over these years has been sufficiently high to keep the disamenity costs of more urbanization roughly constant as a percentage of income. This is certainly a most unexpected result. But although the Nordhaus and Tobin study is an impressive pioneering effort, its conclusion does not settle the basic problems of properly accounting for pollution costs in the measurement of net output. As the authors themselves recognize, their measure of disamenity costs at best includes only a portion of the total welfare costs of environmental pollution. Moreover, their procedure can not take account of the possibility that environmental conditions may have worsened just as rapidly in rural areas as in urban areas over the period covered by their study. If such is the case, their results would clearly understate the effects of environmental deterioration. Thus, the quantitative significance of environmental pollution in affecting measures of the growth rate of net output still remains very much an open question.

Whatever the effect of environmental costs on measured growth rates eventually turns out to be, it will not alter in the slightest the basic philosophical stance of those who believe in the welfare-enhancing effects of economic growth. Carefully restated, this position holds that economic growth, properly measured to take full account of the welfare costs of environmental pollution, is a prerequisite for improving the lot of man.

B. ECONOMIC GROWTH AND WELFARE: THE RADICAL CRITIQUE

A minority—but apparently a growing minority—of economists argue that economic growth has not increased the welfare of human beings and that further economic growth will just make matters much worse. The logical policy position of those who hold such a belief is to call for an end to growth. As noted previously in Chapter 12, the cause of zero growth (of output) is not likely to be a part of the platform of any successful political party in the foreseeable future, but the fact of its political unpopularity does not in itself make zero growth a bad idea. Arguments against economic growth tend to touch upon a wide variety of social issues. In our discussion below, we shall attempt to confine our attention just to the arguments involving environmental issues.

One traditional conservationist argument against the continuation of growth of population and output is that such growth will eventually mean the extermination of many species of flora and fauna. The amount of habitable space on earth is virtually fixed and sites become increasingly scarce as economic growth proceeds. Increased demands for food by a larger and wealthier population cause farmers to make much more efficient use of their land by applying more capital per acre, including the application of more advanced and efficient fertilizers and pesticides. Increased demands for outdoor recreation lead to pressures to achieve higher productivity of the sites suitable for recreational purposes. Military needs for various kinds of facilities even create demands for some of the most unattractive and inhospitable sites on earth. All of these interrelated phenomena follow from the fact that the number of sites is fixed and population and output growth continually bid up the prices of these sites and induce landowners to increase productivity per acre.

One consequence of the increasing scarcity of habitable space is that the survival of species other than man often becomes an apparently dispensable luxury, even in the most affluent society. A farmer attempting to maximize the productivity of a fixed number of acres will not tolerate pests such as coyotes or mountain lions that prey upon his stock or, in any way, hamper his commercial operations. The almost extinct grizzly bear in Glacier Park turns vicious when people seeking to escape the crowds of fellow humans venture far away from normal tourist areas and begin to crowd him in his former wilderness habitat; therefore, he must be destroyed to insure the safety of this recreational area. Nuclear testing causes ecological disaster and threatens the survival of desert flora and fauna. The increasing scarcity of space as a result of continued economic growth thus threatens to make many species extinct, with the consequent loss of irreplaceable gene pools to future generations. Conservationists have traditionally viewed the prospect of the unnecessary destruction of other species with horror. Their view has never been expressed more eloquently than in a famous passage by John Stuart Mill, which deserves to be quoted in full:

There is room in the world, no doubt, and even in old countries, for a great increase of population, supposing the arts of life to go on improving, and capital to increase. But even if innocuous, I confess I see very little reason for desiring it. The density of population necessary to enable mankind to obtain, in the greatest degree, all the advantages both of cooperation and of social intercourse, has, in all the most populous countries, been attained. A population may be too crowded, though all be amply supplied with food and raiment. It is not good for man to be kept perforce at all times in the presence of his species. A world from which solitude is extirpated, is a very poor ideal. Solitude, in the sense of being often alone, is essential to any depth of meditation or of character; and solitude in the presence of natural beauty and grandeur, is the cradle of thoughts and aspirations which are not only good for the individual, but which society could ill do without. Nor is there much satisfaction in contemplating the world with nothing left to the spontaneous activity of nature; with every rood of land brought into cultivation, which is capable of growing food for human beings; every flowery waste or natural pasture ploughed up, all quadrupeds or birds which are not domesticated for man's use exterminated as his rivals for food, every hedgerow or superfluous tree rooted out, and scarcely a place left where a wild shrub or flower could grow without being eradicated as a weed in the name of improved agriculture. If the earth must lose that great portion of its pleasantness which it owes to things that the unlimited increase of wealth and population would extirpate from it, for the mere purpose of enabling it to support a larger, but not a better or a happier population, I sincerely hope, for the sake of posterity, that they will be content to be stationary, long before necessity compels them to it.[5]

More recent arguments against the benefits of economic growth go beyond the conservationist issues raised by Mill. The modern radical critique of economic growth centers on the *fixity* of the environmental resources of earth. The basic point is quite straightforward. The assimilative and absorptive capacities of the earth's air, water, and land resources are finite, and, therefore, sustained economic growth producing ever higher levels of effluents must sooner or later overwhelm these resources. Some writers have developed this point simplistically as a trivial exercise in high school algebra proving that any positive number (effluents) growing forever at a positive compound rate must eventually exceed some other fixed positive number (environmental resource capacities).[6] Of course, it is true that the level of effluents cannot keep on growing forever, but this point evades the real issues of *how* and *when* effluent levels should cease to grow. The answer depends, of course, on

---

[5] John Stuart Mill, *Principles of Political Economy*, Book IV, Chap. VI. Note that Mill talks about the consequences of *population* growth. But since he wrote, it has become clear that *output* growth is the much more important factor in destroying amenity, at least in a relatively sparsely populated society like the United States.

[6] Examples of this simplistic approach are numerous, but perhaps the most publicized is the book by Dennis L. Meadows, Donella Meadows, Jorgen Randers, and William Behrens, *The Limits to Growth: A Report for the Club of Rome's Project on the Predicament of Man.* New York: Universe Books, 1972.

benefits and costs. Such arguments also tend to miss the critical point that the rate of growth of effluents does not necessarily *have* to match the rate of growth of output; society has available techniques, such as effluent charges, to control effluent level emissions within broad limits and tax incentives to encourage the recycling of materials.

On the other hand, the same basic truism can be the starting point for a deeper analysis of the relationship between economic growth and environmental issues. Probably the most sophisticated analysis from this point of view is the *Spaceship Earth* vision of the economist and philosopher Kenneth Boulding. The Spaceship Earth concept is, in part, just a global analogue to the materials balance concept discussed in Chapter 3 of this book. That is, Boulding argues that man must begin to see earth as a closed system, in contrast to the older and still prevalent conception that natural resources are boundless and that man can develop and exploit them without limit. In Boulding's perspective, earth's environmental resources should be viewed as essential, irreplaceable social capital and the major purpose of economic activity should be to conserve this *stock* of capital intact for future generations. In contrast, the more traditional economic view has always been that society should maximize the *flow* of current output. According to the traditional view, the stock of capital society passes on to future generations is determined both by the private market system and by government policies in response to the wishes of the current generation about the allocation of resources between present and future uses. Boulding's analysis is particularly useful in focusing on the issue of whether current market and nonmarket institutions are sufficient to provide for the survival of enough of our precious environmental capital for transmission to future generations. Boulding concludes pessimistically that our society expends environmental capital recklessly in pursuit of the wrongheaded goal of maximizing current output. If he is right, society must alter its basic philosophical position toward the meaning of economic growth. The overriding social goal would be maintenance of environmental resources and would entail acceptance of a lower rate of growth—even a zero rate—of current output toward this end.

One other general criticism of economic growth concerns its harmful effects on amenity, broadly conceived to include all social and cultural factors affecting the quality of life. It is alleged that economic growth has, either directly or indirectly, destroyed the best aspects of life found in less economically advanced ages; in particular, the pleasures of solitude, contemplation, leisurely conversation, creative art, and the like. According to this line of argument, economic growth inundates these civilized pursuits by glorifying materialism and requiring too hectic and frenzied a style of life. To cite just one example, it is clear that the pleasures of a leisurely, solitary stroll are considerably less in modern Manhattan than in a less economically developed time and place. Among the famous economists associated with this view of the amenity consequences of economic growth, the names Bertrand de Jouvenel, Staffan Burenstam Linder, and Tibor Scitovsky are prominent. But the most thoroughgoing reactionary (radical?) in his opposition to economic growth is the brilliant English economist, E. J. Mishan.

Mishan postulates a sharp dichotomy of tastes between what we may call the *modernists* and the *environmentalists*. The modernists desire maximum consumption of goods and services and, therefore, favor all policies that increase the rate of growth of industrial production. They do not mind the disamenity of modern life, and, in fact, even thrive on its noise, confusion, and excitement. The enviromentalists, on the other hand, stand willing to sacrifice many of the comforts and conveniences to be derived from modern production techniques in order to enjoy greater amenity. Mishan poses the question of how society can best reconcile the divergent interests of these two groups.

The answer Mishan suggests is the logical extreme case of zoning, *separate facilities*. The separate facilities solution to amenity problems is the social analogue to the smoking and no-smoking car solution of railroad passenger trains. Instead of either allowing or not allowing smoking in all cars and thereby guaranteeing the dissatisfaction of either one group of passengers or the other, railroads often provide separate facilities so that smokers and nonsmokers can choose the environment in which they desire to travel. Why not, Mishan asks, provide separate facilities for everybody in a society in virtually all aspects of the environment? A large area with tentative boundaries in each state could be set aside initially for people who wished to live in a pollution-free environment. The equilibrium size of the environmentalists' area could be determined by migration over the long run, either expanding or contracting. In this area, total bans on automobiles, power lawnmowers, overhead jet flights, transistor radios, functional architecture, and other disamenities of modern life would be strictly enforced. Outside the environmentalists' area, life would go on for the modernists just as before, except that progress would no longer be hindered by the criticisms of the environmentalists.

Mishan's separate facilities solution to environmental problems is so appealing on its face that only a professional economist could attempt to find fault with it. Who among rational men would not opt to live in the environmentalists' zone, once separate facilities were established? The answer is that only those people willing to pay the unknown costs of amenity would choose to enjoy its environmental benefits. Our guess is that the costs would be unacceptable to all but a few thoroughly dedicated environmentalists. One cost of unknown dimensions of living in the environmental zone would be commuting costs. With automobiles banned —a crucial requirement of Mishan's environmental zone—travel to work could well take up the full working day for those who had to work in the kinds of ecologically disruptive industries that would have to be relegated to the modernists' zone. (Also, emergency transport to expert medical care in hospitals would have to be entrusted to horse and buggy.) Employment for the people who lived in the environmental zone would have to be both compatible with the amenity of the area and tightly integrated spatially with residential areas. All industry dependent on the input of electric power would be uneconomic, given the alternative of locating in the modernist zone. Industries dependent on high-speed and convenient transportation and communications would be ruled out as well. We may speculate that the environmental zone, in equilibrium, eventually would include only universities and the professors and students associated with them, a few similar industries, and, perhaps, a few wealthy retired people. Consumption levels would likely be very low except for those families whose incomes were derived from assets owned in the modernists' zone.

The fundamental problems with Mishan's ingenious proposal lie even deeper, however, than the transportation and related economic difficulties cited above. First, not all environmental problems can be segregated neatly by politically drawn boundaries. Whole regions, encompassing several states, are intimately linked in their ecological balance. It is often economically unfeasible to limit provision of clean air and water to one isolated tract in each state; as public goods, once they are provided for one person or for one small area, they can be provided for all within broad regions at negligible marginal costs. Thus, to achieve true environmental quality within the environmentalists' zone alone would be impossible without the close political cooperation of the modernists. Boulding's Spaceship Earth concept rightly emphasizes the point that all of mankind sinks or swims together in its relationship to the environment.

Even if we could abstract from the fact that it is impossible to escape from environmental problems on this earth, Mishan's scheme would still be unworkable because it would surely lead to a division of our country into two societies as well as two *facilities*. The environmentalists, leading a life of relatively low consumption and high amenity, would have virtually no interests in common with the modernists and their high consumption-low amenity life style. What possible links could unite the two zones as part of one political entity, with the exception of interests in national defense? At best, the relationship between the two zones would be marked by antipathy and contempt for clashing life styles and values. In addition, it is difficult to imagine how a zone of suitable size and convenience could be set aside for the environmentalists without severely hampering the activities of the modernists. Transportation and communications networks in the modernist zone would inevitably impinge on the environmentalists' zone with subsequent political conflict. At the least, noisy and dirty activities in the modernists' zone at the boundaries of the environmentalists' zone would present a source of continuing friction. In short, the coexistence of two such different cultural and economic zones within the same national state does not appear to be politically feasible.

Besides the above practical considerations, Mishan's basic assumption of a distinct dichotomy in tastes has unfortunate elitist overtones; it is more reasonable to assume both that tastes for amenity vary continuously over broad ranges and that these tastes are socially conditioned and subject to change through education and experience. This point is closely related to our previous assertion that the cause of environmental quality involves some potential conflicts between the rich and poor in our society. Schemes to improve environmental quality should not blithely assume that *everybody* is affluent enough to give up the material benefits of economic growth.

The ease with which holes can be picked in Mishan's extreme proposal should not blind us, however, to its fundamental merits in more limited applications. The spatial organization of modern urban life is manifestly unsatisfactory and affords society ample scope for fundamental changes that could benefit everybody. Much can be done to shield human beings from the ugliest, dirtiest, and loudest aspects of the modern city. Although most individuals will have to continue to endure some disamenity as the cost of making a living, enlightened zoning practices can secure greater amenity both on and off the job. Separate facilities can be established to some extent for all people, not just for university professors and wealthy conservationists, by recognizing that individuals, to some extent, compartmentalize their lives as workers, commuters, consumers of goods and services, and consumers of leisure activities at different hours of the day and on different days of the year. Spatial segregation of different activities has enormous potential as a mechanism for general improvements in amenity.

C. CAN GROWTH AND ENVIRONMENTAL QUALITY BE MADE COMPATIBLE?

Sections A and B have presented two sets of apparently irreconcilable views on the desirability of continued economic growth. But the arguments in both sections have intentionally been presented without the usual academic qualifications in order to highlight the conflict between the progrowth and antigrowth camps. This section attempts a partial reconciliation of the two views by suggesting, in bare outline, a hypothetical political economy in which continued economic growth and high environmental quality would be compatible or, at least, much more compatible than past experience would indicate.

Suppose that, by some miracle, the present members of Congress were replaced by a random drawing from the membership files of the American Economic Association. (This is a textbook example, not a political program!) Such a Congress would undoubtedly soon pass legislation that would provide for effluent charges wherever feasible and also for new or higher extractive (severance) taxes on all materials that can be recycled. It would also pass legislation providing subsidies to encourage states and local governments to implement workable supplementary environmental measures such as noise abatement programs, marginal cost (including congestion costs) pricing of transportation facilities, and strict enforcement of existing antilittering laws. Such legislation also would encourage these government units to band together in regional environmental organizations wherever possible to take account of all spillovers across political jurisdiction. The economists' Congress also would establish experiments to find the best mechanisms for efficient allocation of scarce outdoor recreational facilities, and it would provide funds for heavy investment in new facilities, especially for new wilderness areas set aside to preserve scarce species for the future. It might also fund experiments designed to discover wholly new urban spatial arrangements that might increase the overall amenity of life in cities. Let us further suppose that the economists' Congress would discover effective means of making various government bureaucracies effective agents for carrying through the new environmental policies. Perhaps this could be done by designing a complex set of incentives and disincentives for government officials that would lead them to respond effectively to the public interest. Finally, we must suppose that the populace accepts this revolution from above and gives the new environmental measures enthusiastic support.

If we make the further critical assumption that fiscal and monetary policies would be effective in maintaining aggregate demand at a level close to full-employment output, then the major impact of the environmental package outlined above would be a massive realignment of relative prices. To be more specific, the successful implementation of all these environmental policies would mean that the prices of all outputs would have to include the full external (marginal) costs of environmental pollution. We can speculate about a few of the more important expected changes in relative prices.

First, the prices of *goods*, especially heavy consumer durable goods, would rise sharply, relative to the prices of *services*. The reason for this expected change in relative prices is simply that external costs of production are significant for most goods and small for most services. The production of automobiles, for example, involves heavy use of environmental resources largely because of its utilization of steel, other metal, and rubber inputs. The production of medical services, in contrast, is much more labor intensive and involves relatively less use of capital and energy inputs that generate large amounts of effluents.

Second, the price of *energy* to both household and firms would rise sharply, relative to other prices. This price change would be due, first, to the fact that Congress would replace the present depletion allowances with federal extractive taxes on the mining of such fossil fuels as oil and coal. In addition, the full external costs of fossil fuel combustion or the generation of nuclear energy would have to be included in the final price of energy. For example, the heavy taxes on the sulfur content of fuels, called for on environmental grounds, would add to fuel costs, either directly or through the mechanism of the costs incurred by firms to remove the sulfur from fuel prior to use. The day of much higher energy costs has already arrived in the United States; if the environmental measures discussed in this section are implemented, the cost increases could be enormous.

Third, use of *private automobiles* would become much more expensive. The first reason for this prediction was given above—the heavy use of key raw materials and energy at all stages of the production process for automobiles. A second reason would be the higher price of fuel, as all energy costs rise after the implementation of the new environmental program. A third factor would be the new heavy tolls imposed on automobiles using congested highways. Finally, fewer new highways would be built once highway authorities were forced to take account of all the environmental consequencies of proposed construction, and the lessened availability of good highways would make automobile use correspondingly less valuable, or more expensive per mile of desired travel.

What is the relationship of these predicted relative price changes, in a new proenvironmental regime, to economic growth? Assuming again that fiscal and monetary authorities would succeed in maintaining full employment of resources, economic growth would resume after absorbing the shock of the revolution in relative prices, but in much different directions. We take the optimistic view that the pattern of economic growth in this new regime would be compatible with the maintenance of high-quality environmental resources and improved amenity or, at least, much more compatible than under the present system of relative prices.

To be specific, we foresee, first, a reallocation of resources away from goods to services, as consumers respond to the expected change in relative prices. This would mean, for example, less production of consumer durables, such as automobiles and color television sets, and more production of health, education, and welfare services.

We also predict a similar reallocation of resources away from the production of goods and services requiring relatively large energy inputs. Higher market prices for energy would be signals for firms and households to conserve on the use of energy in all forms. We would expect, for example, a steady contraction of heavy goods industries and a diminished use of privately owned household appliances in response to higher energy prices. Instead of every household owning one washing machine with an expected life of less than five years, several households might share the use of one very efficient machine with an expected life of ten years. In general, economic pressures might induce much more communal sharing in the consumption of the services of consumer durable goods.

Third, we predict a revolutionary reduction in private automobile use in response to the change in its relative price. People would have to substitute mass transit, jitney service, bicycles, and even walking, for the automobile. Instead of every household owning two big cars, two or more households might share the use of one small car. In the long run, urban agglomerations might be rebuilt to accommodate the revolution in transportation wrought by the new environmental regime's impact on use of the private automobile.

Fourth, recycling of materials would become a major service industry in the new regime. Extractive taxes and the heavy environmental tax costs on the production of such basic materials as steel and rubber would afford opportunities for large profits to firms that could successfully cope with the technological problems of recycling used materials. The same economic pressures would increase the incentives for individuals to become expert in the repair and maintenance of their own consumer durables. Goods of high quality and relatively great durability would command higher market premiums than they do today.

In brief, these specific predictions lead us to expect that economic growth, under a proenvironmentalist regime, would be service-oriented rather than goods-oriented, as in the past. Because about 60 percent of the American labor force already is employed in service industries, such a shift in the pattern of growth would not be as revolutionary, in its employment aspect at least, as it may appear on first encounter. In contrast to goods-oriented growth, service-oriented growth would take the form of *improvements in quality* rather than increases in quantities produced. In compensation for less growth or even no growth in per capita consumption of many goods, people could expect to receive higher quality medical care, better educations, and improved services of all kinds. We suggest that such a shift in consumption patterns would not only conserve on scarce environmental resources such as air and water, but would also move society towards providing amenities of the kind so deeply desired by Mill, Boulding, Mishan, and others who share their traditional humanistic values.

Is such a revolution in our economic life *politically* feasible in this or any society? The authors do not pretend to know the answer. Much will depend on the environmental education of the next generation of Americans. A great deal will also depend on how successful our society is in redistributing its material prosperity more widely and ending poverty. The cause of a better environment will not gain widespread popular support as long as one-fourth or one-third of the people in our society consider themselves deprived of the material necessities of life. As noted previously in the book, the issues of environmental quality and income distribution are closely linked.

Is such a revolution in our economic life *economically* feasible? Some (politically) radical economists argue that the modern capitalist economy could not cope successfully with a massive reallocation of resources away from heavy goods industries to service industries. Perhaps they are right, although the successful massive reallocation of resources in the post-World War II conversion from military to civilian production suggests that dogmatism on this issue is unwise. And, of course, the full environmental regime could be implemented gradually over a period of years rather than all at once. In our view, social engineering of changes in relative prices is not an environmental panacea, but rather a prerequisite for any substantial progress against environmental deterioration.

D. A NOTE ON THE RESEARCH FRONTIERS OF ENVIRONMENTAL ECONOMICS

This is a textbook, which means that the material presented herein summarizes and synthesizes existing knowledge about environmental economics. But much new exciting work is being done, even as we write, that is expanding the frontiers of this infant social science. This note is directed especially at those readers who have mastered the material in the text and are eager now to think about the major unsolved problems in the field.

The outline of the whole book can serve as an outline for this brief discussion of ongoing research. Chapter 1 of this book (Part 1) introduced the reader to the benefit-cost approach to environmental problems, and the four chapters of Part 2 of the book then fleshed out the theory of determining environmental costs and benefits. This theory is standard microeconomics and was essentially well worked out before the advent of major environmental problems. Economists have found it readily applicable to these problems with few modifications. Further advances in this theory can be expected, but they will probably not be of critical importance in increasing our ability to cope with environmental problems. The partial equilibrium price theory that we developed in Part 2 of the book is already sufficient to give us the theoretical answers to partial equilibrium problems of the environment. The main frontier for economic theory applicable to the environment is in the area of general equilibrium or systems analysis. As noted throughout the book, environmental problems are linked by complex ecological relationships that are not yet well understood. Physical and biological scientists have to work out these relationships and environmental economists have to utilize the results in their own models.

Vast problems remain virtually untouched on the *empirical* side of environmental economics. As noted in Chaps. 6, 7, and 8 of Part 3 of the book, we are just beginning to get a grip on the meaning of the complex quality dimensions of air, water, and other natural resources. Benefit-cost *theory* may be well worked out, but benefit-cost *analysis* is worthless unless we can give some empirical content to the concepts of benefits and costs. Outstanding among the many empirical gaps in environmental economics are identification and quantification of the costs of long-term human exposure to various concentrations of different pollutants in the atmosphere and in food substances. Some of the evidence just recently available on the effects of substances like asbestos is extremely frightening and appears to call for drastic government measures. But we still know very little about the effects of many other potentially dangerous pollutants. For many substances, there appear to be crucial thresholds for human tolerance; that is, marginal social costs become extremely high over some minimum concentration.

Facts are crucial also in filling in the gaps in our discussions of policy issues in Parts 4 and 5 of the book. At this point, we can only hazard intelligent guesses about how well various environmental programs will work, once put into effect. We badly need the social science laboratory of actual experience to put these guesses to the test.

To conclude, environmental economics is still in a primitive stage, especially with regard to its empirical content. We hope that the reader will not regard this fact with dismay, but rather will accept it as a personal challenge.

E. SUMMARY AND CONCLUSIONS

This chapter assesses the relationship between economic growth and human welfare. Economists have, until very recently, generally accepted as self-evident the proposition that growth enhances welfare. This judgment is based on widespread evidence relating growth to vastly increased consumption per capita, greater longevity and better health, and freedom from ceaseless toil.

A growing underworld of radical criticism contests this conventional view of the beneficial effects of growth. Part of this criticism is based on the purely technical point that conventional measures of growth are faulty by their own criteria. But, more fundamentally, the revisionists' case is based on arguments that growth inevitably destroys environmental quality. Some versions of this view argue simplistically that continued geometric growth of output means geometric growth of effluents, and, therefore, that effluent levels will inevitably overwhelm the finite absorptive capacities of environmental resources. More sophisticated radical critics of growth point to its harmful effects on other species, the environmental resource legacy to future generations and various aspects of amenity.

We suggest implementation of a full-fledged environmental program that might mollify some of the critics of growth. This program would consist of a coordinated package of environmental measures that would drastically alter relative price relationships throughout the economy. We predict that growth would continue after such a program went into effect, but along service-oriented lines in contrast to the goods orientation of traditional economic growth. The new pattern of growth hopefully would meet the criticisms of the radical critics.

Finally, we conclude the book with a brief discussion of the research frontiers of enviromental economics. The outstanding theoretical gap in the field is in general equilibrium or systems analysis that could deal with the complex ecological relationships relevant to most environmental problems. Probably more important is the lack of empirical knowledge about the benefits and costs of environmental pollution, especially the long-run effects of various pollutants in the atmosphere and in our foods. Until further research fills these gaps in our present knowledge, environmental economics will remain an underdeveloped science.

QUESTIONS FOR DISCUSSION

1. "The United States is now affluent enough to be able to afford zero economic growth for the sake of preserving the quality of its environment." Discuss critically.

2. Probably the single most important factor causing sustained economic growth is applied technological change. If the government seriously undertook to achieve zero economic growth, it would have to take

measures to inhibit scientific research or at least to prevent the application of scientific advances. Would such measures really improve environmental quality?

3. "Government expenditures to clean up the environment should not be included in NNP because they just alleviate *bads* rather than produce *goods*." Evaluate the logic of this statement. Should household expenditures on aspirin be included in NNP?

4. Some social critics argue that, in the past, too much of the potential benefits of economic growth has taken the form of increased market production and too little has been in the form of more leisure and other nonmarket uses of time. Would you expect this historical pattern to change if the proenvironmental program outlined in Section C were implemented? What would be the effect of an increase in the relative consumption of leisure on environmental quality?

5. Suppose the American people were given a clear either-or choice between two futures: one a simple extrapolation of the past and the other the kind of political economy described in Section C of this chapter. Which do you think they would choose? Why?

SELECTED REFERENCES

BOULDING, KENNETH E., "The Economics of the Coming Spaceship Earth" in *Environmental Quality in a Growing Economy*, ed. Henry Jarrett. Baltimore: The Johns Hopkins Press, 1966. A concise statement of Boulding's ideas. Full of wisdom.

DENISON, EDWARD F., "Welfare Measurement and the GNP," *Survey of Current Business*, LI, No. 1 (January, 1971). An authoritative treatment of how environmental problems are related to the official national income accounts.

JOHNSON, WARREN A. and JOHN HARDESTY, eds., *Economic Growth Vs. the Environment*. Belmont, California: Wadsworth Publishing Company, Inc., 1971. A collection of readings of mixed quality. Emphasizes the radical point of view.

ISARD, WALTER, *et.al.*, *Ecological Economic Analysis for Regional Development*. New York: The Free Press, 1972. An attempt to integrate the ecological consequences and costs of economic development into conventional economic decision making.

KEYNES, JOHN MAYNARD, "Economic Possibilities for Our Grandchildren," in his *Essays in Persuasion*. New York: W. W. Norton & Company, Inc., 1963. A beautifully written classic, well worth reading.

KNEESE, ALAN V., "Research Goals and Progress Toward Them," in *Environmental Quality in a Growing Economy*, ed. Henry Jarrett. Baltimore: The Johns Hopkins Press, 1966. A survey of research in environmental economics.

MISHAN, E. J., *Technology & Growth: The Price We Pay.* New York: Praeger Publishers, 1969. A readable statement of his views by a very original English economist.

NORDHAUS, WILLIAM and JAMES TOBIN, "Is Growth Obsolete," in National Bureau of Economic Research, *Economic Growth. Economic Research: Retrospect and Prospect.* Fiftieth Anniversary Colloquium V. New York: Columbia University Press, 1972. A quantitative analysis of factors that might cause the *true* economic growth rate to diverge from the officially measured rate. Squarely in the traditional, progrowth tradition.

RUSSELL, C. S. and W. O. SPOFFORD, JR., "A Quantitative Framework for Residuals Management Decisions," in *Environmental Quality Analysis,* eds. A. V. Kneese and B. T. Bower. Baltimore: The Johns Hopkins Press, 1972. A systems approach to the waste residual problem employing sophisticated techniques of economic analysis.

Index